O9-BTO-749

WRITING
WORTH READING

A Practical Guide

Abigail E. Weeks
Memorial Library
Union College

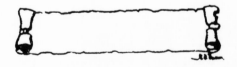

ABIGAIL E. WEEKS MEMORIAL LIBRARY
UNION COLLEGE
BARBOURVILLE, KENTUCKY   40906

WRITING WORTH READING

A Practical Guide

Nancy Huddleston Packer
STANFORD UNIVERSITY

John Timpane

A Bedford Book
ST. MARTIN'S PRESS · NEW YORK

808.042
P119w

Library of Congress Catalog Card Number: 85–61299
Copyright © 1986 by St. Martin's Press, Inc.
All rights reserved.
Manufactured in the United States of America
9 8 7 6
f e d c b a

For information, write St. Martin's Press, Inc.,
175 Fifth Avenue, New York, NY 10010
Editorial Offices: Bedford Books of St. Martin's Press,
29 Commonwealth Avenue, Boston, MA 02116
ISBN: 0-312-89510-0

Typography and design: Anna Post
Cover design: Rogalski Associates, Inc.

ACKNOWLEDGMENTS
Robert Nisbet, "Victimology." Reprinted by permission of the publishers from
Prejudices: A Philosophical Dictionary by Robert Nisbet, Cambridge: Harvard
University Press, Copyright © 1982 by Robert Nisbet.
W. H. Auden, "Law Like Love." Copyright 1940 and renewed 1968 by W. H.
Auden. Reprinted from *Collected Poems* by W. H. Auden, edited by Edward
Mendelson, by permission of Random House, Inc. and Faber and Faber Ltd.
Arthur M. Schlesinger, Jr. From *A Thousand Days* by Arthur M. Schlesinger, Jr.
Copyright © 1965 by Arthur M. Schlesinger, Jr. Reprinted by permission of
Houghton Mifflin Company.
The New York Times Index. © 1975 by The New York Times Company. Reprinted
by permission.
Readers' Guide to Periodical Literature. March 1982–February 1983, from en-
tries under "Educational tests and measurements." Copyright © 1982, 1983 by
The H. W. Wilson Company. Reproduced by permission of the publisher.
Isaac Babel, "My First Goose." Reprinted by permission of S. G. Phillips, Inc.
from *The Collected Stories of Isaac Babel.* Copyright © 1955 by S. G. Phillips,
Inc.
Archibald MacLeish, "Ars Poetica." From *New and Collected Poems 1917–1975*
by Archibald MacLeish. Copyright © 1976 by Archibald MacLeish. Reprinted
by permission of Houghton Mifflin Company.

Preface for Instructors

Students and administrators today increasingly recognize what composition teachers never forgot: writing is at the heart of an education and plays a large role in the lives and careers of most people. Whether students study the humanities or the sciences, their instructors expect them to write well. Lawyers, engineers, and executives in both the public and private sectors focus more and more on the quality of their own writing and that of their employees. The importance of writing is acknowledged in virtually every endeavor. It is no wonder, then, that once again writing is assuming its central place in the curriculum of academic institutions.

Writing, of course, does not exist in a vacuum. Students cannot be taught simply to write, as they might be taught to play tennis or even to operate a computer. Writing is part of the continuum of thinking-reading-writing. The quality of all writing — whether it appears in interpretations, proposals, analyses, or reports — will depend on the quality of the thinking on which it is based. To write effectively, students must first learn to think clearly and critically about significant matters. A giant step toward critical thinking is critical reading. When students engage, even challenge a text, their thinking and their writing will improve. The best writing will come from a scrupulous attention to what one reads and what one thinks. As thinking and reading affect writing, so, too, good writing gives rise to better thinking and reading. Belief in this continuum underlies our thinking about writing.

We wrote the book for students who are not yet fully developed and confident as writers but are intelligent and motivated to learn. We set ourselves two goals. The first was to help these students, whatever their writing task and writing problems. Our second goal was to write in a style that students would find not only understandable but also fun to read.

If we had to choose one word to describe our approach, it would be *practicality*. We believe that specific and practical advice is what today's students need. We have therefore incorporated theoretical considerations only as they are also of practical help, and many are. We discuss writing as both a process and a product, for to write well, a student must understand writing from both sides, those of writer and reader. We pay special attention to revision in this regard, for we see it as a central practical skill. Throughout the book, we have offered advice we think will aid the whole act of communication.

The book is divided into five parts. In each part we include general advice on how to go about the task at hand and careful analysis of examples. The general advice is summarized as "Tips" at the end of a chapter or section. We would not want these tips to be misunderstood. We see no quick and easy — and certainly no mechanical — way to write well. The tips only represent the pieces of advice we hope students will remember. The analyses include both professional and problematic writing. Understanding why a passage succeeds can be informative and encouraging. With problematic writing, we analyze the problem and then show how the writer could solve it. This process of comparison furnishes a model for the kind of close reading we advocate in the rest of the text.

The first part of the book is entitled Cranking Up: The Writing Process and the Reading Process. Its two chapters include detailed case studies that follow one student from invention to revision and another from reading critically to writing an essay on the reading. In the first chapter, we emphasize that revision is often a form of large-scale rethinking, not just another name for editing or moving blocks of text here and there. In the second chapter, we approach the too frequently intimidating concept of critical reading with a series of practical questions that the college reader can apply. Both chapters treat writing and reading as intertwined.

The next two parts cover paragraphs and style. Part Two, The Heart of the Matter: The Paragraph, discusses the paragraph as a concrete unit and as the result of a particular strategy like illustration or definition. It also includes a chapter on how to begin, how to end, and how to title an essay. Part Three, The Art of the Writer: Sentences, Diction, Style, discusses elements of stylistic choice — sentence structure, word choice, and tone. It describes a style appropriate for college writing and shows students how they can achieve it.

The fourth part, The Critical Moment: Persuasion and Argument, because it is so crucial, contains three full chapters. The first introduces a form of argument, the Toulmin model, and shows students how to use it. We have found that students think more clearly and argue more effectively when they understand the importance of evidence and how it is used. Accordingly, Chapter 10 discusses the various kinds of evidence and provides advice on how to use evidence and criteria for evaluating it. Chapter 11 covers the proper and improper uses of induction and deduction — including the familiar logical fallacies — as well as the ethics of persuasion. Here, too, our advice treats writing as well as reading. Understanding how other writers put their thoughts into writing often clarifies the process of argument for college readers. Critical reading is thus crucial to effective argument.

The fifth and last part of the book is entitled Putting It All Together: College Writing and treats three of the most common college writing tasks: the research paper, the essay on literature, and the in-class essay examination. Chapter 12, Writing Research, covers the entire research process from a first trip to the library to the proper format for the final manuscript. It includes three forms of documentation: both MLA forms (parenthetical references and list of works cited, and notes and bibliography) and the APA style. A sample research essay appears with a thorough annotation facing each page. In Chapter 13, Reading, Interpreting, and Writing about Literature, we discuss topics important to all literature, as well as topics specific to fiction and poetry. To demonstrate interpretative methods, we provide a brief case study. Chapter 14, The In-Class Essay Examination, offers advice on preparing for the examination as well as for actually taking it. It includes an excellent sample essay written in class.

The appendixes offer a handbook and a usage glossary. The handbook focuses on grammatical terms and common errors. It includes rules and advice governing punctuation, mechanics, and spelling. The usage glossary treats quandaries about correct usage, diction level, homonyms, and dialect confusions.

The *Instructor's Manual* contains sample syllabuses, suggestions on how to approach the various aspects of writing, and analyses of all the exercises.

We have already suggested our implicit debt to the many writers on composition from whom we have learned. We have also learned from the students in our classes. We wish particularly to thank those at Stanford University who were, perhaps without knowing it, the guinea pigs on whom we tried out many of our ideas and exercises.

Several students must be individually acknowledged: Larry Boyd, Cornelia Condry, Kimberly Corsaro, Christina Gerke, Jeri Shikuma, and Jeff Sloan. We sincerely thank them for letting us use their work and for being such good writers.

We also want to acknowledge the help of the following people: Helen Brooks, Mary Butler, Howard Dobin, Kevin Dungey, Maria-Christina Keller, Barbara King, George Lee, Robert Levine, Dagmar Logie, Dennis Matthies, John McClure, Geoffrey Moore, Joseph O'Mealy, and Ann Swidler. All of them have contributed significantly to this manuscript, providing ideas, criticism, even language. We also wish to thank David Bartholomae, Robert DiYanni, Irv Hashimoto, Michael Meyer, Tom Miller, Shirley Morahan, Mike Rose, and Haskell Springer, who read this book in its early stages and gave us criticism that improved it immensely.

The staff of Bedford Books has been exemplary. We particularly want to thank Charles Christensen for suggesting the book and Joan Feinberg for being patient, persistent, and full of helpful suggestions. Elizabeth Schaaf, Chris Rutigliano, and Susan M. S. Brown have on more than one occasion saved us the embarrassment of a horrendous gaffe. Before writing this book, we had no idea just how large a role an editorial staff plays.

The book, finally, is ours, and we take full responsibility for it. We hope you find it writing worth reading.

Brief Contents

Contents

PART 3   **THE ART OF THE WRITER:
SENTENCES, DICTION, STYLE**   *177*

8. Style and Tone *250*

PART 4   THE CRITICAL MOMENT: PERSUASION AND ARGUMENT *263*

Introduction for Students

*He wins every hand who mingles
profit with pleasure, by delighting
and instructing the reader at the
same time.*

– Horace (65 – 8 B.C.)
Roman poet

*The only thing we have to fear is
fear itself.*

– Franklin D. Roosevelt (1882 – 1945)
President of the United States

No one is born knowing how to write. Unlike breathing, walking, even talking, writing has to be consciously learned. It doesn't come naturally. Most of us don't think in nice, well-rounded sentences and neat paragraphs. In conversation, we don't start out with our main point firmly in mind and immediately back it with proof — often we don't even recognize our main point until halfway through the conversation.

Writing well takes effort. As the Renaissance poet Ben Jonson said, "Who casts to write a living line must sweat." Improving your writing is hard work. So, too, is learning to program a computer, to play tennis or chess, to clone a cell or set a bone. Like all these activities, writing can be very rewarding. You can communicate with your readers, inform them, change their minds, maybe, show them how the world looks to you. Getting it right is worth the sweat. And all the best writers — novelists, journalists, letter writers, people in almost every walk of life — work and work to get it right. Their writing may seem effortless, but then so does Michelangelo's *David*, and that was once just a hunk of rock.

At this point, you may be asking yourself why, in an age of instant communication by satellite or terminal or telephone, you should struggle to write better. We think there are two very good answers to that question, one professional, one personal.

First, the professional. Perhaps computer scientists can envision a world without paper, with everything on a silicon chip. But a world without a written record would be chaos. We would not know where we had been, what we had promised, where we hoped to go. All through our working life, most of us are called on to put our ideas into orderly and more or less permanent form. Police officers take evidence and describe crimes and accidents. Engineers write abstracts of projects they hope to undertake. Executives write reports to the boss and directives to the staff. Lawyers present briefs for judges to study, and judges hand down written opinions. And with every rung of the ladder, people rely more and more on writing.

Second, the personal. We think the second reason is even more important. Writing is a road to knowledge, to knowledge both of the subject of the writing and of the self who writes. We write and we remember better. We write and we understand. Above ِil, we write and we find out what we really think. And the better we write, the better we think.

Many people are afraid of writing. That blank piece of paper can look as resistant as any rock. Many times as we approached a new chapter of this book, we were a good deal less than eager. But because both of us have done a fair amount of writing, we believed we could do it, and we went ahead. You may not yet possess that confidence. Perhaps when you were in the second grade, you overheard your mother or your teacher say something like, "That child will never learn to write!" and you have believed it ever since. Or perhaps writing just did not interest you because your imagination whirled with colors, numbers, animals, plants, music — not with words and sentences. Or perhaps you always assumed you wrote well until that first assignment in Western Civ, when you began to fear you would never understand the hard reading and would never be able to write anything worth reading.

Our experience as teachers and writers tells us that fear is the most pervasive reason people cannot write well. It paralyzes, it stultifies. If you suffer from fear of writing, your first task is to get over it. You can write, if you will. It will require work, yes, but armed with knowledge, seasoned by practice, you can get beyond the fear to the confidence.

For writing is not a mystery. It is, as the English novelist Laurence Sterne observed over two hundred years ago, "when properly managed . . . but a different name for conversation." When you write, you must of course be a little more careful than when you speak, but with the proper management your meaning can be just as powerful.

This book is about proper management. It is about finding something to say that is worth saying. It is about reading more productively and thinking more forcefully in order to write more persuasively. It is about identifying your audience and shaping your language, though not your opinion, accordingly. If you want to improve your organizational skills, you should find some helpful tips here. If you want to make certain once and for all that you know the proper use of the colon and the semicolon, that is here, too. Our aim in writing this book was to provide help with whatever you write, be it an essay, a business letter, a report, a law brief, or an exam.

We don't expect you to come up with a *David*: Michelangelo, Mozart, Shakespeare had a brilliance no one can teach or learn. We do, however, expect you to learn to write what you mean — and with a touch of style.

part one

Cranking Up:
The Writing Process and
the Reading Process

1 / The Writing Process

> *For the things we have to learn*
> *before we can do them, we learn*
> *by doing them.*
>
> *– Aristotle (384–322 B.C.)*
> *Greek philosopher*

Writing is both a noun and part of a verb, a product and a process. Readers look at the product. Does it tell me what I want to know? Is it clear? Do I enjoy reading it? Is the writing worth reading?

Writers, however, must think of the process. Why am I writing? For whom will I write? What will I say? How will I begin? How will I proceed? How can I make it better?

The writing process is a continuing development, a growing through time, one stage shaped by the preceding stage and shaping the following. No two writers will go through the process in exactly the same manner. One person may have a rich fund of ideas but may need to make many drafts and revisions. Another may find that ideas come slowly but that the rest is easy once the ideas are there. And the process will vary according to subject and intention. If, for instance, the instructor gives you an explicit topic, you will not need to find your own. If you must hand in your first draft, you will not go through revision.

Although no one can capture the writing process in a series of rules, writing does fall into four rather loosely defined categories: invention, or getting the ideas; subject and thesis, or saying something; developing, organizing, and drafting, or getting the ideas written;

3

and revising, or getting it right. These categories are not new. Writers have been using them since Aristotle analyzed writing over two thousand years ago. And the categories do not necessarily have to come in this order; sometimes the writer will double back to an earlier category or repeat the whole process. In the next few sections we will discuss these categories.

First, though, we want to discuss two concerns all writers must bear in mind as they write: purpose and audience. No matter what kind of writing you do, you write with a purpose and you write for an audience. These concerns provide the context for the whole process. They govern what writers say and how they say it.

> *Lord, let me shake with purpose.*
> *– James Dickey (b. 1923)*
> **American poet and novelist**

PURPOSE: THE AIMS OF WRITING

Behind all good writing is a writer with a purpose. The purpose is like the destination of a journey. Where do we want to end up? with what effect?

Sometimes our true purpose will emerge in the process of writing. We may need a few paragraphs or even a full draft before we know our destination, as when on a journey we take a wrong turn or even go down a long, wrong road. But when we have our destination in mind, we find the whole process much easier.

Our overall purpose in all kinds of writing is to learn what we think and to communicate it. This means we have to get the facts clear, distinguish the important from the trivial, recognize relationships and hierarchies, and write correct and interesting prose. We also intend to convey a particular kind of information. Aristotle, the first to classify the purposes of writing, said that when we write, our purpose is to report, to explain, or to persuade.

Almost all the writing you will do in school — and most of your writing after you graduate — will have one of these purposes. You may be asked to *report* on the contents of a book or on the performance and results of an experiment. You may be asked to *explain* the causes of war or rust or inflation. You may want to *persuade* someone that the sound of the clarinet is more beautiful than the sound of the oboe or that careerism is destroying education.

Often you will have several purposes within a single piece of writing. In an essay on inflation, for instance, you may need one section to *report* a particular example of inflation — the last twenty years in Israel — one section to *explain* how inflation generally works, and one section to persuade your reader to undertake a specific course of action to stop inflation. Whatever your purpose or purposes, bear it or them in mind as you go through the writing process.

To Report

Good reporting is a faithful, detailed account of something. By faithful, we mean presenting the facts as truthfully as we can. Just as though we were witnesses in a court of law, we swear to tell the truth, the whole truth, and nothing but the truth. We do not repress the unpleasant or the contradictory. We do not distort in order to support a point of view.

By detailed, we mean presenting specific and concrete facts. When statistics are relevant, we cite them. When the story is at issue, we narrate. When how something looked is important, we describe it as exactly and vividly as we can. We try to bring the reader close to the subject.

Sometimes we will base a report on firsthand information, as we might if we were documenting a psychological experiment, describing a sporting event, or narrating an episode from our lives. Sometimes we will base a report on information gleaned from books or articles, as we would if we were narrating a marriage ceremony in Ghana or describing how social security works. However we obtain our information, we must bear our purpose in mind: to tell the facts. And we must remember to be accurate and organized throughout our presentation.

To Explain

Explaining goes beyond presenting simple facts to interpreting, accounting for, and making sense of a subject. If we were only reporting on the Black Death, which historians say killed 20 million people beginning in 1347, we might write,

> Sufferers from the plague exhibited swellings the size of an orange in their groin or armpit. Sometimes victims lasted five days; sometimes they were dead within twenty-four hours.

Something concrete and physical, like the appearance of the victims, can be reported; that is, described and narrated in a straightforward manner. But if something is obscure or complex, the reader will probably need more information, placing the event or idea in a larger context or showing how it functions and why it happened. In discussing the Black Death, for instance, we might want to explain where it came from and how it affected victims, and so we might write,

> The disease was brought to Italy by infected rats from Eastern ports. Fleas carried by these rats infected other rats and people. The plague affected three areas of the body: the lymph glands, the lungs, and the blood.

Now we show what caused the plague and what it caused. We indicate the process and the principles by which it worked. We show the relation of the parts to the whole and to each other. Within the word *explain* lies the idea of making obscure or complex things *plain*.

Explanation is a large part of most college papers. In a chemistry class, you may explain how the nonmetallic element bromine works on metals and on skin or what other elements it combines with to do what. In an American history class you may explain Lyndon Johnson's decision to withdraw from the presidential campaign in 1968. In a communications class, you could explain how Capitol Records' marketing strategies changed in the 1970s. Virtually every paper requires some form of explanation.

To Persuade

Persuasion builds on both accurate reporting and clear explanation. In addition, it requires the ability to identify the crucial issues, muster the supporting evidence, and present the whole so that it appeals to both reason and emotion. Only then will we achieve our purpose: to convince the reader that what we say is reasonable.

Many college papers will require you to take a position on a controversial subject and defend that position. Suppose you wrote about Argentinian politics and wanted to pinpoint responsibility for the troubles of that nation. You would first report the facts and explain the country's political history. You would have to deal with the legacy of the dictator Juan Perón, discuss the rule of the military, perhaps mention the few years of democratic government. You would need to say something about the effect of U.S. policy as well as that of other nations. You would have to reason carefully in order to show the relations between the facts and your assessment of them.

And you would need to handle these touchy issues in a tone that would carry your own feeling and conviction. For when we endeavor to persuade we appeal not only to fact and reason but also to emotion. As the philosopher Ludwig Wittgenstein pointed out, being convinced is an emotional condition, even if reason leads us to it. And so when writing to persuade, part of our purpose must be to get the reader to feel the emotion we feel — joy, anger, indignation. Bear in mind, however, that emotions are a potent tool, volatile and sometimes dangerous. They can be the companion of reason or its enemy. Either way, they cannot be ignored.

TIPS FOR PURPOSE

- Always keep your purpose clearly in mind.
- When reporting, concentrate on being accurate and organized.
- When explaining, remember that you must interpret and make sense of your subject.
- When persuading, bear in mind that you are trying to convince another person and must appeal to both reason and emotion.

EXERCISES FOR PURPOSE

1. Think of an intense experience you have had in the past year and report it as factually and objectively as you can. Think about who was there, what happened, why it happened. In your last paragraph, discuss your ability to be objective about this experience. Would a nonparticipant have reported it differently?

2. Select an activity you enjoy (guitar playing, bread baking, bicycle racing, ballet dancing, and so on) and in a three-page essay ex-

plain how to perform the activity. Cover all important steps; spend more time on parts that are especially difficult.

3. Select an editorial from a recent newspaper and write a letter to the editor disagreeing with the views expressed. Remember that your purpose is to persuade. Mail the letter. If the editor answers, or if your letter appears in the paper, share this with your classmates. Discuss the editor's answer and any letters from other readers. Which points are most convincing? Which least?

4. Read these opening passages from three essays. Can you tell whether the purpose of each is to report, to explain, or to persuade? How? What elements pointed especially clearly to the passage's purpose? Do you trust the writer? Why or why not? Write a paragraph in which you justify your assessment.

The environmental crisis tells us that there is something seriously wrong with the way in which human beings have occupied their habitat, the earth. The fault must lie not with nature, but with man. For no one has argued, to my knowledge, that the recent advent of pollutants on the earth is the result of some natural change independent of man. Indeed, the few remaining areas of the world that are relatively untouched by the powerful hand of man are, to that degree, free of smog, foul water, and deteriorating soil. Environmental deterioration must be due to some fault in the human activities on the earth. (Barry Commoner, *The Closing Circle: Nature, Man, and Technology*)

Niagara Falls is a city of unmatched natural beauty; it is also a tired industrial workhorse, beaten often and with a hard hand. A magnificent river — a strait, really — connecting Lake Erie to Lake Ontario flows hurriedly north, at a pace of a half-million tons a minute, widening into a smooth expanse near the city before breaking into whitecaps and taking its famous 186-foot plunge. Then it cascades through the gorge of overhung shale and limestone to rapids higher and swifter than anywhere else on the continent. (Michael Brown, *Laying Waste: The Poisoning of America by Toxic Chemicals*)

Everyone lives on the assumption that a great deal of knowledge is not worth bothering about; though we all know that what looks trivial in one man's hands may turn out to be earth-shaking in another's, we simply cannot know very much, compared with what might be known, and we must therefore choose. What is shocking is not the act of choice which we all commit openly but the claim that some choices are wrong. Especially shocking is the claim implied by my title: There is some knowledge that a man *must* have. (Wayne Booth, "Is There Any Knowledge That a Man *Must* Have?")

Sagebrush and lizards rattle and whisper behind me. I stand in the moonlight, the hot desert at my back. It's tomato harvest time, 3 A.M. The moon is almost full and near to setting. Before me stretches the first lush tomato field to be taken this morning. The field is farmed by a company called Tejo Agricultural Partners, and lies three hours northeast of Los Angeles in the middle of the bleak, silver drylands of California's San Joaquin Valley. Seven hundred sixty-six acres, more than a mile square of tomatoes — a shaggy vegetable-green rug dappled with murky red dots, 105,708,000 ripe tomatoes lurking in the night. The field is large and absolutely level. It would take an hour and a half to walk around it. Yet, when I raise my eyes past the field to the much vaster valley floor, and to the mountains that loom father out, the enormous crop is lost in a big flat world. (Mark Kramer, *Making Milk, Meat, and Money*)

> *I shot an arrow into the air,*
> *It fell to earth, I knew not where.*
> *– Henry Wadsworth Longfellow*
> *(1807–1882)*
> *American poet*

AUDIENCE: IS ANYONE OUT THERE LISTENING?

Although writing is like properly managed conversation, there is one enormous difference between writing and talking: when we talk, we have that other person sitting there, asking questions, interrupting, responding with body language as well as with words. We probably know something about that other person, including pet prejudices and cherished values. As we speak, we unconsciously adjust what we say to fit the listener.

Similarly, we adjust unconsciously to the audience for some kinds of writing. When we write personal letters, we usually have in mind an image of the recipient and gauge the most effective way to reach him or her. From Italy a student might send a close friend a postcard of the Tuscany countryside, describing a glorious bicycle ride down the mountain in the rain. The student might send her mother a post-card of Giotto's "Madonna and Child," saying she had been to the Uffizi twice and this was her favorite painting. Both true, both wonderful experiences, but different — because the audience is different.

For most people, writing essays is much more perilous than talking or sending postcards. They may not have a clear idea of the purpose or know what the reader needs to be told. They may not even know who the reader is. Too often they simply don't think of their writing as communicating with a reader. They just write. No wonder writing frequently seems scattered, unfocused — it's not aimed at anyone. "I shot an arrow into the air,/It fell to earth, I knew not where." Chances are it got stuck in the trees far from any target.

Sometimes an instructor will set up the target. One instructor we know tells students, "Think of the reader as an intelligent person, familiar with the subject but not expert, and eager to know what you think most important or most misunderstood about it." Another says, "I want you to prove to me you understand the basic concepts." Such statements define the task somewhat. More likely, however, the instructor will merely say, "Write a five- to seven-page paper on some aspect of this subject that catches your fancy." And you start shooting arrows.

Stop. Lay down your quiver and bow until you have set up your target. Make that target as specific as possible. Think about your potential reader. Imagine the knowledge, or the lack thereof, the values, the biases. When you aim your essay — or any writing — you have a much better chance of hitting the bull's eye.

With your target in mind, think about these questions:

What does my audience know and what does it need to know?
What ideas and information do my reader and I share?
Will I need to argue about values?
What level of detail will be necessary?
What response do I want and what can I expect from this audience?
    Respect? Amusement? Agreement? Action? Feeling?
What kind of language will elicit the response I desire?
Are technical items appropriate?
What illustrations and examples will achieve the desired effect?

These questions boil down to two very important ones: How much and what kind of information must I supply to this audience? And what kind of writing will be most appealing?

Suppose you were writing a persuasive essay calling for more nuclear power plants. If you were writing for a professor of physics, you could assume a good deal of scientific knowledge, no doubt more than your own, and a familiarity with the technical terms as well as the background of the debate. You would not, for instance, need to define the difference between fusion and fission unless showing your knowledge was a purpose of the assignment, but you would need to treat the economics of the various forms of energy, a subject in which your professor may not have expertise. And because you were writing for a scientific audience, you probably would attempt to sound objective and judicious.

If, however, you were writing the same essay for a wider, less specialized audience, you would take a different tack. You would probably define in simple terms the difference between the two kinds of nuclear energy. Furthermore, you would make a major effort to examine the safety of nuclear power plants. And when you discussed economics you might mention how savings from nuclear energy could be used for other programs, such as highway construction, child care, and so on. You would probably make an effort to write with more emotion than usual.

We are not suggesting that you shape your opinions and values to please your audience. Your writing would be worthless if it only reinforced someone else's ideas or soothed his or her ego. It becomes worthwhile when it carries your conviction about a significant subject. What is important to you is exactly what your reader wants to know. The goal is to persuade your audience to *your* way of looking at something or *your* plan for doing something. To reach that goal, you must bear your audience in mind throughout the writing process.

TIPS FOR AUDIENCE

- The more concretely you visualize your reader, the better you will be able to provide details that will appeal to that particular person.
- Ask yourself how much background your reader needs.
- As you write, stop occasionally and think carefully about your reader.

EXERCISES FOR AUDIENCE

1. Write an essay favoring a more stringent grading policy for college papers. Decide what points would best make your case. Pitch your argument to the following audiences: the head of your major department; the teachers; your fellow students.

2. Write a short essay in which you discuss how the change in audience affected your argument in Exercise 1. What appeals did you think would work for which audience? Which audience required special appeals, and what were those appeals?

3. Write an essay supporting the notion that your local football or baseball team should never be sold to anyone who would take it to another community. Argue this to the present owner; a prospective buyer; a convention of sportswriters; a convention of mayors, including the mayor of your city and the mayor of a city that wants your team.

4. Imagine that in a fit of hilarity last night, your roommate threw your typewriter out the window. The typewriter is beyond repair. Write letters explaining this event to your mother or father, the dean of the school, and your best friend at another college. Tell the truth, the whole truth, and nothing but the truth. How does your account change for each audience?

> *"Fool!" said my muse to me,*
> *"look in thy heart, and write."*
> *– Sir Philip Sidney (1554–1586)*
> *English poet and statesman*

INVENTION: GETTING STARTED

I don't know what to write. I don't have anything to say. I don't know what the instructor wants. I'd rather be sailing / playing rugby / pumping iron / knitting / purling / doing anything but writing.

As soon as we are required to write on a particular topic, many of us find writing the last thing in the world we want to do and our topic the least interesting. And, of course, the more we resent or fear the task, the more difficult it becomes.

Except for those lucky few whose ideas on practically every subject wait eagerly at the starting gate, most of us need help discovering our way into a subject. Some of us simply cannot get started, or when we do get something down on paper, our writing will likely show our reluctance.

A first step to getting started is to find a way to care about the subject. If the writer does not care, the reader will not care. And caring is almost impossible to fake. Yes, we can be sure the commas are all screwed into place and the topic sentences present and accounted for. Such mechanical or surface correctness is necessary but not sufficient for good writing. Unless we write about something that engages the imagination and intelligence, our writing will be inert, doughlike, dull.

Caring about a subject (and not just the grade on a paper) stimulates the imagination, and that generates energy. Our ideas will find their roots in the world. We may begin to discover connections that enrich our thinking. Our writing will become more enjoyable. Our sentences will get stronger, our paragraphs punchier. Caring leads to good writing.

No matter what the subject, there is apt to be something in it for us. "Nothing in mankind is foreign to me," said Terence. And nothing in humanity need be inaccessible to anyone. Some would probably groan audibly if asked to write on the Spanish-American War, the fight against malaria, or *Moby-Dick*. But in the recesses of our imagination we could probably find a way in which those subjects interest us: large nations bullying small nations; the selfless desire to eradicate disease; the destructive power of obsession, or the courage of seamanship. If we enter a writing task with sincerity and an open mind, we will discover that it can challenge and move us.

In the following pages, we describe a few of the techniques that may help you discover what you think. Not every one will work for all writers or under all circumstances. One technique may be right for one kind of assignment, another technique for a different kind. Try them all until you discover your own way of breaking up the mental logjam.

Brainstorming

Brainstorming usually refers to the way a group of people — movie writers, advertising agents, political advisers — throw ideas and questions at one another, banging out the shape of a project or generating ideas to solve a problem. Writers, too, can brainstorm, alone or with friends. Brainstorming requires an open mind, a fearless attack on a subject, and a tolerance for some temporarily disordered searching.

Although brainstorming follows no set pattern, you might try this four-step process. First, think about the general subject, to the best of your ability ridding your mind of extraneous ideas. Second, jot down as many questions about the subject as you can think of, whether you know the answers or not. Third, narrow in on the questions that spark your imagination and make brief notes on the answers, if any. Don't bother with full sentences or attempt perfect mechanics. Just try to generate a mass of questions and ideas, however outrageous and remote. Fourth, now that you have narrowed your focus, go through the process again in the area you find most interesting. This process may lead you to an idea you want to pursue in an essay.

The following is an example of brainstorming on the subject of secondary education:

> Do other countries have a similar system? What's the point of four years in a classroom? Did teachers once teach everything, like in grammar school? Did they always have special subjects like trigonometry? Why did they make me study 50% of what I did study? Why was I so bored in school? Was it because the outside activities were more interesting? If so, why do they allow that kind of competition for the student's attention? Why athletics? Why that production of *Midsummer Night's Dream*?

After a rather desultory start, the brainstormer warmed to the process and began to get closer to something interesting. He wrote down answers to some of the questions he had asked:

> Never understanding those books
> My parents pressuring me to make good grades
> Sometimes I seemed to try my best not to learn
> Maybe because many other activities competing with studies
> The school even supports them. The track team. And being in *Midsummer Night's Dream*
> I learned a lot being Puck in that play

With the questions at least partially answered, the writer looked over his notes. He decided that "activities competing with studies" needed more thinking. And so he brainstormed again,

Were the outside activities just fun? Or something else?
What about the play?
What do people get out of the debate team or choir?
Would some guys drop out without sports?

Unsystematic as this questioning was, it brought out unexpected ideas or points and perspectives the brainstormer might otherwise have missed. Once he brainstormed "other activities competing with studies," the point he found most interesting, he was only a short jump from beginning to write the paper.

Free Writing

If brainstorming leaves you with a messy lump of questions but no clear direction, try free writing. It is similar to brainstorming, but it can offer a steadier vision of your subject.

Free writing, as developed by Peter Elbow, is based on the notion that writing is a process and that you may need to be in the process, writing and rewriting, to find out what you think and know. This notion has much in common with the saying, "How do I know what I think until I hear what I've said?"

The method is called free writing because you write for a designated period completely free of censorship or editing. You do not stop writing for any reason. You do not think about what you are writing; you just write. Evaluating your ideas or your sentences before or during the writing may abruptly halt the flow of words. Just let yourself go — no one else will read or judge what you write. Try to get as much out as you can, regardless of form. Editing will come later, after you recognize what you really want to say.

You can free-write as long as you like, but of course you should make sure you stick to the designated task and the time you establish. Here is a free-writing procedure that we think works very well:

With the overall subject firmly in mind, write for ten consecutive minutes without lifting your pen. Put down anything that pops into your head, relevant or irrelevant, sense or nonsense. In fact, don't even think about relevance and sense at this stage. Don't judge; keep writing. If your mind goes blank, write, "My mind is a blank on subject X, my mind is a blank on subject X . . . " and keep on writing it until your mind begins to function. Don't let your hand stop writing.

If instead of brainstorming on the subject of secondary education our student had tried free writing, he might have come up with something like this during the first ten-minute period:

> The last thing I want to write about is education it's so general and I can't think of anything except chalkboards that awful scratching sound with the fingernail lots of math equations trigonometry I hated worst except the lit class we read Crime and Punishment was it? it was punishment all right that man murdered the old lady who needs it? I liked Pip though he was okay but not trig I hated my mind's a blank on education just like that fourth question on the final I couldn't even begin I'd rather have been outside the sun was shining but funny old man Puntz really dug that trig stuff his big grin when I finally worked out that problem Puntz was an okay guy and he really liked math but maybe lots of teachers don't like the subject I bet they're bored what would it be like if they switched around and Puntz taught lit and Demoully taught math? Imagine Puntz talking about butchering old ladies.

Time's up.

We recommend a five-minute break after the first effort: Get some water or do a math problem. Then read what you have written. Most of it will usually sound like gibberish. But you will very often find something worth thinking about. Throw away the results of the first step and repeat the exercise, again writing freely without stopping or editing.

> The teachers are interested because that's all they know maybe. Mrs. O'Reilly knew all about butterflies but she was a history teacher. Hard remembering all that stuff they have to remember. And they don't get paid much either. My mind's a blank on education my mind's a blank on education And half the kids are asleep, even tougher when you have to tell them to be quiet just when we were having a good time laughing in trig he had to say everything at least five times and he really must have been bored but wouldn't want us to know he was bored. But that grin when I was right. I was pretty pleased myself. I wonder what he really thought. He probably didn't know what I thought either. Maybe if students and teachers saw the other side it wouldn't be so difficult.

After the second writing, again do something else for five minutes. Then read what you have written, think about it, and repeat the ten-minute exercise.

By the end of the third step, you will probably be honing in on a subject. In our example, the student might be ready to concentrate on the difference between the way a student perceives education and the way a teacher does. After going through the process yet again, he might be ready to state a thesis, the specific point his essay will make:

> To avoid the hostility that sometimes arises between students and teachers, we should initiate informal discussions between the two groups.

The purpose is to keep repeating the exercises until your ideas have crystallized and you have developed a line of thought or at least recognized what material you need. You may need to go through the process four or five times. At the end, flesh out your ideas with the necessary support, arrange them appropriately, revise, and polish.

Free writing doesn't work equally well for all writers. It seems most helpful to those who cannot decide on a thesis and who find themselves blocked when faced with a blank page.

Clustering

Clustering is somewhere between free writing and the more systematic forms of invention. It works best when you have a topic — perhaps one assigned by an instructor — but no clear ideas about it. Suppose you are asked to write about your family, a popular first assignment in a variety of courses, from composition to sociology. If the ideas are not exactly flowing, take a sheet of paper and somewhere near the middle write "My family." Circle the words. Now brainstorm about your family. As other ideas emerge — topics, memories, images, names — jot them down anywhere on the paper:

> Uncle Bill
> Everybody shouting
> Me breaking the picture window
> Girls and boys treated differently
> Nobody turned out as expected

After you have a number of ideas, circle the ones you find most intriguing and begin to make clusters around them. Around "Girls and boys treated differently" you might write "Mother easier on boys" and "Father easier on girls," and you might use "Father easier on girls" to form another cluster, which might include "Changed when Maggie went feminist." Make clusters around each of your subordinate ideas. Now you can do one of two things: note which ideas are connected and brainstorm the connection; or choose a phrase, image, or idea that appeals to you, write it on another sheet of paper, and do the clustering process all over again. If the clustering around "Father changed when Maggie went feminist" interests you, you could start a new sheet of paper with that as the central idea.

As you cluster and connect, you will find your ideas getting more and more specific and insightful. In our example of "Father changed when Maggie went feminist," you might begin a new cluster that would develop into the idea that family relationships necessarily change, especially when children take contrary positions. You might analyze the consequences. By this time you would be fairly close to starting your essay.

Directed Questioning

When you already know what interests you about the general subject but aren't sure how to approach it, try directed questioning. Instead of encouraging your mind to go where it will, with this method you close in on the major points. For when you have your basic ideas in mind, you want to limit and focus, not search and expand. Two directed questioning techniques are the journalistic method and the classical method.

The Journalistic Method. Fledgling newspaper reporters are taught to check their stories for the answers to six simple questions: who? what? when? where? why? how? This method may help you narrow your focus and discover your approach. It will certainly help you order your thoughts and check for completeness. The questions will prove particularly useful when you narrate or describe human events.

Suppose the assignment were to write about a major event of the Civil War and you chose the surrender at Appomattox. The journalistic method would work this way:

> *Who?* Robert E. Lee, commander of the Confederate forces, and Ulysses S. Grant, commander of the Union forces and later president of the United States.

What? The surrender of Lee to Grant, ending the Civil War with a victory for the North.
When? April 9, 1865, almost exactly four years after the war began.
Where? At Appomattox Courthouse in central Virginia.
Why? The Confederate forces were outnumbered and rapidly running out of ammunition and food.
How? When the two generals met on the courthouse steps, Lee offered his sword, but Grant refused to accept it.

Any one answer may spark your interest. For example, you may be drawn to the personalities of the two generals, to the chain of causes that led to Lee's decision to surrender, or to the symbolic importance of offering and refusing the sword.

The Classical Method. Many teachers, most notably Edward P. J. Corbett, suggest that rhetorical devices used by the ancient Greeks and Romans can help today's writers. The ancients analyzed a topic by using definition, comparison, relationship, and testimony. You will get to know some of these devices later as "strategies" you can use to construct a paragraph. Using them to analyze a subject can help you develop ideas about it. If the student who wrote on secondary education had used the classical method, his questions and answers might have followed this pattern:

Definition — What is it? What isn't it? What are its characteristics? What are its parts? Are there concealed implications or values? Are all the terms sufficiently clear?

He might have started with the dictionary definition: "The process of being trained or gaining knowledge through a formal or informal course of instruction." Then he might have gone on to think about that definition:

Suppose I learned how to shoplift — is that education? How can you tell the difference between a good education and a bad one? I think it's what you know. How well adjusted you are to society. Whether or not you have skills so you can support yourself afterward. Some people would not agree. Definitions vary from person to person.

Comparison — How does your subject resemble something else and how does it differ? Are the differences trivial or significant? Is the comparison compelling enough for an entire essay?

Education is like other ways of socializing people to participate in society, joining the army, becoming a member of a club. Going to school is not the only way to get an education. You could listen to informed people, read books and magazines, get some on-the-job training. But school is different. Maybe because so much of what goes on is brain training, which you may get occasionally in these other activities but only incidentally.

Relationship — What preceded and what followed the subject? What were its causes and what were its consequences? What events happened at the same time, and how did they relate to the subject?

What precedes education is not being educated. What happens at the same time? Well: life. While learning one kind of thing in school you learn other things outside. Everything from how to play the xylophone to how to fly a plane. But inside and outside often connect. What follows education is what the debate is all about: happiness? maturity? success? or being a cog in the economic wheel?

Testimony — What has previously been said and written on this issue? Have opinions changed over time? How does your view differ from "received" or conventional opinion? Why? (If your idea is different and you can analyze why, you will be on your way to a strong essay.)

Plenty has been said and written, including "A little learning is a dangerous thing." Ideas about education are always changing. Once teachers would try anything in class, but they are getting conservative. Seems to be a pendulum, from conservative to liberal and back. And that is good. When new ideas are being tried, even when they are really old ideas, students get more interested.

The student would have covered vast territory. Depending on his interests and impulses, he could select any of his answers as a starting point. He could compare the structured learning in school with the unstructured learning out of school, or he could trace the various changes in schoolroom tactics. The advantage of the classical method is that it puts ideas into categories and directs that all-important fund of ideas, daydreaming.

TIPS FOR INVENTION

- There is nothing about which you have nothing to say; you only need to find a way to care about a subject.

- Keep an open mind about all the techniques of invention: brainstorming, free writing, clustering, and directed questioning.
- Remember that one technique may be effective for one kind of task, another for another kind.

EXERCISES FOR INVENTION

1. From the following topics, choose one that interests you and free-write on it for ten minutes: heroes, temptations to lie or steal, being a foreigner, parents, why biology is fascinating. Read what you have written and select the idea you find most interesting. Using it as your starting point, free-write on it for another ten minutes. Stop again and select the most appealing sentence. Free-write on it for a final ten minutes.

2. Write a paragraph in which you describe doing Exercise 1. Was it easier or harder to free-write the second and third times? Did you develop unexpected ideas? Look at your first free writing. What ideas might you have pursued instead of the one you did? Why did you choose the one you did?

3. This exercise takes a partner. Agree on one of the following topics and then brainstorm separately for ten minutes. Compare your notes. List the ideas and images that appear on both sheets. Which seem most promising as writing topics? Choose one of these items and repeat the process. Now each of you write an essay on an item from the second brainstorming list. Compare the two essays and account for differences. What choices did each of you make? Why?

   entering a party full of strangers
   the hazards of exercising
   taking responsibility for your actions
   the value of intramural sports
   the difficulties of choosing a career

4. Cluster ideas around one of these large topics: foreign policy, intercollegiate athletics, imports from Asia, studying philosophy, college education for everyone. From this first cluster, pick an idea and cluster another set of ideas around it. Choose one of the ideas in this second cluster and cluster around it. Write an essay on an idea in your third cluster. Explain your choice.

5. Use the journalistic method to generate ideas on one of the following topics. (If you do not know the answers to some of the questions, consult the reference section of your library.) Compare

your ideas with those of classmates who chose the same topic. After seeing your classmates' work, would you go about the task in a different way? Why?

> Harry Truman's election as president
> special awards at high school graduation
> the Donner Party
> the law of gravity
> a specific athletic event

6. The classical method was originally used to generate ideas from general topics. Try it on one of the following: civil disobedience, faithfulness in marriage, racial diversity, the Third World, social welfare programs. Now write an essay on one of the topics. At the end of the essay, discuss which strategy — definition, comparison, and so on — was most fruitful. Which led you to your topic? Why?

> *There is nothing to write about, you say. Well then, write and let me know just this — that there is nothing to write about.*
>
> *– Pliny the Younger (c. 61–c. 112)*
> *Roman orator and statesman*

SUBJECT AND THESIS: SAYING SOMETHING

Generating ideas is a first step toward writing, but once you have a fund of possibilities, you need to decide which idea or ideas are worth writing about.

In the Introduction we mentioned some of the things we hope you will get from this book, and we started the list with "Finding something to say worth saying." We started there because, of course, that is the most important part of writing. If there is nothing to say, there is no point in writing. All of us know people — and some of us have dear friends — who chatter on about nearly nothing. We put up with it because we love the person or the voice is soothing or the sound serves as a cover for our thoughts. But imagine having to sit still and read that same chatter, word for word, in print. We simply would not go on reading.

Writing worth reading must have both a worthwhile subject and a strong thesis or an interesting angle on the subject. The invention methods we discussed in the previous section may help a writer settle on a subject and develop an angle before actually starting to write. Frequently, however, the something worth saying does not precede the writing. You may begin with an idea, but in the process you may discover what you really think or think through to a better idea. Then you revise to take your new ideas into account. You may find your worthwhile idea before, during, or after your first draft.

The Subject

The subject of an essay is frequently the "given" of the writing assignment. It may be as broad as the titles of the courses: "Soviet-American Relations in the Postwar Period," "Abnormal Psychology," "Classical Greece." More often than not, the instructor will narrow it down: "Soviet-American Relations and the Third World," "Teenage Schizophrenia," "Socrates." Even so, the instructor would not expect you to cover the whole subject in an essay, not even in the big end-of-term paper.

Think of the possible ramifications of "Soviet-American Relations and the Third World." Most of the world is Third World — you could not deal with every country or even every continent. Nor could you discuss every aspect of their relations: military, political, economic, social, technological, and so on. You would have to narrow the subject to a size commensurate with your knowledge, your interests, and the space and time allotted for the assignment.

Every assignment has built-in limits, implicit and explicit. These limits tell you where you can and cannot go. They help narrow the subject. Suppose you receive this assignment in a course called "Classical Philosophy":

> Compare the preoccupations and methods of Socrates with those of pre-Socratic philosophers. Six to eight pages; due in two weeks.

This is a huge topic. Books have been written on the subject and have barely scratched the surface. A whole army of important Greek philosophers lived before the time of Socrates, and of course the great teacher and philosopher Socrates alone is an immense subject.

Your instructor would expect you to *select* one or perhaps two pre-Socratics for consideration. You might decide that Pythagoras is representative and interesting (besides, you have known his name ever since tenth-grade geometry).

You would now have set up the two sides of the comparison: Socrates and Pythagoras. But you would still need to narrow the focus: "preoccupations and methods" covers just about everything. You would limit the number of headings under which to compare Pythagoras and Socrates. You might make a list of the preoccupations the two philosophers had in common:

> the irrational
> problems in perception
> the physical universe

and many more. Which of these topics do you want to analyze? The same constraints operate: your knowledge, your interests, and the space and time allotted.

You may be drawn to "the irrational," just as Pythagoras was. You may "feel" a distinct difference between Pythagoras and Socrates on this subject, but you may not know exactly what that difference is.

At this stage, let the problem percolate. Review all you have read by and about the two philosophers. Compare representative passages from their writings. Review your class notes ("Socrates distrustful of irrational beliefs"). When something strikes you, jot it down. But also let your mind wander (Hey, didn't Pythagoras believe in reincarnation?). Follow your thoughts wherever they lead. Take the brakes off your imagination. Speculate.

When a central concern begins to firm up in your mind, concentrate on it. Write it down so you will be sure not to forget: "What the two philosophers thought about the limits of reason." Having narrowed your subject and thereby set up a manageable comparison, you are well on your way to developing your thesis.

The Thesis

Though some assignments call only for narration or description, most call for *exposition*; that is, analysis and interpretation of a topic.

In an expository essay, the writer makes an assertion about a subject and then sets out to prove it. Proving an assertion demonstrates how students think, how they handle concepts, and how much they understand.

The thesis is the assertion your essay will prove. Stated or implicit, it is your opinion on the subject, your conviction, your evaluation, your discovery, your approach, your point of view. Note the word *your*. The subject belongs to the whole world; the thesis is your stamp on it.

You may not know what your thesis is before you start writing — it may be the result of writing. But when you set about writing your final draft you will certainly need a thesis. An essay without a thesis is like a ship without a rudder. It moves in circles or in zigzags. It rises with the wave and sinks with the trough. It will probably swamp.

Although a thesis may be implicit, an explicit statement of your thesis early in an essay can be helpful to you and your reader. It can help you to bear in mind your destination, and it enables your reader to decide whether you are actually covering the ground you said you would. Usually this explicit statement will occur in the first or second paragraph. From then on, you and your reader can check whether the essay is on course.

In your thesis statement, you identify your narrowed subject and you make an assertion about it. In the essay on Socrates and Pythagoras, for example, you might have this thesis statement:

> Pythagoras was far more willing than Socrates to accept that reason has limits and pitfalls.

Your subject is Pythagoras, Socrates, and their ideas about reason. Your thesis is that Pythagoras was more willing to accept reason's limitations.

A thesis indicates how you view the subject. It lays out the direction the essay will take and the major concerns you will cover. To be effective, it must be succinct and its terms clear. Because the reader will assume the ideas are yours, avoid phrases like "I think" or "I feel" — they clutter your prose and make you sound less than sure of yourself. The thesis is your special twist on the subject; you are the expert on what you think.

You must, of course, get to the narrowed subject before you ar-

ABIGAIL E. WEEKS MEMORIAL LIBRARY
UNION COLLEGE
BARBOURVILLE, KENTUCKY 40906

rive at the sharp thesis. The following examples show the narrowing process operating:

> Assignment: Write about a difficult social situation.
> Broad subject: Smoking
> Narrowed subject: The rights of nonsmokers
> Thesis: Smoking should be restricted to confined areas.

> Assignment: Write about a novel you have read.
> Broad subject: Charles Dickens's *Great Expectations*
> Still too broad: Place in *Great Expectations*
> Narrowed subject: The important places in Pip's early life
> Thesis: The three important places in Pip's early life — the forge, Satis House, and the graveyard — shape Pip's possibilities in life.

Notice that the subjects are sentence fragments, but the theses are full sentences. They make complete statements about each subject. The purpose of the essay is to prove that the statement is justified.

To be interesting and effective, a thesis must avoid four pitfalls: it should not be too factual, too emotional, too grandiose and general, or too trite and obvious.

A thesis is not a litany of cold facts. Facts say nothing about themselves; they simply are. When we write, we show how facts relate and what they mean. In short, we interpret. In a class on twentieth-century European history, the assignment was "Discuss in a four- to six-page essay the Aisne-Marne Offensive." One student wrote this as his thesis:

> On July 18, 1918, a quarter of a million American troops began the month-long Aisne-Marne offensive. This offensive forced the Germans to retreat to the Vesle River. It was followed by the Meuse-Argonne drive. The armistice was signed on November 11, 1918.

This paragraph is all facts you could find in any encyclopedia. The writer did not say why the facts were important. The rest of the essay was a simple chronology. This happened and then this and then this. The facts are cold indeed.

The writer warmed the facts up in his revision:

> On July 18, 1918, a quarter of a million American troops began the month-long Aisne-Marne offensive. This offensive halted what had seemed to be an irresistible German attack, fortified the sagging Allied defenses, served notice of the American presence, and — perhaps most significant — caused widespread dissatisfaction and political unrest in Germany. It was the turning point of the war.

He now had something worth discussing: his interpretation, his opinion. He had the start of a very meaty six-page essay.

A thesis is not a gusher of feeling. We are not against feeling. On the contrary, we are all for expressing it in essays. But feeling alone will not help the cause. Readers will not be stampeded — they can be persuaded. "Computers are fantastic and fun" is not very arguable or scintillating. Neither is "Jeanette MacDonald and Nelson Eddy had the most beautiful voices ever," or "Abortion is a horrible sin and anyone who doesn't see that must be a fool or a knave." These explosions of feeling hardly promise an essay worth reading, one that is reasoned and supported.

In a second effort, the computer fancier tried to modulate her tone:

> Computers are the most fantastic innovation ever to revolutionize human life.

Imagine trying to prove that a piece of hardware is "most fantastic." What about the internal combustion machine, the lever, and the wheel? This thesis is still too large and too emotional for an essay. The writer made a final try:

> Computers have revolutionized human life by drastically shortening the time it takes to perform previously difficult and lengthy intellectual operations.

The writer still has her work cut out for her, but now it is feasible.

The thesis is not a grandiose generality. The thesis is an assertion you can support in the time and space allotted. In a six- to eight-page paper, you can neither prove nor disprove the superiority of capitalism over socialism or vice versa. You can neither prove nor disprove that the novel is dead. These assertions are too far reaching for an essay. Don't claim more than you can support. Be modest.

The thesis is not a recitation of the obvious. No one wants to read that "Senators are subject to pressure from special interest groups." We know that already. We know that slavery is evil, that defense costs money, that science is challenging. Conventional opinions do not a lively essay make. If something is not worth arguing about, it is unlikely to be worth writing about. A good thesis is a controversial thesis. It should not be wild or crazy, but it ought to have a sharp edge.

Sometimes you can turn bland statements of received wisdom —

like those in the previous paragraph — into sharp statements with an argumentative edge:

> Balancing special interest groups is at the heart of the American political system.

> Slavery was essential to the development of democratic institutions in ancient Greece.

> The Star Wars defense plan will save money and lives in the long run.

> The obsessive desire for scientific knowledge is dangerous, as the *Frankenstein* story indicates.

We do not necessarily agree with these assertions, but they do have an argumentative edge, and we would like to read what the writers have to say about them.

Subjects without an Argumentative Edge

Thus far we have been talking about expository essays in which the writer makes an arguable assertion and then sets out to prove it. But thesis statements do not always argue a writer's opinion. You may be asked, in school and out, to do other kinds of writing as well — personal essays, book reports, explications. They narrate or describe, and thus the idea of an argumentative edge does not apply to them. But in all good writing the thesis serves as an organizing principle. Good reporting cannot accumulate and present facts indiscriminately. The writer must determine the most effective way of presenting these facts. Even the simplest reporting, then, requires a thesis to give it form.

Suppose we want to describe the scene outside the window. We cannot include everything, every blade of grass, every leaf on every tree, every movement as the wind passes, every shadow. We need an idea around which the individual facts can be clustered. "Greenness," we might say, "dominates the scene outside the window." That will be our thesis. Now we organize sense impressions into shades of greenness. We can show how the green of the grass compares with the green of the trees and contrasts with the blue of the sky. The statement shapes our essay from the first word. Without it we would probably turn the mass of facts into a mess of words.

What is true of reporting the way something looks is also true of more abstract reporting. We must organize what we report. If, for instance, we are asked to report on inflation in the 1970s, we cannot simply throw the facts — billions of little facts — at the page. We need to find a thesis to organize the material. Should we track the inflation chronologically, using statistics on income, unemployment, and so forth? Should we take a particular family and show how lives are affected? Should we focus on international economics and debt? The possibilities are vast. But once we decide on our thesis, we can begin to arrange the facts.

This sort of thesis must concentrate exclusively on the relevant and the important. It should avoid the incidental and capricious. In the essay on inflation, for instance, we would not discuss the effects on people who drive Rolls-Royces or how much Brazil is in debt to Denmark — neither is particularly relevant or important to the subject.

If we keep the thesis too narrow, however, we risk trivializing our essay. We would drastically reduce the significance of our discussion of inflation if we dealt only with the cost of automobiles or clothing. Our thesis should take an angle wide enough to provide for all we want to say on the subject. If in describing the scene outside the window we want to say something about smog or acid rain, then the narrow notion of color probably will not suffice. We will need to enlarge our focus. We might say, "A pock-marked, straggly greenery dominates the scene outside the window." That statement allows us to consider the effects of pollution. The window provides the subject. The organizing principle is the writer's contribution.

TIPS FOR SUBJECT AND THESIS

- Narrow your subject to a manageable size.
- Be sure your thesis statement is succinct and the terms clear.
- Avoid phrases like "I feel" or "I think" in your thesis statement because the reader already assumes the ideas are yours.
- Ask yourself if your thesis is too factual. Is it too emotional? grandiose? trite?
- In papers that report rather than argue, the thesis statement should be relevant, important, and broad enough to contain all you want to say.

EXERCISES FOR SUBJECT AND THESIS

1. The following subjects are too broad for an essay of 750–1000 words: movies, American children, women in literature, the French Revolution, violence, science fiction, missionaries, DNA. Reduce four of them to manageable size. You need not construct a thesis: this is an exercise in narrowing the subject. Your instructor will ask you to discuss how and why you narrowed the way you did. Be ready to say which narrowed topic is most promising for a paper.

2. For three of the following overly broad assertions, write a thesis statement appropriate for an essay of 750–1000 words. Assert the negative if you prefer. With a partner, compare thesis statements. Test each one by the standards introduced in this chapter. What changes must you make?

   James Joyce was the greatest writer of this century.
   The quality of life ought to be improved.
   Affirmative action is essential.
   Taxes should be reduced.
   Genetic engineering is dangerous.
   Movies are more entertaining than television.

3. Rewrite the following statements to give them an argumentative edge.

   Beethoven is great.
   Doonesbury is an interesting comic strip.
   Waterskiing is exciting.
   In time of war, traitors should be punished.
   Police should be nice.

   Test these thesis statements as in Exercise 2.

4. Evaluate the effectiveness of the following statements as theses for essays of 750–1000 words. Rewrite the ineffective ones to make them workable. Note: you may not know what the writer had in mind — a major flaw in some thesis statements. If this is the case, construct a thesis for the indicated subject.

   Fraternity initiations are like animal aggression.
   The feminist movement threatens the institution of marriage.
   Wood stoves obviate the internal redistribution of thermal energies.
   Violence on television is a complex topic, but in this paper I will attempt to deal with it.
   Private ownership of handguns poses a serious problem.
   City planners may be eliminating the private dwelling.

5. Find an article in the *New Republic, Dissent, Public Interest, The Nation,* the *National Review,* or *Policy Review* and identify its thesis. Write an essay analyzing its effectiveness.

6. Below are opening paragraphs from four essays. Identify the thesis statement if there is one; state the thesis if no single sentence contains it.

> Since my sophomore year at UCLA, I have become convinced that we blacks spend too much time on the playing fields and too little time in the libraries. Consider these facts: for the major professional sports of hockey, football, basketball, baseball, golf, tennis, and boxing, there are roughly only 3170 major league positions available (attributing 200 positions to golf, 200 to tennis, and 100 to boxing). And the annual turnover is small. (Arthur Ashe, "A Black Athlete Looks at Education")

> When in the Course of human events, it becomes necessary for one people to dissolve the political bands which have connected them with another, and to assume among the powers of the earth, the separate and equal station to which the Laws of Nature and Nature's God entitle them, a decent respect to the opinions of mankind requires that they should declare the causes which impel them to the separation. (Declaration of Independence)

> Those of us who grew up in the fifties believed in the permanence of our American-history textbooks. To us as children, those texts were the truth of things: they were American history. It was not just that we read them before we understood that not everything that is printed is the truth, or the whole truth. It was that they, much more than other books, had the demeanor and trappings of authority. They were weighty volumes. They spoke in measured cadences: imperturbable, humorless, and as distant as Chinese emperors. Our teachers treated them with respect, and we paid them abject homage by memorizing a chapter a week. But now the textbook histories have changed, some of them to such an extent that an adult would find them unrecognizable. (Frances FitzGerald, *America Revised: History Schoolbooks in the Twentieth Century*)

> Most people who bother with the matter at all would admit that the English language is in a bad way, but it is generally assumed that we cannot by conscious action do anything about it. Our civilization is decadent and our language — so the argument runs — must inevitably share in the general collapse. It follows that any struggle against the abuse of language is a sentimental archaism, like preferring candles to electric light or hansom cabs to aero-

planes. Underneath this lies the half-conscious belief that language is a natural growth and not an instrument which we shape for our own purposes. (George Orwell, "Politics and the English Language")

> *A man may write at any time, if he will set himself doggedly to it.*
> – *Samuel Johnson (1709–1784)*
> *English writer and critic*

DEVELOPING, ORGANIZING, DRAFTING: GETTING IT DOWN

To get a workable and interesting thesis may take several tries, and you may even change your thesis after you finish your first draft. But when you feel you have a pretty good idea of what you are going to write, it is time to begin to get those ideas clear and to put them on paper.

Writing involves our psychological state and our physical state, so much so that the ease of it depends on how good we feel, how much we expect to enjoy the process, what response we hope for or fear, even our regard for the audience. No wonder it can sometimes not be "free-form fun." As Samuel Johnson suggests, we must sometimes just be dogged about it.

Before you start, plan your attack on the project. Think through your best way of getting down your thoughts. This part of the process will vary from person to person. Some will want to be tightly organized, others will just start writing. Save time and energy by knowing what is best for you.

The following advice should help with any writing task. It contains no big secrets or surefire tricks, only some points that will make your writing more enjoyable during the process and more effective with your audience.

First of all, make it easy on yourself. Start early. Some writers begin halfway between the assignment of the project and the deadline. If they have two weeks, for instance, they start writing one week before the due date. They don't wait until the last minute. Starting early provides a margin for error as well as ample time to perform the task.

Schedule a block of time to write, and do nothing else during that time. When you write in tidbits, you are constantly starting up. This is as hard on writing as stop-and-go traffic is on cars.

Put yourself out of temptation's way. Find a quiet, well-lighted, nonsocial place where you won't be disturbed. Take the phone off the hook. Have a snack or soda nearby.

Keep supplies handy. When you have a head of steam, going off to the store for a new pencil or eraser will undoubtedly dissipate it.

Be sure your references and source materials are easily accessible. Your dictionary should always be nearby. Have a handbook around for questions about writing. If you are using research, check to see that your major sources are with you. Be sure your notes are together, legible, and in order.

Developing

Once you have your general thesis in mind, jot down some supporting ideas. What you are seeking at this point is evidence for your thesis. *Evidence* is whatever the reader will accept without further explanation. It includes numbers, quotations, examples, the word of someone you and your reader both trust, the values you know you share. It is the common ground you and the reader can stand on.

A good source of support is what you generated from brainstorming or directed questioning. Go back over this material and identify the ideas that relate directly to your thesis. Perhaps you should freewrite or brainstorm again, this time with your thesis in mind. Look again for supporting ideas. If what you have seems too general or vague, explain it further with an example or a quotation. The invention techniques in "Invention: Getting Started" can help you develop your ideas as well as discover them.

Evidence also lies in your sources. If you are doing an essay on a novel, refer to the notes you took while reading and then page through the book itself for apt quotations. If you are writing about history, look in your textbook and other readings and rediscover the facts on which you have based your thesis. Be sure to take notes. If you are discussing sociology, develop your ideas by working up a chart or a graph based on some statistics you have collected. Not only is gathering evidence essential to support your thesis, but it can also help you clarify your ideas and organize your essay. (We have more to say on evidence in Part IV.)

Organizing

When you organize, you arrange in a systematic way the ideas and evidence that will go into your paper. Organizing can save you time. It provides a sense of direction in a morass of facts and keeps you on track. It eliminates repetition by grouping ideas so that you can see them clearly. It can show you relations between important points and can help you check your reasoning.

Many writers organize their papers by making an outline. Outlines are helpful, particularly when you have a large writing task before you; they more or less provide a table of contents for your essay. The more detailed and formal your outline, the closer you are to the final shape and content of your paper. But even the roughest outline can tell you something: outline your last free writing, the questions that emerged from brainstorming, or the answers to your directed questioning.

Informal Outlines. Making a rough, informal outline sometime during writing can help you figure out where you are going. For example, you can divide your thesis into its major parts and use each part as a heading under which to group your notes. We call such headings for general areas of discussion "topic headings." Suppose your thesis is "The affluence of American society has changed the values of all but the lowest economic class." Within that sentence lie several topic headings: "affluence," "American society," "all but," and "lowest economic class." Place each of your supporting ideas under the relevant heading. As you write your first draft, this rough outline will help you stay focused, show you where you need more evidence, and keep your main topics and ideas within reach.

Some writers make scratch lists of topics they will cover, brief notes of how they want the essay to progress. This procedure can help you collect all your good ideas so you won't forget them in the rush to finish a first draft. You need not be neat; you need only include all your main points in the proper order. Here is a rough outline of an essay entitled "The Politics of Electoral Reform." It starts, as any good outline should, with a statement of the thesis:

Thesis: The electoral college is unnecessary and potentially dangerous, and we should support efforts to change the system.

system's history
general success
controversy and flaws
problems in system
minorities
federalism
"faithless elector"
main proposals for reform
direct election

Each point appears in a phrase, and the writer has arranged the phrases in the order in which he or she will discuss them. Informal outlines are good for determining general direction and focus. For more detail, however, you may want to make a formal outline.

Formal Outlines.   Formal outlines break down, group, and arrange your ideas far more thoroughly than rough lists can. Formal outlines come in two types — topic outlines and sentence outlines. We call them formal because they are detailed, methodical efforts to set forth the ultimate shape of your paper. In a formal outline you present the major divisions of your topic and the relative importance of your ideas. You identify the major areas of your thesis, divide each area into subordinate parts and, where feasible, subdivide each part into smaller parts. Formal outlines follow the conventional system of numbered and lettered headings and subheadings:

I.
    A.
    B.
        1.
        2.
            a.
            b.
                (1)
                (2)
                    (a)
                    (b)

Items on the same level should be of the same general importance: that is, I should be of equal importance to II, and so on. Whenever you divide a level, you must have at least two parts beneath it. You can't cut a cake into one piece: under I, if you have an A, you must have a B, and so on.

Topic outlines set forth the paper's main topics in words or phrases. Such outlines help you see how you can divide and arrange your main ideas. Here is a topic outline for the essay, "The Politics of Electoral College Reform."

> Thesis: The electoral college is unnecessary and potentially danger-ous, and we should support efforts to change the system.
> I. Institutional success of the college
>   A. Around for a long time
>   B. Largely ceremonial
> II. Flaws in the college
>   A. Inequalities in "winner-take-all" rule
>   1. Inequality of votes
>   2. Inequality of political groups
>   3. Inequality of states
>   B. Potential dangers
>   1. Victory to wrong candidate
>   2. Harmful to "one person, one vote" principle
>   3. Threat to federalist system
>   4. Possibility of "faithless elector"
> III. Plans for reform
>   A. Automatic election plan
>   B. Proportionate plan
>   C. Direct election plan
> IV. Problems with automatic and proportionate election
>   A. Imbalance between majority and minority votes
>   B. Distortion of total national vote
> V. Direct election only fair alternative

Capitalize each item and try to make items at each level grammati-cally parallel (see the Handbook for a discussion of parallelism). No-tice that under IV. the writer had

> A. Imbalance between majority and minority votes
> B. Distortion of total national vote

not

A. Imbalance between majority and minority votes
B. Distorting to the total national vote

Formalizing your outline can tell you where the holes are, which ideas belong together, and which ideas are most important.

If you need more detail still, you may want to try a *sentence outline*. Where topic outlines only identify major items, sentence outlines force you to write a complete sentence about each item. Because you will have to write out exactly what you have to say, your ideas will get nearer to draftable form. Here is part of a sentence outline of "The Politics of Electoral College Reform."

Thesis: The electoral college is unnecessary and potentially dangerous, and we should support efforts to change the system.
  I. By most standards for measuring the success of a political institution, the electoral college seems to have an exceptional record.
  A. It has existed unchanged since the beginning of the Republic.
  B. The college has generally not interfered with the election process, its function being largely ceremonial in most elections.
  II. However, the college is increasingly controversial because of its obsolescence and some potentially harmful flaws.

Notice that each item appears as a complete and detailed sentence. You can add even more detail if you wish. For instance, you could list examples or references as support under each idea, as Larry Boyd did for his essay (pp. 75–76). In any event, you must determine how detailed you wish your outline to be. In general, the more specific and detailed an outline is, the more helpful.

Whatever outline you find congenial, don't settle for your first effort. The most useful outline is born of struggle and trial and error. Constructing it — cutting it down to size, throwing some parts away and keeping others — is a learning process.

You may make several outlines at several different points in your writing. Some writers construct an outline *after* writing a first draft. They use it to check their organization and presentation. Even if you construct one before writing, we recommend doing another before you go on to the second draft. It will serve as a map of what you have done and can indicate what still needs covering and what is out of place.

Drafting

However you organize your material, a time comes when you must start drafting. Whenever we mention drafting in this book, we say that it is or should be the least pressured stage of writing. We say you should let your ideas flow — no one is going to read your first efforts. We talk about drafting as though it were free-form fun each time, a snap compared with the other stages.

Well, that is a bit of an exaggeration. It does not work that way every time. Sometimes getting that first draft on paper is painfully slow. Roadblocks get in the way. Perhaps the subject is genuinely difficult and it takes time to cobble together all the bits of information or fill out each step in a closely reasoned argument. We may spend hours staring at that last sentence without putting down another. Sometimes those very first inkblots are paralyzing. Even James Joyce, a great writer, would stare out the window for hours on end seeking the right word.

Although no method is right for everyone, here are some suggestions for the drafting stage.

1. Keep three basic elements of your paper always in view: your purpose, your audience, and the big picture. Try not to lose the big picture in the little details. Every once in a while, stop and imagine the paper as a whole. Think about your audience. Imagine how the essay will sound, how it will look. Think about your goal. Can you get there from here? Have unexpected ideas revealed a new route to your goal? Consider whether you should revise the rest of your plan.

2. Don't try to write and edit at the same time. Writing a sentence, crossing it out, rewriting it, and worrying over the grammar or the wording can slow you down and endanger your mental health. When you hit on a new twist, you don't need to go back right away to adjust the beginning — you can do that on the next draft. If, however, a start-and-go-back method is the best way for you, then do it. But most of us find it easier and more effective to write now, edit later.

Some writers draft paragraph by paragraph. When they treat the paragraph as the main unit of expression, they get some sense of continuity of thought. Other writers find this continuity only when they write in sections. When they complete a fairly large section and come to a natural break, then they go back to look it over. Still others prefer to write the whole first draft before they reread even one sentence.

By all means, when those blinding flashes of insight tell you, "Hold on! That sentence on page 3 should have read . . . " or "Use that juicy Smith quotation on page 5," obey them. Fix up the suddenly offending passage or at least make a note of it. And if you have an idea you know will work beautifully at the end of the essay, be sure to make a note of that. But what writers need most at this stage is a natural rhythm in writing, not an agonizing halt-and-about-face process. Try to press on.

3. Do not, however, force sections that just will not come. Many writers cannot begin with the introduction: they think it demands too much formality and precision all at once. Yet some cannot get started until that first paragraph is right. Similarly, many dread the conclusion, but a few fashion it first so that they know where they are headed.

Most people find introductions and conclusions the most stressful parts of the writing process. If you feel happiest writing middle paragraphs, go straight to one. Start with a section you think may be easy to write or one for which you have some good ideas. Develop a key point. Don't fret: get to work on a part that interests you. The satisfaction you derive from the easier writing will often speed the harder writing.

4. Read aloud to yourself. When you have come to a natural pause — a paragraph or a section — give voice to your silent words. Reading aloud is a good way to stay in close touch with your writing. It will tell you if you are moving at an appropriate pace and if you are striking the tone you want. Of course, you will revise later, but reading aloud can help you to anticipate your next moves. It may give you some new ideas, reveal rough spots, or encourage you.

5. Recognize signs of tension. This may sound more like therapy than writing advice, but it concerns every writer. Frustration tends to grow slowly for a while and then hit a point where it sends you

through the roof. If you feel frustration building, stop before you explode. Take a break. Take a walk. Take a nap.

Like frustration, fatigue is an enemy of good writing. If you begin to get very tired, rest your eyes and your mind. Stop writing. If your paper is due in two hours, not writing may be hard to do — a good reason to make sure you are never in that position.

6. Regard the first draft as provisional. Few if any writers ever get it right the first time. A first draft is almost bound to be changed, and improved. Be ready — perhaps even eager — to revise.

TIPS FOR DEVELOPING, ORGANIZING, DRAFTING

- Look through your background material and your invention notes for evidence and ideas that need development.
- To save time and energy, find the most congenial method of organizing: informal, topic, and sentence outlines each offer different advantages.
- Identify your major ideas and group less important ideas under them.
- While drafting, bear in mind your purpose, your audience, and the big picture.
- Remember that few writers can write and edit simultaneously.
- Treat your first draft as temporary, subject to drastic change.

EXERCISES FOR DEVELOPING, ORGANIZING, DRAFTING

1. Choose two ideas from a recent invention exercise you've done — brainstorming, free writing, or outlining — and try to develop each one with at least two different kinds of evidence. Write a paragraph describing where you went for the evidence and whether or not it was easy to find.

2. Photocopy the most recent essay you have written and then outline it by all three methods. Write a paragraph describing which method you find most congenial, and why. Turn in the outlines and the paragraph.

3. Imagine that you are sixty years old and have been asked to write your autobiography. Free-write or brainstorm your life-to-be and

then plan how you would go about writing it. Divide the subject into major periods, themes, events, people, or however you want to organize it. Turn in your organizational plan.

4. With a partner, determine the major subdivisions of one of the following theses. Now, using one of the three outlining methods, each of you prepare an outline of a paper arguing that thesis. Compare the outlines. Which kind of outline did each of you use? What differences do you find? Come up with a compromise outline that you will present to the class.

> Smoking should be prohibited in all the buildings on campus.
> The drinking age in this state should be raised by two years.

5. Watch an episode of either a situation comedy or a soap opera on television. Write a short essay in which you organize the events and then explain the episode to someone who has not seen it. In your conclusion, identify the main event or main point of the episode.

6. From the following list, choose the topic that most appeals to you. Construct a thesis, make an outline, and draft an essay — in that order.

> anything that makes you particularly angry
> the virtues and foibles of your mother's or father's family
> allergies you have known
> the value of wearing or not wearing a wristwatch
> the pitfalls of borrowing and lending

> *I'm goin' to change my way of livin'*
> *and if that ain't enough,*
> *Then I'll change the way I strut my*
> *stuff. . . .*
> *– Billy Higgins and W. Benton Overstreet*
> *American popular-song writers*

REVISION: GETTING IT RIGHT

Novelist James Michener once said, "I never thought of myself as a good writer. Anyone who wants reassurance of that should read one of my first drafts. But I'm one of the world's greatest rewriters." Professional writers like Michener do not treat a first draft as sacred, engraved in stone. They know that thoughts rarely march onto the page in perfect order, sentences elegant, phrases vigorous, punctuation accurate. They know that to be a good writer is to be a good rewriter.

Although revision is about as popular as housebreaking puppies, it is the most important stage of writing. We need the spontaneity of the first draft, yes, but the first draft is a *first draft*. First, not last. If we are honest with ourselves, we know we will need a second go, and a third. Revision brings into play everything this book covers, from thinking large thoughts to selecting the proper dot or dash. Like writing, revision is a process. When we revise, we make a series of choices and try out alternatives. We experiment with sentence shapes and with emphasis. We keep on revising until we are satisfied — or have run out of time.

Some people write a first draft and then in the name of revision gussy it up with a few minor changes before presenting it to their bosses or instructors. Here it is, folks: the first-and-a-half draft. That is not revision. Revision follows a slow and objective reexamination of that first draft. It allows us to react to our first thoughts and to refine and expand them.

The Critical Distance

A brand-new piece of writing is like a brand-new baby: it looks perfect. We can no more read our writing objectively than we could list the baby's flaws. We need critical distance. We need to separate ourselves from our creation. Before trying to revise, you should put your essay away for a while. The Roman poet Horace recommended nine years. If you don't have that sort of time, try a few hours. Take a walk, see a movie, practice the flügelhorn — anything that will give your objectivity a chance to grow.

If you would like to know what critical distance feels like, find a letter or essay you wrote two years ago, or five. If you have the sensation of reading someone else's writing, you are feeling critical distance. The perfect writer would treat the first draft like another person's writing — that would guarantee a critical distance. Because most of us are not virtuous enough to attain such a state, we take a long break between drafts.

Once you have achieved some critical distance, return to your first draft. Read it. Read it aloud. Have a friend read it to you. Hearing your written words is almost always surprising. You may even want to interrupt with an occasional "Well, that isn't exactly what I meant." Feel the critical distance grow.

Blowing the Essay to Pieces

If you start revising line by line straight through, you risk seeing the essay the way you first saw it. Good revisers try to break the pattern in order to get a clearer look. They have various ways of blowing the essay to pieces.

Some writers start at the end and work backward. They check the conclusion against their purpose. They compare the ending and the opening to see if they can get to one from the other. Going backward, they note the transitions between paragraphs. They read sentences out of context — and perhaps wonder what they meant.

Other writers make a detailed outline of the first draft to check the order of their ideas. They may write out their topic sentences to see if they make a cohesive paragraph. If there are no missing links in this paragraph, then they know that they have not omitted anything in the chain of argument.

A few actually take scissors to their first effort. They cut it up into sections and arrange them in different combinations. Wrenched from their context, passages lose that "finished" look.

Anything that disrupts the way you are used to seeing or thinking about your writing helps you lose the pride of ownership that makes objectivity so difficult. It allows you to read with fresh eyes.

Once you have established the distance needed for a rigorous examination, you are ready to revise. You will probably want to cross out repetitions, underline good points, write questions to yourself, circle ideas, draw boxes and arrows. Gather some pens or sharp pencils and erasers. If you cut and paste, you will need tape or staples. And you will need plenty of time. This process cannot be rushed.

When the actual rewriting begins, most good revisers start at the beginning and work through methodically.

The Levels of Revision

Revision takes place on two levels, with a number of discrete tasks on each. Keep those levels separate. Trying to do all the revising tasks at the same time can be confusing.

Macrorevising. The most important level of revision is what we might call macrorevising. This level requires rethinking, and here you must be most ruthless with yourself. Think first about your thesis. A strong essay cannot stand on a weak thesis. If your thesis was not worth writing about, find another one.

Check your evidence. Do the examples do what you claim? Do you provide the common ground for you and the reader to stand on? If a weak thesis is a poor foundation for your thought, scanty evidence is a shaky scaffold. If you need more evidence, do the necessary research or brainstorming. And adjust your argument accordingly. Don't try to prop up a rickety argument.

Look at your organization: do the ideas flow and build toward a conclusion? Are the connections clear? Is the emphasis where it ought to be? If your organization is slapdash or haphazard, blow those paragraphs apart and rearrange them.

Microrevising. On the second level of revision, microrevision, we look at our writing phrase by phrase, sentence by sentence, paragraph by paragraph. And we ask hard questions. Is the topic of each paragraph clear, whether stated or implicit? Do all the points relate to the topic? Are the sentences in the right order? Is the meaning of each sentence clear? Is there ample variety? And what about word choice: is the writing concise, concrete, and vivid?

Reading an essay aloud is particularly helpful for microrevision. Be sure you have a pencil handy to mark those places where you question the shape or sound of your prose. If your first draft is too simple or too complicated, you can change it in the second draft.

The last task at this level is pencil editing, correcting grammar, punctuation, spelling, and mechanics. For specific information check the appendix, The Nuts and Bolts: A Handbook, which begins on page 453.

Often, microrevising for style turns into rethinking. If, for instance, you find your illustrations inadequate or uninteresting, you

may try to think up additional ones, and that could lead you to conclude that a point you made really was not justified. You would then
go back and rethink the point and its relation to your whole argument. If excess verbosity or pomposity has made your prose fat, the
slimming process may make your point more visible. Searching for a
better word may lead to a better idea.

CASE STUDY: THE TRUE CONFESSIONS OF AN ESSAY

Here is a true story of how a writer made her way from a first draft
that embarrassed her to a final draft that made her proud. Her task,
set by the instructor, was to define one of a list of terms: creativity,
prejudice, mental health, or mental illness.

Inventing

The student, Kimberly Corsaro, first spent a few minutes thinking
about the terms. Prejudice did not appeal to her; she knew she
would not do a good job if she did not like the subject. Mental illness
was interesting but she felt uninformed about it. She would have to
do research, and that was not the point of the assignment. The point
was to think. Mental health seemed to her a very broad term — too
broad for a short paper. In the end nothing attracted her as much as
creativity.

She began by using the journalistic method of questioning:

Who? Artists
What? God-given talent? physical and tangible? No: imagination
When? Well, any time, all the time
Where? Nowhere, anywhere, everywhere
Why? To express myself, to say who I am
How? Music, poems

This method, she thought, was getting her nowhere. She decided to
free-write her way deeper into the subject.

Creativity — poets and musicians — but don't we all have a bit somewhere? My pictures look like baby scrawls. But funny. My mother's
best friend laughed when I sang that Beatles song. Still, me. Nobody

else. I spend a lot of time in groups do I lose my indiv. or not? Not. That song not the Beatles but Nobody quite like you or something. No two pix alike. Twins even but each person has thoughts nobody else has. Where do I fit? I'm creative. Not just artists.

Corsaro had three ideas she wanted to discuss: her definition differed from most people's; creativity was not limited to artists; she and people like her were creative. She thought she was probably interpreting the assignment in a way her instructor had not intended, but that was all right because the instructor — her audience — liked students to take chances with their writing.

Drafting

Corsaro did not much like making an outline, so she decided that the three basic ideas were enough to go on. She began the first draft.

Most people think of something physical or tangible when they think 1 of creativity. However, the most creative thing that I am capable of doing is neither visible nor concrete. It is my ability to think as an individual.

There are many people who may be artificially talented, but it is 2 through their imagination that we see their creativity. Without thought and imagination from individuals, creativity would be nonexistent and consequently this would be a rather dull and boring place to live.

This is not to say that I or other people do everything differently 3 from others, because that would be an exaggeration. It is very common for people to do things in large groups because they enjoy company and I am no exception. However, you can be yourself and part of a group at the same time. Nobody is you, and you are nobody else. You can see this most clearly if you think about artists. If a group of artists were asked to draw a picture of a house, all the pictures would be different. The theme of the pictures is all the same, but yet all the houses vary.

This is because each artist has his or her own ideas; each perceives a house differently. This is where uniqueness and originality enter into a person.

Everyone has the potential to be creative. It is dependent upon   4
the person to develop his or her own talents. In the cases of some
people, such as artists or musicians, the creativeness is somewhat
obvious, whereas others' talents are less apparent.

Creativeness is the ability to be inventive or to transform   5
original thoughts into something others can enjoy. To most people a
creative work is a painting or great music. While these are good
examples of creativity, it can also be expressed in various other ways,
such as a poet or a writer.

But as I said above, I cannot paint or sing. When I draw it looks   6
terrible, and when I sing everybody asks me to stop. But I do think
for myself, and that is creative. If it was not, I would be thinking
everyone else's thoughts. It can be very difficult to think for yourself, because there are many pressures to conform to other people's ways
of thinking. I try not to do that, though I catch myself doing or
thinking somebody else's way. Sometimes I am glad I have other role
models. If we did not have other people telling us how to think when we
were younger, how would we know how to think at all? But I still think
I put my thoughts together in my own way. That is my creativity.

Corsaro put the essay in a drawer.

Revising

When Corsaro returned five hours later to take a fresh look, she blew the essay to pieces. She looked at the conclusion first. It seemed jumbled. She didn't know how she had arrived there. She checked it against the opening. That opening, she saw, was thin. She decided to make a topic sentence outline of the essay:

Paragraph 1: My creativity is my ability to think as an individual.

Paragraph 2: Without thought and imagination from individuals, creativity would be nonexistent and consequently this would be a rather dull and boring place to live.

Paragraph 3: . . . Which was the topic sentence? The first? The fifth? The last?

The outlining didn't work. She began to read the essay aloud. *She* wrote *that*? The essay started and stopped. She wasn't sure what she meant by certain phrases, like "artificially talented." Some of the writing was really awkward. Her critical distance became so great that she almost ran out of the room. Now she asked herself the hard revising questions.

Macrorevising. Glancing over the first draft, Corsaro was not sure what her thesis was. She didn't want her own creativity to be the central idea. She tried again: imagination, not results or works of art, is the most important part of creativity.

That certainly was better. It sounded like a thesis worth arguing. But had she proved it? It was time to turn to the evidence. Her first bit of evidence had been "Most people think of something physical or tangible when they think of creativity." That was vague, the kind of thing one says for want of something real to say. What she meant was . . . objects, things that people admire. Like what? She knew she needed an example, and her eye found one in the fifth paragraph: "To most people a creative work is a painting or great music."

She decided she should make the examples more specific and emphatic: "Most people think of something tangible — like the Sistine Chapel or Beethoven's Fifth Symphony — when they think of creativity." Would the reader be persuaded? What about adding examples from other arts, Mies van der Rohe's Seagram Building and Laurence Olivier's performance in *Richard III*? No. Piling on examples would not clarify the meaning.

Still, she had not fully established the difference between her definition and the conventional one. After a trip to the dictionary, she wrote: "Dictionaries often define the word as the ability to be inventive, or to transform one's original thoughts into a form others can enjoy." But how did this definition support what she had asserted about "most people"? And then she saw the connection: both defined the word according to the *results* of creativity — what it gives or does rather than the thing itself. They cared about creations, not creativity. In contrast, she was more concerned with imagination itself, a quality possessed by all people, even nonartists.

Now she was ready to state her thesis yet again: creativity exists in each person's particular thoughts and imagination, things most people know very little about.

She now wrote a new second paragraph to focus her thesis:

> I fit the first part of the definition (I have original thoughts) but not the last (I can't transform them into creations other people can enjoy). A person's unique thoughts and imagination are the most important part of creativeness, and that is the part most people know the least about.

With her newly shaped thesis firmly in mind, she began systematically to go through all the paragraphs.

In her original second paragraph she had used the phrase "artificially talented." Five hours later, the phrase no longer made sense to her. She looked up *artificial* in the dictionary: "of a human, as opposed to natural, agency." So what was "human"? Hard work, training, performance. People like Linus Pauling, Leontyne Price, Fred Astaire, Shakespeare. And what was "natural"? Imagination. Natural because we all have it. Eureka. Now she knew what she had intended: Linus Pauling and the rest differed from her in experience, training, and practice, but they shared imagination with her. Imagination existed inside her and, her argument went, everyone. She had clarified her own half-articulated distinction.

She was ready to write a new paragraph, one that related directly to her thesis. Remembering the lessons of the first paragraph, she put in the concrete illustrations for her point:

> There are many people — Linus Pauling, Leontyne Price, Fred Astaire, Shakespeare — whose creativeness shines out through their performance, and that is the product of many hours of hard work and training. But these people had imagination before they were writers, singers, dancers, or chemists. Without thought and imagination from individuals, creativity would be nonexistent and consequently the world would be a rather dull and boring place to live.

She looked now at her old third paragraph. The central idea seemed to be that "you can be yourself even when part of a group." Or was it that "each artist has his or her own ideas"? Whichever, she could not see how it related to the old thesis or the new one. She decided to put it aside and return to it if it fit somewhere later. The decision was extremely important. Corsaro had resisted the temptation to preserve at all costs her original organization.

She had dealt with the human contribution — the hard work — and she had now to deal with the natural. Well, although her own creativity was not *the* central issue, it was a perfectly good example of what she meant by natural creativity. By thinking for herself, she demonstrated her own imaginativeness. She had said this in the original sixth paragraph. Polished and refined, that sixth paragraph could become the new fourth.

And then she saw that the paragraph she had saved had a place after all. She could combine the material about the distinctiveness of artists with the material about how artists work hard in the new third paragraph. She could put the ideas about the distinctiveness of everyone in a new fourth paragraph, and that would wrap up the whole argument.

> I cannot paint or sing. When I draw it looks terrible, and when I sing, everybody asks me to stop. But I do think for myself and that is creative. It is creative because my thoughts are my own and nobody else's. But it is also creative because it is hard to think for yourself. Just as hard as most creative things are. Just think of all the pressures to conform to other people's ways of thinking. Fashions make you want to dress a certain way, and what your friends do is very influential. Then there are your parents and how they think. Just having a thought of your own at all is a creative act.

Although the prose was not exactly elegant, she decided to wait to revise at that level.

She looked at the old fourth and fifth paragraphs and realized they were floating loose. First she examined old paragraph 4. It was simply a summary, and not a very good one, of the whole essay. She was better off without it. When she examined the old fifth paragraph, she realized she had transplanted its heart — the example about painting and music — to the first paragraph.

Now she could make a topic outline of her argument:

Paragraph 1: Most people think of great works of art when they think of creativity.

Paragraph 2: All people share imagination, the most important and yet least understood part of creativity. (Thesis)

Paragraph 3: Artists differ from other people in their dedication to work and training, not natural talent.

Paragraph 4: Having a thought is a creative act.

Paragraph 5: We learn to be ourselves and part of a group.

She felt good about the rethinking.

Microrevising. Now it was time to examine the details and to see how the different parts fit together. Methodically, she examined each paragraph. Her new second paragraph was a problem:

> I fit the first part of the definition (I have original thoughts) but not the last (I can't transform them into creations other people can enjoy). A person's unique thoughts and imagination are the most important part of creativeness and that is the part most people know the least about.

The connection between the two sentences was not clear. Hadn't she heard someplace that two-sentence paragraphs were dangerous because often the connecting links were missing? She wrote in the connecting link:

> I still think I and people like me are creative. That is because a person's unique thoughts and imagination are the most important part of creativeness, and that is the part most people know the least about.

The last sentence looked rather limp. "That is because" is wordy and imprecise, and the word *unique* is overused. But worse yet was the ending: eleven heavy words dragging down the thought. She revised. "A person's thoughts and imagination are the most important, and least understood, part of creativeness." By reducing those eleven words to three and incorporating them in the middle of the clause, she had improved her clarity.

She went on to her new third paragraph. She liked the concreteness of the examples: Pauling, Price, Astaire, Shakespeare, a varied group of creative people. Because they were not known to everyone, she had explained that they were a writer, a singer, a dancer, and a chemist. She realized that the list was not in the right order. She changed it to "chemist, singer, dancer, and writer." Of course, everyone knew Shakespeare was a writer — with him in there, the list wasn't balanced. Examples should be similar. Cross out Shakespeare. Three would suffice.

Corsaro went through the same kind of analysis for the fourth, fifth, sixth, and seventh paragraphs. She put in connecting links, cut back verbiage, added examples, moved always toward the clearer support of her thesis. Once the argument seemed solid, she again read the essay aloud. She was shocked at how often she had said "creativity" and "creative." She had also overused "because" and "people." These repetitions, however, were nothing compared with the many clumps of the lazy verb "to be." She took a red pencil and circled repeated words. By the time she finished, the paper looked as though it had been pelted with buckshot.

As she deleted "to be's" and "peoples," she discovered that her language became more vivid. She noticed that she had concluded the third paragraph with "the world would be a rather dull and boring place to live." A dull and boring sentence. She now had a second chance at that statement. She wrote, "Their actions light up the world." Then she extended the image: "but their imaginations provide the current."

Now she had a transition problem. She needed a new opening sentence for the next paragraph. She was no doubt delighted when she found "Like most of the human race, I have the current but not the light." She went back over the manuscript to check all the transitions. She did not find one quite so brilliant as that, but she locked all her paragraphs more tightly together.

She had spent quite a while marking up her essay and writing out new sentences. Now she stepped back again to look at the whole. She thought about the assignment and visualized the audience. She looked carefully at her style, and then changed some words and rewrote a few sentences.

She went through the essay a final time and made a few more corrections on this working draft. She wondered, finally, if this writing was worth reading. As a last task in revising, she went to work on her grammar, punctuation, spelling, and mechanics. For this part of the revising, she used her handbook and her dictionary.

And then she gazed upon her work, and she found it good.

Was this essay perfect? No. There is no such thing as a perfect draft. Professional writers revise twelve, twenty, thirty times. One of the writers of this book revised a short story over twenty times — the story was published and won a prize. It could have been better. This essay still has awkward moments and almost-but-not-quites.

The writer knew her last sentence was not as strong as it should be. Perhaps she would rewrite it yet again, for her careful revision had paid off handsomely. With revision, her essay had become fuller and more interesting. For us, the essay provides that most exciting reward of reading: the sense of a mind moving.

New Meaning for an Old Word

When most people think of creativity, they think of something 1 tangible--Michelangelo's Sistine Chapel or Beethoven's <u>Fifth Symphony</u>. Dictionaries often define the word as the ability to be inventive, or to transform one's original thoughts into a form others can enjoy. Since dictionary definitions often reflect widespread attitudes, it is not surprising that even Webster's stresses the results of creativity rather than the thing itself.

I have a problem with such definitions--namely that I fit the 2 first half (I have original thoughts) but not the second (I cannot transform them so other people can enjoy them). Still, people like me should qualify, for we all share imagination, the most important, and yet least understood, part of creativity.

We share this gift with stars and geniuses--Linus Pauling, Leontyne 3 Price, Fred Astaire--whose creativity shines through in performance, the product of many hours of training and hard work. What sets them apart is not their natural talent, for many people have fine voices, an aptitude for science, or a sense of melody or rhythm. The true difference began even before they held a test tube, sang a note, or danced a step. It was their outlook, their approach to what they do, and their personal sense of style. Creativity begins when individuals think and imagine. Their actions light up the world, but their imaginations provide the current.

Like most of the human race, I have the current but not the light. 4 When I draw, my pictures resemble nothing in the real world, and when I

sing, everybody asks me to stop. I do think for myself, though. My
thoughts are my own and no one else's--quite an achievement, just as
difficult as many other creative acts. Just think of all the pressures
to conform to other ways of thinking, to accept what others believe.
Parents, teachers, and friends all have their own influences to exert.
Just having a thought of my own is a creative act.

      I do not mean to say I am totally original. Nobody is. If we   5
did not like to do things in groups, we would hardly be human. We also
owe a great deal to the parents, teachers, and friends who teach us how
to think in the first place. But what we learn from them is a sort of
creative conformity: we learn to be ourselves and part of a group at
the same time.

TIPS FOR REVISING

- Unless you are an extremely talented writer, never turn in a first draft.
- Provide yourself with critical distance, that is, separation from your work.
- Read your first draft aloud.
- Don't edit in a straight line: blow your essay to pieces.
- Don't try to revise on the two levels at the same time.
- Stay flexible: be ready to change anything at any time for any good reason.

EXERCISES FOR REVISING

1. Rewrite the essay you have most recently written. Reorganize the sentences in at least two paragraphs; rewrite your opening paragraph; change the last sentence of the essay; change the wording of at least eight sentences. What changes have you made? Why? Do they help? Are there any more improvements you could make?

2. With a partner, select a topic from the list below and separately write a first draft of an essay about that topic. Make an extra copy and then exchange essays. Now revise each other's first draft. Be respectful but pitiless.

an actor you think is bad
your preference for either dogs or cats
a crowd activity you did or did not participate in
student politics on campus
respecting other cultures

3. Compare your first draft for Exercise 2 with your partner's revision. Evaluate the changes. Write a paragraph comparing the two. Give the paragraph to your partner. Be honest but kind.

2 / The Reading Process

*Reading maketh a full man,
conference a ready man, and
writing an exact man.*
– *Francis Bacon (1561–1626)
English philosopher, essayist,
and scientist*

Understanding a text is not an automatic consequence of running our eyes over the print. To read well takes more than eyesight: it takes full engagement of the mind. We can, of course, read some writing without any effort — the sports page or popular novels. We can usually understand this easy-access reading on the first try and without effort. We don't have to puzzle over it or analyze it or reread it. But college reading is by its very nature different. Its purpose is not to divert but to inform and stimulate thought. It almost always requires a second and often a third try, for a serious text builds from thought to thought. Meaning accumulates from page to page. College reading requires, then, that we put our minds in gear and feel the traction as our thought moves over the writer's thought.

We call this process "critical reading." By critical, we do not mean faultfinding or carping over details. We mean a healthy skepticism and a willingness to analyze the text step by step. Critical reading is the act of being respectful but inquisitive when you read the reasoning of other people. In college you must often write about what you have read, and so critical reading and the writing process frequently overlap.

Critical reading helps us to remember. When we read casually, uncritically, we don't nail the text into our memory. When we read critically, however, writing down what we're reading in our own words, the ideas and facts are apt to stick. Being more engaged in the reading, we pay closer attention. We anticipate. We relate one idea to another and notice similarities. As we read, our knowledge accumulates and our understanding grows.

Critical reading also helps us to judge and to evaluate. In this sense, we are all critical in certain areas of life. As soon as an elected official opens his or her mouth, "Oh yeah?" "Who says?" and "So what?" ready themselves for the asking. Each time we see an automobile commercial featuring a sleek cheetah, a brilliant desert landscape, a beautiful woman clad in flowing chiffon, and a virile-looking, handsome man, we feel a scoff coming on.

And we should. We know that politics and commercials are notorious for humbug. Who would vote without knowing what the candidate thought? Who would buy a car because of pretty pictures and suggestions of romance? That wouldn't make sense. And making sense is what being "critical" is all about.

We do not always adopt that critical stance in our reading, unfortunately. We tend to accept what we see in print, forgetting that no matter how well qualified writers may be, they are nonetheless fallible. We cannot assume that mistakes, deceptions, and illogicalities just won't appear in what we read. They will.

A CRITICAL ATTITUDE: ENGAGING THE TEXT

This chapter introduces certain habits of mind appropriate to reading. Some of its terms will be familiar from Chapter 1, because reading and writing are closely related processes. Here you will be learning ways of sifting out the good in what you read and throwing away the bad.

Critical readers share three main activities:

They participate. They do not sit and read passively. Instead, they are active. They make notes, put concepts into their own words, group important topics, relate main ideas. Before starting to read, they map the whole terrain. They look ahead and know what to expect. They summarize or paraphrase, the better to capture the essence of a thought or a text.

They analyze. Developing analytical skills is a — perhaps *the* — major purpose of a college education. To analyze is to break large items into smaller units or to break complex items into simpler components. Critical readers break readings into smaller units, the better to understand and remember them.

They interrogate the text. Critical readers know that almost all writers — whether of textbooks, essays, editorials, or advertisements — are trying to impose their opinions and thoughts on their readers. Critical readers assume neither the best nor the worst, but rather wait to be convinced. They are always on the lookout for sloppy thinking, fogginess, missed steps, and "fast ones" or hidden assumptions. They say firmly but respectfully, "Show me."

AN OVERVIEW: MAPPING THE TEXT

You have a piece of writing before you. It could be a textbook, a newspaper editorial, a magazine article, or a roommate's essay that you have just been asked to look at. In each case, you have a good reason to read critically: you want to learn, you want to understand, or you want to help. The following four tactics will give you an effective way to map the text:

1. When you write, you think about your purpose for writing; when you read, think about your purpose for reading. Do you need to accumulate facts or to understand the development of an idea? How important is the material? Are you studying the text to prepare for an examination, or will you be writing a paper on it?

2. Take a quick tour of the ground to be covered. First, note the title and the author's name and read any information about the author. Next, scan the table of contents. Page through and note any subdivisions, breaks, or illustrations. These are clues to organization and good stops for resting and for recapitulating what you have just read. Then read any headnotes. Note repeated terms and names. Finally, scan the questions, if any, at the end of the chapter or article to determine what the author thinks is important. At this point, although you have not started your actual reading, you are already familiar with the whole piece.

3. Check the length of the piece and estimate how long it will take to read. Don't always try to finish in one sitting. Your brain likes to store information gradually rather than to ram everything in at once. We recommend that when reading textbooks, you read in a fifteen- to twenty-minute chunk, take a short break, and start again.

4. Respond. This may be the most important phase of active reading. You cannot expect to understand and retain what you read if you just turn pages. Some people underline or use marking pens to highlight significant passages. This process has drawbacks, however: it allows the reader to register passively that a word or phrase is important but not how it is important. We once saw a copy of *Othello* that was almost entirely highlighted, because almost every line has something good. You could sit there highlighting all day.

We strongly urge that you take notes, putting what you have read in your own words. Taking notes forces you to discriminate constantly, reducing and reorganizing the ideas to suit your needs. Some people write these notes in the margins of the text. But then the notes remain scattered and are difficult to use and study, and you've ruined a book as well. The best procedure is to put your notes in a separate notebook or on notecards. This method forces you to organize the notes apart from the text, provides you with quick access for review, and gets you one step closer to the writing process if you have to do a paper on your reading.

When you take notes

1. Summarize major ideas and the most significant evidence. Jot down important terms or names.
2. Be selective. Write down only the primary ideas and pieces of evidence. You can go back later to pick up details.
3. Always note page numbers or paragraph numbers for easy reference.
4. Include your agreement with or your reservations about what the text is saying.
5. After completing your reading, make an outline so that you can see how the argument developed and the relation of its parts. (Some readers take their notes in outline form, placing main ideas in prominent positions and listing supporting ideas beneath them.)

Yes, all this is trouble, and yes, it is worth it. Reading critically will vastly enhance both your retention and your understanding.

EIGHT QUESTIONS: EVALUATING READING

As well as mapping the text, truly critical readers ask questions of it as they go along, and they remember the answers. They also question themselves to make sure they stay on track. In this section we discuss eight questions you can ask of any text. These questions should help you stay in control of difficult material.

1. What are they talking about? The Subject

You cannot enjoy a game unless you know who is playing, and you cannot start understanding your reading until you know what it is about. Obvious, perhaps, but too many readers get only a vague idea of the subject before diving in. Your first task is to articulate that subject.

The title will sometimes, but not always, indicate it. "Politics and the English Language" does — "Boring from Within" does not. When a title does not communicate the subject, try the first two or three paragraphs of the essay and then the last two or three. Page through to see if subheadings disclose the subject. Don't go any further with your reading until you know what the subject is. Don't assume you know it. Say it aloud or write it out just to be sure. Or put the subject in the form of a question the whole text will answer: for example, "What is the function of the mitochondrion within the cell?" At the head of your notes, write down your idea of the subject. Now you have made it yours.

2. Why are they talking about it? The Purpose

Writers have different purposes for writing; usually, as we saw in Chapter 1, these purposes break down into three motives: to report, to explain, or to persuade. Sometimes the purpose is concealed and sometimes it is right out front. Some writers — journalists, for instance — have a clear purpose: to report an event or describe a situation or scene. Remember, though, that with the best will in the world no reporter can tell or know everything about an event. In some writing that purports to be pure reportage, we can detect signs of bias and prejudice. Here is an interesting headline from a newspaper:

Fed Official Chides Bad-Mouth Economists

Even allowing for the distortions of brevity, such "reportage" is hard to accept. One "chides" a child; "bad-mouth" suggests an unfair criticism. The headline implies that critical economists behave like little children. Consciously or unconsciously, the writer of that headline meant not merely to report but to persuade. Bias has a way of slipping in, and a good reader will be on the lookout for it.

Much of what you read in college will be not reporting but explaining: *The Rise of the Novel,* "Letter to a Young Surgeon," "Me and My Bike and Why," *Science and the Modern World.* As the titles of their works suggest, these writers are explaining how something came about, how it works, what its consequences are, how to do something. What the work will explain is usually made explicit fairly early. In "Letter to a Young Surgeon," Richard Selzer's first sentence is "At this, the start of your surgical internship, it is well that you be told how to behave in an operating room." The purpose is clear.

In longer works the statement of purpose often summarizes the coming discussion and thus provides a context to help the reader understand the rest of the work. In his study *The Rise of the Novel,* Ian Watt discusses what other people have said and then maps his own direction:

> The present inquiry . . . takes another direction: assuming that the appearance of [novelists Defoe, Richardson, and Fielding] within a single generation was probably not sheer accident, and that their geniuses could not have created the new form unless the conditions of the time had also been favourable, it attempts to discover what these favourable conditions in the literary and social situation were, and in what ways Defoe, Richardson, and Fielding were its beneficiaries.

The rest of the book explains the conditions existing at that time and how the novelists developed from them.

Frequently you will read works whose purpose is to convince the reader that a particular view or course of action is the right one. We can usually discern that persuasive purpose in the first sentence. In his "Letter from Birmingham Jail," Martin Luther King, Jr., begins,

> While confined here in the Birmingham city jail, I came across your recent statement calling my present activities "unwise and un-

timely." Seldom do I pause to answer criticism of my work and ideas. If I sought to answer all the criticisms that cross my desk, my secretaries would have little time for anything other than such correspondence in the course of the day, and I would have no time for constructive work. But since I feel that you are men of genuine good will and that your criticisms are sincerely set forth, I want to try to answer your statement in what I hope will be patient and reasonable terms.

His purpose — to persuade "men of genuine good will" to join his crusade — is clear.

3. What's the big idea?   The Thesis

The Explicit Thesis.   As we have said, the single most important sentence in most essays is the thesis statement, that is, the articulation of the author's main idea. Recognizing the thesis is important for understanding the rest of the essay. You can usually locate i⁻ by reading the first three paragraphs especially carefully. The first paragraph may not contain the thesis; in longer works, especially, you are apt to find it in the second or third paragraph or even further along. There may be anecdotes, accounts of recent controversies, disclaimers, all manner of greetings and promises before the writer hones in on the thesis. Some texts have no explicit thesis. Even so, as you read you will probably feel the subject area narrowing, narrowing, until the author's point becomes clear.

Most frequently, however, an introductory paragraph establishes the subject, narrows it, and then presents the thesis:

> Only in the nineteen-sixties did the textbooks finally end their rear-guard action on behalf of a Northern European America. The civil-rights movement had shattered the image of a homogeneous American society and, for the first time in the twentieth century, raised profound questions about the national identity. The answer given by that movement and accepted as orthodoxy by most state and big-city schoolboards was that the United States is a multiracial, multicultural society. This formula, however, raised as many questions as it answered. Was the United States really like Yugoslavia — a country held together only by a delicate balance among ethnic and cultural groups? Or was there some integration of these groups? Was there a dominant culture — and was that a good thing? Was there some principle of unity that Americans ought to support apart from that of the state? The current texts show signs of struggle with these

questions. The struggle has had no clear outcome, for the social portrait drawn by the texts remains divided and confused. (Frances FitzGerald, *America Revised: History Schoolbooks in the Twentieth Century*)

FitzGerald gives the background for the debate and ends this introductory paragraph with her thesis statement.

Occasionally a writer comes right out and identifies the essay's point or argument with words and phrases that advertise it: "My thesis in this section will be . . . ," "It is, however, more likely that . . . " or "The answer is . . . ." Watch for words that indicate either the assertion of a differing opinion (*On the contrary, Nevertheless*, even *Although*) or a conclusion (*Therefore, Because, For*) — frequently words like these introduce the thesis statement.

The Implicit Thesis. When the thesis is not directly stated, the author will usually manipulate tone and vocabulary to make the main point as obvious as possible without actually expressing it. Identifying implicit theses can be a tricky business, because we could always be wrong about what the author means us to infer. Still, at other times the thesis will shine as clear as day:

Theoretically, of course, modern architecture has been in existence for some time. The Bauhaus, Mies, Fry, Le Corbusier, and others had concealed, here and there in the landscape of Europe, crafted boxes to which pilgrimages were made, and before which mouths were opened to take in or to let out gibberish. The Leninist ideas of the Russian Constructivists and the Bauhaus were taught in schools of architecture, and Le Corbusier's exhortations to tear down Paris and Algiers in the interests of hygiene were being studied by a younger generation of like-minded maniacs. On the whole, however, until the late 1950's nothing much had been done about it, and the occupants of our inner cities slept in relative tranquillity. (Roger Scruton, "Keep This Monster in Its Grave," *London Times*, May 1984)

Notice the phrases *crafted boxes, tear down Paris, like-minded maniacs*. The author trusts his way with words to make his implicit dislike of modern architecture as strongly felt as any explicit statement could make it.

When you have located the thesis, ask the following questions:

1. Is the thesis clear?
2. Does it rest on any vague or ambiguous terms? If so, are these ade-

quately defined later and used consistently throughout the argument?

3. Does the thesis state any important qualifications? Watch for qualifying words and phrases like "sometimes," "may," "might," "perhaps," "with the possible exception of," and "to some extent." If these words or phrases are present, the argumentative edge is not as sharp as it may at first appear.

The Thesis in Reports and Narratives. Not all texts argue for an opinion. Some simply report or explain. In such works, the thesis, determined by the purpose of the book or article, will guide the treatment of the subject. A political science textbook could purport to "discuss various forms of political organization through history." All the information and theory in the book would be organized from that perspective and to fulfill that purpose. For a book describing the various approaches to literary criticism, the author could organize the material around a few important themes that would reappear in each chapter, so that the reader could make a comparison. The organizing principle of a manual for assembling an amplifier might be chronology. Two social scientists undertook to preserve the history of Amoskeag, an old mill in New Hampshire. Their organizing principle? Systematic interviews with former workers and their families.

To set forth something, then, can be its own end — information for information's sake. But the writer must always shape that information.

4. How do you figure? *Main Supporting Points*

Now the real analysis starts. Pay attention to the supporting points under the thesis, the main ideas by which the author hopes to make his or her case. You can sometimes locate these ideas in the topic sentence or main statement of each paragraph. Locate and note topic sentences, especially if the writing is difficult, and note how those sentences tie in with the thesis. This way you can determine how the author is developing and expanding on the thought, and how the essay is unfolding. Ask yourself how each idea supports the thesis, indeed *whether* it does, for this is where the careful reader often notes logical inconsistencies — or finds the real strength of an argument.

In Stephen Jay Gould's essay "Were Dinosaurs Dumb?" (reprinted in his book *The Panda's Thumb: More Reflections on Natu-*

ral History), the author puts forth the thesis that dinosaurs were not so dumb; on the contrary, they were as smart as one ought to expect. He provides three main supporting points:

> Main supporting point 1: Dinosaurs had the right size brain for reptiles of their body size.
> Main supporting point 2: Dinosaurs exhibited intelligence.
> Main supporting point 3: Dinosaurs as a species survived for a relatively long period of time.

Arranging main supporting points in clear relation to the thesis or purpose lets us see the argument in all its twists and turns and provides a clearer entry into real critical analysis.

About main supporting points, ask the following questions:

1. Do the author's main points directly support the thesis?
2. Are they logical and relevant divisions of that thesis? Were you confused or surprised by any of them?
3. Are there any big jumps from point to point? If so, does this fact damage the argument?
4. Does the writer support all points sufficiently?

5. So what? The Conclusion

The conclusion is the payoff to the argument. Locate it — it is usually in the last few paragraphs or the last chapter of a book, but some writers offer it in a next-to-last section and then discuss its implications in the final section. And some studies in the social and natural sciences offer conclusions in the beginning and then show how the authors reached those conclusions. Track the conclusion down and compare it with the thesis. How has the thesis changed in the conclusion? Does the conclusion surprise you? Can you think of alternative conclusions that would follow from the same discussion?

Notice we said "Compare the conclusion with the thesis." Often they are similar; just as often, however, the author has argued the thesis in order to point out a larger significance for his or her essay. The last sentence of Gould's essay on the dinosaur makes an unexpected point:

> Do you know anyone who would wager a substantial sum, even at favorable odds, on the proposition that *Homo sapiens* will last longer than Brontosaurus?

Hardly a person would read that ending without feeling the sudden chill of nuclear anxiety.

Frequently an argument develops from the thesis to the conclusion. Comparing the two is a useful way to keep track of where an argument has led. Here is a very simplified version of the thesis and conclusion of Sigmund Freud's *Civilization and Its Discontents*:

> Thesis: The individual's instincts of aggression and self-destruction inevitably conflict with the prescriptions of civilized life.
>
> Conclusion: The fateful question for the human species is whether their cultural development can master the disturbance these instincts cause in their communal life.

Thesis and conclusion are similar, but they harbor a crucial difference. The conclusion suggests that unless controlled, the conflict could lead to great problems. It makes no sense to accept the conclusion unless you understand the thesis and believe that the argument has adequately supported it. Follow that argument.

If you think creatively, you can sometimes come up with a different conclusion from the one the author has drawn. Here is a familiar argument:

> For five years, five rats were forced to breathe in the smoke of x number of cigarettes. Of the five rats, four died of lung cancer. For experimental purposes the physiology of rats is close to that of human beings.
>   Therefore:

Before reading further, imagine some possible conclusions. The results can be enlightening. Here are just a few:

> You shouldn't do things like that to rats.
> Any human being who smokes x number of cigarettes a day for five years has a 20 percent chance of survival.
> One out of every five rats has a constitution stronger than that of human beings.
> Eighty percent of the rat population will not last twenty years.
> Cigarette smoking may cause cancer in human beings.

All these conclusions follow, more or less validly, from some or all of the evidence. The point of imagining alternatives is that *no conclusions are inevitable; all depend on the author's analysis of the evidence.*

6. Did they prove it?   Evidence

No argument would be more than talk without some hard evidence. (Throughout this book, we have much to say about evidence, and we refer you to Chapter 10 for a detailed discussion.) When you have ascertained the thesis, main supporting points, and conclusion of a work, you must delve even further and evaluate the evidence that backs up every step in the argument. Be especially tough on the evidence provided for crucial points. Ask each bit of proof the following six questions:

1. Is it relevant? Does it directly and unambiguously support the point?

2. Is it accurate? Three things can produce inaccurate evidence. The first is simple human error. The *Manchester Guardian* once quoted the U.S. secretary of the treasury as saying, "We will make certain that there will be calamities in the banking system." One tiny missing *not* invalidated the evidence. If you find errors in quotations or statistics, begin to wonder about the writer. The second cause of inaccuracy is ignorance. Some writers present obsolete research or peddle pop wisdom as fact. The third cause is plain human guile. Writers may disguise or distort the meaning or context of a piece of evidence, the better to fit it into their argument. You must test each piece of evidence to make sure it is accurate.

3. Is it specific and detailed? Vague allusions to "the thinking of Freud" or "the well-known development of South American dictatorships" will never be enough to prove a point. The closer the evidence is to facts, numbers, actual quotations from the text, the better. Demand a thorough analysis of such references as "Freud's notion of the Oedipal complex" or "the strife between the press and the dictatorship of Chile in 1983."

When an author paraphrases rather than quotes another author, be alert. A paraphrase poses tricky questions, since you must trust that it fairly represents the original. Don't just accept it; analyze it. Does the paraphrase sound accurate? Is it enough to make the point believable?

4. Are the sources for the evidence clear? You have the right to know the source of all evidence, and the writer has the responsibility to provide it. We are not suggesting that you look up every reference

or follow every footnote. When you hit a surprising or unclear bit of proof, however, pursue it further. If the source is suppressed or vaguely presented, you may begin to doubt the author.

5. Is there enough support? Only you can decide whether the author has presented enough proof to persuade you. Withhold your assent until you feel ready to give it. Sheer quantity is not the criterion, however. Sometimes you will find that good arguments are based on quite scanty evidence; sometimes a flood of facts will not suffice. Look for the intelligent commentary that makes the evidence relevant.

6. Is the evidence clearly linked to the main point? Or do you have to make a great leap to determine how the evidence actually supports the point? To answer these questions, you must evaluate assumptions.

7. What's behind all this?   Assumptions

An assumption is anything taken for granted. "I'll drive by and pick you up" assumes that the speaker has a car and that it will operate. "My daughter is going to college after she graduates from high school" takes for granted that the daughter will graduate from high school and will be accepted by some college. Our lives are full of unspoken assumptions. Many can remain silent. The speaker need not say "I have a car" or "if my daughter is admitted" — the listener would assume both automatically.

Some jokes depend on a pretty obvious assumption that prompts laughter when we discover it. Will Rogers said:

I don't belong to any organized political party. I'm a Democrat.

As we suggested in our headline example a few pages back, some newspapers hide their assumptions none too well:

Mrs. Williams doesn't wear clothes that excite the fashion industry. She looks like a woman who works for a living.

The assumption is strong: the fashion industry designs clothes not for people who work for a living but only for the rich.

Sometimes a writer writes as though readers agree with certain unspoken assumptions, when in fact many readers might disagree:

Prince Andrew of England has become a folk hero to men precisely because of the strings that are not attached. He attracts as many women as he wants and can jettison them in full view of the public — and get away with it. He flits from flower to flower, virile, cheerful, and irresponsible.

The hidden assumption here is "And that's what all men want — right?" You as critical reader are the one to say "Right!" or "Wrong!" Has the writer soberly reasoned from persuasive evidence or has he or she based the whole passage on crude stereotypes of male desire? When you become aware of hidden assumptions you don't agree with, your attitude toward the argument will change. If you think men can be sensitive people, you won't like it when you see the assumptions behind the Prince Andrew passage.

Hidden asumptions may be all right for humor or fairly harmless in topical journalism, but they can be dangerous in serious written argument. Important assumptions should be explicit and detailed, for then the reader can judge their validity. If we do not agree with a writer's assumptions, we will never agree with his or her arguments.

In the following examples, we present the same assertion supported by three different bits of evidence. In each case, there is a hidden assumption. Before reading the analysis, try to put the assumption into your own words. Determine whether the assumption is valid, and whether the writer should make it explicit.

> Soviet behavior around the world is hostile to the United States. Russian troops just blew up the Washington Monument.

The hidden assumption is that any foreign power that blows up the Washington Monument is hostile to the United States. This assumption is obvious and acceptable, and the author need not make it explicit.

> Soviet behavior around the world is hostile to the United States. Russian-made missiles have been sighted in Cuba.

The hidden assumptions are that these missiles are threatening to the United States and that anything Cuba does Russia instigates. Most, though not all, readers would find such assumptions acceptable. Cuba is 90 miles from the United States, and sighting Russian missiles there is cause for thinking Russia is involved. Many people would agree without further explication.

> Soviet behavior around the world is hostile to the United States. The Russians invaded Afghanistan.

The hidden assumptions are that America has important interests in or near Afghanistan and that this invasion intentionally threatens those interests. Their validity is shaky. The Washington Monument is right at home and Cuba only 90 miles from our shores, but Afghanistan is half the world away. Perhaps the author thinks that the USSR plans to cut the United States off from the oil fields of the Middle East and that the invasion is one more step toward this goal. If so, these are exactly the kinds of assumptions that the author must write out.

> Soviet behavior around the world is hostile to the United States. The Soviets persecute those who practice their religion.

The hidden assumption is that because the United States allows freedom of religion, religious persecution in Russia is a strike at our values. The assumption is unacceptable. The Communist system has always precluded religious practice, even in times of friendship between the two countries. Once we make this assumption explicit, we reveal a hole in the argument. Now the author must either find evidence to provide the connection between Soviet policy on religion and hostility toward the United States or give up this line of argument.

Most evidence is neither as self-evident as the first example nor as invalid as the last. The middle two examples represent the middle ground where you must evaluate.

To track down hidden assumptions, follow these lines of questioning:

1. Subject all arguments to intense scrutiny at the beginning to determine whether you share a starting point with the author. If you disagree with the assumptions on which the argument is based, you will probably not accept the rest of the argument. If, for instance, you believe that desirable social change can come about peacefully, you probably will disagree with an essay based on the assumption that change will come only with revolution.

2. Try to determine the assumptions behind definitions. Do you agree with the way the author defines terms? It would be important to know, for instance, whether or not behind the word *revolution* was the notion *violent*.

3. When the tone or angle of the piece strikes you as unusual or unexpected, look for hidden assumptions. Sometimes authors hide personal bias or prejudice in an argument. To discover it may not make the argument invalid, but it will certainly help you understand the writer.

4. When you suddenly find yourself confused about why this point appears here or why that evidence is discussed, stop reading. Trace your confusions back to their source. Were there missing steps or strange twists? You may have spotted a dark corner in which an unacceptable assumption hides.

5. Ask yourself if the author connects the evidence clearly and naturally to the main assertion. If he or she does not state assumptions explicitly, are they fairly obvious and acceptable? If the author does state assumptions, do you find them reasonable?

6. When you isolate assumptions, always ask yourself whether you share them. Do you find them biased? naive? unreasonable? Or are they what you would assume in the same instance?

8. Was it all worth it? The Whole Essay

When you have finished reading, sit back and take stock of the book or essay and decide what you think of it. Page back through and pause at important points. Carefully examine the evidence. Think about the definitions. Think about the overall argument: was it closely and persuasively reasoned, or were you forced to make some pretty strenuous leaps across the gaps? Was the conclusion justified? When you read critically and actively, you will be in a good position to evaluate even the most illustrious authors, for you will have a deeper understanding and a more secure memory of what they wrote.

CASE STUDY: GETTING WRITING FROM READING

The following is a description of the way one student, Larry Boyd, read a difficult essay and, by mapping the text and using the eight questions outlined in the preceding section, was able to turn his reading into a serious and highly satisfying written response.

The purpose of the reading was clear: Larry Boyd was to write a paper on the essay "Victimology" by Robert Nisbet. In his initial overview, he learned that the essay comes from Nisbet's *Prejudices: A Philosophical Dictionary*. That book is a collection of short essays under topics like alienation, permissiveness, uncertainty, and war.

Nisbet is Albert Schweitzer Professor of the Humanities, Emeritus, at Columbia University in New York. According to the blurb, he has written several books that seem to be on similar subjects, such as *The Quest for Community* and *The Twilight of Authority. Emeritus* means he is retired.

Boyd could see that the essay was a little over three pages long. It had no chapter headings or breaks. He found no questions at the end. As he quickly turned the pages, he picked up one piece of useful information for mapping ahead: the word *victim* appeared frequently, once in italics. Another repeated word was *liberal.* Boyd checked the dictionary to be sure he knew what *liberal* meant: "Having, expressing, or following political views or policies that favor civil liberties, democratic reforms, and the use of governmental power to promote social progress; having, expressing, or following views or policies that favor the freedom of individuals to act or express themselves as they choose."

Because the essay was short, Boyd thought he could read and take notes on it in about thirty minutes. The second reading would probably be shorter, the third shorter yet. He gathered three pens — no point in having to search around if one went dry — and put his notecards by the book on his desk. He was ready to read and to write.

Victimology

This word will not be found as yet in most dictionaries and doubtless will strike the sensitive ear harshly. But so far as meanings go, this word has as much prima facie right to existence as *criminology*, the study of criminals and what they have in common. It only later occurred to students of crime that victims in the aggregate might also be shown to have a good deal in common.   1

There are those who victimize — dominating parents, older brothers and sisters, employers, police, asylum tenders, and physicians as well as common ordinary felons. Victimizing comes more easily and naturally to some than to others in the population. But so does victimhood come more easily to some than to others. Clinical psychologists assert that some people need and subconsciously enjoy being victimized, being exploited, browbeaten, tightly ruled. It is as natural for them to be victims as for others, of different temperament, to be victimizers.   2

Although interest in the class characteristics of victims of crimes goes back to the founders of criminology in the nineteenth century, it was not until the middle of the twentieth century that victimology   3 became a specialty within sociology and social psychology. The scientific research conducted so far leaves no doubt that the study of victims of thefts, robberies, rapes, assaults, murders, and other crimes is almost as rewarding and illuminating as is the study of criminals. The inescapable fact is that just as there are murderers, so there are murderees. Without victims there can be no victimizers, and temperaments of certain individuals have been shown to lead to ways of behavior which come close to inviting victimization, such as theft, rape, or assault. This does not mean that people conspicuously lacking in the stigmata of victimhood do not also suffer victimization of every kind. It is simply a matter of statistical probability. The majority of those who are mugged on the city streets have in common certain attributes which are less likely to be found among those never or rarely mugged. In sum, precisely as one cannot learn all there is to be learned about leadership without attending also to followership, so with peccadilloes, cruelties, sins of man against man, and crimes: the victim is as important to a knowledge of crime as is the perpetrator.

But there is very different and wholly political meaning today to   4
the words *victim* and thereby *victimology*. This meaning is inseparable from the welfare Leviathans that have been built up in the West during the last century or two. The source of this meaning is the do-gooder and uplifter that became widespread in the nineteenth century. Those who were poor, unemployed, chronically drunk, and even criminal in tendency were, by some sociological legerdemain, decreed to be victims — of society. This form of thinking allows two victims for any given crime and no victimizer or criminal. The individual robbed, raped, or slain is certainly a victim, but so is the robber, rapist, and murderer a victim — of circumstances, of poverty, of broken family, in sum, of society. Few things please the liberal heart more than a victim, especially that of society, and when a choice has to be made between the rights of the victim who was robbed and the victim of society who did the robbing, the right-thinking humanitarian almost tropistically sides with the latter.

In this special, very modern social sense of victimhood, there can   5
be no end to the process of creating victims. At this moment, at least 75 percent of the American people are victims. From the point of view of the ardent women's liberationist, all women, or some 51 percent of the population, are victims. Add the blacks, Hispanics, Indians, farmers exposed to drought, unemployed, mentally disturbed, pupils in the public schools, and many other groups in the population, and even an estimate of 85 percent might seem absurdly low. Wealth and high status are no protectors. A new species of victimhood has just been publicized with excellent market results: children

of celebrities. They too must be seen as victims. In wife beating there is manifestly a female victim, but the subtlety of the victimological mind should never be underestimated. The husband administering the beating is also a victim — of childhood, say, in a wife-beating home atmosphere — and cannot properly be held accountable.

Accountable! Human society is ultimately possible only when 6 people are accountable for their actions, that is, responsible. The moron who murders, the poverty-stricken who steals, the clinical sadist who tortures and mutilates, the psychologically disturbed who rapes, the insane who slaughters boys by the dozen after sodomizing them, assassins and would-be assassins of Presidents and other high officials of state — all of these are manifestly the causal agents of their various crimes and are recognized as such. Once they would also have been declared responsible and accountable for their crimes. They would have been duly punished by execution, sometimes in a manner as painful or nearly as painful as that inflicted upon their victims. Punishment would have been swift and public, for punishment can exert its cathartic effect upon a community that has been grievously violated only if the punishment is observable by all.

Correctly did Maistre maintain after the Revolution in France that 7 the executioner is the necessary symbol of the social order. If everyone is a victim of some sort, even a Gacy in Chicago who sodomized, strangled, and buried under his house some three dozen boys and men, then there are no criminals. If there are no criminals, there cannot logically be any punishment. Nor can rehabilitation be the goal, since most students of the rehabilitation process, even at its most expert and humane, pronounce it a failure.

There is no substitute for punishment in a social order, and that 8 means holding human beings accountable, treating them as human and therefore responsible. Concern for human rights is rampant these days, but a right is possible in the strict sense only for beings who can be rationally regarded as responsible. The celebrated dignity of man oozes away in an atmosphere where man is so little prized for his unique mental and moral qualities as to be classified from the start a victim. Rights, duties, responsibilities, restraints, consciences, moral codes, all of these are visibly softening and decaying under the influence of victimology — no longer a specialty of criminology but a gigantic malaise of Western society.

More victims, of a different order, have appeared during the last 9 year or two on the American scene: college students, writers, artists, and musicians. They are all victims, it is said, of the federal government's effort to reach a balanced budget without placing punitive taxes on other citizens. For many years government loans were available to nearly all students who requested them; often these loans were not paid back, with government agencies reluctant to prosecute lest they seem to make victims of the delinquent. Now when something of a cut is made in the funds for loan use, or at least a slight deceleration in the rate of increase of these funds, thousands of new victims, the middle-class students, suddenly appear.

Similarly, although the budgets of the National Endowments of the Arts and Humanities rose in the fifteen years between 1965 and 1980 from 10 million to around 170 million each, the result has been only to create more victims, among artists, writers, and musicians. Testimony before Congress by a best-selling novelist, himself acquainted with grants by taxpayers, tells the story: "The truth is, if you are going to take away the lunches of school children, payment to miners with black lung, store front legal assistance, you might as well cut the budget of poets, artists, and musicians. You cannot rip up the texture of our national life and expect it to survive. . . . What does it matter if our theaters go dark or if the libraries close their doors. . . . I recognize a simple undeniable eviction procedure in which most of us are the widows and orphans. . . . As a writer of fiction, I could not relate or tell of this. I could not get away with a portrayal of such sanctimonious cruelties." The entire reason for this bleat was simply that a few million dollars were to be lopped from the proposed increases in the budgets of the two endowments. One wonders how Dreiser, Cather, Hemingway, Faulkner, and Cozzens were able to do their writing in an era when there was no endowment, or how the scholarship of McIlwain, Kittredge, and their many peers across the country came about without such endowment. The truth is that they were victims, and egregious ones for they did not even know they were victims. 10

But Americans do now. By the year 2000, the whole of American society will be composed of victims, or so perceived by the prophets of liberal cant, and perceived no doubt the same way by those aggressive enemies abroad who in their own Soviet-communist garrison states do not recognize victims. 11

Boyd's first set of notes looked like this:

Paragraph 1 — Victimology not found in most dictionaries.
Paragraph 2 — Some people are victimizers, some are real victims; vic-hood comes easily to some, need to be victimized.
Paragraph 3 — But v-ology new, 1950, soc and psych. New political meaning to v today: everybody.
Paragraph 4 — "Do-gooder" and "uplifter" source of vic. Even crim considered vic of society. (N doesn't like that.) Fault of the "liberal

heart." (Big theme here.) Libs side against society. (Some libs do.) Libs behave "tropistically" (Dictionary says "tropistical — in the manner of a reflex reaction." That's a dig.)

Paragraph 5 — Lots of vics. Maybe 85% too low; even rich kids!

Paragraph 6 — Human society only possible when *"Accountable"* (N. getting excited. This section seems to be his main idea.) Everybody "manifestly the causal agents of their crimes" and once were "accountable." Punishment "swift" and "public" — cathartic for all.

Paragraph 7 — Maistre: executioner as symbol of social order. (Wow!) Rehabilitation a failure.

Paragraph 8 — Concern for human rights rampant today (ironic!); rights only possible if responsible. (Dictionary says a right is "something to which one has a just claim; power or privilege to which one is justly entitled.") Vic: "gigantic malaise of Western society."

Paragraph 9 — Even middle-class students, artists vics because of balanced budget effort.

Paragraph 10 — How did writers manage before, when didn't know they were vics? (More irony — or is this sarcasm?)

Paragraph 11 — Aggressive enemies: Soviet "garrison states" — will see us as victims. Scary ending.

In these notes, Boyd summarized the essay for himself, adding some useful dictionary definitions and impressions of the author's attitude. Armed with his set of notes, he was ready to write out his answers to the eight questions.

1. Subject: Why we like to identify people as "victims."

2. Purpose: Ultimately to persuade the reader that identifying people this way is foolish and even dangerous. First, of course, Nisbet has to show the reader that victimology is popular and to explain how it got that way.

3. Thesis: Mostly implicit, but the strongest statement of it is

Rights, duties, responsibilities, restraints, consciences, moral codes, all of these are visibly softening and decaying under the influence of victimology — no longer a specialty of criminology but a gigantic malaise of Western society.

In other words: our obsession with victims is a sign that many things are wrong with our way of living.

4. Main supporting points:

We are almost as interested in victims as in criminals.

Sociology and social psychology refer to many kinds of people as victims of society, including criminals; so they think every crime has two victims: the crook and the victim of the crime.

All sorts of political groups see themselves as victims.

But if everyone is a victim, there is no accountability, and accountability is what makes society possible.

But there is no substitute for punishment — it gives the criminal what he deserves and makes the real victim feel better.

No wonder morality is decaying under this maliase.

5. Conclusion: If they listen to the liberals, soon all people will consider themselves victims. Then Nisbet has this image of the Soviets, who don't believe in victims, looking at us in the year 2000. Scary. Does that mean we would have decayed completely and would be open to attack?

6. Evidence: Nisbet calls on history, recent events, a congressional report. But sometimes he doesn't really document his sources. Who are the "students" (does he mean scholars?) who think rehabilitation is a failure? Nisbet could probably say. He seems to know a great deal. There's a ring of truth to it.

7. Assumptions: Nisbet sort of blames the social sciences and the liberal heart for beginning this trend, and he seems to look down on people who think of themselves as victims. Does that mean he thinks they aren't really victims? Aren't minorities really victims of the system? Or a person who really tried to get a job and couldn't and then stole something to feed his kids?

Still, he brings most of his assumptions to light when he starts talking about "accountability." His main assumption is that accountability is essential to society.

8. The whole essay: Overall, it's pretty convincing. I see what he means and I agree with a lot of it. What he says about punishment bothers me. Public executions? I don't agree with everything he says. In fact, he isn't talking about victims — he's talking about liberals. They're his real gripe.

After this analysis, Boyd was thoroughly familiar with Nisbet's essay and was ready to respond to it. He had been particularly struck by the fact that the essay was not really about what the title indicated. With that thought in mind he went back over the essay and took detailed notes. He jotted down additional memorable phrases, steps he now saw were important to the argument, things that struck him as significant. Notes are the relay station between reading and writing. From our notes, we select examples, distill what we need from the text, and remind ourselves of our thoughts.

Although raw notes are extremely useful when we turn reading into writing, they are not a good basis for organizing an essay. Notes taken while reading follow the shape of the reading, and adhering closely to them usually makes for a poorly constructed essay. Successful essays seize on a significant point and organize the thinking around that. An argument's shape must take priority over the shape of the text.

Boyd's first step away from the reading's organization was his answers to the eight questions. On the basis of what he learned from these answers and the essay topic he decided to pursue, Boyd edited and reorganized his notes and hammered out a thesis for his response.

An outline can help at this point. It allows the writer to devise a general structure and then to place useful quotations and ideas from the reading under relevant headings. Although it won't provide the argument, it will show it clearly.

After going over his reorganized notes, Boyd knew how he would support his ideas, and he hashed out the following outline, to which he added notes on quotations he would use to support his points. Though quickly done, this outline organized his ideas and his notes and prepared him to write.

Thesis: Nisbet's essay is not really about "victimology" but about liberal ideas and institutions that Nisbet thinks produce such thinking.

    I. "Victimology" really an ironic attack on "the liberal heart" and the consequences of liberal social views
       "welfare Leviathans" (para. 4)
       rehabilitation "a failure" (para. 7)
       victimology appeals to the "liberal heart" (para. 4)
       concern for human rights "rampant these days" (para. 8)
       liberals "bleat" (para. 10)
    II. Argues for a social order of accountability, punishment for misdeeds, and responsibility.
      A. Accountability

society "possible only when people are accountable for their actions, that is, responsible" (para. 6)
even "moron who murders" accountable (para. 6)
- B. Punishment
  "cathartic effect" of punishment (para. 6)
  punishment "as painful . . . as that inflicted upon their victims" (para. 6)
- C. Responsibility
  without it, dignity of man "oozes away" (para. 8)
  "rights, duties, responsibilities," etc. (para. 8)
- III. Much truth in Nisbet's argument
  - A. Problems with welfare state
  - B. Inconsistency in society's view of criminals
- IV. Some not true
  - A. Overstates his criticism
  - B. Executioner a bad symbol: executioner as "necessary symbol of the social order" (para. 7)
- V. Things not as bad as he says: "garrison states" (para. 11)

After he had completed his outline and had reviewed it to make sure his ideas still held up, he started writing. Several drafts later, he had this version:

Victims of Victimology

"Victimology" is a word that has not made most dictionaries yet, but Robert Nisbet thinks it should. He thinks we need such a word to capture America's growing obsession with victims. On the surface, he argues that America is becoming a society full of people who consider themselves victims and that this indicates many of the main problems of American life. As more of us come to consider ourselves victims, he argues, society will become weaker and weaker, until it collapses along with all human dignity. However, Nisbet's central issue is not victimology as such but rather the "prophets of liberal cant" who are responsible for such thinking.

Nisbet attacks the "welfare Leviathans that have been built up in the West during the last century or two." Many recent liberal American causes come in for similar criticism, including women's liberation, minority rights, and prisoner rehabilitation. He says, for example, that the last is simply a "failure."

Nisbet's worst sarcasm is at the expense of "the liberal heart." He never defines exactly what that heart is, but it seems to stand for the way liberal people view the relation between the individual and society. Nisbet traces liberalism to the "sociological legerdemain" of the nineteenth century, which first made it popular. This way of thinking enabled early liberals to describe social relations and, according to Nisbet, get them all wrong. The liberal, he says, unthinkingly sides with the individual against society:

> Few things please the liberal heart more than a victim, especially
> that of society, and when a choice has to be made between the
> rights of the victim who was robbed and the victim of society who
> did the robbing, the right-thinking humanitarian almost tropistically
> sides with the latter.

This mistake of always putting the individual against society leads to many problems. The liberal heart mixes up criminal and victim until some very important values become confused. This is why, in Nisbet's words, "concern for human rights is rampant these days." Liberals "bleat" about victims when the think society is not doing enough.

Nisbet rejects the idea that society should somehow do everything for its members. Thus, the central passage in his essay concerns his idea that "human society is ultimately possible only when people are accountable for their actions, that is, responsible." This includes everyone, rich or poor, sane or insane, "the moron who murders, the poverty-stricken who steals." Instead of making excuses for everyone, society should uphold the dignity of its members and enforce responsibility by punishing criminals, no matter what the explanation behind their crimes.

Punishment is the American institution Nisbet discusses most. It is, he says, good for society. It defends and upholds the dignity of human beings. He looks back to the days when punishment was "swift and public," sometimes "as painful . . . as that inflicted upon [the] victims." Nisbet probably does not think much of forbidding cruel and unusual punishment. He is also probably frustrated by the lengthy trials and long delays that characterize the legal system today. Above all, he probably thinks that American society does not punish criminals with a force equal to their crimes.

Nisbet's definition of the word <u>victim</u> ties in with his emphasis on responsibility. A victim is someone who has had his or her rights taken away and has been stripped of dignity. If we all consider ourselves victims, "the celebrated dignity of man oozes away":

> Rights, duties, responsibilities, restraints, consciences, moral codes, all of these are visibly softening and decaying under the influence of victimology—no longer a specialty of criminology but a gigantic malaise of Western society.

This is the climax of his essay, the place where Nisbet not only defines <u>victimology</u> but also reveals that he is really talking about the decline of our way of life.

Much of what Nisbet has to say about America is definitely true. As we have learned, there have been many problems with the so-called welfare state in America since World War II. Many programs like Social Security have grown too large and cost too much, leading people to question the ideas that created these programs in the first place. American society has also shown inconsistency and unfairness in the way it views criminals and victims, sometimes seeming to show more sympathy for the criminals.

Nisbet overstates his case, however, and some of his ideas are poorly based. I do not agree with what he says about cutting student loans.

Many students would never go to college if they could not get some financial aid, and needing financial aid does not mean they think they are victims. The government should cut the defense budget before doing away with student loans. Or it could cut some White House salaries. Although Nisbet is right when he says that some people have portrayed women and minority groups as victims of society, he takes the idea too far. Most women and minorities do not want to be thought of as victims. They only want to get the very rights Nisbet is talking about.

Although I disagree with the extreme position Nisbet takes, I agree that accountability is important to American society. Even here he takes the idea too far when he says the executioner is "the necessary symbol of social order." Few people would want to identify with such a symbol. Perhaps some other symbol, like the builder or the teacher, would be better for an accountable society.

If things were really as bad as Nisbet thinks, we would, as he says, be in danger from "those aggressive enemies abroad who in their own Soviet-communist garrison states do not recognize victims." But things are not that bad. Nisbet is criticizing the few who make the newspapers, not the millions of people who just lead their lives the best way they know how and would never think of themselves as victims.

TIPS FOR READING

- Read critically; that is, participate, analyze, interrogate the text.
- Before starting to read, leaf through the text to get some clues about its most important ideas.
- To help both understanding and retention, take notes on what you read.

- Summarize the main ideas and the most important supporting ideas.
- Use the eight questions to analyze the text.
- Closely follow the way the thesis develops into the conclusion.
- Evaluate both the relevance and sufficiency of the main supporting points.
- Pay particular attention to the writer's purpose and assumptions.
- Consider the entire argument when you have finished reading.

EXERCISES FOR READING

1. In a large general encyclopedia, follow all the steps under "Mapping the Text" for one of these entries: Rabindranath Tagore, Omar Khayyám, Lao-tzu. What is the writer's purpose? What is the article's thesis or organizing principle? Are there hidden assumptions that should have been explicit? What is your overall evaluation of the article? Write a short essay on your reading of this text.

2. In the library you will probably find copies of *Dissent, Policy Review, New Criterion, the Nation,* or the *National Review.* Using the eight questions, analyze an article from one of these journals. Was the article persuasive? Should the author have added anything or made the assumptions more explicit? Write an essay evaluating the article.

3. Using the *Readers' Guide to Periodical Literature,* the *Humanities Index,* the *Social Sciences Index,* or the index to a major newspaper, locate one article or column for and one against one of the following controversies of the not-too-distant past:

> establishment of a new court just below the Supreme Court to cut down on the Supreme Court's work load
> a constitutional amendment to ensure a balanced budget
> the quality of large cultural awards like the Pulitzer Prize or the Nobel Prize in literature
> a "flat rate" income tax
> women in high office
> the Olympic ban on professional athletes

Analyze the two articles. Would you have preferred a clearer thesis in either? Was the support adequate? Do you think either should have made its underlying assumptions more explicit? Your answers to these questions could take the form of either a short essay or an in-class report.

4. Identify any questionable assumptions in the following statements:

> The cause of cancer is stress.
>
> When a new president for this college has been selected, we hope he will be reliable, responsible, intelligent, and wise.
>
> The true self, the inner self, has no need for order, power, control, or systemization.
>
> Fred is a tough competitor and always comes out on top, and so I think he should be our leader.
>
> You should not eat candy because it causes cavities.

5. Below are some definitions. What assumptions underlie them? Do you agree or disagree with any of the definitions? Where you disagree, can you come up with your own definition?

> *Graft*: The main element in any smoothly running government
>
> *Immorality*: What you do that I wish I could do but cannot
>
> *Free enterprise*: The same thing as greed
>
> *Liberalism*: The guilty conscience of people who are well off
>
> *Conservatism*: Defending old ideas in the absence of new ones

6. *Time, Newsweek, U.S. News and World Report*, and the *New York Times* "Week in Review" cover some of the same topics. Choose a topic prominent in last week's news and analyze how it was treated in these four publications. Write an essay on the different treatments.

part two

The Heart of the Matter: The Paragraph

3 / The Structure of the Paragraph

Sentences are not emotional but paragraphs are. . . . I found this out first in listening to Basket my dog drinking.

– Gertrude Stein (1874–1946)
American writer

Some people write paragraphs by charging ahead in a straight line, one sentence after another, not one look back until they run out of words. Then they indent five spaces, draw a deep breath, and start another idea. This may be fine for a first draft, when you are still sifting ideas, but it won't do for a finished essay. No reader would be able to follow the thoughts, and all would be reluctant to try.

No matter how wonderful our ideas are, we still need to organize and package them into paragraphs. We need to put our pieces of evidence into order so that the reader will know what we are claiming and whether we can prove it. Suppose you took a sackful of coins to the bank and demanded a twenty-dollar bill. Before anyone would believe you really had twenty dollars in change, you would have to sort the coins into those thick paper wrappers, perhaps red for pennies, blue for nickels, and so on. That is what paragraphing is all about: sorting, separating, combining, packaging.

A paragraph contains both a main point and support for it. The main point provides a summary or explanation or interpretation that links the paragraph to the whole essay. The support is the quotation, the fact, the observation, the belief that your reader accepts. It is what needs no further proof. Support is the foundation of the paragraph. When the foundation is strong enough, the main point is sturdy and secure. It then provides support for the thesis of the whole essay — and you get the twenty-dollar bill.

In the following passage, Malcolm Cowley carefully combines his pieces of evidence to make a complete package:

> The vanity of older people is an easier weakness to explain, and to condone. With less to look forward to, they yearn for recognition of what they have been: the reigning beauty, the athlete, the soldier, the scholar. It is the beauties who have the hardest time. A portrait of themselves at twenty hangs on the wall, and they try to resemble it by making an extravagant use of creams, powders, and dyes. Being young at heart, they think they are merely revealing their essential persons. The athletes find shelves for their silver trophies, which are polished once a year. Perhaps a letter sweater lies wrapped in a bureau drawer. I remember one evening when a no-longer athlete had guests for dinner and tried to find his sweater. "Oh, that old thing," his wife said. "The moths got into it and I threw it away." The athlete sulked and his guests went home early. (Malcolm Cowley, "The View from 80")

The first sentence identifies the main point. It is a statement of the idea that governs the paragraph. The other sentences provide support. Cowley turns first to the ex-beauties and then to the ex-athletes. He demonstrates why it is "easier . . . to explain, and to condone" the vanity of old people. This support makes a strong foundation. We do not need details about the scholar and the soldier. This support carries us to the common ground.

THE TOPIC SENTENCE: DECLARING YOUR INTENTIONS

Every paragraph has a single main idea that controls its content and its development. All the sentences in the paragraph are related to that main idea. When a single sentence expresses the main topic, we call that sentence a topic sentence. The topic sentence binds all the other sentences in support of the main idea. Usually the most general sentence in a paragraph, it states what all the other sentences will combine to prove.

Cowley's first sentence in the example we just discussed tells us that his subject is the vanity of old people. After reading this sentence, we expect an explanation, and that is exactly what we get. Look at these topic sentences and think about the expectations they create:

> In astronomy, although the sun, moon, and stars continue to exist year after year, yet in other respects the world we have to deal with is very different from that of everyday life. (Bertrand Russell, "Touch and Sight: The Earth and the Heavens")

> The intellectual interest of a child in the riddle of sexual life, his desire for knowledge, finds expression at an earlier period of life than is usually suspected. (Sigmund Freud, "The Sexual Enlightenment of Children")

> The modern business organization, or that part which has to do with guidance and direction, consists in numerous individuals who are engaged, at any given time, in obtaining, digesting or exchanging and testing information. (John Kenneth Galbraith, "The Technostructure")

Each of these sentences makes a promise to the reader: this is what the following evidence will support. What exact form that evidence takes — example, comparison, analysis, definition — is often suggested by the topic sentence as well. We might expect, for instance, that Galbraith will describe how exchange and testing go on, that Freud will give some examples of the child's desire for knowledge, that Russell will analyze some of the differences between astronomy and everyday life. However the writer presents the evidence, the topic sentence tells us what the evidence means.

In all these examples, the topic sentence was the first sentence of the paragraph, and that position is most common. It is not, however, the only position. A topic sentence can come anywhere in a paragraph.

Frequently, a first sentence serves as a transition from the previous paragraph, and the topic sentence appears in the second or even the third sentence. This arrangement occurs in an essay urging a more creative approach to business planning. After a paragraph describing some failures of "rational" planning, the authors write:

> Now, all of this is apparently bad news for many who have made a life's work of number crunching. But the problem is not that companies ought not to plan. (Thomas J. Peters and Robert H. Waterman, Jr., "Analytic Ivory Towers")

The first sentence is a transition. The rest of the paragraph supports the topic announced in the second sentence.

Sometimes a topic sentence in the middle holds together apparently disparate ideas:

> Glasses of tea with tin covers were brought, and a plate piled high with steaming corn on the cob, and then a plate equally laden with a kind of roll. It was the Indonesian ritual of welcome, the display of abundance. It called for a matching courtesy in the guests. No one wished to be the first to eat or drink; and it often happened that the tea, say, was drunk right at the end, when it was cold. (V. S. Naipaul, *Among the Believers*)

Here, the topic sentence ("It was the Indonesian ritual. . . .") is right in the middle of the paragraph. It governs both what comes before and what comes after, and it ties disparate evidence into a single bundle. It explains the meaning of the occasion of welcome in its cause and its effect. Both fit comfortably under the main point, *ritual of welcome*.

Naipaul could have divided the main point into two parts and written two short paragraphs: one to deal with the conduct of the host and the other with the conduct of the guest. Instead, he preferred to write one amply demonstrated paragraph. He devised a topic sentence to cover everything he wanted to say, and he put it in the middle of the paragraph, as a linchpin. There is logic and grace to this method, but to use it well takes planning.

When the topic sentence ends a paragraph, it summarizes the evidence and focuses the reader's attention on what that evidence has shown. It clarifies and unifies the preceding sentences. In the following passage, Wendell Berry describes how he set about turning land into a farm:

> In the early spring of 1965 I had planted a small orchard; the next spring we planted our first garden. Within the following six or seven years we reclaimed pastures, converted the garage into a henhouse, rebuilt the barn, greatly improved the garden soil, planted berry bushes, acquired a milk cow — and were producing, except for hay and grain for our animals, nearly everything that we ate: fruit, vegetables, eggs, meat, milk, cream, and butter. We built an outbuilding with a meat room and a food-storage cellar. Because we did not want to pollute our land and water with sewage, and in the process waste nutrients that should be returned to the soil, we built a compacting

privy. And so we began to attempt a life that, in addition to whatever else it was, would be responsibly agricultural. We used no chemical fertilizers. Except for a little rotenone, we used no insecticides. As our land and our food became healthier, so did we. And our food was of better quality than any that we could have bought. (*Recollected Essays: 1965–1980*)

That last sentence is like putting the sum of a column of figures at the bottom. The reader says, Ah, now I know what all these ideas add up to.

When we wait until the end to state the significance of our evidence, however, we may find that we have not focused our thoughts sufficiently: the sentences may have run out of control. One thought has reminded us of another, and that of another, and so on, until we have lost touch with the main point. Our line of argument may begin to waver. And our reader, abruptly arriving at the final sum, may have to retrace the steps to be sure they were added correctly. Write paragraphs with topic sentences at the end, of course, but double-check them.

Not every paragraph must have a topic sentence. Sentences may combine in such a clear way that no explicit statement of the topic is necessary. Look at this paragraph without a topic sentence:

Suddenly it comes, the flaming globe, blazing on the pinnacles and minarets and balanced rocks, on the canyon walls and through the windows in the sandstone fins. We greet each other, sun and I, across the black void of ninety-three million miles. The snow glitters between us, acres of diamonds almost painful to look at. Within an hour all the snow exposed to the sunlight will be gone and the rock will be damp and steaming. Within minutes, even as I watch, melting snow begins to drip from the branches of a juniper nearby; drops of water streak slowly down the side of the trailerhouse. (Edward Abbey, "The Most Beautiful Place on Earth")

Abbey does not need to explain the significance of these natural images. The writing itself — lyrical, even enraptured — provides the interpretation: the experience is sublime. To decide whether you need a topic sentence, read your writing as a reader would. Is your point clear? If not, find a topic sentence.

Sometimes a paragraph will find its topic sentence in the last line of the previous paragraph. In "The View from 80," Cowley ends one paragraph with

> We start by growing old in other people's eyes, then slowly we come to share their judgment.

and in the next paragraph, he provides the evidence.

> I remember a morning many years ago when I was backing out of the parking lot near the railroad station in Brewster, New York. There was a near collision. The driver of the other car jumped out and started to abuse me; he had his fists ready. Then he looked at me and said, "Why, you're an old man." He got back in the car, slammed the door, and drove away, while I stood there fuming. "I'm only 65," I thought. "He wasn't driving carefully. I can still take care of myself in a car, or in a fight, for that matter."

Likewise, writers will often continue a topic in a second or even a third paragraph without any additional topic sentence. In an essay comparing our fears with those of the Eskimo, Loren Eiseley begins one paragraph this way:

> For what is it that we do? We fear. We do not fear ghosts but we fear the ghost of ourselves. We have come now, in this time, to fear the water we drink. . . .

He finishes that paragraph with a series of things we fear and then goes to a new paragraph and continues listing our fears:

> We fear the awesome powers we have lifted out of nature and cannot return to her. We fear the weapons we have made, the hatreds we have engendered. We fear the crush of fanatic people to whom we readily sell these weapons. We fear for the value of the money in our pockets that stands symbolically for food and shelter. We fear the growing power of the state to take all these things from us. We fear to walk in our streets at evening. We have come to fear even our scientists and their gifts. (Loren Eiseley, "The Winter of Man")

The topic sentence controls the development of both paragraphs.

Paragraphs containing only a topic sentence also occur occasionally; their main idea is so obvious that it needs no further support. Frequently these one-sentence paragraphs are rhetorical questions, as in this example from Eiseley's essay:

> Has the wintry bleakness in the troubled heart of humanity at least equally retreated? — that aspect of man referred to when the Eskimo, adorned with amulets to ward off evil, reiterated: "Most of all we fear the secret misdoings of the heedless ones among ourselves."

Almost always, however, you will need to flesh out the topic sentence with a series of supporting sentences.

The best writing has a variety of constructions and should never be mechanical. Having the topic sentence at the beginning can, however, be reassuring for inexperienced or uncertain writers. There, it can help keep the writer on track and serve as an ever-present reminder of what the writer is saying. Like a compass or direction marker, it can help the writer check progress during the writing. It can help the reader as well. Bearing it in mind, the reader can check off the supporting ideas one by one. By the end the reader can intelligently evaluate the author's point.

One further advantage: a bold and intriguing topic sentence up front can excite readers and entice them into the paragraph. When you are constructing your topic sentence, make it interesting so that your reader will want to read on.

TIPS FOR THE TOPIC SENTENCE

- Ask yourself if the topic sentence actually does predict or encompass the whole paragraph.
- Putting a topic sentence at the beginning of the paragraph can help you stay on course.
- If you place the topic sentence at the end of a paragraph, ask yourself whether all the sentences lead to it.
- If you place the topic sentence in the middle, be sure it covers both the first part of the paragraph and the last.
- If a paragraph does not have a topic sentence, make sure the subject is clear to the reader.
- Word your topic sentence so that it will make your reader eager to go on to the rest of the paragraph.

EXERCISES FOR THE TOPIC SENTENCE

1. Below are pairs of sentences, one a topic sentence for a paragraph and the other a piece of support. Identify the topic sentence in each pair.
   a. Blessed are the children who always eat the same flavor of ice cream or always know beforehand what kind they want. It's a sad thing to observe a beautiful young child who has always been perfectly happy with a plain vanilla cone being subverted by a young schoolmate who has been invited along for the

weekend — a pleasant and polite visitor, perhaps, but spoiled by permissive parents and scarred by an overactive imagination. (L. Rust Hills, "How to Eat an Ice Cream Cone")

b. Perhaps the finest painting in the church is Lorenzo Lotto's *St. Anthony Giving Alms* in which the warm colour scheme seems to have been derived from the soft Turkish carpets which play a prominent part in the composition. Although the church is not as rich in paintings as in sculpture, it contains several of note. (Hugh Honour, *The Companion Guide to Venice*)

c. The Beatles could afford not to grow up because a certain childlike magic had always been central to their appeal. They were bound up with the decade in more ways than one, for the sixties were a period that believed in magic and innocence, that had a touching faith in the omnipotence of individual desire. (Morris Dickstein, *Gates of Eden: American Culture in the Sixties*)

d. Early one morning the sub-inspector at a police station the other end of the town rang me up on the phone and said that an elephant was ravaging the bazaar. It was a tiny incident in itself, but it gave me a better glimpse than I had had before of the real nature of imperialism — the real motives for which despotic governments act. (George Orwell, "Shooting an Elephant")

2. Each of the following statements could serve as a thesis for an essay. For each, write four topic sentences suitable for supporting paragraphs. Exchange your sentences with a partner and discuss the differences.

Attempting suicide should/should not be a crime.

The government should/should not provide funds for abortions for women on welfare.

Freshmen at this institution should/should not be required to take a sequence of courses on Western civilization.

This institution should/should not participate in intercollegiate athletics.

3. Write paragraphs on four of the following topics: the seasons, sports, traveling, listening to music, gambling, cousins or aunts and uncles, dieting, required subjects in school, the cost of education. In one paragraph, put the topic sentence at the beginning; in another, at the end; in the third, in the middle; and in the fourth, don't use a topic sentence at all. Otherwise, treat the topics any way you wish.

UNITY: BEING ONE IN SPIRIT AND PURPOSE

When a paragraph is unified, every idea, every fact, every opinion contributes to the main idea announced in the topic sentence. Unity means no extraneous ideas are dropped in, however witty or arresting. Unity gives paragraphs power by making the main point more easily understood and therefore more convincing.

The following paragraph comes from an essay whose thesis is "Most country and western performers are mockeries of real cowboys." All the sentences work as a unit.

The clothes that country and western performers wear bear little resemblance to those of the authentic cowboy. The cowboy's hat was made of rough leather to protect him against the relentless, corrosive western sun. Bandanas also protected the cowboy from the sun and served as swabs to mop up the inevitable sweat; they were made of plain cotton cloth. Chaps and boots, rough leather like the hats, were not ornaments: they helped ease chafing of the legs and thighs during the rough riding the cowboy did each day. From these homely and practical garments, country and western singers have somehow derived a costume of black velvet hats, alligator boots, satin pants, and phosphorescent bandanas. Perhaps they figured that cowboys wore fancy clothes in their spare time, to go to the local square dance. Whatever their reasoning, the result is a travesty of history. And of common sense. I can't picture any self-respecting horse allowing a hot-pink, rhinestone-studded dude to get within ten feet, let alone to ride him out on the range.

The writer took one way — clothes — in which country and western singers are mockeries of real cowboys and then fully developed it. The topic sentence at the beginning ties the paragraph to the thesis of the essay and indicates exactly what will follow. All the other sentences come under a clear and cogent heading: cowboy clothing. The writer has resisted the temptation to talk about hairdos, accents and voices, or music (she takes them all up elsewhere). After all, there is a good and ample point to be made — and much fun to be had — just with clothes. Such a sharp, consistent focus illustrates the virtue of unity.

We must resist beguiling, even fascinating, associations that will lead us away from our main idea and probably right out of our paragraph. Imagine a paragraph with consecutive sentences on these subjects: paint, color, green, blue, blues, jazz, rock, stone, stoned . . .

and then the paragraph is out on a limb with no tree attached. We have rarely seen paragraphs that aimless, but we have seen some in which the writer just drifts down the stream of consciousness. Here is a fairly tame example:

> When we think about animal experimentation, we should look at the animals used. Because so many are required, only abundant species are chosen. Scientists may test a drug on anything from a small mouse to a monkey. Testing is helpful to scientists because it enables them to study the effects of new chemicals. Limiting tests to cell and tissue cultures only is inadequate. Scientists can find out a good deal from tissue analysis, but drugs do not act the same way when other kinds of tissue are absent. Not even with the capabilities of computers can scientists discover enough about the effects of drugs. Tests on experimental animals are still our best means, short of human trials, of learning how drugs work in human bodies.

The topic sentence promises a discussion of the lab animals, and for the next two sentences that is what we get. But the word *testing* in the fourth sentence diverts the writer from her point, and she drops the animals. If the student had compared each sentence with the topic sentence, she would have seen right away that at her fourth sentence she had begun to go astray. In the fifth and sixth sentences, she discussed another kind of test, and in the seventh, quite far afield, she points out the inadequacy of computers. The closing sentence brings us back to animals but makes a point not anticipated in the topic sentence.

In the revision, the writer refuses to be diverted and concentrates on supporting her main point.

> When we think about animal experimentation, we should look at the animals used. Because so many are required, only abundant species are chosen. Scientists may test a drug on anything from a small mouse to a monkey. They choose animals that share certain biological functions with human beings. By observing the effect of drugs on these animals, they can learn something about the effects of the drugs on human beings. This kind of testing is still our best means, short of human trials, of learning how drugs work in human bodies.

TIPS FOR UNITY

- Remember that all ideas must relate to the main point.
- If you have a topic sentence, check each sentence in the paragraph against it to be sure you have not changed the subject but have stayed on track.

EXERCISES FOR UNITY

1. Here is a disunified paragraph. Revise it for unity, cutting out extraneous material and correcting it when it begins to digress. To revise effectively, first identify the topic sentence and measure the paragraph's direction against it.

The apparent advantage of dialogue over lecture as a way of teaching critical thinking is that it can involve students in more than one viewpoint and help them develop their own ideas. But even Plato, usually acknowledged as a master of the dialogue form, sometimes fails to bring off this advantage. In "The Cave," for example, he has Socrates question Glaucon about the nature of life, but Plato makes Glaucon such a yea-sayer that the reader never gets a proper interplay of ideas. It is like a class in which the teacher asks leading questions but will only accept one answer — one that agrees with his. Students sense that they are being unfairly manipulated and are not being taken seriously, and soon most will lapse into indifference. The teacher then complains to other teachers that the Socratic method is a waste of time. Some of his more open-minded colleagues may protest that the method must be properly used, but the old guard nod sagely to one another as if to say, "Another one of us has come of age." Life is full of such rites of passage, and in some circles they pass for wisdom. But education of this sort never got anyone out of the cave.

2. The following two paragraphs lack unity because their authors have gone off on tangents. In each case, identify the point at which the paragraph gets off track and then compose a new ending starting at that point.

Popular fiction focuses on a few basic fantasies, continually re-adapting them to the latest fashions in the culture. In the 1950s, for example, the private eye was the basic adventure hero, in the 1960s it was the spy, and in the 1970s the ex-Vietnam veteran against organized crime. But each hero faces essentially the same challenges — rich and powerful supervillains — and has the same resources — hand-to-hand combat skills, inventive intelligence, and that most crucial of all ingredients, sex appeal. Indeed, whatever the decade of their flourishing, these heroes always succeed in seducing women. And this is what their readers want to experience vicariously. In airports, on trains, at bus stops, you see mild-mannered and well-groomed men, briefcases in hand, reading the latest stories. Who would suspect the brutal and lascivious fantasies exploding within their brains? As Gilbert and Sullivan once observed, "Things are seldom what they seem."

There is great power not only in the denotative meanings of words but in their connotations as well. Consider, for example, this familiar phrase: "We hold these truths to be self-evident." Ask yourself, how is this different from "We hold these truths to be sacred and undeniable"? Thomas Jefferson himself actually wrote the second phrase. The Continental Congress, however, delegated the task of writing the Declaration of Independence to five men, including John Adams and Benjamin Franklin. Adams had suggested that Jefferson write the document by himself, in part because Jefferson was known to be a good writer, in part because he was a Virginian and Adams wanted to secure Virginia's support for the rebellion. Who actually changed the wording, though, we do not know.

3. Examine a recent essay of yours paragraph by paragraph for unity. Do any paragraphs fail to adhere to their topic sentence? Do any end far away from where they began? If you find examples of disunity, revise them.

COHERENCE: HANGING TOGETHER

Now you have a strong topic sentence and a number of supporting sentences. So far, so good. However, some paragraphs that are unified may still lack coherence. Coherence means that the sentences within a paragraph are clearly connected with one another. They hang together. One thought logically and naturally follows another, and each piece of support is completed before the next one is begun.

In this paragraph from "Letter from Birmingham Jail," Martin

Luther King, Jr., maintains coherence in a passage of rich detail, subtle thought, and moving argument.

> In your statement you assert that our actions, even though peaceful, must be condemned because they precipitate violence. But is this a logical assertion? Isn't this like condemning a robbed man because his possession of money precipitated the evil act of robbery? Isn't this like condemning Socrates because his unswerving commitment to truth and his philosophical inquiries precipitated the act by the misguided populace in which they made him drink hemlock? Isn't this like condemning Jesus because his unique God-consciousness and never-ceasing devotion to God's will precipitated the evil act of crucifixion? We must come to see that, as the federal courts have consistently affirmed, it is wrong to urge an individual to cease his efforts to gain his basic constitutional rights because the quest may precipitate violence. Society must protect the robbed and punish the robber.

This statement of conscience gains power with each sentence. Each idea builds upon the one before it and increases the intensity of the argument. All the questions point to that completely persuasive reference to the crucifixion in the fifth sentence. A reversal of that order — starting with Jesus and ending with the robbed man — would have been anticlimactic and even confusing. At the end King wraps up his thought by referring back to the robbed and the robber. Every sentence illuminates the main idea. In addition, each sentence seems to rise from the one before it and to reach out for the one after it. The ideas grow as if organic, and with each sentence the impact builds.

When a paragraph is coherent, thoughts and ideas develop continuously, and the relationships are clear. The current of thought flows. There are no jerks, no backing and filling, no long leaps from the period of one sentence to the capital letter of the next. Coherence means that the proper order is maintained, continuity preserved, and the transitions firm.

Order

Sometimes incoherence results when sentences or thoughts appear out of sequence or when the writer drops an idea, only to pick it up later. Look at this paragraph from an essay arguing for changes in rules governing football:

> The technique of tackling known as "spearing" — charging helmet first into the opposing player's body — ought to be outlawed. Getting speared is very much like getting hit with a cannonball. Yet ballcarriers are likely be in the forefront of those resisting this rule change. Why do we allow spearing to continue? And if the tackler hits at the wrong angle, he can break his back. Playing with pain has become a sign of manliness. But it isn't just pain that is at stake. A tackler could give himself a concussion — padding can only absorb so much shock. There are, in short, things in this world of more value than demonstrating manliness through enduring pain — things like maintaining the health of one's body for an active life, not just for a few "playing years." The modern helmet is as hard as iron, and with 250 pounds of charging linebacker behind it, the impact is awesome. At best the ballcarrier will come out with a bruise, but it is all too likely that the blow will break a rib or even puncture a lung. Football has been plagued from the outset by a macho image.

It is all in there — the ballcarrier, the tackler, the danger, even the threatened values — but not in the right order. The writer has not finished one thought before he starts another. He does not, for instance, complete the description of the damage to the runner, and so he has to come back to that subject at the end. And the mention of the tackler surprises us. The whole paragraph zigzags back and forth among its various ideas. Dizzying shifts and turns like these call for rearrangement, which the writer undertakes in his revision.

> The technique of tackling known as "spearing" — charging helmet first into the opposing player's body — ought to be outlawed. It jeopardizes the health of both the ballcarrier and the tackler. For the ballcarrier, getting speared is very much like getting hit with a cannonball. The modern helmet is as hard as iron, and with 250 pounds of charging linebacker behind it, the impact is awesome. At best the ballcarrier will come out with a bruise, but the blow could break a rib or even puncture a lung. Nor does this practice leave the tackler unscathed. If he hits at the wrong angle, he can break his back, or, because padding can only absorb so much shock, he may give himself a concussion. Yet players themselves resist rule changes in their interest. Football and individual football players have been plagued from the outset by a macho image. Playing with pain has become a sign of manliness, and perhaps it is. But there are things of more value than

such manliness; for instance, the health of one's body over an entire lifetime.

Now we know that the paragraph will treat both ballcarriers and tacklers. The writer has grouped all the sentences referring to the ballcarrier and then all the sentences referring to the tackler. The sixth sentence is a bridge between the two. The writer presents the ideas in an appropriate and logical order, and we can follow without stumbling and falling.

Ways to Maintain Order

Unfortunately, we know of no hard and fast rules for maintaining order. Bear in mind three patterns — chronological order, order of climax, and order of difficulty — as you organize your paragraphs.

Chronological Order. Sometimes material we write about quite naturally follows according to *when* the various parts or events occur. If you were writing about history or explaining a process or a cause and effect relation, you would very likely find chronological order essential. To vary from it might confuse your reader. In any case, maintaining chronology can be an effective ordering method. The following passage comes from an essay by Roy C. Selby, entitled "A Delicate Operation":

> After making certain there was no bleeding, the surgeon closed the wounds and placed wire mesh over the holes in the skull to prevent dimpling of the scalp over the points that had been drilled. A gauze dressing was applied to the patient's head. She was awakened and sent to the recovery room.

Reverse those sentences and see what you get. The chronological order saves us from thinking for a moment that the patient was awake during the operation.

Order of Climax. Sometimes you can present your evidence so that the paragraph rises to a peak. If, for instance, you have three points, you can arrange them so that the paragraph develops from interesting point, to more interesting point, to most interesting point. Speech writers, novelists, and musical composers are well aware of the advantages of this order. They build toward a climax of increasing tension and interest.

You should go to almost any lengths, short of distortion, to avoid a sudden drop in tension, or anticlimax. Anticlimax creates confusion and a sense of disorder. The following paragraph brims with marvelous details, but it suffers from anticlimax:

> Living in England for two years convinced me that the Who was rock's most representative group. Their music was challenging, violent, as repetitive and insistent as the throb of a broken jaw. That music, at times the closest thing to pain I had ever heard, seemed to be me and say me. Their lyrics spoke of the undeniable facts of life at eighteen: you are caught in the middle, not a schoolboy and not ready to be a working man, old enough to want power and young enough never to have it. The Who looked like skinny, awkward kids: defiant pairs of deep, hungry eyes, a chipped tooth here, a huge nose there.

In revising, the writer evaluated the impact of each sentence, and then arranged them in order of climax:

> Living in England for two years convinced me that the Who was rock's most representative group. They looked like skinny, awkward kids: a huge nose here, a chipped tooth there, defiant pairs of deep, hungry eyes. Their lyrics spoke of the undeniable facts of life at eighteen: you are caught in the middle, not a schoolboy and not ready to be a working man, old enough to want power and young enough never to have it. Their music was challenging, violent, as repetitive and insistent as the throb of a broken jaw. That music, at times the closest thing to pain that I had ever heard, seemed to be me and say me.

Now the writer had a much more dramatic, entertaining, and coherent paragraph.

Order of Difficulty. To ease into an intricate or controversial idea, you can begin with an idea the reader is most likely to understand or agree with. Once you have secured that point, you can go on to the harder points. When the reader is with you point by point, the reading seems more coherent. When the reader has to fight the ideas, the writing may seem disorganized. Going from less difficult ideas to more difficult ones can help organize not only paragraphs but whole essays.

The following paragraph is from an essay claiming that people the author calls "optionaires" start life with a wider range of opportunities and advantages than others. This passage, like the whole essay, contains ideas difficult for many to accept, but the writer ordered them to make that acceptance easier:

> There is some recognition among optionaires that the country has minority groups of nonwhite citizens who are excluded from the affluent society because of racial prejudice; a handful of people from these groups is admitted into affluence and their membership is touted as evidence of America's inherent equality of opportunity. But the vast majority of people in the nonaffluent society — more than 140 million Americans — are generally ignored. (An exception is just before election time, when optionaires running for office remember the existence, and voting rights, of the nonaffluent until all the ballots are in.) (Celeste MacLeod, "Some People Always Make It: The Optionaires")

MacLeod starts with the generally accepted idea that, yes, the country does suffer from prejudice. The reader will sadly accept that, and may even feel moral in acknowledging it. The writer then points out that not only minority citizens but also millions of whites are ignored. She ends with the idea that "optionaires," of whom the reader may well be one, actually manipulate nonoptionaires for their own ends. That little bit of sugar on the first sentence helps the bitter pill of the last to go down. Had the order been reversed, the reader might have rejected the whole idea out of hand.

Thoughts Descending a Staircase.   However a paragraph is ordered, the steps between ideas should be gradual enough for the reader to step from one idea to the next. Sometimes paragraphs suffer from the steep staircase. The steps are all there, but they seem dangerously far apart. Rather than moving easily, readers feel as though they are for a moment dropping into space. Such is the case in reading this paragraph, in which a student discusses Carl Sagan's essay, "The Abstractions of Beasts":

> Research indicates that certain kinds of monkeys have considerable language skills. Carl Sagan deals primarily with three chimpanzees — Lucy, Lana, and Washoe — who were taught Ameslan (American Sign Language) and developed vocabularies ranging from 100 to 200 words and eventually were capable of constructing phrases. James Dewson and other colleagues found that chimpanzees have a language center in the neocortex of the left hemisphere of the brain, just as human beings do. Apes are thought to transmit extragenetic or cul-

tural information. Differences in group behavior have been documented among chimpanzees and other related species.

Although all the sentences relate to the topic, something seems to be missing. How does the reader get from the three chimps to James Dewson? What is the connection between cultural information and differences in group behavior? The last four sentences are piled one on top of the other without relation to the first or to each other — like pancakes tossed on a plate. And one thing a paragraph should not be is a pile of sentences tossed anywhere.

Recognizing the gaps between the ideas and the apparent discontinuity of his thoughts, the writer went back to work. He provided elaboration of some ideas and even additional sentences. These changes help us to descend through the paragraph.

> Research indicates that certain kinds of monkeys have considerable language skills. Carl Sagan deals primarily with three chimpanzees — Lucy, Lana, and Washoe — who showed considerable linguistic talent. When they were taught Ameslan (American Sign Language), they were able to develop vocabularies that ranged from 100 to 200 words and eventually to form phrases. Medical research provides further support for the idea that chimpanzees are capable of linguistic tasks. James Dewson and other colleagues found, for example, that monkeys have a language center in the neocortex of the left hemisphere of the brain, just as human beings do. This center may explain why their language capacity is far beyond that of other lower mammals. In addition, investigators think apes transmit extragenetic, or cultural, information that differs from tribe to tribe depending on the environment and what is needed to survive. Differences in group behavior among chimpanzees and related species have been documented. Such differences could come about, some investigators claim, only through language skills.

In the revision the writer does more than merely list pieces of evidence about the monkeys and the neocortex. Recognizing that the steps between the main idea and some of the concrete evidence are too steep, he builds intermediate steps. The intermediate step in the second sentence allows us to move gracefully from the main idea to the Sagan research. The intermediate step in the fourth sentence eases us from the Sagan research to the evidence on the neocortex. These two steps help us descend through the paragraph. The last sentence is not so much a new step as an elevator: it carries all the freight back up to the topic sentence. Without it, and without those intermediate steps, all that evidence would lie inert in the basement of the paragraph.

We can think of the paragraph as a staircase the reader can smoothly descend, one foot safely on a step before the other foot moves. If the steps are too steep, the reader must jump and may fall. We must build in the intermediate steps — those statements somewhat less general than the topic sentence, somewhat more general than the evidence, that make for continuity of thought.

Transition

Even when our ideas are in the appropriate order and our thoughts are continuous, we still must provide transitions between sentences. In a well-made paragraph, each sentence, while introducing a new thought, almost always refers back to something in the previous sentence. This reference eases the reader from one sentence to the next and creates a sense of thought flowing and evolving.

Look at the King paragraph on p. 99. The second sentence asks a question about the first. The third repeats the question in a more concrete form. The fourth and fifth continue the questioning in the same form. It is as if each sentence reaches back for an idea from the previous sentence and then modifies it. The thoughts are continuous, the connections clear.

The natural progression of old and new, however, may not be quite enough, and we will need to reinforce our transitions explicitly. The transitions in the following paragraph need a good deal of reinforcement.

> Housing prisoners one to a room is a controversial proposition. Some citizens oppose it as unwarranted luxury. Our society is already too permissive with criminals. Army recruits live in barracks. There are very real and practical advantages to it. Hardened criminals would have fewer opportunities to corrupt first offenders. Violence would decrease. Prisoners would have a chance to reflect on their past actions. Talk about the proposition is academic. Taxpaying citizens are in no mood to underwrite experimentation in any area of government service. It might have ended up saving money, not to mention lives.

Although the "something old, something new" holds, this paragraph is difficult to follow. Does *it* in the second sentence refer to *housing* or to *proposition*? Who thinks there are *practical advantages, some citizens* or the writer? Do the third, fourth, and fifth sentences support or contradict each other? Does *it* in the last sentence refer to *government service, experimentation, talk,* or *proposition*? This paragraph cries out for transition reinforcement.

A writer can reinforce the transitions between thoughts in four ways:

1. by repeating words and phrases
2. by shifting to pronouns and demonstrative adjectives
3. by using parallel construction
4. by inserting transitional flags.

In revising, this writer used all four methods.

> Housing prisoners one to a room is a controversial proposition. Some citizens oppose such housing as unwarranted luxury. They say that our society is already too permissive with criminals. Furthermore, they say, army recruits have to live in barracks. On the other hand, there may be real and practical advantages. The proposition, for example, would provide less opportunity for hardened criminals to corrupt first offenders. It would offer less opportunity for violence. And at the same time it would provide more opportunity for prisoners to reflect on their past actions. Unfortunately, talk about these advantages is academic. Taxpaying citizens have made it clear that they are in no mood to underwrite experimentation in any area of government service. Nonetheless, the proposition might have ended up saving money, not to mention lives.

Repeated Words and Phrases.   When a writer repeats a word or its synonym from sentence to sentence, the reader recognizes that the same subject is being discussed. That recognition ties the two sentences together. The revised paragraph on housing prisoners contains many examples of this kind of reinforcement. The synonym *criminal* takes the place of, and makes more emphatic, the word *prisoner*. Notice how *they say* is repeated, as are *opportunity, proposition, advantages,* and *citizens*. These words are like Velcro, binding the sentences together.

Sometimes repeating a word throughout a paragraph tightens the connections:

> Experience, intelligence, and personality would not be enough to elect a person president. There must be money. Money influences delegates. Money buys airtime. Money pays for television advertisements. Money pays for hairstylists and speech coaches. Money pays for the campaign directors, whose main job is to find more money.

Pronouns and Demonstrative Adjectives. The revised passage on housing prisoners uses both pronouns (*it, they*) and demonstrative adjectives (*such, that*) to aid coherence. When readers see a pronoun, they will expect that the writer will say more on the same subject and that the ideas will accumulate, as in this example:

> Your basic president is a man who combines the common and the uncommon. He is white and he stands somewhere around six feet tall. He is always religious, or at least a member of a religious organization. He is almost always a millionaire.

What holds true for pronouns also applies to demonstrative adjectives such as *this, that, these, those,* and *such.* The paragraph on presidents goes on to say:

> These qualities do not prevent his being an astute politician with many supporters. Those supporters get him to the White House, and, if he is at all competent and lucky, keep him there.

Read these sentences substituting *the* for *these* and *those.* Although you can figure it out, your reaction time is just a little slower. Your eye climbs back through the sentences, seeking connections that the demonstrative adjectives make plain.

Parallel Construction. Later we will discuss parallel construction in regard to both diction (see Chapter 7, Working with Words) and grammar (see the appendix, The Nuts and Bolts: A Handbook). Here we want to point out that repeating a grammatical form links sentences and helps to make a more coherent paragraph. Responding to the repeated pattern and the repeated rhythm, the reader makes connections more easily.

This passage from John F. Kennedy's inaugural address is an excellent example of the power of parallel construction:

> To those old allies whose cultural and spiritual origins we share, we pledge the loyalty of faithful friends. United, there is little we cannot do in a host of cooperative ventures. Divided, there is little we can do, for we dare not meet a powerful challenge at odds and split asunder.
>
> To those new states whom we welcome to the ranks of the free. . . .

And on he went, holding firmly both his sentences and his audience.

Transitional Flags

Frequently, transitional flags, such as *furthermore, however,* and *for instance*, will hold two ideas together and make explicit the logical connection. They explain whether the previous idea is being modified, qualified, amplified, or contradicted.

Before we discuss transitional flags in depth, we want to make two important points. First, you will not need to plant a verbal flag in absolutely every sentence. Whole paragraphs, in fact, can flow along without a single *however, thus,* or *furthermore*, just on the strength of a strong topic sentence and implicit relationships among ideas. In fact, overused, explicit transitions make writing wooden and mechanical. But carefully and sparingly employed, they make writing tight, emphatic, and clear. Second, transitional flags carry a meaning and function of their own. They help determine the meaning of a sentence. Thus, you must be sure to choose a word that does exactly what you intend.

Here are eight relations that transitional flags can signal, with examples under each relation.

Number. *First, second, third, finally.* If you have a series of complex ideas, you can give your reader a sense of order by rating the ideas as a list and numbering them. To show that you are closing the list — or to show that you are ending a narrative — you can use the word *finally.*

In becoming a successful owner of securities, follow these four basic steps. First, learn to read Standard & Poor's monthly stock guide, which shows price/earnings ratio, long- and short-term debt, and so on, of many companies. Second . . . Third . . . Finally, be prepared to tolerate some wrong judgments.

Addition. *And, furthermore, moreover, in addition, besides.* When you attach another idea to a point already made, use one of these words or phrases.

> And everything will be crystal clear. Moreover, your writing will be smoother.

Comparison. *Similarly, likewise, in the same way.* One of these words or phrases will tell the reader to notice that two ideas are alike.

> Western explorers have always misunderstood the foreign cultures they "discover." In the same way, most American and European listeners fail to comprehend Indian music and think of it as a mixture of nasal caterwauling and groaning strings.

Contrast. *Even so, still, nonetheless, but, yet, notwithstanding, nevertheless, however, on the other hand.* To signal the reader that a new idea differs from the previous idea, insert one of these words or phrases.

> Babe Ruth was overweight, bandy-legged, often drunk, and always slow. He became, nevertheless, one of baseball's greatest hitters.

Example. *For instance, for example, to illustrate, in particular.* When you use an example to support a statement, flag the example.

> Earning a college degree in the sciences is only one of many ways to a promising future. You could inherit your father's oil well, for instance, or score 100 points a game for your high-school basketball team.

Concession. *Of course, to be sure, granted, given that, no doubt.* Concessions are an important part of any argument. They demonstrate that you are aware of other ways of looking at questions.

> More wars have been fought in the name of money than in the name of religion. Granted, millions have suffered and died for their reli-

gious beliefs. But behind every religious purge we can usually find an economic motive.

Summary. *Briefly, in short, in conclusion, in sum, to sum up.* These signals warn your reader that you have ended your argument and want to make it a bit plainer by summing it up.

Templeton's writing style is full of dense sonorities, a polished perfection that serves to avoid the untidy, irrational moment. In short, it stinks.

Consequence or conclusion. *Thus, and so, as a result, consequently, therefore, hence, accordingly.* These words and phrases provide a sense of finality. We want to caution you, however, against using such words inaccurately. Be sure you don't claim a conclusion you haven't earned. For example, we could not in all conscience now write

Thus have we exhausted the subject of transitions, and you therefore know all you ever need to know.

With this brief survey, we have not earned either the *thus* or the *therefore*.

As their name indicates, transitions assist the flow of your thought from one sentence or phrase or clause to the next. They are the bridges over which your thought moves. Rather than asking your reader to jump the gap between thoughts, you provide a bridge.

Coherent writing conveys the reader smoothly and considerately from thought to thought. Much of your writing will do this naturally, but when rereading and revising your writing, watch for the gaps or missed connections that could cause your reader to stumble. Working for coherence will help your reader understand and will also help you chart the progress of your thought.

TIPS FOR COHERENCE

- Finish one idea before you take up another so that you won't have to double back.
- Ask yourself whether you should arrange your ideas in chronological order, order of climax, or order of difficulty.
- Ask yourself whether the thoughts are clearly continuous from

one sentence to the next or whether you should provide intermediate information.
- Be both sparing and accurate with transitional flags; make sure
you earn your *therefores* and *moreovers*.
- Remember: few considerations in writing are as important as how
you get from one idea to the next.

EXERCISES FOR COHERENCE

1. Underline everything in these two passages that aids coherence,
particularly all transitional words.

Sport may be the toy department of life, but one of its abiding
compensations is that, at least on the field, it is the real thing. Much
has been done in recent years in the attempt to ruin sport — the
ruthlessness of owners, the greed of players, the general exploita-
tion of fans. But even all this cannot destroy it. On the court, down
on the field, sport is fraud-free and fakeproof. With a full count,
two men on, his team down by one run in the last of the eighth, a
batter (as well as a pitcher) is beyond the aid of public relations. At
match point at Forest Hills a player's press clippings are of no help.
Last year's earnings will not sink a twelve-foot putt on the eigh-
teenth at Augusta. Alan Page, galloping up along the quarterback's
blind side, figures to be neglectful of that quarterback's image as a
swinger. In all these situations, and hundreds of others, a man either comes through or he doesn't. He is alone out there, naked but
for his ability, which counts for everything. Something there is
that is elemental about this, and something greatly satisfying. (Joseph Epstein, "Obsessed with Sport")

In Mexico, orphaned when he was eight, my father left school
to work as an "apprentice" to an uncle. Twelve years later, he left
Mexico in frustration and arrived in America. He had great expectations then of becoming an engineer. ("Work for my hands and my
head.") He knew a Catholic priest who promised to get him money
enough to study full time for a high school diploma. But the promises came to nothing. Instead there was a dark succession of ware-
house, cannery, and factory jobs. After work he went to night
school along with my mother. A year, two passed. Nothing much
changed, except that fatigue worked its way into the bone; then
everything changed. He didn't talk anymore of becoming an engineer. He stayed outside of the school while my mother went inside
to learn typing and shorthand. (Richard Rodriguez, "The Achievement of Desire")

2. Go through a recent essay of yours and locate a passage near the middle of that essay. If you can, find a passage you recall writing with special ease. Now read that passage closely. How did you get from sentence to sentence? What is it about your sentences that made transitions possible? Look carefully for passages *without* either repeated words or transitional flags.

3. Revise the following pairs of sentences so that something old and something new are in the second sentence of each pair.
   a. In the nineteenth century, being well padded with flesh was a sign of beauty. My friends like the slender look.
   b. Football games are not called on account of weather. Rain fell and they postponed the third game of the World Series.
   c. Pug dogs are fawn colored. Siamese cats are fawn colored.
   d. Genes are the elements that determine human inheritance. Some people believe we may eventually abuse our ability to change things that were not defects in the first place.

4. Revise the following passages to improve coherence.

   One writer suggests that solar power is the answer to our energy needs. Nuclear power should be our source of energy is what the other writer argues. Solar power is too expensive for many homes. No commercially viable power source has been devised on a scale large enough for private use. Nuclear power is used on a national scale.

   Antivivisectionists are opposed to any scientific experimentation on animals. The desire for new and safe cosmetics does not justify the pain and death necessary to test various products. Scientists want to learn the effects of chemicals and drugs on human beings.

COMPLETENESS: POSSESSING ALL PARTS

A good paragraph conveys a feeling of fullness, of having said all that needed saying and of coming to a natural ending. For a conscientious and interested reader, few things are more frustrating than to come upon a skimpy, fleshless paragraph like this one:

   The God of the Old Testament is uncompromising in the demands he makes on humanity. Commanding Abraham to sacrifice Isaac is a case in point. The fate of Job is another. There is no reasoning with the All-powerful.

That's it. Good-bye. Hope you enjoyed it. Thinking the job is done, the writer turns off the burners, and in the meantime we have only that appetizing opener. Remind us of Abraham, we want to say. How is his story "a case in point"? What had Job done and what happened to him? And then there's that fine last sentence (like many of us, this writer is less good at middles than at beginnings and endings): how did we get there? We may have other unanswered questions. In the Book of Hosea, didn't God compromise a little? We are left hungry. We have been fed fragments of thought, an appetizer, nothing solid.

Whether such writing is a result of impatience, stinginess, or timidity, we of course don't know. But we do know that no writer should force the reader to fill in information. When we write an illustration, we should indicate exactly what is being illustrated and exactly how it relates to the main point. When defining a term, we must show how the term can be used. And when the point is complex, we must supply more than a thin gruel. We must be nurturing, and give our reader a healthy diet of explanation.

Here is another paragraph that leaves the reader hungry:

> Another change I would like to see in our college curriculum is a program consisting of a traditional departmental major and an interdisciplinary minor. Each student would be matched with a faculty adviser who shared to some extent the student's special interest. Working together, they would construct a program that, having been reviewed and endorsed by the appropriate body, would have the same status as any other minor.

Nice plan, isn't it? All those big ideas in three little sentences. The trouble is, once again we are left with many questions. How would the student and the adviser work together? Casually? Systematically? Any papers required? Would the arrangement be left to the instructor or to this vague "body"? Finally — and this is the biggest unanswered question — what advantages does this program have that would justify the change?

Why did this intelligent student ignore all these questions? We think we have the answer: the proposal is complex and controversial, and he probably wanted to avoid the trouble. That is impossible in making a proposal or arguing for an idea. There is no point in dodging complexity. Your audience will expect not avoidance but explanations. And there is no point in trying to hide controversy. It will out. In this revision, the writer provided a complete presentation:

> Another change I would like to see in our college curriculum is a program consisting of a traditional major and an interdisciplinary minor. Each student would first of all have to be matched with a faculty adviser who shared to some extent the student's special interest — for example, ceramics in the Renaissance. They would make a list of the college's relevant offerings — for example, "Renaissance Art," "Social History of Italy," and "The History of Design." They would then construct a program equal to the number of hours required for the present minor. Once this program was reviewed and endorsed by the appropriate administrative body, it would have the same status as any other minor. In this way, a student could graduate with a degree that reflected both traditional discipline and individual spirit.

Now the third, fourth, and fifth sentences provide specific details about the proposal. And the sixth explicitly responds to the eternal "So what?" and provides closure — that is, the feel of completion as well as the fact of it.

The feeling of closure is important. Readers often take away from the paragraph the thought expressed in the last sentence. Although no degree of eloquence in the wrap-up will make a sickly paragraph look healthy, that last sentence can contribute to the feeling that everything is there, everything has been fully demonstrated, now everything makes sense. A strong last sentence gives readers a feeling of replenishment.

How do you know when enough is enough and not too much? No hard and fast rules exist but we cannot remember as teachers ever writing in the margins of an essay, "You are explaining too much" or "This paragraph is too detailed." Our experience tells us that writing is one area in which fat is generally better than skinny. The healthiest paragraphs are, of course, those that are exactly right — and you'll have to learn to identify them by trial and error, because we don't have any surefire advice.

TIPS FOR COMPLETENESS

- If you find that your paragraph's point is complex or controversial, so will your reader. Explain.

- Your concluding sentence should provide a sense of closure, of wrapping up the argument.
- As you would if your paragraph were a baby, prefer fat to skinny.

EXERCISES FOR COMPLETENESS

1. Here are three skinny paragraphs. Study each one, determine where the gaps are, and fill them in, providing missing material and connections. Feel free to rewrite any of the sentences if that will help. After you finish revising, be prepared to discuss what you added and why.

   America's many foods take their characters from their countries of origin. Spaghetti is a good example, as are tacos and burritos, which are both spicy and hot. And we must not forget the hamburger, one of America's most popular foods.

   Children learn language by imitating their parents. At first, all a newborn can do is cry, but then it can see better. It starts imitating its parents, and soon it can make sentences by itself. Now it is a member of society.

   Roads are becoming a real problem for modern cities. Many cities have grown too fast. They build new roads. As those fill up, soon they have no place to put more roads. Public transportation is the only solution.

2. Find a recent essay of yours and look for skinny paragraphs. Revise it, adding what is needed. What did you add and why? (You can do this with a partner, too: exchange recent papers and look for skinny paragraphs. Then take your own paper back and revise it. Or you can revise a skinny paragraph in your partner's essay.)

EMPHASIS: ACCENTING IMPORTANT IDEAS

As is probably clear by now, the best writers (or the best rewriters) know their paragraphs inside out. They can distinguish their major points from their minor points, their topic sentences from their supporting statements. Furthermore, they know that they must devote more detail and greater emphasis to their major points. They decide who are the stars of the show, they bring them front and center, and they direct the spotlights accordingly. The minor players stay in the shadows.

We too must stage our paragraphs; we must decide which idea stands where in what light. We need to determine how to provide the right emphasis. These decisions usually boil down to choices about extent of discussion and placement.

Extent of Discussion

The intuition of some writers about the extent of a discussion is just about perfect. They seem to know instinctively exactly which points to play up and which to play down. But for most of us, this is a tricky business. We worry that if we do not hammer a point home, the reader may miss it altogether. But we know if we spend too much time on a minor point, we may knock our argument out of shape and distract the reader.

Some decisions are easy. You need not slave to prove that IBM is innovative. You can just say "Always innovative, IBM . . . " and everyone will read on. In fact, if you begin citing examples as proof, your readers will see that you are wasting time. But if you argue that IBM always borrows ideas from other companies, you will need a whole book to prove your assertion. We have to be wary of too little discussion as well as too much.

In the following paragraph, the writer argues that our sense of time depends on how involved we are in what we are doing. The notion of "psychological time" is interesting. The writer, however, has become enamored of roadside attractions and lost sight of the important points. The result is that much of her evidence supports tangential ideas.

Our sense of how fast time passes indicates our involvement in what we are doing. In any activity — like studying at the library — we experience periods of absorption punctuated by periods of disengagement. Then we usually glance around, or perhaps actually get up for a drink of water, take a walk, or go to the bathroom. These breaks may hark back to the survival instinct, readily witnessed in films of animals in the wild pausing in the midst of feeding or drinking to take a look around and sniff the air. Even while dashing across the plains, the whole herd may stop as though to take its bearings. When we do look around, we check the time. We compare the reading with what time we expect it to be. Intense involvement can distort our expectation. We can be so absorbed in an activity that we are not aware of time passing, and we expect that a normal interval has passed when it has been longer. We get the idea that time passed swiftly. But who ever heard of a clock going faster at one time and then slower at another?

Unity is not the problem here. Every sentence is about interrupted time. Nor is coherence a problem. The ideas follow closely one after the other, the transitions are clear and smooth, the ideas rich and complex.

Yet the writer weakens this potentially fascinating theme by incorrectly emphasizing certain parts. The paragraph bulges out of shape. So much time is spent describing the lessons of the wildlife documentaries that a reader may begin to think the subject is the sense of time of animals. The writer jams discussion of the real subject — the disparity between clock time and perceived time — into a few short sentences. At the end, she seems to be on a mad dash out of the paragraph.

The revision retains the virtues of the original but improves on its wandering ways:

> Our sense of how fast time passes indicates our involvement in what we are doing. In any activity — like studying at the library — we experience periods of absorption punctuated by periods of disengagement in which our minds pull back from the immediate situation. We glance around at our surroundings, and we usually manage to check the time. When we do, we compare the reading with what we expect it to be, based on our normal span of involvement. For some this may be twenty minutes, for others forty; but however long, it tends to remain fairly constant. Intense involvement, however, can extend this time markedly; when we are intensely absorbed we have little sense of time passing. When we check the clock, we discover that it is much later than we expected. Thus, we get the idea, patently illogical, that time itself has passed swiftly.

In revising, the writer sorted out her main idea (that our perception of time depends on how involved we are) and added to the two major supports (the normal expectation of time passing and the effect of absorption). She de-emphasized everything else. Removing her reference to the animals was painful: this was the writer's favorite material. Nevertheless, out it went, and with it the improper emphasis.

Placement of Major Points

Placement creates emphasis. Your major points — the ones you want the reader to keep in mind — should come at the beginning and the end of your paragraphs. In writing, as in life, those are the most emphatic places to make a statement. The minor points should come in the middle sentences.

Writers work hard on beginnings for two reasons. First, they want to be sure the reader goes on reading. If the opening sentence is not interesting, the reader may skip the whole paragraph. Second, writers know that the reader will probably scoop up an emphatic opening idea and carry it all the way through the paragraph. So it is best to put a strong statement right up front, and to say it well. The art of the opener — of constructing a grabber, a hook — is one to be mastered. The following paragraph opens with a dull, unemphatic, and imprecise sentence:

> Many of us spend hours every week listening to television. After the networks have finished trying our patience, the local stations demand equal time. We are shown products guaranteed to automate and begadget the most mundane household tasks. We are subjected to "Amazing!" shaves and "Miraculous!" washes. If we tried all the beers we are invited to taste, we would float down the avenue — and get run over by all those fast cars our neighbors have been seduced into buying. To close the evening, Cutprice Records presents its Infinite Original Hits: Do you remember this? and that? It is not the commercials that interrupt the programs, but the programs that interrupt the commercials, ever more briefly.

The paragraph itself is not bad, but who would get to it after that dull start? And what is the paragraph going to be about? What major idea does the writer want us to carry forward? All this writer needed was a snappier and more informative opening:

> The barrage of commercials never ends.

The word *barrage* alerts us; the word *commercials* tells us exactly where we are going. An emphatic opening sentence acts like a magnet, drawing the other sentences toward it.

The other traditional place for emphasis is the end of a paragraph. In some ways this position is even more important. Leave 'em laughing, says the comedian. The last sentence provides the momentum into the next paragraph. If it is a bore, the reader will be reluctant to continue. If it is well constructed and dynamic, it will provide the impetus for going on. The following paragraph comes from an essay on the character of Mortimer in *Henry IV, Part I.*

> As one of the original rebels against King Richard, Mortimer should be most faithful to the rebel cause. But after his marriage, he seems more devoted to his bride than to the rebellion. When his comrades urge him on to battle with "to horse immediately," Mortimer responds, "With all my heart." The context, however, makes it clear that this response is halfhearted at best. The irony becomes apparent when he somehow never makes it to battle. Mortimer is unable to stay loyal.

Everything is there: a topic sentence, evidence, good organization — everything but emphasis. The paragraph has a point, but it is not pointed; it doesn't seem to be going anywhere. No thought, no energy concentrates at the end to carry the reader onward. In revising this otherwise good paragraph, the writer replaced that last uninspired sentence with an emphatic sentence.

> Mortimer thus betrays the rebel cause.

Just as the *barrage* sentence exerted an upward surge, this new ending exerts a strong forward pull. It properly focuses the reader's attention on the significance of Mortimer's fickleness. Without it, the reader hardly knows what is important.

TIPS FOR EMPHASIS

- Differentiate important support from unimportant details.
- Ask yourself if you need to add emphasis to the important points.
- Limit discussion of unimportant details, even if you find them fascinating.
- Sentences expressing major points should come at or very near the beginning and the end of the paragraph.
- Minor points should go in the middle of the paragraph.
- On your first draft, underline the most important point in a representative paragraph, and if it is not properly placed, change it. (If you had a problem, do the same with all your paragraphs.)

EXERCISES FOR EMPHASIS

1. The following paragraphs have improper emphasis. This may show up either as too much discussion on a particular subject or misplaced discussion. Revise each to correct this problem, deleting unnecessary elaboration or adding what is missing. Be prepared to answer the question: what did you change and why?

> Pulling a person out of quicksand is a delicate process. You must lie on the nearest solid piece of ground. The ground can be wet or even a little sandy, but you must test it to make sure it will hold when you start pulling. Wind your rope around one shoulder. Two-thousand-pound nylon test is the best, though conventional silk-wound or hempen rope will do. Some rescuers have used their own belts, but these must be of leather rather than the weaker synthetic materials. The whole question of exactly what material to use is sorely debated. Then throw the rope and pull the victim out.

> A good diplomat must possess three essential qualities: discretion, social grace, and political savvy. Without discretion or political savvy, the diplomat will be a liability in times of international tension. Without social grace (a knowledge of local habits and customs, easy affability), the diplomat will be a bore at parties and will fail to build that system of informal contacts so crucial for keeping abreast of local developments. For this ′reason, the diplomat should purchase full sets of silverware and tablecloths and practice eye contact and conversational skills. Spare no expense: stingy diplomats make poor impressions.

2. Here are three theses, each followed by a list of points. Choose one thesis and determine which of the points you would emphasize most in a paper on that topic and which ones you would emphasize less. Arrange the points according to your choice, with most important point last; then write a paragraph using your rearranged list as an outline. Devote two additional sentences to the point you feel is most important. Give less important points one additional sentence. If you wish to leave a point unemphasized, do not add to it. Be ready to explain which points you emphasized most and why.

    a. Richer countries must sacrifice to help poor countries. Time is running out.

    The richer countries can afford it.

    It is hard for any sensitive person to go on watching the famine and suffering without doing something about them.

Poor countries cannot help themselves.

The individual sacrifice would not be very large.

b. Space exploration has had many benefits.

It has expanded the human imagination.

It has helped humanity develop new technologies that it would have been impossible to develop on earth.

It has allowed women, minorities, and people from many other countries to join in a great project.

c. Most popular music is based on a strong rhythmic beat and not much else.

Writers design their songs that way to capture the dance market.

If you actually listen, many of the melodies are undistinguished and indistinguishable.

The words are usually vapid as well.

4 / Beginning, Ending, Titling

Of all my verse, like not a single line;
But like my title, for it is not mine.
That title from a better man I stole:
Ah, how much better, had I stol'n
the whole!

> *– Robert Louis Stevenson (1850–1894)*
> *Scottish novelist and poet*

Two of the most misunderstood kinds of paragraphs are the two most important of your essay: the opening and the concluding. They are your social paragraphs, the ones in which you establish and leave your most significant impressions. Too cautious, too timid, an opening can make your essay a chore to be endured, like a dutiful visit to a sick relative. But overdone, too assertive, and your essay will seem rude, as if you just barged in, shouting "Here I am!" A poor conclusion can seem equally dreary or impolite, depending on whether you repeat the same conversation upon leaving that you had upon arriving or run off without even saying good-bye.

THE FIRST PARAGRAPH: A BOLD BEGINNING

Some opening paragraphs sound like an ancient truck trying to warm up on a very cold day. Old trucks don't offer a very enticing ride, and neither do essays that begin in a dull, unpromising fashion.

An introductory paragraph has four goals:

to grab the reader's attention
to identify the central issue or subject
to establish the writer's thesis
to create the tone of the essay.

The way you start will determine how your reader responds to your essay. It is so crucial that many writers draft it only after they have finished the essay and can put all their energy and artistry into it. And all the good writers we know rewrite that first paragraph again and again. They don't want the engine to die before the reader even turns the corner into the rest of the essay. If you have trouble getting that first paragraph right, wait until you finish the essay before writing the opening. In any case, you will probably need to rewrite it.

Some openings read as though the writer wants to postpone unveiling his or her thought until the last possible moment. First there is a litany of generalities that we already knew and didn't want to hear again ("Human beings are rational creatures, and yet their behavior is not always explicable." Oh?). And then the apology ("I don't pretend to know everything about human nature" — as though anyone did). Such openings usually indicate lack of confidence. When we aren't sure of something, we delay committing ourselves. We walk our thought around the block a few times. We hide behind generalities, platitudes, and other distractions. We hem and haw. The reader gets suspicious: what am I being asked to buy? do I really want to buy it?

An introduction should interest the reader first in the subject and

your thesis. Although you may need to give more background in a later paragraph — perhaps the second — it is only courteous to indicate in this first paragraph the general area you will discuss and how you will approach it. You should provide enough background so that the reader can place the thesis in its proper perspective, but not so much that the reader is swamped or confused.

The Shape of the Opening Paragraph

The thesis statement can appear in the first sentence or in the last or even in the middle of the opening paragraph. In fact, it does not have to be in the very first paragraph at all (but it is a good idea to state it fairly early). Nor must you begin with a series of generalizations. You could start with something descriptive or narrative and then show how this description or narration gives rise to the thesis. Anything that works goes — if it grabs the reader's attention and leads right into your essay.

One especially effective shape for opening paragraphs is the *funnel*, so named by Sheridan Baker. The wide end of the funnel is the first sentence, a focused generalization that provides the necessary context and the subject. Each succeeding sentence narrows the subject. The last sentence is the thesis statement, the least general statement in the paragraph. Lewis Thomas provides a clear model of this shape in the opening paragraph of an essay entitled "How We Process Information."

> According to the linguistic school currently on top, human beings are all born with a genetic endowment for recognizing and formulating language. This must mean that we possess genes for all kinds of information, with strands of special, peculiarly human DNA for the discernment of meaning in syntax. We must imagine the morphogenesis of deep structures, built into our minds, for coding out, like proteins, the parts of speech. Correct grammar (correct in the logical, not fashionable, sense) is as much a biologic characteristic of our species as feathers on birds.

Here Thomas moves from the general idea of genetic endowment to the concept of DNA to the linguistic notion of "deep structures" to his thesis in the last sentence. The ideas rush through that funnel into the rest of the essay just as water rushes through the narrowed nozzle of a hose.

Not all essays open with a funnel. Lewis Thomas begins another of his essays, "Natural Science," by stating its point in the first sentence.

> The essential wildness of science as a manifestation of human behavior is not generally perceived. As we extract new things of value from it, we also keep discovering new parts of the activity that seem in need of better control, more efficiency, less unpredictability. We'd like to pay less for it and get our money's worth on some more orderly, businesslike schedule. The Washington planners are trying to be helpful in this, and there are new programs for the centralized organization of science all over the place, especially in the biomedical field.

The rest of the paragraph tells us exactly what the first sentence means.

Sometimes the thesis is implicit, never actually stated:

> Miss Nims, take a letter to Henry David Thoreau. Dear Henry: I thought of you the other afternoon as I was approaching Concord doing fifty on Route 62. That is a very high speed at which to hold a philosopher in one's mind, but in this century we are a nimble bunch. (E. B. White, "Walden")

From these few words opening an essay about White's visit to Walden Pond, where Thoreau had lived a hermitlike life, we know that the thesis is the difference between Thoreau's time and the writer's.

Another possible way to begin an essay is the multiparagraph opener, which unfolds in more leisurely fashion. The first paragraph may provide historical background, an extended definition, or a series of illustrations or facts that are then developed in the second paragraph. The following opening reaches its thesis statement at the beginning of the third paragraph:

> About 225 million years ago, at the end of the Permian period, fully half the families of marine organisms died out during the short span of a few million years — a prodigious amount of time by most standards, but merely minutes to a geologist. The victims of this mass extinction included all surviving trilobites, all ancient corals, all but one lineage of ammonites and most bryozoans, brachiopods, and crinoids.
>
> This great dying was the most profound of several mass extinctions that have punctuated the evolution of life during the past 600 million years. The late Cretaceous extinction, some 70 million years ago, takes second place. It destroyed 25 percent of all families, and cleared the earth of its dominant terrestrial animals, the dinosaurs and their kin — thus setting a stage for the dominance of mammals and the eventual evolution of man.
>
> No problem in paleontology has attracted more attention or led to more frustration than the search for causes of these extinctions. (Stephen Jay Gould, *Ever Since Darwin*)

The multiparagraph introduction can be graceful and appealing, as this one is. It slides the reader deep into the essay. Remember, though, that regardless of length or shape, the goal of the introduction is a clear and comprehensive statement of the thesis and an attractive invitation to the reader to join you in exploring it.

The First Sentence

Perhaps the most important single sentence in an essay is the first one. An excellent opening sentence is like the first bite of a superb dinner: it stimulates the taste buds and starts the digestive juices flowing. But if the first taste is badly seasoned or poorly cooked, no one will be eager for the next. Here are some ways to provide a good appetizer.

A Sharp Quotation.   A statement like Sir Isaac Newton's "Errors are not in the art but in the artificer" could introduce an argument favoring genetic engineering. When using a quotation, however, be sure you don't choose one that is overused.

A Revealing Anecdote, Historical or Personal.   An essay by Roland Barthes analyzing the significance of the Eiffel Tower begins,

> Maupassant often lunched at the restaurant in the tower, though he didn't care much for the food: *It's the only place in Paris,* he used to say, *where I don't have to see it.* ("The Eiffel Tower")

The humor of this opening entices the reader.

An Interesting or Illuminating Fact.   An essay on highway safety could start, "Between 1958 and 1968, more Americans were killed on the national highways than on the battlefields during the Vietnam War." Anyone who hadn't known that would now surely want to know more.

An Arresting Image.   An essay on breeds of dogs begins, "He had eyes like Junior Mints, a body like a chorizo sausage, a tail that could have pulled wine corks, and, while his slavish retainers grasped the edges of the bed to keep from tumbling to the floor, he sat like a king in the middle of a $500 silk comforter." Building a thesis on that would not be difficult.

A Provocative Opinion Asserted Provocatively.   Your position can either be supported or refuted: "American doctors have lost their halos, for very good reasons." Remember, though, it is one thing to be provocative and another to be outrageous. You need to arouse interest without offending.

Pitfalls to Avoid

We have made some suggestions for good beginnings, but we have hardly exhausted the subject. Indeed, the possibilities are almost limitless. Having said that, we now want to identify some openers that are to be avoided at almost any cost.

The Obvious Definition. One paper on Marx's *Communist Manifesto* began, "Society is defined as a voluntary association of persons for common ends, and government, which exists in society, is defined as the organization or agency through which a political unit exercises authority." The writer could have safely assumed that the reader knew terms this basic.

Facts Nobody Needs to Be Reminded Of. A paper on John F. Kennedy's foreign policy need not begin "John F. Kennedy, who served as President of the United States . . ." or "Conduct of foreign policy is the responsibility of all Presidents of the United States, and so it was with John F. Kennedy." These are tedious.

Platitudes. Too many essays begin with sentiments like "The processes of life are awe inspiring" or "Despite thousands of years' experience of the horrors of war, we seem no closer to controlling our destructive impulses" or "Poetry can be important to our lives." True statements all, but hardly promises of an exciting essay.

Apologies and Excuses. "Ricardo's economic theories are extremely difficult to explain, but I will do the best I can . . ." does not increase the reader's confidence in the writer. And "This essay will be short, because I began it only five hours before it was due . . ." may seem clever to the writer, but it probably will not amuse the instructor. Some apologies and excuses are honest expressions of insecurity, others are mere manipulations. Spare the reader both.

TIPS FOR THE OPENING PARAGRAPH

- Remember that the goals of a beginning are to get the reader's attention, to identify the central issues, to establish the writer's thesis, and to create the tone.

- Put a lot of thought into your first paragraph, and especially your first sentence. Make them as inviting as you can.
- Don't dawdle — get started.
- A funnel is a good way to begin, but it is not the only way. Choose the form that suits your subject and your style.
- Avoid obvious definitions, well-known facts, platitudes, apologies, and excuses.

EXERCISES FOR THE OPENING PARAGRAPH

1. Here are four thesis statements, each of which sets forth a controversial or unpopular position:

   > In light of the recent upswing in violent crime, police officers should use more force during arrests.

   > Insurance companies are to blame for putting doctors out of business with their high malpractice rates.

   > American children are growing up largely ignorant of the way the federal government functions.

   > Minority children need more scientists and intellectuals and fewer athletes and musicians as role models.

   Choose one statement and compose an opening paragraph for an essay arguing for or against that thesis. Your paragraph can be as long or short as you please, but it must start with a provocative or attention-grabbing sentence that employs one of the strategies outlined in "The First Sentence," and end with the thesis statement.

2. Find a recent essay of yours and examine the opening paragraph. Is it effective? What do you think of the first sentence and the way the paragraph unfolds? Revise your paragraph to improve it.

3. Exchange your revised opening with a classmate's. Write a paragraph comparing the effectiveness of the two.

CONCLUSIONS: FINISHING IN STYLE

We won't claim that your concluding paragraph is as important as your opening one — if you don't give your readers a good start, they probably won't make it to the end. Nonetheless, it is crucial, for it is your last chance to make a good impression.

A conclusion has three goals:

to make one last effort to convince the reader
to suggest larger implications than you could reasonably assert before
    you presented your evidence
to provide a satisfying sense of closure.

Ending on the Right Note

When so much is riding on your essay, you do not want to leave the impression of limping or skulking off. You want to appear dynamic and confident, fully engaged and in control. Without appearing smug, you want to be seen — figuratively, of course — brushing the dust off the palms of your hands after a job well done.

To achieve this poise, follow two general rules: never apologize and never brag. If a writer apologizes, the reader is very apt to think the whole journey through the essay has been a waste of time. And when a writer brags that he or she has proved a large notion or accumulated a great deal of information, the reader is apt to be annoyed — and inspired to find holes in the argument and faults with the writing. Be honest and modest: don't claim more than your argument fully justifies. A concluding tone of judicious assurance can finish off your essay in style.

The Larger Implications

If you have done your job in the middle of the essay — developing your argument while staying close to the thesis — by the end you should be ready to push your thinking — and your reader's — a little. After all, what you have said surely has some importance beyond the limits of your thesis. You should now be able to tell your reader how the thesis opens a window on a larger idea.

A student in an art history class was asked to write a paper on painting. She narrowed the topic to her favorite painter, Vincent van Gogh, and then to a favorite painting, "Chair and Pipe." Her thesis was "The physical quality of van Gogh's brushstroke and use of paint emphasizes the concrete and material reality of his subject." Through the body of the paper she analyzed the painting. In her last paragraph she wrote that "Chair and Pipe" may have led other painters to employ similar techniques reflecting the density of their subjects. She did not have to prove this observation; she only had to suggest it. Her analysis gave her the right to this larger observation.

In a criminal justice class, a student wrote an essay arguing for automatic jail sentences for anyone driving with a blood alcohol count of over 0.5 percent. In the body of the paper, she carefully presented and analyzed information on both sides of her subject. She discussed the effects of the alcohol count on the nervous system, the experience of countries with stringent laws, the increase of alcohol consumption, and the increase in teenage drinking. She admitted negative implications. In her conclusion, she stated that despite problems, the compulsory jail sentence was worth a try. That assertion would hardly have surprised an attentive reader — it was probably assumed in the writer's thesis. But this writer wanted to go beyond the thesis and make an impression on her reader, and so she enlarged her argument:

> Many Americans seem willing to forbid smoking in public places, to insist that guns be prohibited, and to institute a nationwide speed limit of 55 miles per hour. Surely the time is right to go after the deadliest killer of them all — driving under the influence.

By shifting the focus to other kinds of socially dangerous behavior, she provided some thought-provoking analogies and expanded the implications of her paper. And she left a strong impression.

An accomplished conclusion, then, often goes beyond the essay. It sets the thesis in a larger context, and that larger context helps to clinch the argument, for then the reader understands the importance of the ideas.

Pitfalls to Avoid

A good conclusion adds to an essay; a bad conclusion detracts. Many last paragraphs, unfortunately, seem mechanical, embarrassed, lazy, or frenzied. Here are the major pitfalls you should try to avoid in your endings.

The Waste Basket Ending. Some writers sweep up all the overflow points they could not fit into the body of an essay and present them in the last paragraph. In an essay on the founding of Israel, a writer concluded: "The Palestinians are Sunni Moslem. The Sunnis are one of the great divisions in Islam, the other being Shiite. The two groups separated over the succession to the leadership of Islam following the death of Mohammed." Those facts might have been interesting if the writer had developed them in the essay, but tacked on in the last paragraph, they only confused the reader. Don't throw into your conclusion bits and pieces that didn't fit elsewhere.

The Fade Out. Have you noticed how some people can tell a fascinating story but seem to lose heart as they get to the end and let their voices dwindle away? Some writers end essays that way. The following concludes a very good essay on how children learn to use language: "Researchers have so much more to discover in this area that I have to admit that we have only scratched the surface. Whatever we say now will be superseded very soon." Those last sentences seem to say, "Maybe this wasn't worth writing after all. Sorry I took your time." An essay should end on a note of confidence.

The Wild Surmise. We have noticed that when students fear that their essays are not important enough, they often write a concluding paragraph that leaps far beyond the evidence to a grandiose pronouncement. The concluding paragraph of an otherwise excellent essay on Nigerian bureaucracy suddenly claimed, "From this we see the utter futility of tying aid to underdeveloped nations to the adoption of western standards." All because of limited experience in Nigeria? How much better it would have been to conclude with "If the Nigerian experience is typical of the Third World, perhaps we ought to re-evaluate the strings we attach to our foreign aid." Qualified claims are better because they are so much likelier to be true.

The Mirror Image. Because the mirror image is perhaps the most common error students make in endings, we saved it for last. The writer repeats the thesis and summarizes the main points, as in this example:

> As I said, professional athletes should be allowed to participate in the Olympics. They would add quality to the games. The hypocrisy

now rampant would decrease. The Soviet athletes would no longer enjoy an advantage resulting from having "government jobs." We should act immediately to change the Olympic rules.

This kind of conclusion is dull and mechanical. If you have done your job in the body of the essay, you do not need to repeat the whole argument in the last paragraph. The best conclusions do not carry the thought backward but forward.

The conclusion can be one of the most effective parts of your essay. Let it be an elegant and creative farewell.

TIPS FOR THE CONCLUSION

- Your closing is not an afterthought. Pay as much attention to it as to your opening.
- Keep in mind the three goals of an essay's conclusion: to make one last effort to convince the reader, to suggest larger implications than you could reasonably assert before you presented your evidence, to provide a satisfying sense of closure.
- Try to appear poised and confident in your conclusion; never apologize and never brag.
- Reach for larger implications, but don't go outside the realm of your essay.
- Avoid the wastebasket ending, the fade-out, the wild surmise, and the mirror-image closings.

EXERCISES FOR THE CONCLUSION

1. Here are the last paragraphs of three professional essays. Can you tell what each essay was about? What hints do you find? What techniques did each author use to make his ending more effective? What do you think of the last line of each paragraph?

   "Like bone to the human body, and the axle to the wheel, and the song to a bird, and air to the wing, thus is liberty the essence of life," José Martí, the Cuban poet and patriot, wrote. "Whatever is done without it, is imperfect." (William Pfaff)

   Still, beyond all this is another laugh entirely, that neither condemns, praises, ridicules, nor conspires, but sees into the essential nature of a slip of the tongue and consequently sympathizes. After all, most human endeavor results in a slip of the something — the best-laid plans gone suddenly haywire by natural blunder; the chair, cake or painting that turns out not exactly as one imagined; the kiss or party that falls flat; the life that is not quite what one had in mind. Nothing is ever as dreamed.

So we laugh at each other, perfect fools all, flustered by the mistake of our mortality. (Roger Rosenblatt, "Oops! How's That Again?")

So I will try here to be exact. I wish my father had done more headlong, more elegant inventing. I believe he would respect my wish, be willing to speak with me seriously about it, find some nobility in it. But now he is dead, and he had been dead two weeks when they found him. And in his tiny flat at the edge of the Pacific they found no address book, no batch of letters held with a rubber band, no photograph. Not a thing to suggest that he had ever known another human being. (Geoffrey Wolff, "Memories of My Father")

2. Write an essay on one of the following topics — but write the conclusion on a separate sheet of paper: competition in college, not knowing a foreign language, wanting to live comfortably, a pet fear, or taking dares. Hand your essay to a partner and have him or her write a conclusion for you. Then compare your conclusion and your partner's for each paper. What are the weaknesses and strengths of each closing? Which suits each paper better?

THE TITLE: ISSUING THE INVITATION

The title is probably the last thing you write for an essay, but it is the first thing the reader sees, and it ought to be attractive. No title at all or something like "Assignment 3" or "Second Sociology Paper" is pretty unappealing. Even "Hemingway's *The Sun Also Rises*" or "The Albigensian Heresy" won't arouse a reader's wild enthusiasm. These titles are too broad and shapeless.

You need a title that says, "I know something interesting — come and find out." A title like "Four-Letter Words Can Hurt You" or "Running and Other Vices" or "Shakespeare without Tears" intrigues readers and even softens them up to enjoy the essay. Even "Authorial Intervention in *The Sun Also Rises*" and "The Albigensian Heresy and the Rise of Preaching" tell something about their essays and provide the reader with an entryway.

A title should be an honest advertisement. Something cute and snappy but irrelevant forces the reader to double back and readjust his or her expectations. When "Six Months behind Bars" turns out to refer to a summer spent mixing drinks at a fancy resort, the reader will feel tricked — justifiably. Similarly, a serious essay shouldn't have a frivolous title. If, for example, the subject is geriatrics, a title like "Everything You Always Wanted to Know about Death — But Were Afraid to Ask" would offend many people. The essay must deliver what the title promises.

A well-chosen title will indicate not only tne subject but also the tone of the essay. Think for a moment about what your expectations are for these titles: "A Dog's Eye View of Man," "Motherhood — Who Needs It?", "The Reach of Imagination." Which essay would you expect to be the most serious? Which would you expect to be confrontational? Titles can — and in these examples do — represent both the thinking and the approach of the essay.

You can find titles in a variety of places. Sometimes a title will come from within your essay. A nice turn of phrase or a recurrent theme may say it all. Or you might pull a quotation out of the text or the subject you are writing about: "I beg your pardon — I know exactly what to think" comes from Jane Austen's *Pride and Prejudice* and could serve as the title for a study of the character who made this statement. General Douglas MacArthur said, "I shall return" when he was forced to leave the Philippines at the beginning of World War II; that quotation would nicely introduce a paper on the Battle for the Philippines.

Sometimes you can find a good title outside your immediate subject. Hundreds of writers have used the Bible and Shakespeare as sources for titles. Peter Cohen wrote *The Gospel according to the Harvard Business School*; his ironic title tells much about his approach. If you were writing about the difficulty of starting college, you might find a title in the words of the Latin poet Vergil: "Look with favor upon a bold beginning." Finally, you may use a twist on an old saying, like "Two Birds in the Bush" for an essay about Stanley and Livingstone, or a phrase from a song, like "My Country, Taint of Thee" for an essay on environmental pollution. In short, you can find a title anywhere. The trick is to find one that fits the essay.

TIPS FOR TITLES

- Choose a title that is inviting and appealing.
- In devising a title, think about both the content and tone of your essay.
- You can find a title in your essay, in the work or subject you are discussing, in literature, or even in popular sayings.

EXERCISES FOR TITLES

1. Match the description of an essay in column A to the corresponding title in list B. Why did you make the match you did?

A	B
Suggests that the English people fight famine by dining on Irish babies	1. The Importance of Being Ordinary
Compares the tools and methods of different plastic surgeons	2. Was Paul Revere a Minute-Person?
Details a month in the life of a professional art appraiser	3. A Modest Proposal
Draws up a program of absolutely essential education	4. The Cutting Edge
Argues that we should not change our use of English just to avoid sexism	5. In the Eye of the Beholder
Discusses how the rich and famous try to be just like other people in order to improve their public image	6. Is There Any Knowledge that a Man Must Have?

2. Here is a partner exercise. Write an essay that describes eating, compares people who listen to people who watch, or discusses your personal tastes in humor. Then give it to your partner to title. Do you think the title works? Does it capture the essence of your essay? Why or why not?

5 / Strategies for
Developing Your Thoughts

I hate definitions.
– Benjamin Disraeli (1804–1881)
British prime minister and author

So far we have discussed the qualities a paragraph should have, such as unity and coherence, but not what a paragraph is good at doing. We have acted like the salesperson who tells you that an automobile has style, speed, and comfort without telling you that it can accelerate, stop on a dime, and handle those tight corners. What are paragraphs good for? They are good for taking a thought and developing it. In paragraphs you can describe your thought, tell stories about it, give illustrations of it, analyze it as a process, trace its causes or effects, divide or classify it, compare or contrast it with another thought, define it. All these "strategies" make your ideas grow before your readers' eyes.

The strategies work together. In writing any essay, you will call on more than one. When you write a comparison and contrast essay, you may well need a paragraph or two of definition, illustration, or cause and effect. You will almost certainly need description: to compare two actors or two automobiles, you would need to describe them. Even within a paragraph, you will often mix the strategies. The definition of a word like *patriotism* — which you will find on page 174 — requires comparing and contrasting, cause and effect, and illustration. A good process analysis is a kind of narration. And so on.

The kind of strategy you use depends on your purpose. Describing a Zulu war dance is different from defining *surrealism*. In analyzing a poem, you would probably not — though you could — compare it with and contrast it to another poem. With each task, you will have to decide what strategy or strategies to employ. And after the decision comes the performance. There are wrong ways and right ways, awkward ways and smooth ways, to use each of the eight strategies outlined in this chapter.

DESCRIPTION: SHOWING IT

When we put mental images into words or transmit what our senses tell us, we are describing. Our everyday lives are filled with description. "Meet me by the broken copper fountain under the gnarled old tree that gives off a pungent, almost acrid smell." We frequently use description in our college work as well. In a film class, the instructor might assign the description of a scene from a movie; in a history class, a battle or a political event; in a law class, a court trial or an accident.

Description is one of the most basic and important strategies. We can use it by itself or to support one of the other strategies. A narration almost always includes passages of description. A definition also frequently contains description.

What Description Is

In the following passage, James Agee describes the great movie comedian Buster Keaton:

> No other comedian could do as much with the dead pan. He used this great, sad, motionless face to suggest various related things: a one-track mind near the track's end of pure insanity; mulish imperturbability under the wildest of circumstances; how dead a human being can get and still be alive; an awe-inspiring sort of patience and power to endure, proper to granite but uncanny in flesh and blood.

Everything that he was and did bore out this rigid face and played laughs against it. When he moved his eyes, it was like seeing them move in a statue. His short-legged body was all sudden, machinelike angles, governed by a daft aplomb. When he swept a semaphorelike arm to point, you could almost hear the electrical impulse in the signal block. When he ran from a cop his transitions from accelerating walk to easy jogtrot to brisk canter to headlong gallop to flogged-piston sprint — always floating, above this frenzy, the untroubled, untouchable face — were as distinct and as soberly in order as an automatic gearshift. (James Agee, "Comedy's Greatest Era")

With this vivid description, Agee re-creates in our mind's eye the brilliant comedian. First he sets up the angle from which we will view Keaton's deadpan face. Then, like a camera zooming in on a scene, he moves us closer and closer to the details of Keaton's face, body, and performance. He provides us with concrete detail. We see the eyes moving in the immobile face. We see the movements of the short-legged body and arms. In the seventh sentence, he brings the whole description — face and body — brilliantly alive in a specific, and typical, scene: Keaton running from the cops. And always the deadpan face, the organizing principle of the passage.

Agee wants us to share his vision of Keaton. And so he avoids the vague and the abstract. Notice the words *statue, frenzy, soberly, gearshift*. Each calls up a distinct image. He uses the word *mulish* before *imperturbability*, so we think of the dumb, unyielding mule. When we read "easy jogtrot to brisk canter to headlong gallop to flogged-piston sprint," we conjure up images associated with these words. The picture unfolds in our imagination: Buster Keaton's motion accelerating from casual to smooth to pounding to mechanical.

At every step of the way, Agee had choices to make. He might, for instance, have written "a donkeylike imperturbability" — a donkey is about as stubborn as a mule. But *donkey* would call up the unwanted association of almost frivolous stupidity. A mule is mulish, but it is not a jackass. Think about why Agee chose the word he did.

As the Elizabethan playwright John Heywood said, "Enough is as good as a feast." Agee did not write "a large, jutting, rough-edged hunk of gray granite." The single word *granite* sufficed. And he did not write "his short-legged body with its somewhat long and rather stiff torso and sloping shoulders." He knew that a few well-chosen details would suffice to suggest a complete picture and that unimportant details would only confuse.

Agee made a point with this description: the source of Buster Keaton's power and appeal is that face. By the end of the passage, we can understand why he found Keaton so wonderful. This is exactly what good description does: it conveys an idea and the images it is based on from the mind of the writer to the mind of the reader. When the description is good, the idea lives in the reader's mind.

Writing Description

The writer's task is, as Joseph Conrad said, "by the power of the written word, to make you hear, to make you feel — it is, before all, to make you *see*." The details we choose for a description are crucial. They must be vivid enough to call up images from the reader's store of remembered impressions and sensations. Good description demands the exact, the concrete, and the familiar. Abstract or imprecise words make for slower understanding and are generally less effective.

A writer of description needs to create images, yes, but even the most vivid and precise description is pointless unless it serves a larger idea. The details must add up to something, an impression, an effect, like Agee's idea about the source of Keaton's appeal. Only when we select details with our idea in mind will the reader *see*.

The following passage describes a great painting:

The *Mona Lisa* is a portrait by Leonardo da Vinci of an Italian woman about whom we know little. Her hands are folded in her lap. She is looking out of the painting, wearing her famous smile. She has on dark clothes and is poised at a window. Her hair is mostly straight. The surface of the painting has deteriorated so that closer examination is difficult.

This description is too vague. It doesn't tell us, for instance, whether the folded hands are tensely gripping each other or are loose and relaxed. The phrase *her famous smile* could mean a death's-head grin for all we know. Furthermore, some of the details seem irrelevant: it doesn't matter that the subject is Italian, and without a doubt we do not need to be told the name of the painter. The relations between smile and clothes and window are unclear. The condition of the painting's surface appears as an isolated fact. The details are too disorganized to make a point. Indeed, there was apparently no point be made.

The revision is considerably better:

Everything in the *Mona Lisa* communicates serene repose. Her hands, folded loosely, and her gaze, neither avoiding nor confronting the viewer, indicate a woman at peace with herself and the world. Her smile bespeaks inner contentment, not an effort to entertain or impress the world. Da Vinci reinforces this mood of quiet by using muted hues — dark hair, dark clothing, the distant, obscure valley. Yet even here there are bits of brightness, in both the wisp of curl framing the subject's face and the river behind her. Time itself has supported da Vinci's theme, for the deteriorating surface of the painting thwarts the microscopic examination that would set mood aside to analyze structure. One must instead absorb the *Mona Lisa* whole, and in this way, perhaps, come away a bit more serene oneself.

Now we can see the kind of smile it is, the hands as part of the whole, the window as framing the river. We understand that the hues reinforce the meaning of the smile. All the details are relevant. Finally, the writer has reminded us so subtly of the painter's name that we are not offended.

TIPS FOR DESCRIPTION

- Use details vivid enough to call up an image in the reader's mind.
- Emphasize important details; suppress unimportant ones.
- Make sure there is a point to the description; have it contribute to a larger idea.

EXERCISES FOR DESCRIPTION

1. Think about a movie you have seen recently and conjure up a particular scene. Focus in on just one moment in that scene, as if you were selecting one frame of film for a publicity still. Describe that frame in vivid, concrete detail and suggest the overall impression it makes. Now change one major detail — the general appearance of a character, the number of characters present, the setting, the

dominant color. How would the change affect the overall impression?

2. Think back over your childhood and recall an object you especially cherished. Describe it as objectively as you can from your present perspective. Now describe it as you think you saw it when you were a child. What is the difference?

3. Describe an object that has become something of a symbol of the American way of life; for example, a McDonald's or a football. In the course of your description, emphasize details that strike you as important, and explain their significance in relation to your interpretation of American culture.

4. Go to the library and find a photograph of one of the following people. Photocopy it and describe it in a paragraph. All the paragraphs will be reproduced and distributed in class and the photocopies will be passed around. Members of the class will try to match the descriptions to the photocopies.

Billie Holiday	Robert E. Lee
Jim Thorpe	Shirley Chisholm
Calvin Coolidge	Golda Meir
Jean Harlow	Indira Gandhi
Marie Curie	Charles Darwin

NARRATION: TELLING IT

"Where did you go?"
"Out."
"What did you do?"
"Nothing."

When we tell what happened, even if it was "nothing," we narrate. A narration is a sequence of events, an account of what happened, whether real or invented. Short stories and novels are narrations. But so is a joke, an anecdote, or an autobiography. We use narration in all kinds of essays. We narrate when we summarize the plot of a novel, tell what happened during a rebellion, or trace the course of a disease. We also narrate a lab report or a summary of a research project.

After description, narration is the most basic writing strategy. Frequently, we use it in conjunction with other strategies. When we write a descriptive piece, we almost always narrate part of it. Often our examples are narrations. And we may use narration in definitions, process analysis, and cause and effect.

What Narration Is

In the following passage, George Orwell skillfully narrates a poignant but challenging event:

> We set out for the gallows. Two warders marched on either side of the prisoner, with their rifles at the slope; two others marched close against him, gripping him by the arm and shoulder as though at once pushing and supporting him. The rest of us, magistrates and the like, followed behind. Suddenly, when we had gone ten yards, the procession stopped short without any order or warning. A dreadful thing had happened — a dog, come goodness knows whence, had appeared in the yard. It came bounding among us with a loud volley of barks, and leapt round us wagging its whole body, wild with glee at finding so many human beings together. It was a large woolly dog, half Airedale, half pariah. For a moment it pranced round us, and then, before anyone could stop it, it had made a dash for the prisoner and, jumping up, tried to lick his face. Everyone stood aghast, too taken aback even to grab at the dog.
>
> "Who let that bloody brute in here?" said the superintendent angrily. "Catch it, someone!" ("A Hanging")

This brief passage is a crucial part of an essay in which Orwell recounts the events that led him to reject capital punishment. Though brief, it helps Orwell drive his points home, for the passage is a powerful narrative in its own right. The scene is deftly set. Action and language work together. The action is continuous, from "set out" to "Catch it, someone!" Something is always happening, and every happening contributes to the point. The passive prisoner is never the grammatical subject of a sentence, yet we cannot forget him for a moment. When the dog gives the prisoner the canine kiss of love, one "pariah" accepts another. The dog offers a sympathy that we and perhaps the officials in the narrative like to associate with human beings.

As this passage unfolds, we become uneasy. By its end, we may find ourselves pondering a serious moral question: what love should we offer criminals, outcasts, pariahs? This question takes on life not in a sermonette but in a narrative.

Writing Narration

The building blocks of good narration are the same as those of good description: a point to be made and concrete, relevant details. You must have a purpose for your narration, a feeling, an insight, a point you want to make. To help the reader get the point, you should concentrate on the most illuminating events. You let the story unfold scene by scene. Using vivid detail — concrete nouns, active verbs, exact adjectives and adverbs — you re-create the narrative in the reader's imagination. You *show* rather than *tell* the story, as though the reader were actually watching and listening. And you arrange the scenes so that they rise to a climax, a dramatic high point.

The following passage attempts to narrate an important event in the life of the writer:

> When we came back from the store that Christmas Eve, I realized I had been given too much change from my final purchase. I showed the money to my brother and then to my father. My father didn't like it and he made me give back the money. My brothers and sisters all laughed at me. I should have returned the money myself, without father's having to tell me.

This narrative is an abstract and general summary of happenings, lacking in details that might spark the reader's imagination. There is no dialogue, no contrasts, no drama. The writer tells everything and shows little — and yet many important questions are ignored: we don't really know why the father took the narrator back to the store or why the siblings laughed. As for the point, at the end the writer tries to incorporate a neat — far too neat — little moral. But does the story only want to tell us to be honest? Do we really need to be reminded of that?

In the revision the writer thought through what point she wanted to make. Then she made an effort to visualize the happenings and present them as vividly as she could.

When the salesclerk gave me back my change, I thought she had given me too much. At age five, I didn't count money very well, and so when we got home, I showed the coins to my brother. "I gave her fifty cents," I said, "and she gave me this."

"That's sixty cents," he said in an admiring voice I seldom heard from him. "You're smarter than I thought." Beaming with pride, chortling over my new fortune, I went sailing in to my father to receive his praise.

"The salesclerk gave me too much change," I said.

With deliberation, he went over all my purchases with me. He examined my dog-eared Christmas list and the sales slips. "Get your coat," he said.

The news flashed through the house, and, as my father and I prepared to leave, my brothers and sisters hid behind the banisters and silently mocked me.

"Honor," my father said as he closed the front door. "Honesty," he said as we walked to the car. "Fairness," he said as he started the car. "These are virtues without which civilization cannot endure. Money," he went on as we backed away from the curb, "may threaten virtue but must never be allowed to defeat it. Let this be a lesson to you." And in truth it was, though I could not have said in what.

For her revision, the writer developed four scenes: with her brother, with her father in the house, with her brothers and sisters behind the banisters, and with her father in the car. We watch the people act and hear them talk. The writer explains the return trip to the store and makes clear why her siblings laughed. Furthermore, the scenes now build to the climax. Perhaps the greatest improvement, however, is in the point of the story. Now it is left ambiguous, as it should be. Sibling rivalry, parental instruction, honesty, the joys of praise and of money — all are inextricably mixed in the young narrator's mind. The whole narrative supports that point.

TIPS FOR NARRATION

- Before writing, decide what point your narrative should have.
- Choose events, details, and language to support your point.
- Show, don't tell; develop scene by scene.
- Build to a climax.

EXERCISES FOR NARRATION

1. Report an incident, at home or at work, as if you were giving information to a specific person; for instance, a police officer or supervisor. Think about what kind of detail the audience needs. Think about the purpose.

2. Narrate a story having to do with one of the following feelings: pain, fear, hunger, affection, hope. Do not name the feeling. Let your choice of events and the words you use communicate it.

3. Make up an encounter in which you and a stranger have a disagreement. Be sure it has a climax and a point, but don't state the point. In a follow-up paragraph, describe how you selected the key events to make the episode climactic. Now state the point and evaluate your skill in conveying it.

4. Write a page narrating one of the following events:
   high-school commencement
   your arrival at college
   registration for classes
   the first meeting of this class
   the first social occasion at school

   Now exchange your essay with a partner, each analyzing the other's essay. Based on your partner's critique and your own increased focus on narration, rewrite your essay.

ILLUSTRATION: MAKING IT SPECIFIC

When we see a questioning look on our listener's face, we instinctively provide an illustration, an example of what we mean. "Ingmar Bergman is excellent at portraying intricate family relationships — in *Autumn Sonata*, for example, he captured mother-daughter rivalry." In much of your college writing, you will need to provide illustrations. When you make a point about a work of literature, you must go to the text to find illustrations for it. When you generalize about a historical event, illustrations clarify your meaning. They support your assertion about a work of art, a social phenomenon, a laboratory procedure.

Illustrations serve three purposes. First, they clarify your thought by bringing the general idea to a more easily understood specific level. Second, they help prove your idea by showing that, at least in this particular instance, your assertion is reasonable. Third, they make reading more entertaining. Nothing brings the reader and the writer together quite so quickly and effectively as the well-chosen illustration.

What Illustration Is

The writers of the following passage state a point and then make it more specific by providing illustrations.

> Under the stimulus of his interest in geometry, Hobbes [the English philosopher of the seventeenth century] familiarized himself with all the latest developments in science. He made the acquaintance of Galileo and his work, during the years 1634–1637, and became his disciple. Indeed, Hobbes applied Galileo's assumptions — such as those concerning bodies in motion, and the distinction between primary and secondary qualities — and methods to all fields. In fact, much of Hobbes' basic achievement was to turn Galileo's physics into a metaphysics. (J. Bronowski and Bruce Mazlish, *The Western Intellectual Tradition*)

This paragraph consists of an assertion about Hobbes followed by illustrations. The assertion is abstract; the illustrations are specific. The authors realized that they could not list every bit of scientific knowledge Hobbes had. They therefore chose illustrations that indicated the depth and range of his knowledge. They began with Galileo because he was perhaps the most significant scientific figure of the age. In the next paragraph, they discuss the influence of other scientists.

The support becomes more and more specific. When, for instance, the authors say that Hobbes "applied Galileo's assumptions," they then provide more specific illustrations of that statement: "such as those concerning bodies in motion and the distinction between primary and secondary qualities." Without the illustration, the point might be vague and unconvincing. Readers might not know what kind of assumptions the authors had in mind. Step by step, the authors establish the common ground, until by the end the reader will agree: yes, Hobbes knew science.

Writing with Illustration

Writers cannot present their illustrations willy-nilly. As with all strategies, they must plan and arrange illustration carefully. Each illustration must be relevant to the subject and should follow the same sequence as the point it supports. It should also be accessible and familiar to the reader. This may require, as it did for Bronowski and Mazlish, illustrations to support illustrations.

In this paragraph, from an essay analyzing the distinctive qualities of various movie stars, the writer uses illustrations in his discussion of Humphrey Bogart:

> Humphrey Bogart occupies a unique and permanent place in the imagination of the American moviegoer. The key to his success lies in his ability to portray a complex character, at once a ruthless, utterly self-seeking loner, and a tender, even sensitive, defender of the weak. In *The African Queen*, Bogart is a buffoon and Katharine Hepburn is the tough one. In *The Desperate Hours*, Bogart displays love for his brother but cruelly jeopardizes the family he holds hostage. When he dies, we feel both relief and a touch of sorrow. Fredric March plays the father, who is loving and selfless. In *To Have and Have Not*, Bogart is again both hard and sensitive. Lauren Bacall is as usual honest and humorous. Moviegoers still value the qualities Bogart represented and look for them in today's actors. But we can no more imagine a new tender-tough Bogart than we can a new Garibaldi riding through the Italian countryside, unifying his country.

Did you feel this paragraph going awry? Did you think that the illustrations were not persuasive? The writer has a great many details, but he has not selected them wisely or arranged them well. Notice that he reverses the description of Bogart from tough-tender to tender-tough and then back to tough-tender. Once we establish an order, we ought to stick to it. Otherwise the reader's eyes will be flying up and down the page, looking for home base.

Many of the details are irrelevant. The references to Katharine Hepburn and Fredric March distract the reader. The writer has an interesting point about Bogart as a buffoon; however, he introduces his support far too early — before he has developed his main idea — and muddles the discussion. The comparison in the last line is far-fetched. Few readers would easily connect Garibaldi, the nineteenth-century Italian revolutionary leader, with Bogart, the twentieth-century actor.

The reference to *The Desperate Hours* is obscure. The writer should have expanded on this important but unfamiliar illustration. He should have broken the illustration down — as Bronowski and Mazlish had done in their discussion of Hobbes — until reaching that specific fact the reader could understand and accept.

Still a Bogart fan, the writer went back to the writing desk:

> Humphrey Bogart occupies a unique and permanent place in the imagination of the American moviegoer. The key to his success lies in his ability to portray a complex character, at once a ruthless, utterly self-seeking loner and a tender, even sentimental, defender of the weak. A good example of this character can be seen in *The Desperate Hours*. In this movie, Bogart's willingness to destroy his fellow convict, to pistol-whip the innocent father of the family he holds hostage, and to jeopardize the lives of the family exists side by side with his love for his brother and, finally, his unwillingness to harm the little boy in the family. In *To Have and Have Not,* Bogart again plays the tough-tender guy, but his toughness is softened by Lauren Bacall's irony and his sentimentality undercut by her honesty. Bogart did not always play the same role, of course — in *The African Queen* he is a weakling and a buffoon until near the end — but he was always most appealing in his tough-tender guise. Moviegoers still value the qualities Bogart represented and look for them in today's actors. But we can no more imagine another tough-tender Bogart than we can another ironic-honest Bacall.

Revised, the paragraph reads smoothly and persuasively. The writer maintains the tough-tender order all the way. He sticks to his subjects, and where needed he elaborates with illustrations of the illustrations. At the end, he illustrates his point by a comparison with the well-known Lauren Bacall.

TIPS FOR ILLUSTRATION

- When providing illustrations, follow the same pattern as the idea the illustrations support.
- Be sure your illustrations are clearly related to the point.
- Use illustrations that your reader will find easily understandable.
- If necessary, offer illustrations of your illustration.

EXERCISES FOR ILLUSTRATION

1. Find a passage in one of your textbooks in which the author illustrates a point. Be ready to present the passage to the class and answer these questions:

   > Why did the author use the illustration or illustrations?
   > Would fewer or more illustrations have improved the passage?
   > How could you make this passage more effective?

2. Think up two illustrations for each of the following statements:

   > Money is the root of all evil.
   > Shyness can be an asset.
   > Buying stocks can be hazardous to your financial health.
   > Politics is the art of the possible.

   Exchange your illustrations with a partner. Choose one of the statements and write a paragraph analyzing the difference between your illustrations and those of your partner. Which are more accessible? Which need to be more specific? How would you make your partner's illustrations better?

3. Take your most recent essay and find places where you need more illustrations of your point. Rewrite the essay accordingly.

PROCESS ANALYSIS: EXPLAINING HOW IT WORKS

Process analysis is a special kind of narrative, one that concentrates not on a particular episode but on *how* something happens. We often use process analyses to instruct. If we want to teach someone how to use a computer, how to dissect a frog, how to get there from here, we focus on the process. Without process analysis, we could not teach anyone how to do anything.

We also use process analysis to explain. Scientists use process analysis to explain how a strand of DNA, deoxyribonucleic acid, replicates. Economists use it to explain how bank clearinghouses work. If psychologists wish to explain the development of human personality in the infant, they would probably call on this strategy. It is important in virtually every academic discipline.

The following passage instructs novices in how to save work when using WordStar, a word processing program:

> Every half hour or so, while editing a file in WordStar, type ↑-K ↑-S. This will save everything you have typed so far on the disk and

return you to the top of the file. After the computer has finished saving the file, type ⬆-Q ⬆-P to return to where you were before.

When you have finished an editing session and are ready to turn off the computer or remove a text diskette, save the file by using ⬆-K ⬆-X, which will write your file on the disk and return you to the operating system. The computer will display a "B⬆" prompt (because you changed the logged drive to B: after you entered WordStar — see step 4.c above). *Do not remove any diskettes* until you have returned to the operating system and the red lights on both disk drives are off. If you wish to do other things on the computer (i.e., not using WordStar), type A:<RET> to log in Drive A. (Tiro Project, "Instructions for Start-Up, Disk Handling, and File Maintenance")

This analysis of how to operate WordStar is unusually good. Bearing in mind the purpose — to save edited material — the writer breaks the process into major elements and deals with each as an entity, a miniprocess: analyzing first how to save what you have typed during an editing session and then how to save work when you are finished. Within each major element, the writer narrates the process step by step and shows how each step is related to the previous one.

Rather than saying "Do this, do that," the author explains consequences. He interrupts the analysis to fix the process in the reader's mind by summing up the process so far. He indicates exactly when to take the next step. These signals increase the user's understanding and retention, the goals of any instruction.

The writer avoids unnecessary detail. He does not spend words telling the user to press the control key with the index finger or to sit up straight. He sticks to the essential, makes the language simple and direct, and keeps technical terms to a minimum. The most nervous, inexperienced user would have no trouble following these directions.

When we use process analysis to explain, the goals are similar: to set forth the process in all its richness, to make clear the sequence of states or steps, and to present the analysis so that the reader can easily understand and remember it. The following passage is a process analysis of the investment plan known as a living trust:

Of the small percentage of people who use some version of the trust, only a small percentage, in turn, use the "living trust," which is the type that often carries with it the biggest benefits. The concept is simple: the property goes to the trustee (family member, lawyer, banker) today while the donor . . . is still alive. The property is managed as an investment, for income purposes and growth of principal, until the donor dies. It is then automatically distributed to the heirs of the donor — or retained in trust for their benefit — according to the precise wishes of the donor as spelled out in the trust agreement. This distribution is made free of the complications of a formal will. . . . (Joseph L. Wiltsee, *Business Week Guide to Personal Business*)

The writer has broken down the process into the major components of concept, management, and execution of the trust. He explains each of these components in detail. After reading this analysis, we understand the purpose of a living trust, we see the steps involved in setting it up, and we have a good idea of the results. We are better equipped to make an informed decision about the advantages of the investment.

Writing Process Analysis

Process analysis may seem easy because it is, like most writing, a written version of a natural way of thinking. We often wonder how things happen or work, and if we can figure them out, we think we should be able to explain them. As with most writing, however, a gap exists between understanding a process and effectively conveying it in writing. And sometimes in our headlong rush to get it down, we fall into that gap.

The first step in writing process analysis is to articulate its purpose or its ultimate goal. If you are telling someone how to put together a bicycle, you cannot assume your reader will figure your purpose in time to make sense of what you say. The purpose determines both the order of the presentation and the emphasis each part receives. The second step is to divide the process into major elements and treat minor elements within the context of the major ones. In explaining the assembly of a bicycle, you would divide the process into some major elements — assembling the frame, fitting the gears, attaching the wheels — and discuss the minor elements as subdivisions. If you tried to deal with one operation after another without grouping — bolt 1, bolt 2, bolt 3, and so on to bolt 25 — the reader would have a difficult time understanding and remembering.

You will need to decide which details are essential to your analysis and which merely confuse the issue. You don't want your reader to get bogged down in excess, but you do want to provide an adequately concrete analysis. Because a process is a sequence of steps or operations, you need to show how one step is related to the previous and the following steps. Clear transitions help to keep the order in focus. It is also important to stop every once in a while and recapitulate briefly where you are in the process.

The final step is to suit your language to your audience and purpose. You would not discuss circumference/velocity ratios on a bicycle with someone who merely wanted to get the thing on the road. But do not hesitate to use special terms when they are the best way to convey your meaning; just be sure to define them clearly the first time they come up.

When process analysis goes wrong, the writer usually has not articulated the overall purpose or explained the parts in terms of the whole. Those are the problems in this analysis of essay grading.

> Grading an essay is not a single, unified process but rather a summing up of many separate evaluations. Are the paragraphs unified, coherent, properly proportioned, and complete? Does the essay state a clear thesis and back it up with sound arguments? Are the words it uses effectively chosen and spelled right? Do the sentences make sense? Are they grammatical? Does the paper have an introduction that directs the reader to the argument and a conclusion that puts the argument in its most significant context? Is the paper neat and professional in format? All these questions and more pass through the minds of evaluators as they try to funnel things down to a single, comprehensive, fair grade. But perhaps the hardest task lies ahead — justifying the grade to the writer who earned it.

Reading this analysis is not going to help anyone understand the grading process. The writer has put down a shopping list of thoughts; she has not divided the subject into major elements. The passage fails to establish the relations of the parts to each other and to the whole. What, for instance, has "sentences make sense" to do with "neat format"? Furthermore, the writer provides no divisions or signposts to guide us through. We have no idea of the essay's purpose.

In her revision, the writer addressed all these problems.

> Grading an essay is not a single, unified process but rather a summing up of many separate evaluations. To understand why, we must take a closer look at writing from the reader's point of view. There are, essentially, three qualities that readers have traditionally sought

from good writing: sound logic, effective rhetoric, and good grammar. That is, they expect what they are reading to have a clear meaning substantiated by legitimate support, to present its meaning directly and pleasantly, and to do so within the conventions of standard English and traditional publishing format. Already, in other words, the grading involves not one but three different assessments. But the problem is even more complicated than that. Readers focus on many different levels of writing. Quite close up, they focus on individual words; a little further along, on the sentence and the paragraph; and from a still greater perspective, on the writing as a single, unified entity. Success at one level does not necessarily carry over to any other. One can, for instance, write excellent sentences yet have a disastrous essay. In short, the grader is making not one but as many as twelve separate evaluations to be funneled into a single, comprehensive, fair grade. But perhaps the hardest task lies ahead — justifying the grade to the writer who earned it.

We can see improvement from the start. Perhaps most important, the second sentence provides a purpose for the passage: to understand why grading involves a series of separate evaluations. In the third sentence, the writer divides the whole process into major components. In the fourth sentence and eighth sentence, she defines some terms. She pauses in the fifth and the last sentences to regroup. Because of these signposts the reader does not lose the way. The writer has considerately defined, grouped, and related the parts.

TIPS FOR PROCESS ANALYSIS

- Tell your reader the purpose of your analysis.
- Group individual elements into major components; treat the minor components in the context of the major groups.
- Use only essential details. Provide clear transitions between stages of the process.
- Pause occasionally to summarize where you are in the process.
- Be sure your language is appropriate for your audience and purpose; where necessary, define terms.

EXERCISES FOR PROCESS ANALYSIS

1. Choose something you do well — playing a musical instrument, operating a machine, waterskiing, playing tennis — and write an essay in which you explain to a novice the skills necessary for this activity. At the end, describe the perfect practitioner of your activity and identify all the qualities that make for that perfection.

2. Outline a plan for a major enterprise, such as converting the campus food service to a student-run operation, setting up a summer camp for blind children, or developing a transportation system for the campus. Your purpose is to persuade the authorities, who know nothing of this plan, that they should institute it as soon as possible.

3. Write a paragraph in which you explain first to a ten-year-old and then to a contemporary one of the following:

   a checkmate in chess
   a full house in a poker game
   a suicide squeeze in baseball
   a particular body position that signals defensiveness
   an *entrechat*

   Specify the functions of each part in relation to the overall strategy, attack, or defense involved.

4. Choose one of the following topics and, after you have done the necessary research, write a process analysis of it:

   how an Individual Retirement Account works.
   the courting rituals of the praying mantis.
   how one becomes a Methodist minister.
   how continental drift works.
   what a "rite of passage" is.

CAUSE AND EFFECT: EXPLAINING WHY IT HAPPENED

Cause and effect analysis answers the question *why?* Why did you ruin the peas? I left the burner on too long. Why is Joe in the hospital? He had a car accident. Why did he have the accident? He was driving too fast, the roads were wet, and there was a sharp curve. Breaking down a train of events into causes and effects can be a powerful analytic tool. It can help us to understand not only small, simple events, like our examples, but also large, complicated ones. When California passed New York as the nation's most populous state, experts argued over the causes and the effects of the demographic redistribution. Economists use it to explain the stock market crash in 1929. Futurologists attempt to analyze the effects of technology: what will life be like when people shop and pay bills and even entertain via television and computers?

Cause and effect analysis helps answer two fundamental questions about an event. The first is, Why did something happen? To answer that, we look for causes. What factors, for example, allowed California to surpass New York in population? Did people move to California because of the weather? because of the decay of cities in the East? because the international economic focus was shifting from Europe to Asia? The second question is, What happened because of it? To answer this question, we look for effects. What changes resulted from the migration to California? Has the California style of living become more attractive than other styles of living? Has the quality of life in California declined because of overcrowding? What has happened to the agricultural industry as a result of the greater demand for housing?

Because this form of analysis is so important to understanding our world, instructors often assign cause and effect essays. A psychology instructor may assign a paper on the causes of neurosis. A history instructor may assign one on why the Weimar republic collapsed. A physics instructor may ask for an analysis of the effects of ultraviolet radiation on the skin. Most research projects include cause and effect passages to support their theses, because almost always we want to know why. And most argumentative essays contain some cause and effect analysis as well.

What Cause and Effect Is

In the following passage, a close observer discusses why Richard M. Nixon cut a poor figure in the television debates with John F. Kennedy in 1960.

The Vice President [Nixon], to begin with, suffers from a handicap that is serious only on television — his is a light, naturally transparent skin. On a visual camera that takes pictures by optical projection this transparent skin photographs cleanly and well. But a television camera projects electronically, by an image-orthicon tube, which is a cousin of the x-ray tube; it seems to go beneath the skin, almost as the x-ray photograph does. On television, the camera on Nixon is usually held away from him, for in close-up his transparent skin shows the tiniest hair growing in the skin follicles beneath the surface, even after he has just shaved. And for the night of the first debate, CBS, understandably zealous, had equipped its cameras with brand-new tubes for the most projection possible — a perfection of projection that could only be harmful to the Vice President. (Theodore H. White, "Round Two: The Television Debates")

White does not claim here a single cause but identifies several — some more important than others, but none sufficient to bring about the effect by itself. Nor does he simply list all the causes. "Here they are: transparent skin, television photography, CBS eagerness. One, two, three. Out." He goes beyond naming to explaining. He points out, for example, that the image-orthicon tube is like an X-ray tube in that it seems to photograph beneath the skin. So that we can better understand each cause, he provides background — causes of the causes. In addition, he explains the chain of causes, the way they are related to one another. He shows how transparent skin when projected by the image-orthicon tube makes for a poor picture, a problem compounded by the newness of the tube.

White does not overdo his analysis. His purpose is not to indicate from which side of his family Nixon inherited transparent skin, the history of photography, or the origin of network competition. He concentrates on damage to Nixon's image so that the reader could understand it. Had he gone deeply into background issues or remote causes, he would certainly have lost his focus.

Writing Cause and Effect

In constructing a cause and effect argument, you start with a situation and work your way forward to the effects or backward to the causes. This process can be an intellectual adventure, and may include both research and speculation. A good way to begin is to brainstorm and then organize the individual possibilities into large groups. This way you can distinguish essential elements from incidental ones. Organizing your ideas can help clarify relationships, establish a hierarchy of importance, and ensure that your analysis is comprehensive.

Beware of oversimplification. We often think that we have discovered *the* cause or *the* effect when in fact we have only come upon one of several. Complex phenomena have more than one cause or result in more than one effect. Even a simple effect like "I ruined the peas" cannot be explained simply by saying "I left the burner on too long." Of course, if the focus was only on the agent — or *precipitating* cause — of the ruin, "I left the burner on" would be enough. In most cases, however, we would need to explain why the burner was left on: the telephone rang and I answered it and it distracted me because it was long distance, there had been an accident, Joe was injured . . .

In constructing a cause and effect essay, you must also distinguish between *remote* causes and close or *proximate* causes. Proximate causes contribute directly and forcefully to the effect: "The telephone rang" is a proximate cause and must be included in any explanation of burning the peas. To say "The peas were ruined because Joe was in the hospital" would not make much sense: what has Joe's being in the hospital to do with burning the peas? You must include the proximate cause of each effect: "The telephone call informing me that Joe was in the hospital distracted me, and I left the burner on too long, ruining the peas."

Remember the old saying "For want of a nail the shoe is lost, for want of a shoe the horse is lost, for want of a horse the rider is lost"? Causes happen in chains, and every cause has causes. Yet there is a limit to how far we want to extend our search for causes. In explaining the peas, we could say, "The peas were ruined because Joe's mother didn't discipline him when he was a child." Joe's recklessness may indeed go back to being overindulged by his mother, but mentioning his upbringing as a cause of ruining the peas only confuses the issue.

How far back to go is a matter of judgment. And purpose is the key to making that judgment. If the purpose is to explain the ruined peas, we do not need to state that Joe's mother did not discipline him. If, however, the purpose is to explain Joe's recklessness, we probably do need to talk about his mother's overindulgence.

Purpose also determines how far we should go seeking causes. We cannot include everything that may have contributed — we may have burned those poor old peas in part because the range light was dim, we were tired, and we have always loathed peas. Even though these facts contributed marginally, we clutter up our reasoning by trying to be all-inclusive. We should mention only causes that contribute significantly.

Sometimes we mistake coincidence for cause. We think that because something happened either before or at the same time as the effect, then that something caused the effect. (See "The Logic of Argument" in Chapter 11.) "Joe never had an accident until he got that convertible. Obviously convertibles aren't safe." This is patently illogical. The convertible did not cause either the accident or Joe's recklessness. You must limit your discussion to causes that have real agency.

When cause and effect analysis fails, it is usually because the writer has not sorted out the essential elements from the nonessential, or has not thought through his or her purpose. Such is the case in the following paragraph from an essay on the changing status of women in American society:

> The main reason that women improved their position is that the media focused so much attention on the women's liberationists at the beginning of the 1970s. Sexual emancipation also contributed, as did fairer hiring policies in business and government. A liberal political climate and a succession of Democratic presidents and Congresses in the 1960s cleared the way for the climb, as did the invention of the Pill. Women in high places — like Golda Meir, Indira Gandhi, Margaret Thatcher, Geraldine Ferraro, senators and representatives, business executives, university presidents — became role models. Rising divorce rates also contributed. Of course, many minorities of other sorts were seeking their rights at the same time. Many women were not interested any longer in the traditional roles of housekeeper, wife, and mother. Women had been a large part of the war effort during the Second World War, and afterward more women started going to school and earning higher degrees.

It is all in there somewhere — yet something is missing. The writer has a good list of causes but does not evaluate his findings. Which causes does he think are important, and why? All the causes receive the same treatment. Nor does the writer differentiate between causes and effects. In the first sentence, media attention is called the main reason, but media attention was probably an effect of the change, not a cause. It was without doubt not the main cause.

The writer establishes no chain of causation and does not show

how the elements he lists are related. Is there, for instance, a connection between women participating in the war effort and women not being interested in traditional roles? between the contraceptive pill and sexual emancipation? The writer does not say. By slapping the causes on the page without grouping them or analyzing the chain in which they figure, the writer fails to provide a clear explanation of how this enormous social change came about.

For the revision, he decided that the two most important causes were women's experience in industry and contraception. He clustered his other causes around these and showed how they were connected.

> The improvement of the position of women in American society resulted from many events occurring in the last half of the twentieth century. During World War II, the country and women themselves learned that women could perform well in an industrial society. This success led to a demand for greater opportunities in education and employment. With the advent of effective contraceptive devices, especially the Pill, women began to feel that they were not bound to motherhood. This sexual emancipation became a symbol for other kinds of freedom: freedom to pursue education and a career, and freedom to reject the traditional roles of housekeeper, wife, and mother. When the civil rights movement focused national attention on the rights of minorities, people began to see more clearly that women, too, had been denied rights. The liberal political climate of the 1960s and 1970s led to fairer hiring policies in business and government. And, as though they had been waiting in the wings, there emerged a group of prominent public women — Golda Meir, Indira Gandhi, Margaret Thatcher, senators and representatives, business executives, university presidents — ready to show younger women the path to the halls of power.

Improvement begins early with a very firm topic sentence that brings previously scattered points into order, sets forth a hierarchy of courses, and controls the rest of the paragraph. Notice that he maintains clarity by dealing first with the more remote cause — the experience during World War II — before turning to the recent chain of events. And he completes the analysis of causes before going on to the effect. By careful use of transitional devices — "This success," "this sexual emancipation," "women, too, had been denied rights" — he indicates relations between the various ideas.

TIPS FOR CAUSE AND EFFECT

- Start off with a list of all possible causes and then narrow it down to the important ones.
- Distinguish between significant causes and incidental ones.
- Resist the temptation to look for an only cause or single effect.
- Differentiate between remote causes and proximate ones.
- Use your purpose as a guide to determine how far back to go in the causal chain.
- Separate real causation from coincidence.

EXERCISES FOR CAUSE AND EFFECT

1. Here is a list of words often used in causal arguments: antecedent, component, condition, consequence, constituent, determinant, element, factor, influence, ingredient, issue, occasion, prerequisite, result. Look each one up in your dictionary and determine the distinctions among them. Which identify the most important causes? Arrange the words in ascending order of importance.

2. For each of these effects, determine a remote cause and a proximate cause.

   your being in this writing class
   your living in this state
   the fact that you speak English
   your choice of the clothes you are wearing
   what you did last Saturday night

3. Here is a list of possible causes for the increased suicide rate among Americans aged fifteen to twenty-four from 1960 to 1977:

   political and social decline of America since 1960
   trauma of the Vietnam War
   alienation from society
   economic policies of the government
   unemployment
   racial tensions
   sexual and love-related matters
   parents too permissive
   parents too strict
   migration to big cities
   lack of clear and consistent values

   Which do you think are proximate causes? Which are remote? Which do you reject? Put them in ascending order of significance.

4. Write a mini-research essay (using at least three books and two periodical sources) on one of the following effects:

> the rise in the number of American bison since 1911
> the upward trend in sports salaries
> why Americans are eating fewer meals at home
> the constant appeal, whatever the economic situation, of diamond rings
> the disappearance of the dodo bird
> the overthrow of the Somoza regime in Nicaragua

Determine the importance of each cause and argue for your interpretation.

CLASSIFICATION AND DIVISION: PUTTING IT IN ITS PLACE

When we divide, we start with a single entity and break it into its parts. Without some kind of division, we could not develop ideas about a subject. To say something useful about the practice of medicine, we might first divide it into its functional components: diagnosing, treating, curing, and preventing disease. Once we have divided the whole, we may need to subdivide: diagnosing includes use of sight to observe the patient, touch to determine abnormalities, hearing to examine functioning of lungs and heart, and microscopic, chemical, and bacteriological examination of blood and urine. And we could divide subdivisions further.

Dividing is often the first step in the other strategies. When we write description, narration, process analysis, cause and effect, or definition, we almost always begin by dividing the whole subject — the whole picture, the whole event, the whole world — into parts. Even when we compare and contrast, we divide items into their attributes. And division is at the heart of the strategy we call classification.

When we classify, we sort individual items into categories based on shared attributes or qualities. First we define the categories. If we were classifying dogs, we might set up categories based on size: small, medium, large. Once we have set up the category, we can make general observations about all the individual items within that category. We can say small dogs eat less, bark more, learn quickly, or whatever we find to be true of small dogs. Now when we meet up with a small dog, we can say that it will eat less, bark more, and learn quickly — because those are attributes of individuals in the small dog category.

By putting any phenomenon into a classification, we often understand it better. A new government takes over a country, and we immediately want to place it: is it in the Soviet sphere of influence, the American sphere of influence, or neutral? We hear music on the radio, and without even thinking we shuffle it into a known category: rock, country and western, classical, soul.

Fields of knowledge are often defined by what they classify and how they classify it. In biology, animals are classified according to family, genus, and species. In geology, rocks are classified as igneous, sedimentary, and metamorphic. Often instructors ask students to apply what they have learned by classifying individual items into the proper categories. Is this poem lyric or narrative? Is that note A sharp or E flat? Is a rabbit really a rodent like a rat? These categories are all given, ready-made. Often, however, you must invent your own classification.

What Classification and Division Are

In this passage Eric Berne suggests that human personality is based at least in part on which layer of the body — inward organs, muscles, or nervous system — is most developed in the individual.

We can thus say that while the average human being is a mixture [of brains, muscles, and inward organs], some people are mainly "digestion-minded," some "muscle-minded," and some "brain-minded," and correspondingly digestion-bodied, muscle-bodied, or brain-bodied. The digestion-bodied people look thick; the muscle-bodied people look wide; and the brain-bodied people look long. This does not mean the taller a man is the brainier he will be. It means that if a man, even a short man, looks long rather than wide or thick, he will often be more concerned about what goes on in his mind than about what he does or what he eats; but the key factor is slenderness and not height. On the other hand, a man who gives the impression of being thick rather than long or wide will usually be more interested in a good steak than in a good idea or a good long walk. (Eric Berne, *Mind in Action*)

This classification conveys the sense of a creative mind making meaning of the world he experiences. Like all good classification, it is based on significant aspects of the subject: body type and personal interests. To categorize according to a trivial or irrelevant quality — for example, surnames or color of hair — would provide little useful information. Whether a person is named Jones or Domjanovich says nothing about the influence of body type on personality, which is Berne's topic. Preference for steak over walks says a good deal.

Whenever we classify, our categories should all contain the same kind of information. Otherwise, an individual item might fit in more than one category. If Berne's categories had been, for instance, "red heads," "people named Jones," and "North Dakotans," he might well have found that some red heads named Jones live in North Dakota. Berne's categories are mutually exclusive; that is, human beings can be placed in only one category.

Berne also made sure that his classification was comprehensive enough to include all individuals in his subject. Notice that at the beginning he limits his subject: "while the average human being is a mixture, some people are mainly 'digestion-minded' . . . ." He then goes on to classify the "some people." We are left with the impression that his three categories pretty much cover the limited subject without trivializing the differences they identify. From his classification, we gain insight into the relation of body type and personality.

Writing with Classification and Division

Classifying people, places, ideas, and acts is natural, but doing it well requires care. First of all, decide on the point of the classification. Be sure you can state the purpose served; in fact, articulate it so that you will have it clearly in mind. Second, settle on a principle of classification. For Berne, the principle was the relation between body type and personality. The principle should divide the whole subject in categories into which all the individual items can fit. Then define the categories so that they will not overlap: an item should fit into only one category.

When writing, be sure you describe the categories in the same terms. Decide which characteristics differentiate the categories, and then describe all the categories with these differentiating characteristics. And, of course, these characteristics should be significant to the subject and relevant to the point you are making.

When a writer ignores these guidelines, a first draft may look like this:

> The men at this college fall into categories. First are the hackers, who are round-shouldered and bleary eyed from all-night sessions with the computer. Next are the fraternity boys, many of whom come from well-off families. Next are the athletes who are shaped like V's and call women *babes* and *chicks*. Next are the men who wear jeans and sneakers. Next are the hard-working types who will probably go to law or medical school. Then there are the men who spend most of their waking hours drinking beer or smoking dope. And finally there are the ones who wear their shirts open down to their navels and have a little gold chain nestling in their chest hair.

This classification is not a success. Its problems are twofold: lack of a clear purpose or unifying point and failure to hit upon a consistent principle for grouping the men on campus. Individuals are not confined to a single category. Some hackers may have money, some athletes may wear jeans and sneakers. Furthermore, the categories do not exhaust the subject: where are the foreign students, the married students, the commuters?

The writer went back for a second go. First, she came up with a point: from their clothing, an observer can tell a good deal about male students, how they view themselves and what their aspirations are. Next, she *divided* the whole topic into categories that were mutually exclusive. Luckily, a natural division stood waiting: preppy, jock, grind. When she asked herself if the categories exhausted the whole, she decided she had to add one more: others.

With her point clear and categories established, she was ready to write.

> We can learn a good deal about college men from their clothes. The preppy's uniform — a boat-neck sweater over a blue cotton button-down shirt above a pair of wrinkled chinos above Top Siders — says he comes from the best suburbs and the good prep schools. For him, college is a rehearsal for the good life. The giant V-shaped jock wears a shiny shirt so tight you can see his tattoo and pants so form-fitting you can see the freckles on his knees. His shoes say Nike, Adidas, or Puma. He, too, is rehearsing: for pro scouts, big bucks, adoring fans. Those who want to advertise that they are grinds also do it through the choice, or lack of choice, of their clothes. No-

tice the row of pens or the calculator hooked to the pockets of white, probably polyester, shirts, wash-and-wear pants, hard-soled shoes and maybe mismatched socks. These men take their studies very seriously.

As extremes of fashion, these three stereotypes make clear what is also true for the others, whose nameless sneakers and nondescript jeans make them harder, but not impossible, to read. The way a college man dresses indicates an attitude — toward performance in school, toward social acceptance, toward the future beyond school.

In this draft each category is treated in the same manner: description, then interpretation of clothes. The last sentence makes the categories significant, for now we see that they have helped to convey a meaningful point about students and clothing.

TIPS FOR CLASSIFICATION AND DIVISION

- Decide first on the point or purpose of the classification.
- Choose a significant principle of classification and stick to it.
- Make sure your categories are mutually exclusive.
- Describe all the categories in the same fashion.
- Make sure all the individual items fit in your categories.

EXERCISES FOR CLASSIFICATION AND DIVISION

1. Create classifications under the following headings:

women's shoes	babies
fast foods	religions
middle-class people	airliners
forms of government	sports played with a ball

2. Write an essay about living arrangements for students in your school. Free-write or brainstorm until you have a thesis. Divide the subject and then develop a system of classification that allows you to support your thesis.

3. Choose one of the following abstract terms:

language	wars
classification	beauty
goodness	immorality

Find a way to divide it and classify its components.

4. Divide your class on the basis of three different principles. Although you need not place individuals in categories, be sure each system of classifying is comprehensive and each category exclusive. Be prepared to share your systems with the class.

COMPARISON AND CONTRAST: SHOWING LIKENESS, SHOWING DIFFERENCE

We would not make an important decision without deliberately and carefully comparing and contrasting one possibility with another. In deciding which college to attend, or whether to attend at all, most people would consider as many aspects of the choice as they could think of — cost, social life, sports, and, of course, academic challenge. They would then determine how the possibilities compared and contrasted. Once they had evaluated differences and similarities, they could make a more informed, intelligent choice.

In college essays and examinations, students are often asked to compare or contrast two or more possibilities: investment in equities, bonds, or real estate; reproduction in amoebas and paramecia; the treatment of Hell in Milton's *Paradise Lost* and Marlowe's *Doctor Faustus*; the views and actions of Presidents Kennedy, Johnson, and Nixon in the Vietnam War. The possibilities are unlimited, for everything can be compared with something else. Sometimes our point will be to show the depth of our knowledge, at other times to make a choice and back it up. Where an alternative presents itself, comparison and contrast can make it clear.

What Comparison and Contrast Are

Here is a complex but carefully controlled comparison:

An orange grown in Florida usually has a thin and tightly fitting skin, and it is also heavy with juice. Californians say that if you want to eat a Florida orange you have to get into a bathtub first. California oranges are light in weight and have thick skins that break easily and come off in hunks. The flesh inside is marvelously sweet, and the segments almost separate themselves. In Florida, it is said that you can run over a California orange with a ten-ton truck and not even wet the pavement. The differences from which these hyperboles arise will prevail in the two states even if the type of orange is the same. In arid climates, like California's, oranges develop a thick albedo, which is the white part of the skin. Florida is one of the two or three most rained-upon states in the United States. California uses the Colorado River and similarly impressive sources to irrigate its oranges, but of course irrigation can only do so much. The annual difference in rainfall between the Florida and California orange-growing areas is one million one hundred and forty thousand gallons per acre. For years, California was the leading orange growing state, but Florida surpassed California in 1942, and grows three times as many oranges now. California oranges, for their part, can safely be called three times as beautiful. (John McPhee, *Oranges*)

In this passage — from an essay describing the history, sociology, and delights of the orange — McPhee compares orange growing in Florida with orange growing in California in terms of a range of aspects. He describes a specific aspect of Florida's orange growing industry and then compares it to the same aspect of California's orange growing industry or vice versa. He develops the paragraph aspect by aspect: skin and juice of the fruit, rainfall, production rates, beauty of the fruit.

Writing Comparison and Contrast

Common though comparison and contrast is, it must be done carefully. Remember that comparison and contrast supports and clarifies your ideas, but you still need a thesis. When, for instance, you compare and contrast the three presidents' involvement in Vietnam, you might say something like, "A comparison of the three presidents indicates that though Kennedy seldom receives blame for the war, his actions were at least as blindly chauvinistic as those of Johnson and Nixon."

Maintaining a consistent pattern or focus is also extremely important. Attribute by attribute is one way of patterning a comparison and contrast. Whatever attributes you identify in one item you must also identify in the others, and in the same order. Another way is to present one item, describe all its relevant attributes, and then do the same for the items with which you are comparing and contrasting it. If McPhee had used this method, he would probably have written a paragraph about Florida oranges, describing skin, juice, weather conditions, quantity, and appearance, and only then turned to California oranges, and dealt with skin, juice, weather conditions, and quantity. He would have made sure that both items received the same treatment in the same order.

Unfortunately, unless the writer stays alert, he or she may mix the two methods, as happens in this paragraph on typical food in the region of Spain called Catalonia:

> *Boeuf à la Catalane* is a mixture of beef chunks and rice simmered in stock. The taste is rather bland, unlike that of *paella*, which is an eating adventure. Of course, knowing a dish is nutritious always makes a person feel good. Julia Child has a good recipe for *boeuf à la Catalane* in *Mastering the Art of French Cooking. Paella* comes from a word meaning "cooking pot." It is made of rice cooked with a saffron-flavored stock, which gives it its yellow color. You can add to it almost anything available in the market: chicken, sausage, shrimp, mussels, olives, peas. *Boeuf à la Catalane* provides sensible, undemanding pleasure. *Paella*, however, combines a lot of flavors. Although both are essentially rice casseroles, there are differences between them.

This comparison and contrast is certainly hard to follow. It jerks the reader from idea to idea and across gaps of reasoning. It has no apparent plan. The first sentence dishes up a stew of facts about one item but announces no overall purpose. The item-by-item pattern is interrupted in the second sentence by the intrusion of an attribute of *paella*. Then the writer sends us back to the beef. Information that appears with one item does not appear with the other. In the fourth sentence, for instance, the writer indicates where to locate a recipe for *boeuf à la Catalane*, but neglects to give the same information for *paella*. The attributes of *paella* appear in the fifth, sixth, and seventh sentences, but in a different order from that in which the beef dish was described. The reader's head is spinning.

In the revision, the writer presents similarities and differences in a more organized way:

> *Boeuf à la Catalane* and *paella* are both Catalonian rice casseroles, yet one could hardly imagine more dissimilar dishes. *Boeuf à la Catalane* is a mixture of beef chunks and rice, simmered in stock, wine, and herbs. The taste, while pleasant, is a little bland. The real satisfaction is knowing that one is eating a nutritious meal. For *paella*, the rice is flavored with saffron, which gives it its yellow color. Other ingredients depend on what is available at the market; typical

additions might be chicken, sausage, shrimp, mussels, olives, and peas. Each bite brings a different flavor. In contrast to *boeuf à la Catalane, paella* is an eating adventure. Both dishes represent aspects of Catalonian culture.

This revision shows all the virtues that characterize effective comparison and contrast writing: consistency, clarity, and parallelism. The writer treats *boeuf à la Catalane* completely first, then moves to *paella*, which she treats in exactly the same manner. At the end, the writer makes a concluding statement that ties together both sides of the comparison and contrast.

TIPS FOR COMPARISON AND CONTRAST

- Be sure you have an overall point and make it clear, preferably at the beginning.
- Make sure the form of your comparison and contrast is consistent throughout, either item by item or attribute by attribute.
- Provide the same kind of information in the same order for all items or attributes.

EXERCISES FOR COMPARISON AND CONTRAST

1. Write a brief consumer report comparing and contrasting two brands of a product you would like to buy, perhaps a car, a computer, a stereo, or even blue jeans, pizza, detergent, or shampoo. Justify buying one brand over the other.

2. Select a news story and compare and contrast the way two newspapers or magazines presented it. Draw conclusions as appropriate.

3. Using illustrations, compare and contrast two abstract words that are often taken to be synonymous — happiness and joy, sorrow and despair, solitude and loneliness, boredom and apathy, and so on. Don't forget to establish an overall purpose.

4. Write an essay on the kinds of social encounters you prefer. To illustrate your preference, think about two families that you visited recently. Narrate the two visits to provide comparison and contrast.

DEFINITION: ESTABLISHING WHAT A WORD MEANS

Virtually every serious essay contains words or phrases that need defining. Whether you write about art or science, world affairs or personal affairs, you will probably need to define some term. What is it? What is it not? What are its uses? What are its characteristics? Can I recognize it on the street if I see it? Can I recognize it in this essay?

In college writing, we often need to use complex terms — meiosis, abstract expressionism — and we must define them so that our readers will have the same idea we have. Most often we can define in a single sentence ("Crime is conduct forbidden by law and resulting in punishment"), but when the term is especially complicated, it can take a paragraph or even a whole essay. "Revising" in Chapter 1 contains an entire essay devoted to the word *creativity*. The context as well as the word will determine the lengths to which you must go in defining it.

What Definition Is

A formal definition — like those found in dictionaries — has three parts: the name of the thing to be defined, the class to which it belongs, and the quality that distinguishes it from other members of its class. Formal definitions are useful for fairly straightforward words. A cheetah, for instance, "is a large cat native to Asia and Africa, possessing tawny fur with black spots and long back legs that make it unusually swift." For the most part, you will not need to define concrete words such as *chair* or *painting*. If, however, what you say can be applied only to a particular item, you can add a limiting word or two: I mean a wing chair, a cubist painting. An informative adjective can often locate an idea in a proper context.

Simple definitions like these, however, are not adequate for complex terms or terms used in special ways. The formal definition of *modernism*, for instance, would be "a movement supporting modern practices, trends, ideas, and so forth, or showing sympathy with any of these." With that definition, we would not get a very deep understanding of the great cultural movement called modernism. To define that term would probably require paragraphs.

Sometimes, though, we can define a rather complicated or mysterious term briefly right in the text and then go on with what we are saying. In the following sentence a writer parenthetically defines the technical term *stagflation*.

> Worries about stagflation — that is, economic stagnation at a time of inflation — depressed private investors and the U.S. stock market in general during the late 1970s.

Now the writer can use *stagflation* with confidence through the essay.

Even a summary of complex ideas can serve as a definition. In the following sentence, Schopenhauer's belief is summarized:

> At one time Nietzsche was deeply influenced by Schopenhauer's belief that reality is blind force expressed in human beings as the will to live.

The reader now has some idea of what Schopenhauer's philosophy is. Of course this summary hardly does justice to Schopenhauer. If his philosophy were important to the whole discussion, the writer would have to devote much more time to defining it.

Figures of speech — metaphors, similes, analogies, and the like — often sharpen our definitions and can make them unmistakable:

> To succeed in business in the 1950s and 1960s, some women felt they had to suppress their womanliness, as had the Amazons who sliced off their right breasts to improve their aim with the bow and arrow.

We may not agree with the writer, but we certainly know what she meant by "suppress their womanliness." (For a discussion of figures of speech, see "Writing with Flair" in Chapter 7.)

Greater difficulty comes with words that have several meanings or meanings that are confusing or controversial. The writer must define these terms precisely. Suppose, for instance, that a writer says, "Nude sunbathing is normal." *Normal* has many meanings. It could mean "conforming, adhering to, or constituting a usual or typical pattern, level, or type" or "functioning or occurring in a natural way" or "average in intelligence, ability, and emotional traits, or personality" — and other definitions from mathematics and chemistry are also possible. We see a world of difference between "average," "natural," and "conforming to the usual." Which does this writer mean? Einstein was natural, and he conformed to a type, albeit the type called "genius," but he was far from average. Was he "normal" or not?

We can resolve any confusion in several ways. We can substitute a more specific phrase: "Nude sunbathing is accepted at certain beaches on Mykonos." We can provide a context that makes the use clear: "Nude sunbathing is normal among indigenous populations on some South Sea islands." Or we can stipulate — that is, simply assign — the meaning: "By normal, I mean typical behavior at that time and place."

When we *stipulate*, we say in effect, "Exactly *this* is what I will mean when I use the word." We specify a condition of our argument, and the reader must recognize that condition or miss the argument. Stipulating is particularly useful for limiting the range of a discussion. When, for instance, we say, "Crime is conduct forbidden by law and resulting in punishment," we exclude behavior that is not forbidden by law and does not result in punishment.

Terms like *normal, average, natural,* even *crime* are tough enough, but some words are dynamite and a lighted match. Words like *fascism, patriot,* and *Christian* can arouse great passions. To use them well, you must define them with care. Even with these loaded words, you can stipulate a definition: "By Christian, I mean any person who is actively engaged in a Christian community of believers" or "By Christian, I mean any person who has been baptized." These two definitions exclude people who are members of other communities (Buddhists, Jews, and Moslems, for example) or who define themselves through rituals other than baptism (trances, ordeals, or rites of passage, for example). You have set the limits of the term and can go on from there.

You cannot, however, go very far, because you have lost many of the value connotations of the word *Christian*. You cannot now say, "Anyone who accepts abortion is not a good Christian" or "Anyone who fails in generosity to the poor is not a good Christian," because you did not allow for those exclusions in your definition. You have to stay within your stipulation.

Writing Definitions

Few things are more challenging than establishing meaning, and nothing is more important. When we want to communicate meaning in writing, we must define all terms that the reader may not know or that we may use differently. As a first step, check the dictionary, but then go beyond it. You can seldom get a truly complicated or subtle understanding without thinking about the connotations of a word. You may even need to trace the history of its usage and examine how it is used in a particular context.

Definition often involves the other strategies. You may need to divide the word into its components and classify it according to its distinguishing characteristics. To get at its essential meaning, you may need to compare and contrast it with similar words. Except for the most obvious definitions, you will almost certainly need to provide illustrations. Remember that in definition, as in all strategies, you are trying to bring your reader to the common ground, to establish a meaning that the reader will accept. Thus, even with abstract terms you need to be as specific and concrete as possible.

To deal with attitudes toward war of the World War II and Vietnam generations, a student defined *patriotism*.

> In evaluating the two generations, we should think about whether or not they were patriots. *Patriotism* is love of country and a willingness to sacrifice for it. During the Vietnam War, many young Americans refused to take up arms to fight for their country, some going so far as moving to another country, others serving time in jail. The generation of 1941 was more patriotic and willing to fight for the country.

Did you feel disappointed, as though you had been promised steak and had been given white bread? What are "love of country" and "willingness to sacrifice"? This simple, and abstract, definition is inadequate for such a highly charged issue.

Once he had achieved some critical distance, the writer recognized that what he had written was platitudinous. He spent a few hours doing research and discovered that the meaning of *patriotism* has varied from place to place and time to time. During the American Revolution, the idea of "patriot" was purely affirmative. Writing about the Boston Tea Party, John Adams said, "There is a dignity, a majesty, a sublimity, in this last effort of the patriots that I greatly admire."

Across the water, however, the word had a different meaning. In eighteenth-century England, it meant "a factious disturber of the government," and the contemporary writer Samuel Johnson said, "Patriotism is the last refuge of a scoundrel." Were Johnson and Adams talking about the same thing? What *were* they talking about? The writer then looked up material on attitudes toward World War II and the Vietnam War. He discovered that veterans of World War II had accused the anti-Vietnam demonstrators of not being "patriotic" because they did not support all the decisions of the President and the Congress. But many of the men who refused to fight in Vietnam claimed that a true patriot would not support a cause that destroys the values the country cherishes. They felt that they were the "true" patriots.

The writer decided to brainstorm the subject. Why should we let other people in government determine our lives? What would happen if we had no obligations except to our own ideas? Could a country continue if every citizen could, in the name of the higher "patriotism," decide what laws to obey? What would happen to society if we all refused to pay taxes when we didn't like the way the money was spent? The result would be chaos.

After absorbing all these ideas, the student tried again to define the word *patriotism*:

> In 1941, patriotism meant an immediate response to the war effort; such a definition was understandable and reasonable in light of the clear threat posed to the nation by the belligerent forces of Japan and Germany. In 1965, the threat in Vietnam was neither as clear nor as present. Patriotism meant upholding certain values like questioning authority and refusing to serve in what was considered by many to be an unjust war. For our time, perhaps we should put these two experiences together and define the word anew. In a society like ours, patriotism cannot be blind, or we chance losing the very values that have established our country. At the same time, we cannot expect to enjoy the privilege of those values without being willing to sacrifice to maintain them. Patriots, then, will be critical of their country for the country's own good, and yet be ready to sacrifice for it when reason, combined with the force of events, tells them they must.

The writer went far beyond the dictionary to gain his understanding of the word. When it came to writing, he was explicit about the different definitions, stating exactly how the experience of the two generations differed. Notice the careful comparison and contrast of the two. The writer divided the concept into its two parts: the willingness to sacrifice and the necessity to uphold values. Thus did he make a fairly complex definition clear to the reader.

TIPS FOR DEFINITION

• Use the dictionary, but go beyond it to connotations and subtle meanings.
• Be as specific and concrete as you can.
• Use the other strategies to help you define.

EXERCISES FOR DEFINITION

1. Research and define one of the following words or phrases: *anima, balance of power, karma, law of supply and demand, Occam's razor, Planck's constant, surrealism, transubstantiation.* In a short essay, describe the process you went through in formulating your definition.

2. Define from your own experience one of the following words: apathy, discipline, egotism, fantasy, insecurity, negotiation, nostalgia, power, success, wealth. Narrate an experience of yours that illustrates your definition. If you think your definition may be unusual, account for the difference.

3. Trace the different definitions of the word *law* in this section of the poem, "Law Like Love," by W. H. Auden.

> Law, say the gardeners, is the sun,
> Law is the one
> All gardeners obey
> To-morrow, yesterday, to-day.
>
> Law is the wisdom of the old,
> The impotent grandfathers shrilly scold;
> The grandchildren put out a treble tongue,
> Law is the senses of the young.
>
> Law, says the priest with a priestly look,
> Expounding to an unpriestly people,
> Law is the words in my priestly book,
> Law is my pulpit and my steeple.
>
> Law, says the judge as he looks down his nose,
> Speaking clearly and most severely,
> Law is as I've told you before,
> Law is as you know I suppose,
> Law is but let me explain it once more,
> Law is The Law.
>
> Yet law-abiding scholars write:
> Law is neither wrong nor right,

Law is only crimes
Punished by places and by times,
Law is the clothes men wear
Anytime, anywhere,
Law is Good morning and Good night.

Others say, Law is our Fate;
Others say, Law is our State;
Others say, others say
Law is no more
Law has gone away.

And always the loud angry crowd
Very angry and very loud
Law is We,
And always the soft idiot softly Me.

4. For a classtime game: All students in the class will be asked to write a definition of each of the following words: omphaloskepsis, ngwee, constringe, doss house, deodand, oxytocic, primipara. The instructor will secretly give one student the correct definition. All the students will read out their definition, and the class will try to decide which is the correct one.

part three

The Art of the Writer: Sentences, Diction, Style

6 / *The Sentence from Many Angles*

> *Backward ran sentences until reeled the mind.*
> – *Wolcott Gibbs (1902–1958)*
> *American writer and humorist*

You could not write an essay, you could not write a paragraph, indeed you could not express a thought at all without sentences. You could say a word, and thus denote a thing or even identify a concept, but you could not say anything about that thing or concept. A sentence expresses the basic unit of thought. By its construction, it discriminates among ideas and signals what is important. Its very form affects its meaning.

Some writers seem to think sentences exist fully grown somewhere in the corners of the mind and will come when called. It isn't that easy. Sentences don't write themselves: we have to do the work. Words are in our heads, but we have to put them together to make a whole thought.

PARTS OF A SENTENCE: THE BASIC THOUGHT

Deep in every complete sentence there exist always a simple subject (S) and verb (V) and frequently a direct object (O) or a complement (C). These compose the spine of the sentence.

S	V	O/C
Raccoons	harassed	farmers.
I	like	Ike.
Sugar	is	sweet.
Khrushchev	blinked.	

The subject is the topic of the sentence. *Raccoons* is the topic of the first sentence. The verb indicates an action or state of being. *Like* indicates the action in the second sentence; *is* indicates the state of being in the third. The *direct object* receives the action. *Ike* receives the action *like*. The *complement* names, identifies, or describes the subject. *Sweet* describes *sugar*.

Not all sentences contain an object. In *Khrushchev blinked*, he didn't blink anything — he just blinked. The thought and the sentence are complete.

Some sentences contain both an indirect object (IO) and direct object. The indirect object indicates to whom or for whom the action was done:

S	V	IO	O
The hamburger	cost	us	money.

Spines provide the substructure for thought, and often they are all we need. "I love you," "War is hell," and "You shut your mouth" hardly require embellishment.

MODIFIERS: ENRICHING THE THOUGHT

Usually we want to go beyond the simple statement to ask subtle questions, voice reservations, describe in detail what we see, give complicated commands, explain with precision. The unembellished subject-verb-object/complement will seldom convey a complex meaning.

Here is a sentence that cries out for elaboration.

The people supported a law.

This sentence contains nothing to catch our interest, let alone hold it until the next idea emerges.

We can enrich the sentence by adding adjectives, adverbs, phrases, or clauses:

Long before pollution reached international proportions, *the people* of Dortmund, West Germany, *supported a law* making public health a higher priority than any other political consideration.

Although still there, our original sentence is hardly recognizable, for now we have added modifiers that explain, qualify, and amplify the central thought. We know when the people passed the law, where they lived, and what the law said.

Modifiers depend on the spine to support them. Without it, they would collapse in a heap. But the spine without modifiers could be uninformative or even confusing. What, we may well ask, did "I like Ike" mean and why did people like him?

Adding Adjectives and Adverbs

We can hang a modifying word on any part of the spine. Suppose our sentence is

Raccoons harassed farmers.

We can make this sentence more pictorial and more exact by adding an adjective to modify the nouns or an adverb to modify the verb:

The marauding raccoons harassed the farmers.
The raccoons gleefully harassed the farmers.
The raccoons harassed the hot-tempered farmers.

We can combine these possibilities and write a fairly lively sentence.

The marauding raccoons gleefully harassed the hot-tempered farmers.

Now we have told our readers more about the raccoons, the harassment, and the farmers.

If we wish, we can add more than one adjective to any noun and more than one adverb to any verb.

Crusty, cantankerous Khrushchev blinked rapidly twice.

Building with Phrases and Clauses

So far we have added fairly simple words as modifiers. But we can also attach more complicated modifiers — phrases and clauses — to sentence spines.

A *phrase* is a group of words lacking either a subject or a verb. We can hang phrases on any part of the spine:

> *Blue from the cold,* the mountain climbers plunged *into the Jacuzzi.*

> *To get even for the harsh and petty measures of the Roman officials,* the Visigoths rebelled *against Rome.*

We do have to be sure, though, that we hang phrases close to the words they modify. We might confuse the reader if we wrote

> The mountain climbers plunged into the Jacuzzi *blue from the cold.*

Is the Jacuzzi blue from the cold?

A *clause* is a group of related words containing both a subject and a verb. Clauses come in two varieties. One variety, called *independent*, can stand as a complete sentence.

> Babe Ruth started his baseball career as a pitcher.

The other variety, called *dependent*, cannot stand alone.

> After Babe Ruth pointed his bat at the center field bleachers

Although this clause contains a subject and a verb, it is not a complete thought, and it needs an independent clause to support it.

> After Babe Ruth pointed his bat at the center field bleachers, he hit a home run.

Dependent clauses, like phrases, can be attached to any part of the spine:

> The conquistador Balboa, *who was the first European to view the Pacific from the Western Hemisphere,* claimed the entire Pacific coast for the Spanish crown.

> *While he was preparing an expedition to Peru,* Balboa was accused of treason.

Again like phrases, clauses must be placed close to the part of the spine they modify. We would confuse our reader if, for instance, we wrote

> General Lee presented his sword to General Grant, *which he had carried throughout the Civil War.*

Lee most certainly did not carry Grant throughout the Civil War. (For a further discussion of phrases and clauses, see the appendix.)

Modifiers carry information, and where and how they carry it makes all the difference. We must follow the rules of syntax, grammar, and usage. And, of course, we must show restraint and choose our modifiers carefully. Piling on modifier after modifier can make near-gibberish of writing:

> On a cold and rainy January morning, in a fit of pique, and blue from the cold, marauding raccoons who had reconnoitered at dawn gleefully harassed the furious, hot-tempered farmers, which was their way of getting even for harsh and petty measures.

The human mind simply cannot sort out so many ideas and images at once. A few well-chosen modifiers will make the point more clearly and forcefully. A single sharp image may have more impact than a lengthy description. Often a simple noun is better all alone. *Gorilla* hardly needs *hairy* or *scary,* and *howled* hardly needs *wildly.* If, however, the gorilla is bald and simpering, add the modifiers.

TIPS FOR MODIFIERS

- Modifiers — adjectives, adverbs, phrases, and clauses — explain, qualify, or amplify the thought that the spine of the sentence expresses.
- Place modifiers as close as possible to the part of the spine they modify.
- Show restraint: use only as many modifiers as the spine can easily carry.

EXERCISES FOR MODIFIERS

1. Make these sentences livelier by modifying each at three places, using adjectives or adverbs.
   a. Mother wrote a book.
   b. Politics is absurd.
   c. The boss provided us with transportation.
   d. The crane hit the pavement.

2. Modify each of these sentences with both a phrase and a clause. (Make up attributes and events if you need to.)
   a. I study metallurgy.
   b. The hurricane destroyed the house.
   c. Sherman attacked Atlanta.
   d. The Spartans defeated the Athenians.

3. Modify each of these sentences by adding at least one adjective, one adverb, one phrase, and one clause.

> **a.** Harry Truman succeeded Franklin Roosevelt.
> **b.** Economics is dismal.
> **c.** The instructor flunked me.
> **d.** Sigmund Freud wrote *Interpretation of Dreams*.
> First, let yourself go. Make them as wild as you like. Then revise the sentences to make them acceptable for a school essay. But keep them lively.

COORDINATION AND SUBORDINATION: SHAPING THE THOUGHT

Modifiers are only one way of shaping and directing sentences. Now that we have seen how they work, we can begin to look at the others. In this section, we discuss how to structure the sentence.

The Simple Sentence

The simplest construction is a simple sentence. It consists of a single independent clause.

The Irish elk is a deer.

Leonardo da Vinci invented the bicycle.

The simple sentence can have a compound subject:

In 1940, *Sammy Baugh* and *the Washington Redskins* lost the National Football League championship to the Chicago Bears by a score of 73–0.

It can also have a compound verb:

The Scottish poet Robert Burns *wrote* the words to "Auld Lang Syne" but *did not write* the music.

Both these sentences contain only one independent clause.

The simple sentence can express complicated ideas and contain a good deal of information:

Woodrow Wilson, the twenty-eighth president of the United States, had been a practicing lawyer, a professor of political science, president of Princeton University, and governor of New Jersey.

The simple sentence can convey much information; it can also come right out and say what is what. From it the reader can quickly pick up the main idea. (For more on simple sentences, see the appendix.)

Young children use simple sentences almost exclusively. Their writing sounds like this:

> Dear Mom and Dad,
>
> I am having a lot of fun at camp. We learned how to swim yesterday. Then we went on a hike. We got on top of a mountain. It was high. You could see a long way. I got dizzy. I like Counselor Howard. I don't like the food so much. Give Frisky a big kiss. Say hi to Grandma.
>
> Love,
Patty

What gives such writing its charm — and makes it sound childish — is its way of putting the same emphasis on everything. Each sentence runs in a straight line, from locomotive to caboose. Patty writes with clarity and directness, all right — even Grandma could hardly miss the meaning — but her prose lacks variety and depth. No one, of course, would criticize a nine-year-old for this kind of writing. Readers, however, expect mature writers to be able to use not just the hammer and the saw but all the tools of the trade. And they expect the right tool for the job.

Coordination

Rather than having a string of choppy sentences, an older Patty could combine her simple sentences into compound sentences.

> We learned how to swim yesterday, and then we went on a hike. I like Counselor Howard, but I don't like the food so much.

A compound sentence contains at least two independent clauses and no dependent clauses. Patty now expresses her experience more clearly. She shows the relations between ideas. She points out how camp activity is structured and how one event immediately follows another. Finally, to show the range of her experiences, she combines a like and a dislike in one sentence.

This process is called *coordination*. When we coordinate sentences, we are saying that the clauses enjoy the same importance. They are co-stars and deserve equal billing. (For a further discussion of compound sentences, see the appendix.)

By placing two independent clauses in the same sentence, we imply that they are so integrally connected that they must perform in the same show. The two independent clauses should reinforce each other; each thought should benefit from being coupled with the other.

> Give me liberty or give me death.
>
> Candy
> Is dandy
> But liquor
> Is quicker.
>   (Ogden Nash)

If the two ideas are not closely related, they should not be in the same sentence. When we hook together disparate ideas, our sentences tend to fly apart:

> Michelangelo painted the Sistine Chapel, and Pope Julius II was a great patron of the arts.

These two clauses have no apparent connection.

Even if both parts of the sentence treat the same subject, the parts may not mesh.

> Leonardo da Vinci painted *The Last Supper*, and he was a Florentine.

The connection between these two ideas is too casual to justify putting them together.

To connect independent clauses, insert between them either a comma and a coordinating conjunction or a semicolon. (Without one of these devices, you would commit the error called a comma splice. See the appendix.)

Coordinating conjunctions (*for, and, nor, but, or, yet, so*) indicate the relation between the independent clauses. Each carries its own logic. You would not use *and* when one clause contradicts the other. You would not use *yet* when you meant *nor*.

Writers sometimes face the decision of whether to use a conjunction or a semicolon.

> The pollsters predicted a close election, but the smart money predicted a landslide.
>
> The pollsters predicted a close election; the smart money predicted a landslide.

Often this choice is a matter not of grammar but of intuition. The semicolon signals a closer relation between the two clauses. It rivets the reader's attention on the connection. Even if the comma and conjunction seem more natural to you, try a semicolon occasionally. It will give your clauses a tighter link.

Subordination

A prose consisting only of simple sentences and coordination can tire your reader. Even though you may add interesting modifiers, the basic beat goes on until the reader goes away. Coordination also can be quite confusing. It does not tell the reader how thoughts dovetail or which are more important.

Remember our tortured sentence about the raccoons and the farmers? Suppose we had presented the information this way:

> It was a cold January morning, and it was rainy, too. It was dawn, and the marauding raccoons reconnoitered. They were blue from the cold, but they were piqued. They were determined to get even. The farmers' measures had been harsh; they had been petty. The raccoons harassed the farmers. The farmers were furious; they were a hot-tempered bunch. And, oh yes, the raccoons were gleeful.

This series of independent clauses fails to identify what is important and what is not. Everything comes at the reader willy-nilly. For all its silliness, our original involuted sentence makes better reading. Intelligent readers will make some educated guesses about the priority of each bit of information. But why should they have to do the work? It is the writer's responsibility to make the point clear and to indicate relative importance, to *subordinate* the less important ideas to the more important. As coordination indicates equal significance of ideas, subordination indicates that one idea is more significant than the other.

> Although it was a cold, rainy January morning, the raccoons were determined to get even with the farmers.

From this sentence the reader knows that the weather and time of day are less important than the raccoons' determination.

When we subordinate, we bring the main idea front and center in an independent clause and push less important ideas back into a dependent clause. The main idea should *always* appear in the independent clause. The subordinate ideas depend on and are secondary to that main idea.

> When his Ninth Symphony was first performed, Beethoven had been deaf for five years.

The main idea is Beethoven's deafness. Had the writer considered the Ninth Symphony the main idea, he or she would have put it in the independent clause.

> After Beethoven had been deaf for five years, his Ninth Symphony was performed.

The writer could clearly improve the next sentence by subordinating one idea to the other:

> Hunger had finally driven him wild, and Big Foot Sam began to stalk the Milwaukee suburb.

There is nothing wrong here — except that there is no weighing of the ideas. Is the hunger more or less important than the stalking? And what is the connection between them? The intelligent reader figures out the meaning and silently rewrites:

> Because hunger had finally driven him wild, Big Foot Sam began to stalk the Milwaukee suburb.

These two ideas inhabit the same sentence because one is the condition out of which the other comes.

You can have more than one subordinate idea in a sentence, and you can put them in different places, depending on meaning and style.

> Muhammad Ali, *who had won the heavyweight title from Sonny Liston and again from George Foreman,* became the first man to win it three times *when he took it from Leon Spinks.*

To join a dependent clause to the independent clause, use either a subordinating conjunction or a relative pronoun. (One of each appears in the Muhammad Ali sentence.) The subordinating conjunctions you are most apt to read and use are: *after, although, as, because, before, if, in order to, since, so that, unless, until, when, whenever, where,* and *while.* Each of these indicates a particular relation between the dependent clause and the independent clause — what caused what, when, where, why, and how.

> *Although* he never learned to juggle, Raoul had a certain unwashed charm about him.

> The postman refused to deliver the mail *because* my dog Frank bit him on the rump and tore his britches.

(Caution: some of these words also function as prepositions — *before the vending machine, because of you, since Tuesday*. To identify a clause, look for both a subject and a verb.)

The relative pronouns are: *that, which, who, whom,* and *whose.*

The question *that* this essay poses has baffled all the critics *who* have wrestled with it.

Some sentences contain both a subordinating conjunction and a relative pronoun:

Because a small, barred window *that* looked down on the prison yard provided the only light in the cell, he could not read.

As these examples demonstrate, subordination can create flexible, energetic, precise, and subtle sentences. Subordinated sentences can be either *complex* — having one independent clause and one or more subordinate clauses — or *compound-complex* — having at least two independent clauses and one subordinate clause. For further discussion, see the appendix.

TIPS FOR COORDINATION AND SUBORDINATION

- When two thoughts are equal and reinforce each other, coordinate them in a single sentence.
- Remember that over-coordinated prose sounds childish.
- Use subordination to convey the relative importance of thoughts.
- Put main thoughts in independent clauses and subordinate thoughts in dependent clauses.

EXERCISES FOR COORDINATION AND SUBORDINATION

1. Combine each of the following groups of sentences to make one sentence.
   a. Inflation most drastically affects the lives of people on fixed incomes. These people depend on Social Security. The Social Security laws provide for increased payment based on the cost of living. We should protect that part of the law.
   b. Each year, the swallows come back to Capistrano. They come

in the summer. They are small birds. In flight they are graceful. Their plumage is an iridescent black or blue.

c. The obelisk is a monument. It is four sided. Usually it is made of a single piece of stone. It tapers toward the top. In ancient Egypt, obelisks were dedicated to the sun god.

d. The Mississippi is a mighty river. It is sometimes as thick and brown as mud. It curls like a snake in motion. It is one of the world's greatest waterways. Vast cities have been built on its banks.

e. San Marco is a church in Venice. It contains beautiful mosaics of stone, glass, and gold. Its foundations are in watery soil. The air is damp. These factors threaten the permanence of the art-works. They also threaten the stability of the church.

f. The channel catfish will eat almost anything. It is a scavenger. It is a predator. It can find food by sight and also by touch and taste with its fleshy barbels. You can bait your hook with min-nows. You can also use frogs and chicken innards. Artificial lures attract the channel catfish. It is omnivorous.

2. Revise the following sentences as directed:

    a. The boss turned her back, and Carl and Tony stuck out their tongues. (Use subordination.)

    b. Margaret Mead was able to throw herself into tribal life because she possessed remarkable gusto. (Make into a simple sentence.)

    c. After he took a fabulous bite out of the Big Apple upon his ar-rival in New York, he was hooked. (Use coordination.)

    d. There is no other drink as potent as the zombie, and I know that from recent, painful experience. (Use subordination.)

3. In a few sentences, discuss each change you made, stating whether it was an improvement or not, and why.

4. Revise the following to make subordinate sentences:

    a. I played the piano, and Mary sang.

    b. Galileo had artistic ability and might have turned out to be a painter or a musician.

    c. Williams voted for Phillips and so Phillips won the election.

    d. Many old people watch the actions of the young with nostal-gia, regret, and sometimes horror, but few young people take an equally strong interest in the old.

    e. A history of philosophy and theology could be written in terms of grudges, wounded pride, and aversions, and it would be far more instructive than the usual treament.

    f. She came up behind the man, and she looked gaunt in the gray, shapeless garment and the sunbonnet, and she wore stained sneakers.

EMPHASIS: STRENGTHENING THE THOUGHT

Some sentences have punch; others do not. And should not. An essay that came on like gangbusters all the time would soon exhaust and irritate the reader. Reading it would be like listening for hours to a prize fight. You want variety. You want some sentences to start with a punch, some to end with a bang, a few to proceed evenly from start to finish.

In speaking, we usually start with our subject and then amplify it as thoughts occur to us. Written sentences often follow this pattern.

> Bats are obliged to make sounds almost ceaselessly, to sense, by sonar, all the objects in their surroundings. (Lewis Thomas, *The Lives of a Cell*)

We call this pattern *loose*, because the structure is rather casual, or *cumulative*, because information piles up along the way. As the sentence progresses, the main idea becomes clearer.

Occasionally, a writer may so distribute the emphasis that it first falls on the main idea and imperceptibly shifts to the subordinate clause:

> I go for all sharing the privileges of the government who assist in bearing its burdens. (Abraham Lincoln, Letter to the Editor, *Sangamon Journal*, New Salem, Illinois)

The emphasis seems more or less equal throughout, first falling on the main idea and then on the added material. You will find many elegant loose sentences.

Ending with a Bang

All of us want occasionally to make a truly emphatic statement, to cue the trumpets and train the spotlights as the big point arrives. The big moment will very likely occur at the end.

> Take the money and run.

> Those who make peaceful revolution impossible will make violent revolution inevitable.

Reverse the order of the ideas and they lose that strong emphasis:

> Run after you take the money.

> Violent revolution will be made inevitable by those who make peaceful revolution impossible.

A sentence generally wants to get somewhere. It wants to gather momentum as it travels. Remember Beethoven and his Ninth Symphony?

> Beethoven had been deaf for five years when his Ninth Symphony was first performed.

This loose sentence is grammatically correct but hardly emphatic. Suppose we had written it this way:

> When his Ninth Symphony was first performed, Beethoven had been deaf for five years.

Here we have the same words, same ideas, same independent clause, same dependent clause, but a different order and greater impact. The notion of the great composer's deafness is not slipped in but slammed home.

When the emphasis comes at the end, we call the sentence *periodic*. The early elements of the sentence push toward the climax. The strong, final element serves as a springboard into the next sentence.

In the passages that follow, we discuss four versions of an opening sentence for a paragraph in praise of the lowly hot dog. Each sentence contains the same set of ideas, but the arrangement of those ideas makes each sentence quite distinct.

> The most American of all foods is still the hot dog, which is a thought that makes great chefs bristle.

This is a loose sentence and not a particularly good one. Few readers would realize that the writer intended to praise the hot dog. That homely object lies buried in the middle, where the main clause dies a murky death. Highlighted, unfortunately, is a weak, barely breathing *which* clause. This clause reads like an afterthought, or a thought the writer did not know how to include.

> The most American of all foods is still the hot dog, although great chefs bristle at the thought.

This is also a loose sentence but a much better one. It still reverses the flow of energy and sends the reader backward looking for the target, but the *although* at least indicates that something contrary, and therefore perhaps interesting, may follow.

> Although great chefs bristle at the thought, the hot dog is still the most American of all foods.

This is a periodic sentence, the more emphatic structure. Unfortunately, this version does not take full advantage of the construction. That hot dog is obviously the point of the sentence — not the chefs, not American foods — and the writer ought to place it in the most prominent spot.

Although great chefs bristle at the thought, the most American of all foods is still the hot dog.

Now the reader gets the full impact of the idea.

Sometimes you simply cannot place your main idea at the end, however. The sense of the sentence may dictate otherwise:

Because he was rich, he thought people adored him.

He thought people adored him because he was rich.

These two sentences do not express the same thought. You would probably dislike the fellow in the first version but pity him in the second. Placing the modifying clause near the word it modifies is as important as strong emphasis.

Opening with a Punch

Although the ending is the most emphatic part of a sentence, the beginning is a close second. When you start your sentence with a strong idea, you step right out and say, "Here it is, folks—take it or leave it."

The cold grave is the fate of humankind.

That sentence packs a wallop from the first word. To reverse it would be to weaken it.

The fate of humankind is the cold grave.

Even for less stunning assertions, the opening can make a reader sit up and take notice.

Be cheerful while you are alive.
Stealing apples can lead to trouble.

Some writers muffle a strong opening idea in a construction that weakens the impact:

There isn't anyone who can stop him now.

is less emphatic than

> No one can stop him now.

and

> It was frequently said that lust for applause was his worst fault.

is bland compared with

> Lust for applause, it was frequently said, was his worst fault.

In that revision, the writer buried the least interesting idea in the middle.

The Second Spotlight. Even when you write a periodic sentence, putting your main idea at the end, start off with the second most important idea. Read these two sentences:

> Because every day the city sees the influx of thousands of people, Mexico City is a sprawling mess.
>
> Because thousands of people enter the city every day, Mexico City is a sprawling mess.

Sprawling mess is, of course, the most compelling idea in the sentence and rightly goes at the end. But *thousands of people* is the second most compelling and should have the second spotlight, the beginning.

Revising for Emphasis

The Limp Sentence. Limpness (not a technical term) in a sentence can have three causes. First, it can come from adding a weak and unnecessary phrase or clause to a sentence:

> Hamlet hated King Claudius, so it seems.
> But through all the trouble, he loved his mother, in a way.
> He was of several minds, so to speak.

With phrases like these, even the best sentence will sag.

Second, limp sentences may result from using a *passive voice* construction. In these constructions, the subject of the sentence is not the actor but the recipient of the action:

> Yesterday all my hair was cut off by John the barber.

The reader must go back to the beginning of the sentence to find the target of the action. In the meantime, the sentence loses both energy and emphasis. Had the writer followed the natural flow of the simple English sentence, this one would have read:

Yesterday John the barber cut off all my hair.

(For further discussion of passive voice, see the appendix.)

Third, ending with a preposition can make a sentence limp. Note the difference in emphasis between

Toxic waste dumps are hazards to keep away from.

and

Toxic waste dumps are hazards to avoid.

That *from* at the end makes the idea trail off weakly, while *to avoid* provides a firm closing.

You should not twist your sentences into knots just to avoid this construction. To tease pedants, Winston Churchill said that to worry about ending sentences with prepositions was something "up with which I will not put." It is not a crime — it is just not a strong finish.

The Anticlimax.   Anticlimax will undermine even the most interesting sentence. When you write a sentence of several more or less equal elements, watch your order of presentation. That order can make or break your sentence. The obvious, and easy, way to present a list is chronologically. But not all items occur in sequence, and indeed sometimes strict chronology leads to anticlimax, as in this sentence:

She flew a balloon in France; she hunted lions in Africa; she fought a revolution in Chile; she drove a taxi in Philadelphia.

Philadelphia? a taxi? Fortunately, the revision does greater justice to an exciting career:

In Africa, she hunted lions; in France, she flew a balloon; in Philadelphia, she drove a taxi; and in Chile, she fought a revolution.

This new order is called the *relay race* because, as on most relay teams, the second best leads off and the best runs the last lap. Driving a taxi takes, as it should, a less important position even though it occurred after the other events.

The writer also improved this sentence in another way. In the original, place comes last in each clause and thus receives the emphasis. But what happened is more interesting than where it happened. In revising, the writer put the action at the end of each clause. *She fought a revolution* provides a fitting climax.

Equal Emphasis: Treating Ideas Alike

So far we have seen sentences in which one idea dominates and therefore deserves the most emphasis. Now we turn to sentences in which two or more related or similar ideas deserve equal billing. We create such sentences by means of parallelism and correlatives.

Performing on the Parallel. In parallel construction equal or similar ideas are presented in the identical grammatical form.

> I came, I saw, I conquered.

Follow Caesar's lead: put parallel ideas in parallel grammatical form. Parallel construction requires that all like elements be treated in the same manner. They should be expressed in the same grammatical construction, whether clauses or phrases, passive or active voice.

> The farmer takes a wife, the wife takes a child, the child takes a nurse, the nurse . . .

Because of the parallel construction of this traditional song, children have no difficulty understanding the story. Without parallel construction you might get something like this:

> The farmer takes a wife, the child is taken by that wife, and it in its turn has an opportunity to choose its nurse, and then a choice is made by the nurse . . .

In this version, the ideas do not function as an organized team, but rather as a motley mob of straggling thoughts.

Maintaining parallelism is particularly helpful in comparing and contrasting two things. Though the following example contains all the elements of a comparison, the writer has presented them in a confusing manner:

> The Sahara was a verdant region in 10,000 B.C., but seven millennia later you would have seen fewer lakes and forests.

Not only is the sentence limp, but also the reader must reorganize elements to figure out exactly what it says. The revision is clear and forceful.

> In 10,000 B.C., the Sahara was a verdant region, but by 3,000 B.C. it had become a desert.

Verdant region and *desert* offer a sharper contrast; using dates for both periods of time makes the point clearer; repetition of the subject-verb construction underscores the comparison.

In constructing a list of complicated thoughts, we will ignore parallelism at our peril, as the writer of this sentence discovered:

> The main priorities of Hitler's campaign were encouraging the German people, and fewer debts, the subjugation of France, and he wanted to become the sole power in Europe.

This is a jumble. The reader has to get in there and straighten it out.

> The main priorities of Hitler's campaign were to encourage the German people, to reduce the German debt, to conquer France, and to become the sole power in Europe.

Now the reader will grasp Hitler's goals more easily.

Although in parallelism all parts must have the same construction, they need not all possess the same length or cadence. Here is a parallel sentence in which one element is much fuller than the other:

> For its well-being, Mississippi depends largely on agriculture, but for its well-being, Georgia depends on business, commerce, and manufacturing as well as agriculture.

Maintaining Your Balance. Balance is a stylistic variation on parallelism. In a balanced sentence, the length and rhythm, as well as the grammatical elements, are the same in both parts. We could find no better illustrations of balance than in the orations of Brutus and Mark Antony over the body of Caesar in Shakespeare's *Julius Caesar*.

> Not that I loved Caesar less, but that I loved Rome more. . . . As he was valiant, I honor him; but as he was ambitious, I slew him.

With these balanced cadences, Brutus sways the Roman crowd. In opposition, Antony uses the same technique with even greater effect.

> The evil that men do lives after them,
> The good is oft interred with their bones.

The reader feels the exquisite tension of perfect balance — that of an elegant gymnast on the high bar.

We cannot write like Shakespeare, but we can strengthen even our everyday sentences by balancing the ideas. A sentence like

> Although Stephen Douglas triumphed in the debates, the presidency went to Abraham Lincoln.

can become

> Although Stephen Douglas won the debates, Abraham Lincoln won the presidency.

and

> He had a passion to discover things and that pushed him onward, but he was held back by a fear of failure.

can become

> His passion for discovery pushed him onward, but his fear of failure held him back.

Revised, the sentences are balanced.

Joining with Correlatives. When you are working out on the parallel bars or trying to balance on the high beam of a sentence, you can find help by turning to correlative conjunctions: *either . . . or, neither . . . nor, both . . . and, not only . . . but also, whether . . . or.* These pairs firmly tie two thoughts together by showing exactly how they are related.

> Both Joe Louis and Rocky Marciano were great heavyweights.
> Either he would get his way, or he would not play.
> Neither screaming men nor rivers of blood could stop the war.
> Francis Bacon was not only a philosopher but also an essayist and a statesman.

When you use these pairs, you show that the two parts of your thought are equally important. You can forge a stronger and more emphatic bond with correlatives than with the coordinating conjunctions, like *and, but,* and so on.

Bonding carefully is both grammatically and stylistically important. When using correlative conjunctions, make sure the grammatical form used with the first phrase or clause is repeated in the second. It is incorrect to write

> Either you are part of the solution or part of the problem.

It should be

> Either you are part of the solution or you are part of the problem.

or

> You are part of either the solution or the problem.

By using correlatives, you can strengthen gramatically correct but uninspired sentences. You can, for instance, change a rather dull sentence like

At Abu Simbel, Ramses II built an immense temple in his own honor and he built another one as an honor for Queen Nefertari.

to the livelier

At Abu Simbel, Ramses II built not only an immense temple to honor himself but also one to honor Queen Nefertari.

Caution: The words *both, either,* and *neither* are not always correlative conjunctions; they can also function alone as pronouns or adjectives.

Because both played well, either side could have won, but neither was overwhelming.

TIPS FOR EMPHASIS

- Remember that the place of greatest emphasis is the end of the sentence.
- The second most emphatic position is the beginning.
- Avoid limp sentences and anticlimaxes.
- When you express more than one important thought, put them in parallel grammatical form.
- Balance elements in a sentence to emphasize the equality of the thoughts.
- Correlative conjunctions can help tie thoughts together, but when you use one of the pair, you must use the other.

EXERCISES FOR EMPHASIS

1. Change the following sentences so that the emphasis comes at the end:
   a. The mayor acts as though she dislikes street vendors more than anybody in the United States.
   b. The airport is where I would like this taxi to take me.
   c. Virtually all agree that we must find a new source of fuel to be able to meet our increasing energy demands in the future.
   d. The paintings of Giorgione are enjoying a period of immense popularity because there is an exhibition at the museum of his works.
2. Rewrite the following sentences so that the emphasis falls at the beginning:

    a. What it is that's important is doing your homework.
    b. A bad way to bring about change is mob rule.
    c. The languages of the Bantu and the Arabs combined to form Swahili.
    d. People are telling the truth when they say he is conventional.

  3. Rewrite these sentences to emphasize the most important point.
    a. Born in the fifteenth century, Lucrezia Borgia had her second husband murdered, although she was the daughter of a pope.
    b. Cotton has been spun, woven, and dyed since prehistoric times, including long before Europeans settled in the Western Hemisphere.
    c. Pacifists, celibates, and egalitarians, the Shakers have virtually vanished as a religious group, although they were a relatively popular offshoot of the Quakers in the nineteenth century.
    d. Copper is a useful element because it is a good conductor of heat and is used in alloys like brass and bronze, in addition.

  4. Revise the following sentences to make them parallel, balanced, or both. Where appropriate, use correlative conjunctions to bind the two parts.
    a. Women should earn just as much as the opposite sex, and I think they also ought to be able to feel as good about themselves as females.
    b. People should save their money so that they can put it in investments of one kind or another, but money earning something would be important, too.
    c. Although he thought he was probably extremely prejudiced, behaving in a fair manner was something he knew he was capable of doing.
    d. He was an excellent plumber, and I was surprised to learn that he worked really well doing carpenter work.

VARIETY: CHANGING THE PACE

There may come a time in your writing when you want to take a chance and try something different, something you haven't tried and don't see very often in your school reading. When that mood strikes, go ahead. Dive in. Here we describe two ways to vary the construction of sentences — inverting the natural order and using fragments.

Inverting the Natural Order

A writer's natural inclination is to move through a sentence from subject to verb to object—along the way, of course, hanging modifiers on the spine. Most of the time, this is how you will construct your sentences. But occasionally you may want to try an unusual construction, like

A genius he isn't.

By inverting the natural order, you undercut your reader's expectations and quicken his or her interest. Used sparingly, inversion can transform a bland sentence into a sharp one. Compare

We shall always have the poor with us.

with

The poor we shall always have with us.

Using Fragments

A sentence is a fragment if it lacks either a subject or a verb, or if it contains a dependent clause but no independent clause.

Walking fast in order to get home by dusk.
The building designed by Frank Lloyd Wright.
Because I said so.

Although they are grammatical errors — sentences must contain both a subject and a verb — fragments sometimes appear in published works; we have used a few in this book. Employed rarely and carefully, a fragment can add a little zing to writing.

Had you gotten off the Harbor Freeway and driven into Watts before the 1965 riots, you would have seen the scars of official indifference. For Watts had been forgotten by those responsible for the city. On either side of the freeway you would have seen once-pleasant houses now with broken windows and crumbling walls, once-verdant gardens now junk heaps, a once-prosperous commercial area now half-occupied and wholly dilapidated. You would have seen teenagers — and adults — lounging against liquor stores, with absolutely nothing in the world better to do. What were the elements that turned their quiet lethargy into violent rebellion? *A very hot summer day. Some radio and television stations hungry for news. A handful of frightened police officers. A small event.*

When experienced writers use fragments, they prepare the ground so carefully that the reader understands the ideas very well and can supply the missing words without thinking.

An occasional and deliberately designed fragment can intensify a thought and add complexity to a paragraph. But you must take great care to lay the groundwork and make sure that the meaning is clear and the writing smooth. We have a peculiar rule for writing fragments: don't ever write a fragment unless you know that is what you are doing.

Summing Up the Sentence

Short sentences are fine. They say what they came to say. Then they leave. They are clear. They are direct. They are efficient. They can be punchy. But they can become exhausting. Too many in a row will not do. Your readers will get irritated. They will put down your writing. You will lose them. Try again.

And so the time comes when you wish you had written, not sentences with more wit, for your sentences were clever enough; and not even stronger sentences, for those short ones were as strong as an uppercut; but longer sentences, sentences that took their time getting to their appointed end, sentences that stopped every so often en route to the period to consider not only where they had been but also where they were most likely to be going. However, and this is an important point, the simple act of writing longer sentences, as tantalizing as it may be and as much as it seems to promise greater complexity of thought, wider command of all possible aspects of the subject matter, and that adroitness, that panache, that *je ne sais quoi* for which every writer strives, frequently fails to deliver and all too often becomes a way of stretching out the little you have to say over as many words as you can find to stuff into the sentence in an effort to avoid having to come to the end of saying that little. Your readers will get irritated. They will put down your writing. You will lose them. Try again.

Mix up your sentences. Add a little variety to your writing. Try not to have the same shape sentence after sentence. Include all four constructions: simple, compound, complex, compound-complex. Perhaps a fragment. Why not try an occasional question? Don't get stuck in one rhythm like a skipping phonograph record. Have some long sentences, some medium, some as short as a word. Don't try to dazzle your reader with the brilliance and power of every sentence, but make sure your reader occasionally sits up and takes notice.

TIPS FOR VARIETY

- Be a little adventurous: invert the natural order.
- Try a fragment occasionally.
- Change your pace by mixing up constructions, sentence length, and placement of emphasis.

EXERCISE FOR VARIETY

1. Rewrite the following to give it variety.

The young people in our culture seem to be suffering from a lot of anxiety. This anxiety has many causes. The young people fear they will not have jobs. They won't be able to afford to own houses. Children are expensive. If they have them, will they be able to educate them? And of course they worry about nuclear bombs. When they travel, they worry about terrorism and anti-American feeling abroad. Some people tell them they are lucky anyway. It is possible that they are lucky. But maybe they are not so lucky.

7 / *Working with Words*

> . . . *to go* live *among the* little
> housekeeping *words, the*
> swaggering street-corner *words,*
> *the* honest, working, *money-*
> *saving words, all the forgotten and*
> *neglected citizens of the sacred*
> *and half-forgotten city [of words].*
> – *Sherwood Anderson (1876–1941)*
> *American writer*

When we write, we are always choosing words. Most of our words just appear on the page, without our quite knowing where they come from. Crucial moments arise in writing, however, when we consciously rack our brains for exactly the right words. *Diction* is the art of choosing that right word. It is the art of finding words that will present our thought exactly, clearly, and attractively.

Although words are neither good nor bad but only used well or badly, every word counts. We want to repeat that: every word counts, the ones that just appear on the page and the ones you worry over. Note the different meanings in these sentences:

A dog has fleas.
The dog had fleas.
The dog has the fleas.
The dog has ticks.
The cat has fleas.
The dog has the cat.

Every single word, including the verb as it changes and the article *the*, carries specific meaning. In simple sentences like these, we have no problem. We know whether we mean all dogs or only this one, fleas or ticks, and so on, and we write accordingly. As the ideas become more complicated, however, so does the job of choosing the right words to fit them. As we write and revise, we fret over our choices, conscious and unconscious.

Writers have in common with musicians a reliance on their hearing. We have all known people who have such perfect pitch that they can tell what note the doorbell hits when it rings, and we have all known people who sound as though they are moaning for help when they sing "Jingle Bells." Similarly, some people have a talent, a good ear, for words. They instinctively go for the right one at the right time. What they say sounds right and what they write looks right. Most of us, however, are not so blessed. We have occasional attacks of sickly word choice. A few of us even seem to suffer from chronic tin ear, invariably putting the wrong preposition with a verb or derailing a sentence with the wrong noun.

Like our ear for music, our ear for words can be trained. People who thought they couldn't carry a tune have learned to sing — albeit not in the Metropolitan Opera. And people who thought they could never be happy with pen in hand have learned to write well. This chapter should help you to train your ear and your eye.

Our first piece of advice is this: read and read and read some more. You should read in all directions, but be sure you read good writing. If you are a speed reader, slow down and listen to the words. Try to feel their shape and size and strength and rhythm. Notice the company they keep. When an excellent stylist uses a phrase that you have never used, say it aloud several times and use it in a sentence. Analyze a superb essay. If the words seem strange or awkward, write them down in a notebook. Try them out.

In this chapter, we will discuss working with words to attain precision, economy, vigor, appropriateness, and flair.

WRITING WITH PRECISION

All good prose is precise. Good writers won't settle for a word that is nearly or almost what they mean. The word must convey exactly what they mean. As a soprano would be embarrassed to hit C-

sharp when she meant to hit C, so a careful writer avoids words that
will not communicate a precise meaning.

Connotation and Denotation

Most words have a number of different meanings, or shades of
meaning. Take the word *gross*. It derives from the Latin *grossus*,
which meant "thick." It still means thick. But it has also developed
many additional meanings. To accountants and economists, it means
an overall total, as in *gross national product*. To merchants, it means
twelve dozen of anything ordered. To many people, it means anyone big or overweight. To college students, however, it has come to
mean something disgusting. If we say, "That person is gross, isn't
he?" you might reply, even though he weighs 300 pounds, "On the
contrary, he is the nicest person I know." Because the word *gross*
has one meaning for you and another for us, we would not be communicating.

Words both *denote* — indicate or point to something in the world
— and *connote* — suggest a range of meanings surrounding that
something. Denotation is the explicit meaning. Connotation refers
to all that is associated with the word, the feelings and references it
calls up.

Let's look at the word *government*. According to the primary dictionary definition, *government* means "an organization that exercises authority over a particular political unit." That is its denotation,
on which everyone would agree. Its connotations vary, however.
When some people think of *government*, they think of exorbitant
taxes, corruption, and officials meddling in their private lives. To
them the word connotes something bad. But when others think of
government, they think of law and order, care for the poor, protection and security. To them, *government* connotes something good.

Connotation is composed of the suggestions and feelings that
each word carries with it. It is molded by a word's history — is it
from Old English, like *half-wit*, or from Latin and Italian via French,
like *prestidigitation*? Each word has been shaped by the way people
habitually use it. For instance, people have *hangovers*, but roofs
have *overhangs*. Even a word's physical properties — like sound and
length — help determine its connotation. Think of *niggle, smug,* and

rump as opposed to *worry, self-satisfied,* and *derriere.* Because of all these shades of suggestion, English has few if any exact synonyms, that is, words with precisely the same meaning. Brothers and sisters, yes, but no identical twins.

If a word has several near-synonyms, chances are that each, while denoting the same thing, will connote something slightly different. *Police officer* denotes the same thing as *cop, flatfoot,* and — to those who disliked them in the late 1960s — *pig,* but the connotation worsens with each synonym.

Word choice depends on the situation and the writer's purpose. Was the officer who gave you the speeding ticket a *pleasingly plump police officer* or a *fat pig?* The first phrase has a touch of delicacy and respect; the second suggests you think you were framed and want to fight.

Simple choices, like that between *police officer* and *pig,* don't cause much trouble. When the words are more abstract or remote, however, diction becomes a fine art. Welfare recipients receive *handouts, payments,* or *entitlements,* depending on who is talking. We constantly read, hear, and use phrases like *nuclear freeze, affirmative action,* and *Third World,* and words like *materialism, socialism,* and *gay.* All are loaded with connotation. Handle with care: be sure both you and your audience know exactly what you mean.

We don't have a formula for choosing the right word every time. Good word choosers develop their skill through years of training. We do, however, have a few suggestions.

1. Handle overloaded words with care. Some words, like those just listed, have acquired such a weight of meaning that no two people would agree on their proper definition; writers who use them without thinking risk confusing and misleading their readers. Still, we can hardly talk about politics without using words like *democracy, liberty,* or *equality.* Therefore, our next suggestion:

2. Define your terms. If, for instance, your essay is on entitlement programs, don't assume that your reader will correctly interpret the phrase *safety net.* Fairly early in the essay, provide a definition: "By *safety net,* I mean a package of government benefits that would bring the recipient's income to the government-designated poverty level." (See "Definition: Establishing What a Word Means" in Chapter 5 for a model of a longer definition.)

3. Use your dictionary. It can help you choose the word with the right connotation.

Your Friend the Dictionary

The great dictionary maker himself, Samuel Johnson (1709–1784), said, "Dictionaries are like watches; the worst is better than none, and the best cannot be expected to go quite true." While it may not "go quite true," a good dictionary can be a writer's valuable friend, and most writers keep one close at hand.

You may be surprised at all you can find in a dictionary. It will give you preferred pronunciation — sometimes you have a choice, as with *pajamas* and *advertisement*. It will tell you where to divide between syllables — is it *in-nards* or *inn-ards*? It will provide synonyms and antonyms. If it is a fairly good dictionary, it will also trace the derivation of a word, whether it comes from Greek, Latin, Old English, or another language, and what prefix or suffix is appropriate for it — whether, for instance, we *legitimize* or *legitimate*.

The surprise about good dictionaries is that they can inform us about not only denotation but also connotation. The word *tolerate*, for example, has several meanings in most dictionaries: (1) to allow without opposing or prohibiting; (2) to recognize and respect the rights, opinions, and practices of others; (3) to bear or put up with someone or something not especially liked. Follow these denotations a bit and you will arrive at the word's various connotations: indifference, appreciation, mild hostility.

The *Oxford English Dictionary*, known familiarly as the OED, is a veritable education in itself. It contains nearly a half million English words and over a million and a half quotations illustrating their use at various times in history. It traces the development of words and their meanings in detail. Not many of us can afford to own this publication, but almost every library has a copy. Browse through the OED and learn more about the wonderful world of words.

In that corner stands the dictionary, in this corner the thesaurus. The latter is popular with writers because it contains synonyms (and often antonyms) for words.

At this point, we want to flash a giant caution sign. A thesaurus is a good servant but a bad master. What it gives you are all the rough equivalents for your word; what it does not give are differences in connotation. Beware: a near-synonym may have the proper denotation but a wrong connotation.

Some writers are afraid of repeating a word, so they run to the thesaurus for a synonym. Or they fear that their vocabulary doesn't sound intelligent enough, and the next time *policeman* pops up in an essay on crime prevention, it appears as *constable* or *minion of the law*. Imagine a love letter:

Dear Laura,

I have been sitting next to you all day and just can't believe how pretty you are. Your voice is like music, and your eyes are like moonlight. I know that beauty isn't skin deep, for I saw you laughing at our teacher, which shows good sense. I think we could get on well together. Let me know what you think.

Love,
Name Withheld

Fearing that Laura would find his note unexciting, the writer scurried to his thesaurus. There, of course, he found all sorts of replacements for his plain words. The trouble was, the resulting stew of mismatched words would have sent even the most receptive Laura into paroxysms of laughter.

Dear Laura,

I have been straddling you daily and simply cannot fathom how comely you are. Your vociferation approximates a sonata, and your peepers resemble lunar illumination. I comprehend that pulchritude isn't subcutaneous, for I ogled you sniggering at our pedagogue, which illustrates beneficent cranial capacity. I formulate in my mind that we would have a positive response to each other. Inform me of what you reason about.

Charity,
Name Withheld

This writer is not necessarily stupid — he just doesn't trust his natural, comfortable vocabulary. Luckily for him, his pedant/instructor/educator intercepted the missive/epistle/correspondence and saved him some embarrassment/incommodity/loss of face.

If you use a thesaurus, use it along with — not in place of — your dictionary and your own imagination. Use it to remind yourself of what you already know — to draw out a word momentarily forgotten or to help you find a more exact word. Don't use it to inflate your language.

The Idiom

Do we go to town or downtown or uptown? Should we nurse our cold or nurture it or nourish it? When we are under the weather, are we out in the rain or inside the house? When we pass an exam, do we say hello? Few dictionaries and no thesaurus will answer these questions. Nor are there any rules that will predict their answers. When a word is chosen and in what context is a matter not of decree but of accepted usage — idiom.

Idiom refers to the way native speakers speak a language and good writers write it. Idiom is the customary way people put words together, the peculiar twist that a group gives to its language. Americans look under the *hood* of the car and put their tools in the *trunk*, while the British look under the *bonnet* and put their tools in the *boot*. Southerners say, "I'm fixing to eat dinner," but you would not hear that sentence from a northerner.

For nonnative speakers, idiom is the hardest part of a language to master. It does not follow rules the way grammar does. In answer to the question *Who wants to shampoo the Great Dane?* most of us will cry, *Not me* — bad grammar but good idiom. And *Cecil spent all his hardly earned cash* is good grammar but bad idiom. Nonnative speakers often use words that seem fine to them but are simply not idiomatic: *I have traveled a long space* or *I cannot tell you how much indignation I feel to this proposal.* Both sentences sound wrong, but try to say why. Try to explain why a student can be *late* or *tardy* for school but why a party may begin *late* in the afternoon but not *tardy*. Or why a case of pneumonia, though it is always *bad*, is never *reprehensible*, but a mean act is both.

If you grew up speaking English, its ins and outs are second nature to you. Even so, you may still be uncertain about some idioms. Again, use your dictionary if a phrase you have written does not sound right to you. And keep an ear out — not *on* or *in* or *at* — for the often irrational twists and turns that idiom takes.

Specificity

To write with precision means to prefer the specific to the general term. The difference between specific and general is the difference between *Aunt Tabitha* and *woman*, or *bow tie* and *item of clothing*. A specific word refers to the individual item, the thing itself. A general word encompasses all the items of a kind or class.

The specific and the general are not opposites but matters of degree. In the following lists you can see increasing specificity:

> crime, felony, murder, first-degree murder, the murder of Jesse James
>
> food, meal, entrée, chicken Kiev, the chicken Kiev I burned last night

As our words become more specific, the ideas they refer to become more concrete, an image in the mind of the reader. The reader can imagine the prostrate body of Jesse James and the burned chicken Kiev. The more concrete the language, the closer the reader will come to understanding what you mean. And to enjoying what you write.

Sometimes writers use abstract terms when they could replace them with something hard and specific. It happens all the time.

> Albany sent fire-fighting equipment to the scene of the fire.

A few concrete images can make the sentence more visual, more interesting, and more informative.

> Governor Cuomo ordered bulldozers, fire trucks, and air transport carriers to the forest fire near Elmira.

A sentence like

> Emperor Nero of Rome was obese.

is not incorrect, but

> Emperor Nero of Rome weighed 360 pounds.

is much more interesting. The writer bores us with

> An official said that the United States suffered recently from economic problems.

but might get us to read further with

> The United States suffered from record-setting trade deficits and high interest rates in the late '70s, according to Genevieve duPres of the Treasury Department.

In these sentences, the writers changed abstract nouns (*equipment, problems*) into concrete nouns (*bulldozers, trade deficits*), vague descriptions (*an official, recently*) into concrete terms (*Genevieve duPres, the late '70s*). *Obese* only skittered across the surface of Nero's fatness; the revision gives us the fat emperor pound for pound.

Sometimes we use abstract words like *truth, beauty,* or *goodness* without thinking about them. When we do, our audience may have only the vaguest idea of what we mean. If communicating ideas is what writing is about — and it is — we had better find ways to clothe our thought in terms that precisely convey it.

Remember our failed love letter? How likely was it that Laura would know what "we would have a positive response to each other" meant? A positive response could be anything from a passionate embrace to a belly laugh.

Writers need not express difficult ideas in abstract terms or dress them in vague and high-toned language. The evolutionary biologist Stephen Jay Gould handles abstract concepts as a scientist but grounds them in the concrete. In discussing Freud's idea that to ensure civilization, human beings must "renounce more and more of our innate selves," Gould writes,

> Freud's argument is a particularly forceful variation on a ubiquitous theme in speculations about "human nature." What we criticize in ourselves, we attribute to our animal past. These are the shackles of our apish ancestry — brutality, aggression, selfishness; in short, general nastiness. What we prize and strive for (with pitifully limited success), we consider as a unique overlay, conceived by our rationality and imposed upon an unwilling body. Our hopes for a better future lie in reason and kindness — the mental transcendence of our biological limitations. "Build thee more stately mansions, O my soul." (Stephen Jay Gould, *Ever Since Darwin*)

Gould makes these complex ideas clear by using specific, familiar language. Having clarified what Freud meant, he can now refer simply to "Freud's argument." He concludes with a line from a once-popular poem by Oliver Wendell Holmes.

An abstract term can serve as shorthand for a set of specific ideas or images. Once you have made your point clear, you will often use an abstract term to stand for that point. In a discussion of the fire in Elmira, for instance, you would not continue to say "bulldozers, fire trucks, and air transport carriers." You would just say "the equipment." First, however, be sure you bring your ideas out into the concrete world you share with your reader.

TIPS FOR PRECISION

- Consider both what a word denotes and what it connotes before you use it.
- Read all the information about a word in the dictionary.
- Resort to a thesaurus with a critical eye and consult it along with, not instead of, your dictionary.
- Be as concrete and specific as you can.

EXERCISES FOR PRECISION

1. For each of the following pairs of synonyms, write a sentence in which either would fit: *hold/grasp, evening/dusk, throttle/choke, obsequious/humble, humiliate/embarrass, refuse/garbage, teeth/dentures, inebriated/drunk, crazy/insane.* Discuss the connotations and analyze how the sounds of these words do or do not reinforce their meanings.

2. For each of the following phrases, provide at least three synonyms that carry different connotations:
   a. unwillingness to change one's mind
   b. an object that costs less than one expected
   c. not telling the truth
   d. one's parent of the opposite sex
   e. a member of the House of Representatives

3. Go to a large dictionary, preferably the OED, and look up the following pairs of words: *empathy/sympathy, enormity/enormousness, notoriety/notoriousness, uninterested/disinterested, ensure/insure.* Write a paragraph comparing the meanings of each pair.

4. Practice using a large dictionary by investigating the derivations of the following words: *engineer, sarcasm, gossip, oxygen, circle, correspondent.* Write a paragraph about two of them, tracing their meanings from their earliest usage to the present.

5. Make the following sentences more concrete or specific:
   a. The creature took the food into the room.
   b. Attendance at secondary educational institutions has been correlated with participation in athletic endeavors.
   c. The woman took down the garment and concealed it about her person without the store personnel's awareness and then went to the escalator and descended.

> **d.** When exposure and malnutrition are present, support from various levels of government should be forthcoming.

WRITING WITH ECONOMY

Some people write as though they believe that the more words, the better the writing. Of course, that is not true. We have all read passages in which the writing sags from sheer volume of verbiage.

Good writing is efficient. By efficient we mean possessing two qualities: precision and brevity. In the previous section, we discussed precision and how to achieve it. In this section we discuss how to be brief and economical with words.

Excess Baggage

> "Under the impression," said Mr. Micawber, "that your peregrinations in this metropolis have not as yet been extensive, and that you might have some difficulty penetrating the arcana of the modern Babylon . . . in short," said Mr. Micawber in a burst of confidence, "that you might lose your way . . ." (Charles Dickens, *David Copperfield*)

Mr. Micawber takes twenty-nine words to say what he could have said in six. He is a spendthrift with words. In contrast, good writers work with tight budgets. They look for that one word that will do the work of ten. This stinginess is much to their credit, for in English the longer and the more repetitious the statement, the weaker.

Here is a sentence from a student paper that is laboring under a great deal of excess baggage:

> Carl Sagan opens up an area of interest to me with the content of his essay, which cites explanations of how monkeys can be observed to learn to communicate through the use of language.

Even the most physically fit reader would sweat under that load.

The writer repacked. If the area is *of interest to me*, then it is *interesting*, period. The *content of his essay* is nothing more than *his essay,* so *content*, farewell. *Can be observed to learn* is really an empty suitcase, because the focus is not on someone's observing, but on the monkeys' learning. *The use of language* is only a long way of saying *language*. So now the writer had

> Carl Sagan opens up an interesting area with his essay, which cites explanations of how monkeys can learn to communicate through language.

From thirty-four words down to twenty-two without losing a thing. With such success, the writer became a little bolder and began to change some verbs and nouns around. *Cites explanations* became *explains*. Then she realized that *opens up an interesting area* could be tucked into the word *interesting* and tagged onto *essay*. She was down to thirteen words, and a much more vigorous sentence.

> In his interesting essay, Carl Sagan explains how monkeys can learn to communicate.

> In the next few pages, we discuss the kinds of surplus that you can easily jettison.

Blah Phrases. Sometimes your prose will be invaded by blah phrases, groups of uninteresting words that contribute nothing to your sentence. Whenever you see tiny words in your sentences, beware. *It, that, of, do,* and many more are waiting to weigh down your sentences. They form flocks: *due to the fact that, in the event that, it is also of importance that, when it comes to, in the matter of, has to do with.* Flocks of tiny words can be a bad omen in writing. They burden your reader.

> Due to the fact that the death of the previous captain had to do with a quarrel over a black hen, the effect is that of providing a preview of what Marlow himself will face in the future.

We can eliminate many of these tiny words.

> Because the previous captain died after a quarrel over a black hen, Marlow understands what he will face.

Frequently, we can translate a flock of tiny words into a single one: *in the event that* can become *if, has to do with* can become *concerns,* and *when it comes to* can usually shrink to *when.* As in the example, *due to the fact that* can become the simple *because.*

Blah phrases do not necessarily consist of tiny words; they are often simply long ways of expressing things. Sometimes they conceal perfectly good ideas.

> Lincoln decided that he would go to Ford's Theater to see the play even though he had been somewhat disturbed by thoughts that there might be some kind of danger if he went.

We can often find energetic one- or two-word substitutes for these limp strings.

> Despite his premonitions of danger, Lincoln went to Ford's Theater to see the play.

Twenty blah words at the end of the original have condensed to five crisp words beginning the revision.

In revising, we can often condense overlong modifying clauses or phrases — especially *who* or *which* clauses that end a sentence — into an adjective or shorter phrase with the same meaning and then embed that adjective elsewhere in the sentence. Finding an equivalent will sometimes take some imagination; just as often, though, it is quite easy.

> The emperor, who had been drinking to the point of intoxication, staggered here and there through Rome, until he eventually found a place to sleep in the garbage dump, which all the Romans used.

can easily become

> The emperor, drunk and staggering through Rome, eventually slept in the Roman garbage dump.

Redundancy.   *Redundant* refers to words used when the meaning is clear without them. We culled this from a newspaper:

> We will do all we can to do everything in our power to see that the incumbent does not return to the White House as president for a second term.

We certainly got the point, but we could have gotten it more quickly and enjoyably if we hadn't had to push our way through all the unnecessary verbiage. After all, *all we can* is *everything in our power,* and if the incumbent returns as president, that will be a *second term,* and surely it will be to *the White House.*

Repetition is not bad in itself and can sometimes come in handy. We may want to emphasize a point by repeating it, as in "I said no, No, NO!" — but we should be on our guard. Redundancies are useless repetitions; they creep into speech and once there are hard to extricate. How many times have you heard *the general public* instead of *the public, the stadium's total capacity* instead of *the stadium's capacity, personally I think* instead of just *I think,* or *my close personal friend* instead of *my friend?*

Redundancies appear in several guises. Often writers use a modifier for a noun or verb that already contains the modifier's meaning.

Thomas Edison was the original inventor of the electric light bulb.

Inventor means "originator," and the only thing we call a *light bulb* is electric. We should settle for

Thomas Edison invented the light bulb.

Sometimes writers pile on adjectives with the same meaning.

She did not strike him as an open-minded, impartial, or objective judge.

These adjectives mean about the same thing. Any one alone is ample.

She did not strike him as an impartial judge.

Occasionally an idea already implied in one part of a sentence is made explicit elsewhere.

Unlike his friend Cassius, who seems to have made his decision quickly in comparison with Brutus, Brutus has made his decision slowly, as his opening words show.

Because this sentence obviously presents a comparison, the phrase *in comparison with* is redundant. The writer can imply Cassius's quickness by focusing on Brutus's slowness.

Unlike Cassius, Brutus has made his decision slowly, as his opening words show.

This problem is harder to identify and avoid than simple one-word redundancies; the best prevention is to pay close attention to the meaning of your sentence. Develop your "redundancy detector." Weed out useless repetitions in pursuit of spare, efficient English.

Long, Running Jumps and Expletive Openers. Look for excess baggage in the beginning of the sentence. Some sentences take a long run before leaping into the thought. In the following sentence, so many words run by that the reader would have to watch the replay to remember the subject:

Clearly, activity in the oil industry over the last ten months is indicative of the fact that, far from being on a decided wane, the efforts of OPEC and cartels like it are all the more likely to continue.

The sentence improves with a shorter run.

Oil profits for the last ten months show that, far from waning, the success of OPEC and cartels like it is likely to continue.

That was a loose sentence. The problem of the long running jump is particularly acute, however, in periodic sentences that begin with a subordinate clause or a lengthy phrase.

Even if it were true that you and your mate enjoy a perfect marriage, it would still be just as true that, if certain sociologists are to be believed, there are 125,000 other possible mates who would suit you just as well.

From the revision, we realize that the sentence contains an interesting idea.

Even if you and your mate enjoy a perfect marriage, certain sociologists claim that 125,000 other possible mates would suit you just as well.

Many long, running jumps start with *It is* or *There are*. This opening is called the *expletive*, meaning that *It* or *There* acts as the formal (though not the real) subject of the sentence. Sometimes expletive openers are the most appropriate way to start a sentence. They are, for instance, wonderful for pointing out things that simply exist. The first line of Jane Austen's *Pride and Prejudice* is

It is a truth universally acknowledged, that a single man in possession of a good fortune must be in want of a wife.

And sometimes no other opener can capture just the right mood.

There is a tavern in the town, in the town. . . .

Frequently, however, the expletive seems to obfuscate more than it clarifies, as in this sentence regarding intervention in international currency markets:

There were occasions when there was agreement to intervene and to intervene in a coordinated manner. There was some concerted intervention after January 31 and last week.

Sometimes the expletive only condemns the reader to additional words that postpone the moment of truth.

It is true that many people believe there are some ways in which football has become the national pastime.

The revision is compact, like a running back.

Many people believe football has become the national pastime.

We can hardly talk without the expletive, for it gives us time to shape our thoughts. But when we write, and therefore have time to revise, we ought to cast away unnecessary baggage, and that often means the expletive. We are not suggesting that you never use *It is* or *There are* — they have their uses. You just should not overuse them or fall back on them to avoid a little extra effort or thought.

Qualifiers Vague, Timid, or Loud

Three kinds of qualifiers — vague, timid, and loud — are often verbal fillers rather than informative elements in a written sentence.

Vague Qualifiers.   Often writers use words like *very, actually,* and *really* to pump up adjectives. But these vague qualifiers frequently have the opposite effect. The unadorned

That rhinoceros was huge.

suggests more hugeness than

That rhinoceros was really very huge.

How big is *very*? How real is *really*? It was huge, period.

By overusing vague qualifiers, we diminish the power of language. The word *terribly* once meant "in a manner to cause fear and dread," as in *The wounded rhino closing in on me roared terribly*. Now we blithely say, *I had a terribly good time at your tea party*. The word *terribly* is, like the rhino, wounded, but it lacks the energy to roar. We can no longer convey in a single word "in a manner to cause fear and dread."

We are not suggesting that you should or could make every sentence absolute (few get close enough to say, *The rhino weighed 847 pounds and head to tail measured 9.33 feet*). And we are not saying you should rid yourself of every *very*. If *very* is as close as you can get to what you mean, and the context makes the meaning clear, then you should use the word. But do not lean on vague qualifiers to avoid making careful assessments.

Timid Qualifiers.   Counsins to the vague qualifiers are the timid qualifiers. How big is *a bit*? To what degree is *somewhat*? Is *a lot* the same as *a good deal* or is it more like *much*? How much is *rather*?

Like their kin, these words pop up almost unbidden. They may save you the work of being precise, but they can blur your writing. If we say, *East German swimmers are rather superior,* what do we mean? Do we mean that they won one more race than the competition, or that they won all the races but by a narrow margin? If we say, *Our friend is somewhat of a hypochondriac,* do we suggest one major complaint a week or a dozen minor ones each day?

No writer can do without timid qualifiers; indeed, they keep prose responsible. They are reminders of the imprecision of estimates and the tentativeness of opinions. You should not pretend to a certainty you do not possess. But use these qualifiers only when they convey your thought as precisely as possible.

Loud Qualifiers. Loud qualifiers also add verbiage without much meaning. "Oh wow! That is absolutely the most *fantastic* thing I ever heard! That's just *incredible!*" Perhaps you know people who talk like this. You may even like their enthusiasm. But when they talk this way all the time, complete with exclamation points, italics, flashing lights, and explosions, you probably begin to wonder what they find important.

The problem with constant emphasis, whether in writing or in speech, is that it fails to make distinctions. What did the person find so *fantastic* and *incredible?* Did someone rise from the dead? That is indeed incredible. Did a rich uncle die, bequeathing an island off the coast of Greece? That does sound like a fantasy. If, however, the writer just attended a movie, maybe it was only *good,* or — to be more informative — maybe *the acting was effective* or *the camera work helped convey the mood. Incredibles* and *fantastics* do not tell what somebody thinks. "How was the movie?" "Fantastic!" "But how was the movie?"

Careful writers avoid artificially emphatic words. They try to convey their enthusiasms without shouting. They want to show their readers exactly what excited them.

Wasteful Constructions

The requirements of the thought should determine the size and construction of a sentence. Overextended, a sentence can appear awkward or even incomprehensible.

> When he was in the village, he saw the timbered houses, which had been built by the colonists, who brought the style from England, and they were now occupied by the aborigines, who had entered the village after the colonists had retreated.

In revising, the writer wisely broke the sentence into two:

> When he was in the village, he saw the timbered houses, which had been built by the colonists in a style brought from England. Ever since the colonists had retreated, the aborigines had occupied the houses.

The passage gains in both clarity and strength. Never do violence to the complexity or subtlety of your thought, but when you can shorten and simplify, do so.

The English language offers numerous ways to compress thoughts without changing meaning. Sometimes you can move elements around and substitute a few words for a long clause.

> Dirty tricks in political campaigns are as old as the American republic, and they will probably be around until its end because they have frequently been effective when politicians have resorted to them.

Compressed, the sentence is easier to read:

> Frequently effective, dirty tricks in political campaigns are as old as the American republic and will probably be around until its end.

The writer combines the two independent clauses into one main clause. *Frequently effective* takes the place of *because they have frequently been effective when politicians have resorted to them*. The writer does not mention *politicians* because the reader can assume the word from the main clause.

We can also use appositives to condense. *Appositive* refers to a word or group of words placed beside a noun or noun substitute to supplement its meaning. An appositive can take the place of a wordy clause.

> Cairo, which is the largest city on the African continent, has a daytime population estimated at 12 million, which is 2 million more than its estimated nighttime population.

can become

> Cairo, Africa's largest city, has a daytime population estimated at 12 million, 2 million more than its estimated nighttime population.

Changing a dependent clause to an adjective phrase can often create a shorter, more energetic sentence.

Philadelphia, which is called the City of Brotherly Love because it was founded as a Quaker colony, served as the American capital during the Revolution.

can become

Founded as a Quaker colony and called the City of Brotherly Love, Philadelphia served as the American capital during the Revolution.

You may have noticed that many of the changes we recommend get rid of a *which* clause. As a general caution, beware the *which* clause, which is much overused, which is a shame, which is an example. *Which* clauses tend to inefficiency as well as windiness.

We are not suggesting you should excise all clauses that begin with *which*. Here, for instance, is an elegantly turned sentence.

Punishment, which is inflicted by all civilized societies, is not a virtue but a necessity.

No serious writer could do without the word *which*. But when saving words, check the *which* clauses.

TIPS FOR ECONOMY

- Look for blah phrases and cut them out of your prose.
- Remove, delete, and get rid of redundancies and saying the same thing twice.
- Remember that expletive openers are often not necessary.
- Watch out for vague, timid, or loud but empty qualifiers.
- Remember that the complexity of a sentence should be determined by the complexity of the thought.
- When you can shorten and simplify without distorting meaning, do it.
- Look for the *which* clause when you are searching for excess.

EXERCISES FOR ECONOMY

1. Reduce the following sentences to a minimum without losing sense:
   a. In view of the fact that she is a person who is likely to monopolize the conversational talk, men and women alike have experienced a wish to go elsewhere and in fact do go elsewhere when she is speaking.

    b. It is unbelievable for you to say that if a person who smoked marijuana regularly did not fear that he or she might come into conflict with the law in an unpleasant manner and subsequently serve time in a jail, marijuana would very likely be smoked in public places more often than in fact it now is.

    c. When people are a bit too quick to do things, it is a fact that they often end up making an awesome mess of what they are trying to do.

    d. It is a fact that many human beings, including both men and women, who stay up late at night seeking excitement in its very many guises and in all ways driving themselves a bit too much, may find that later in life their chances to live to a ripe old age have been in point of fact fabulously curtailed.

2. Exchange with a partner two paragraphs from an essay you wrote for an earlier assignment. Revise each other's paragraphs for economy. At the same time, revise your own paragraphs. Discuss the effectiveness of the changes.

3. Find two- or three-word substitutes for the italicized parts of the following sentences:

    a. My father was a *person who was born and lived in Italy before he came to the United States.*

    b. *He uses a lot of words that repeat each other.*

    c. My mother married *when she was very young and in fact was not even twenty years old.*

    d. Franklin Roosevelt *was the thirty-second president of the United States and was the only president to be reelected three times.*

4. Write a sentence or two describing four of the following subjects:

    a. baking cookies or bread

    b. a track-and-field event

    c. the last election

    d. tying your shoes

    e. balancing a stick on your forehead

    f. walking a dog without a leash

Use as many words as you can and still make sense. Try to include all the kinds of excess baggage. Afterwards, revise the sentences to convey the same information in as few words as possible.

5. Using appositives, revise these sentences to make them less wordy:

    a. Auburn is a university in the state of Alabama, and it has an agricultural school and an architectural school.

    b. Abraham Lincoln, who was a citizen of Illinois though he was born in Kentucky, was the sixteenth president of the United States.

    c. The Napa Valley, which is famous for its many varieties of wine, is located just north of San Francisco.

WRITING WITH VIGOR

Some writing seems crisp and energetic; other writing seems limp and tired. We have already dealt with some of the causes of limp, tired writing, like imprecision and verbosity. Here we give direct advice on how to make your writing more vigorous.

Be Active

The verb makes things happen in your sentence. It provides muscle. It generates energy. If your sentence begins to sag, blame the verb. If it zings home its meaning, credit the verb. Your choice of verbs can make all the difference in your sentences.

Active and Passive Voice.   English verbs come in two voices: active and passive.

    The firefighter grabbed the hose.
    The hose was grabbed by the firefighter.

The first sentence is in the active voice. The subject (*the firefighter*) performs the action (*grabbed*). The second sentence is in the passive voice. The subject of this sentence (*the hose*) receives the action (*was grabbed*). The passive consists of the past participle of a verb (*grabbed*) preceded by some form of the verb *to be* (*was*).

For good reason, most good writers prefer the active voice. It is clearer and more direct, and it packs more punch. Also, it immediately identifies the responsible actor.

    Bill struck Tom.
    Professor Beerbohm spilled coffee on my term paper.

We know exactly and immediately who did what to whom. Passive voice tends to be unemphatic and wordy.

Tom was struck by Bill.

It is sometimes evasive:

Coffee was spilled on my term paper.

Thus does Professor Beerbohm escape blame.

Much official writing resorts to the passive voice, frequently erasing all signs of personal responsibility.

It has been decided that farm subsidies must be decreased.

This sentence makes it sound as though a disembodied law of nature made this fiscal decision rather than the people announcing it. If they recast their sentence in the active voice, they would have to admit that

We have decided to decrease farm subsidies.

Some student writers employ the passive because they think it sounds more important.

It is agreed by most scholars that the superego was meant by Freud to be portrayed as a force by which the id is prevented from getting what it wants.

Four passive constructions in a single sentence are not so much weighty as wooden. In an effort to remove all evidence of the passive, the student revised the sentence.

Most scholars agree that Freud meant to portray the superego as a force that prevents the id from getting what it wants.

She reduced thirty words to twenty-two and wrote a much clearer, more direct, more active, more enjoyable, and more informative sentence.

The passive voice is not always bad. You should not tie yourself into a pretzel to avoid it. Sometimes it is awkward to state the subject of the sentence. If you just want to say

Los Angeles is well supplied with water.

it would distort your meaning to twist the sentence into active voice this way:

Canals, conduits, pipes, and a series of reservoirs supply ample water to Los Angeles.

Sometimes we do not know the subject of a sentence. It is only natural to write

The game at Candlestick Park was called on account of fog and rain.

instead of

National League officials called the game at Candlestick Park on account of fog and rain.

When used with finesse and restraint, the passive voice can even add variety to prose.

The slumbering household was slowly awakened by the twittering of tiny birds.

The problem is misuse. Pseudoscientific and pseudoofficial prose is everywhere, tempting writers into the passive voice. Resist. Write in the active voice whenever you can.

Vigorous Verbs.   Many dynamic verbs are vanishing into extinction. And some of the best are being converted into nouns, leaving the work of sentences to weak, deflated verbs. In this sentence,

The police made an investigation into reports of explosions near the Capitol.

the writer has turned a fine verb — *to investigate* — into a noun — *investigation* — and the uninteresting verb *to make* has taken over the action. Result: more words, less action. The rewrite,

The police investigated reports of explosions near the Capitol.

saves three words and restores the action.

Some writers apparently abhor the powerful and direct use of good verbs. According to them, people don't *need* things: they *are in need of* them. People do not *approve* of things: they *give their approval* to them. We could change

She made a face.	to	She winced.
He goes on a bit.		He chatters.
I have admiration for		I admire
You will show deference to		You will defer to

Writers are sometimes seduced from the specific by fancy sounding verbs, like *interact, relate, impact,* and *deal with.* Unfortunately, in meaning almost anything, verbs like these mean almost nothing.

I interacted with Alex yesterday.

What did the writer do with Alex? Did she kiss him? stab him? hand him a subpoena? All these would be *interactions*, but no one knows exactly what happened.

Likewise, *impact* as a verb has almost no impact.

> Brazil's failure to meet its debt obligations has impacted upon American interest rates.

Was the effect good or was it bad? You can always replace *impact* with a more specific action:

> Brazil's failure to meet its debt obligations has driven up American interest rates.

Perhaps less blatant but still debilitating is writing that contains an abundance of general-purpose verbs like *go, seem, do, make, have,* and *become.* While useful beasts of burden, these verbs cannot carry the specific meanings that vivid prose demands. As much as possible, good writers choose verbs that tell exactly what the action was. Here is a sentence much in need of a good verb:

> To ingest plant fiber has a positive effect on the risk of heart disease.

As readers, we must use our imaginations to find our way through this. Just what does *has a positive effect on* really mean here? Is there a verb out there that will say the same thing? Perhaps *decreases* will do; it is certainly more active than *has* and tells us something more precise about those plant fibers.

> To ingest plant fiber decreases the risk of heart disease.

> When you revise your prose, seek verbs with energy.

Not *to be*. You may have noticed that forms of *to be* crop up frequently in inactive sentences. This verb links the subject of the sentence to a word or words that describe the subject's condition.

> Max is a friendly Doberman pinscher. He really is.

> The town with the lowest zip code number in the United States is Agawam, Massachusetts.

> I am Gunga Din.

The little verb *to be* is one of the most necessary verbs in English. Many sentences would not be without it. For instance, you couldn't convey a complete thought by saying

> I hungry!
> The baby disgruntled!
> The bathtub overflowing!

With so many forms of *to be* around, however, writers can fall into the habit of using them for almost everything. Verb deflation frequently occurs because we use forms of the verb *to be* followed by a noun followed by a preposition.

> This argument is demonstrative of
> This episode is an example of

These sentences have lost the services of the vigorous verbs *demonstrates* and *exemplifies*.

We tend to overwork the verb *to be* in other ways as well. We can turn a static condition into an action by writing

> Demosthenes spoke more effectively than Cato did.

instead of

> Demosthenes was a more effective speaker than Cato was.

We can make

> If it had not been for the unfair taxes the British imposed, there might not have been an American Revolution.

shorter and more energetic by writing

> Without unfair British taxation, the Americans might not have revolted.

Very long and complicated sentences often rely too heavily on forms of the verb *to be*.

> Stein is saying that American governing philosophy is in a situation where it is becoming an area that is under the domination of men who are not really sincere about what is good for the public, men who are attracted only by what is advantageous to them and to the special interests that it is their function to represent.

As this sentence shows, when a writer overuses the verb *to be*, other problems frequently emerge. The revision, short and to the point, eliminates many *to be*s, the passive voice, and verbosity.

> Stein maintains that the men who have dominated American governing philosophy are less interested in the public good than in their own advantage and that of the special interests they represent.

In revising a first draft, try circling each occurrence of *to be* (don't forget to include *is, am, have been,* and other forms) and search for a better word. You won't be able to change every one (nor should you), but try especially hard to reword when you see bunches of circles.

Prefer People

Imagine being confronted with the following sentence:

> Renouncing a former state to obtain real existence is an adjustment requiring understanding of what is seen, comprehending its causes, and coping with it.

Can you figure out who is doing the renouncing, or who must adjust, understand, comprehend, and cope? The sentence is depopulated, yet the writer seems to be writing about human beings.

Now look at the sentence:

> In order to renounce their former state and improve themselves, clients must understand how they perceive the world, why they perceive it that way, and how they can cope with it.

Although a little longer, the sentence is much clearer and more interesting. We know who is doing what.

Why did the writer depopulate that sentence? Perhaps he thought impersonal prose sounded more serious. But aren't you more interested in reading about what people do or have done to them? Wouldn't you rather read *The actor playing Othello made the audience weep* than *The performance of the role of Othello brought tears*? Even a small move toward putting people in a sentence can make a difference. People add strength and vibrancy to your sentences.

Impersonal writing can be both boring and confusing, like this passage on how tennis players should choose the food they eat.

> Careful selection of foods containing all the proper nutrients is important for maintaining health and adequate energy. Whether food is prepared at home or eaten out, resistance to disease can be increased and energy rate maximized through careful nutritional food selection.

Tennis players, anywhere? Not a person within a mile of those sentences, although people ought to be doing almost everything in them. You have probably spotted some of the ways the writer has kept the passage impersonal: overuse of the passive voice, nouns where there might be verbs, too many *to be*'s. It doesn't make you want to rush out and try the diet, does it?

A revision puts the people back where they belong.

> To stay healthy and full of energy, tennis players must select foods that contain all the proper nutrients. Whether they cook their meals

at home or eat out, they can better resist disease and maximize their energy by carefully choosing nutritional foods.

We do not think every sentence must contain a person. It would be absurd, perhaps impossible, to try to stick people into sentences like

Art is the accomplice of love. (Remy de Gourmont, 1858–1915)

or

Land is immortal, for it harbors the mysteries of creation. (Anwar Sadat, 1918–1981)

When people are involved, though, good writers put the people in. And they put them in as human beings, not as abstractions or congregations. We wouldn't say *members of the student body* or *members of the electorate.* We would say *students* and *voters.* We ought to follow this natural inclination when we write.

We can go a step further and use the good old names for occupations and professions. When we write *teacher* or even *professor,* we picture a human being, perhaps even someone we know, but when we refer to a teacher as an *educator,* we imagine a faceless bureaucrat. When we write *banker,* again we picture a person, but when we say *financial executive*, we don't even pretend a human being is concealed inside that gray eminence. Indeed, our prose takes on a slightly gray quality itself.

We don't advise you to make everything in your writing sound chatty. As we discuss in Chapter 8, there is a tone appropriate to college writing, and chatty it isn't. But neither is it depopulated. When possible and where appropriate, keep your prose alive with people.

Say It Straight

Even with energetic verbs and people, prose can be flat and uninteresting. Often, the problem is indirectness. Many of us apparently like to hold off saying what we came to say or try to conceal our thought beneath a variety of indirect constructions. Just as English tends to move straight ahead from subject to verb to object, it also works best when it goes straight to the point. Our moral here is "Say it straight." You must help your readers: they don't have time to play hide and seek with your thoughts. You can help them understand your meaning by hacking away the underbrush.

We discuss here three bad habits that often block understanding.

Disclaimers. No doubt you have read *opinions to the contrary not-withstanding, it is conceivable* (or *arguable* or *possible*) *that one might say, an opinion might be hazarded that,* and phrases like these. They may seem like security blankets, but they are more like smoke screens. Some of these disclaimers self-destruct if you think about them; our two favorites are *needless to say* and the immediately comic *needless to repeat.*

Weak-Hearted Negatives. As George Orwell pointed out in his essay "Politics and the English Language," overuse of the negative is a form of circumlocution — "talking around" your meaning. Orwell quotes this sentence:

> I am not, indeed, sure whether it is not true to say that the Milton who once seemed not unlike a seventeenth-century Shelley had not become, out of an experience ever more bitter in each year, more alien to the founder of that Jesuit sect which nothing could induce him to tolerate.

Once you untie all the negatives, you have the following (we think):

> Out of an experience more bitter each year, the Milton who once resembled a seventeenth-century Shelley had come to resemble the founder of that Jesuit sect which nothing could induce him to tolerate.

Less outrageous, but more frequent, is the use of the negative to evade an unpopular opinion: *They did not honor their debts as they had promised* instead of *They reneged,* or *She did not play her clarinet very admirably* instead of *She played her clarinet terribly.* In each case, the first may sound more polite, but the positive is stronger and clearer.

Think of the statements *The president was not inarticulate,* or *The book is not uninteresting.* The reader has to cancel out the double negative and even then cannot be sure what the sentences mean. Was the president articulate or only just a cut above mumbling? Is the book interesting or just this side of the trash basket?

Euphemisms. Writers of euphemisms substitute neutral terms or agreeable words for words with strong or unpleasant associations. They say *salvage engineers* when they mean *junk dealers, remains* when they mean *corpse, fib* when they mean *lie,* and *water closet, comfort station, necessary room,* or almost anything else when they mean *toilet.*

Euphemisms sometimes spare feelings — to say *I'm sorry your mother passed on* might be gentler than to say *I'm sorry your mother died.* Too frequently, though, people slip in soft words to conceal meaning. Hitler used the term *rectification of the frontier* when he forced thousands of people to march miles from their homes; some organizations have referred to murder, execution, or assassination as *termination with extreme prejudice.* These phrases conceal the awful truth: Hitler uprooted large populations; people were killed.

You should try to say exactly what you mean in the most honest manner you can. Try to be graceful rather than crude, of course, but say it straight.

TIPS FOR VIGOR

- Prefer the active voice to the passive.
- Seek vigorous, fresh verbs, and avoid tired, general ones.
- Don't overuse forms of *to be.*
- Put people in any sentences where they can fit.
- Avoid disclaimers, weak-hearted negatives, and euphemisms.

EXERCISES FOR VIGOR

1. Rewrite the following sentences to make them more vigorous:
   a. The decision was announced by the referee and the loud cheers were emitted by Jack Dempsey's supporters.
   b. Open-heart surgery will be performed on me tomorrow.
   c. Absconding with the family heirlooms was the accusation made against Señor Ortega by Señora Isabella.
   d. Asia was overrun by Genghis Khan and the hordes of warriors who had been enticed by him to join his army.

2. Replace the weak verbs in these sentences with more energetic ones.
   a. He made a very tasty sauerbraten and then gave a party.
   b. My cousin went through India in eight days and then came home in a big hurry because she had a job to go to.
   c. Admiral Darlan, who had been the head of the French navy during the Second World War, seemed to become a different

person when he became minister of defense in the Vichy government.

d. My decision was to go to the head of the department and to make a strong case for a raise in what I got in my job.

3. Reread an essay you've written recently and circle every use of the verb *to be*. Then revise the whole essay, using *to be* as little as possible.

4. Revise the following sentences to make them more direct:

a. One is not unwilling to hang-glide although one is not unfamiliar with the difficulties one may encounter.

b. When in the vicinity of vipers capable of making what might be called a fatal attack, I have a tendency to experience unpleasant emotions and to prepare to exit as quickly as possible, in a manner of speaking.

c. Once the animal custodian picked up the little dog, it was not unlikely that in a short period of time the underground engineer would be called in to perform, if he has not been intemperate with alcohol lately, though far be it from me to claim to know about his private habits.

WRITING AN APPROPRIATE PROSE

All of us want our prose to express our sensitivity, our distinctiveness, and our taste. At the same time, we want what we say to fit both the audience and the subject. Yet we sometimes slip into language that does not express what we mean, let alone who we are. In the pages that follow, we examine five ways to avoid sour notes writers can hit.

Choosing Slim Words over Fat Words

Remember that Mr. Micawber said in twenty-nine words what he could have said in six? With this lovable old duffer, Dickens poked fun at people who invariably choose the impressive polysyllabic word rather than the short, familiar one. Mr. Micawber is not alone. You will find inflated language in legal, bureaucratic, academic, technical, and editorial writing.

Winston Churchill said, "Short words are best and the old words when short are best of all." Practically all great literary stylists agree. Yet some writers think that the more complicated and unusual the language, the more serious the thought. Windiness is not elegance, however, and difficulty is not profundity. It is no more elegant and profound to say *Precipitation appears imminent* than to say *It's going to rain.*

Many of the shorter, plainer words in English come from Old English: they preserve the Anglo-Saxon in our language, growling out practical and durable monosyllables: *house, thief, stone, want, help.* Such words are concrete, familiar, and useful. *I want to get an ice cream cone* is more direct and understandable than *I want to procure a frozen gelatinous confection; get* is the functional word you need in this sentence, not the overdressed *procure,* and that *gelatinous confection* sounds nauseating.

The thesaurus provides a list of synonyms for *get,* including *procure, secure,* and *acquire.* These words came into English later than *get,* via Latin and French. Like most travelers of this route, they are longer than their Old English near-equivalent and have connotations that *get* does not. The dictionary tells us that *get* is a "very general term and may or may not imply initiative." *Procure,* however, suggests "effort in obtaining something"; *secure* implies downright "difficulty in getting"; *acquire* has it easy by comparison, implying "an addition to what is already possessed." Good writers would neither abandon *get* just to have more letters and syllables nor use *get* when they mean *procure* or *secure.*

Keep in mind this simple rule from George Orwell: "Never use a long word where a short one will do."

This does not mean that you must speak in Tarzanlike monosyllables. Longer is better when that is the clearest way to say something. Here is Orwell writing clearly but not in monosyllables:

> Now, it is clear that the decline of a language must ultimately have political and economic causes: it is not due simply to the bad influence of this or that individual writer. ("Politics and the English Language")

No one would call that sentence pretentious. The "long words" (*language, political, economic, ultimately, influence, individual*) are all familar ones, and Orwell obviously uses them because they are the ones he needs. No other words mean what those words mean.

If we used only one-syllable words, our essays would be about as subtle as telegrams. Long words often help us to be precise and to convey the right nuance.

Karl Marx said that rich people keep poor people from being free.

is direct, but

Karl Marx's economic theories depict the efforts of the powerful capitalist classes to oppress the workers of the world.

tells us more, and more exactly. *Capitalist classes*, for example, suggests more than just money, and *oppress* implies both action and purpose. The longer sentence is true to Marx's thought. Orwell would have agreed with this corollary to his little rule: use a long word when it, and only it, is the word you need.

Another rule we think Orwell would have agreed with is: when two words bear more or less the same meaning, select the one more familiar and natural to you and your reader. Prefer *limit* to *circumscribe, the rest* to *the remainder,* and *use* to *employ*. Remember that English has a great heritage of short, direct, familiar words. They are where the language began. When we need to be clearest in our writing, they are waiting for us. Readers tire of long parades of peculiar or pompous words, and they become suspicious of the writer who uses them. Writing can be both simple and intelligent. Use complex words only when they carry just the shade of meaning, just the distinction you want.

Prioritizing Dejargonization

Technical terms emerge in every discipline. They take the place of lengthy descriptions or definitions. In law, we speak of *torts* and *liability* and *double indemnity*; in computer science of *interface systems, bits,* and *bytes,* and in economics of *balance sheets* and *cartels.* Of course, we must use the terms of the discipline we are discussing.

A problem emerges, however, when technical terms are used unnecessarily or inappropriately. Then they are *jargon*, a special language often unintelligible to anyone outside the group that devised it. Can you, for instance, figure out this Hollywood jargon?

> The veepees and the exex of the new org were skeeded to orb the Europix in an all-day sesh.

Or this psychological babble?

> The process of representational guidance has been found to be essentially the same as response learning under conditions where an externally depicted pattern was followed by a person who is then *directed* through a series of instructions to enact novel *response* sequences.

Both these examples are comical, but the second sometimes fools readers because it sounds academic.

Often prose riddled with jargon is depopulated, and the passive voice dominates. Common words, like *direct*, receive a special twist. The writer piles adjectives one on top of another in the interests of precision. Business writing can come up with some whoppers.

> Problem determination procedures indicated that parallel reciprocal mobility was supported by management options.

And we wouldn't want you to think that English studies are lagging behind in the jargon race.

> Plot is the structure of action in closed and legible wholes; it thus must *use* metaphor as the trope of its achieved interrelations, and it must *be* metaphoric insofar as it is totalizing.

Thus many writers abandon the common language and common usage in favor of a private language that is bewildering to outsiders and often incomprehensible even to other professionals. Jargon poses a threat to the most basic principle of writing: communication between people.

Whether you write about an engineering project, a painting, or a computer project, you should try to avoid jargon. Always strive to write so that any literate person with an interest in the subject could understand you. Write in standard, vigorous English.

Giving Clichés the Kiss of Death

Clichés are a dime a dozen. Some people use them right off the bat, even though they may have a sneaking suspicion that brave souls would give them the cold shoulder. But make no bones about it, good writers have other fish to fry and could care less. That's the bottom line.

A cliché is a worn-out saying or expression, an expression we have heard so much that it no longer creates an image for us. The first time they appeared, the clichés in the paragraph above offered fresh images or fresh views. *The kiss of death*, for instance, was what Alfred E. Smith said when he learned that William Randolph Hearst was supporting Smith's opponent in the election for governor of New York. Smith suggested that Hearst's help was like Judas kissing Jesus and would lead to political death. His opponent lost. At the time, the expression was fresh (fresh enough to go down in Bartlett's *Familiar Quotations*). Since then, however, overuse has exhausted it.

Most clichés started out as efforts to make an idea vivid. A speaker or writer puts a new twist on something to illuminate it. When the twist is pithy, others adopt it — we can imagine Smith's supporters chortling as they repeated *the kiss of death*. The original context soon fades; mechanically and thoughtlessly, however, writers keep using phrases that have lost their point. Whenever fresh expression fails, out trots the cliché.

When people string several clichés together, the result can be hilarious: "He is one of those people who stand up and tell it like it is and go against the powers that be whenever they have their turn at bat." "My target is to explore every avenue to relieve the bottleneck in our backlog of orders." The mind reels.

Another form of cliché is the trite expression. *Gone but not forgotten, easier said than done, better late than never, in a very real sense* are a few of the ubiquitous phrases out there enticing us into dreary prose. They may once have carried thought, but now they only carry ennui.

Akin to the trite expression is the automatic pairing of a noun with a particular adjective. In this group we find *solemn oath, heavy burden, forseeable future, crushing blow*. The list could go on and on.

The attraction of clichés is that they are ready-made. Rather than struggle with a fresh image, we reach for the nearest cliché. Using them may be excusable in speech — we are often in a rush to get our opinion stated. Writing is different. We — and our readers — have time to examine our prose. When we state even the most imaginative and reasonable idea in clichés, it will seem flabby and vague. Precision in thought and energy in expression are what good writing is all about, and that means getting rid of clichés.

Using Slang — The Language of Our Crowd

Slang refers to the special and spontaneous language a group develops. It revitalizes and rejuvenates the standard language. It keeps English slightly off balance and prevents it from becoming rigid. Like the unmannerly, vital yokel who crashes the tea party, slang brings in energy. Words like *zoo on* or *dogging* when we mean *insult, munch machine* when we mean *big eater,* or *fried* when we mean *extreme* all add vitality to what we say.

Slang is not universal or standard throughout society. People on different blocks in the same neighborhood — not to mention people on different coasts or people in different social or cultural groups — may use words to mean quite different things. *Get wasted* means to drink too much, to take too many drugs, or to be killed, depending on where you are. In the 1960s *uptight* meant one thing to whites and another to blacks. The word *fag* has meant, at various times to various people, an underling, a cigarette, and a homosexual.

Slang is often a signal that a person belongs to a certain group: youth, jazz lovers, the political left, the country club. Creating new words or giving old words new meanings helps form a group's identity. Although some slang expressions filter into everyone's vocabulary, they usually take a long time to do so, and by then the originators have probably gone on to other slang words.

Most slang changes quickly. The slang our grandparents used — *scram, lollapalooza, nix, rats!* — has a pleasantly old-fashioned sound today. Even slang from the 1950s and 1960s has lost its currency: think of *Mary Jane* for *marijuana,* or *groovy* (itself a word resurrected from the 1940s) for *good.* Sometimes it seems that contemporary slang fades before we learn to use it. Occasionally slang achieves a desirable effect in writing.

With their vote in the municipal runoffs, the residents of Bedford-Stuyvesant have told the all-white city council, "If you can't hang with it, stroll."

College writing generally requires a level of diction offensive to none and understandable to all. You should write *bewildered* rather than *freaked out, overwhelmed* instead of *blown away,* and *frustrated* rather than *bummed* — or are our examples already out of date?

Avoiding Sexist Language

We have all heard obscene words connoting sexual assault. Hearing them, we must assume that the speaker intends to express intense hostility toward women and even a desire to inflict pain. Such words seem to indicate either the user's personal problems or an insensitivity bordering on the pathological. Fortunately, few adults employ ugly sexist language.

Not all sexist words are so overtly or deliberately cruel and crude, however. Words like *bird, doll, tomato,* and *broad* can be affectionately intended. Even so, they carry connotations that to some suggest a less-than-fully-human person, a plaything. (With no more grace and sensitivity, women on occasion use similar words to denote men — *hunk* and *stud* come to mind.) Innocent though many may think these words, they are insidious. Not only do they encourage disrespect for the opposite sex, but also they reflect slovenly thought and speech.

Sexist assumptions permeate our language. Without any intent to insult, many of us might say *the lady veterinarian* or *the female lawyer,* for example, though we would never say *the gentleman veterinarian* or *the male lawyer.* We tend to call hypothetical doctors *he* and nurses *she.* In the higher-ranking professions, the male seems to be the norm and the female the aberrant. Many positions of leadership and responsibility contain masculinity in their denotative words: *chairman, congressman, policeman, fireman.* Yet we know that women can and do hold positions of high prestige and responsibility in all these fields.

In addition, many grammatical conventions favor men and ignore women. Traditionally, it is grammatically correct to say *A writer must choose his words carefully* or *To each his own.* Some people think these constructions suggest that the female was an afterthought, to be subsumed under the dominant category "male."

Some of our common expressions seem to support this bias toward males. The rallying cry of the American Revolution — "All men are created equal" — seems to exclude women. Some people argue that the term *man* encompasses the entire species and that objections to its use are foolish. But others note that during the time of the Revolution the "equal" did not include women, for they were not allowed to vote or serve on juries, and a married woman could not dispose of her own property without the consent of her husband.

These usages reflected the society in which they grew, a society dominated and documented by males. The complaints that females may have had about the laws and the language would not have been well known or recorded. Society has changed drastically, and so has language.

The English language is now, as always, in a state of flux, growing and adjusting to new perceptions. Recognizing that sexism has no place in intelligent prose, sensitive writers are trying to get rid of it. Unfortunately, sexism in language is much easier to criticize than to weed out, but we have five suggestions for writing non-sexist prose.

1. Avoid stereotypes about men and women. Treat both sexes with respect and appreciation, and treat individual people as individuals. Think of all the exceptions there are, for instance, to the stereotypes *insensitive men* and *irrational women.*

2. Keep your writing free of gender-determined words, from obscenities to apparently innocent terms like *man and wife* and *co-ed. Man and wife*, for instance, suggests that women are an attachment; *co-eds*, that they are an afterthought.

3. Avoid sexist usage. Find broader, more inclusive terms for words that denote only males. Instead of *policeman,* say *police officer.* Instead of *chairman*, say *chairperson.* If that usage sounds awkward or condescending, say *chair* or *head.* The point, of course, is to avoid the implication that only males hold high positions.

4. Steer clear of what many people consider sexist grammar. When you write about a nonspecific person, an anyone, use the plural instead of the sexist masculine singular pronoun. In place of *A writer should choose his words carefully,* say *Writers should choose their words carefully.* Shifting to the plural means that you avoid the suggestion of sexism without resorting to either the ungrammatical *a writer should choose their* or the questionable *s/he.*

5. Be ever gracious and inclusive: when you cannot avoid the singular, write the unobtrusive *he or she, him or her, his or hers.*

TIPS FOR APPROPRIATE PROSE

- Prefer short, plain words to long, fancy ones.
- Avoid jargon; strive to write so that any literate person can follow your thought.
- Get rid of clichés.
- Keep slang out of your writing.
- Replace sexist language with language that includes both sexes.

EXERCISES FOR APPROPRIATE PROSE

1. Revise these sentences by removing jargon, clichés, and slang.
   a. Incrementally compatible programming will always impact on total management options.
   b. Although the horror movie freaked me out, I thoroughly enjoyed the evening, most particularly when I flashed on the fact that I cannot relate to that other dude because he does not give me ego reinforcement. That's when I decided to be up-front with you, sweetie pie.
   c. What you say may be true, but if I hear that bromide one more time, I will flip.
   d. The Bard of Avon was a great writer and had a mind like a steel trap.

2. For fun, construct two sentences using at least two of the following words in each sentence: *dialectical, functioning, heuristic, conceptualized, metonymy, partial need factor, systematized, reciprocal, time-phase, feedback, logistic, hermetic.* Be sure your sentences *mean* something. If you don't know the words, look them up in the dictionary.

3. Eliminate the sexist bias from the following sentences:
   a. Three students — a man and two girls — were murdered in their composition class because they had misplaced a modifier.
   b. The lawyer's husband lets her travel alone, but a senior partner would have his own reasons for objecting.
   c. The dean presented awards to both John Smith and Ellen Jones. Smith's was, of course, for athletics and Ellen's for art.
   d. The proper study of mankind is man.

WRITING WITH FLAIR

Although much of our book has been cautionary — don't do this, don't do that — we don't want you to write safe, stodgy prose. Be adventurous and courageous in your writing. Take chances, even if you risk failure. At that, you may be shaking your head: why should I take a chance of falling on my face? That question has four answers.

One, nothing communicates what we are and how we think more powerfully and completely than prose. It tells what we value and why. Stodgy prose therefore implies that the writer is stodgy.

Two, good writing leads to good thinking and vice versa. As you strive to interest your reader, you challenge your own thinking. Struggling to find an image or an exact phrase may open up a new range of thought.

Three, almost all A papers in the world possess personality and imagination. Aim high. Stretch toward excellence.

Four, writing with flair is more fun.

Although you should never sacrifice sense and integrity, you should actively seek the vivid. Indeed, vivid writing will often add to sense and integrity. The following three passages demonstrate some different ways of employing vivid language. The first was written by a funny man who obviously enjoys his words.

There is no question that there is an unseen world. The problem is, how far is it from midtown and how late is it open? Unexplainable events occur constantly. One man will see spirits. Another will hear voices. A third will wake up and find himself running in the Preakness. How many of us have not at one time or another felt an ice-cold hand on the back of our neck while we were home alone? (Not me, thank God, but some have.) What is behind these experiences? Or in front of them, for that matter? Is it true that some men can foresee the future or communicate with ghosts? And after death is it still possible to take showers? (Woody Allen, "Examining Psychic Phenomena")

The humor in this passage is provided by the sudden invasion of the absurd. Allen juxtaposes two different worlds, that of psychic phenomena and that of daily concerns. The incongruity of the two is unexpected and forces the reader to look at ideas anew.

The strength of the second passage comes not from the collision of ideas but from the strings of memorable images or mental pictures used to describe the prose of President Warren Gamaliel Harding.

. . . He writes the worst English that I have ever encountered. It reminds me of a string of wet sponges; it reminds me of tattered washing on the line; it reminds me of stale bean-soup, of college yells, of dogs barking idiotically through endless nights. It is so bad that a sort of grandeur creeps into it. It drags itself out of the dark abysm (I was about to write abscess!) of pish, and crawls insanely up the topmost pinnacle of posh. It is rumble and bumble. It is flap and doodle. It is balder and dash.

But I grow lyrical. (H. L. Mencken, "Gamalielese")

This writing is a feast of vivid writing. We have no doubt about the author's attitude and the attitude he wants his audience to take. Mencken is certainly having fun, and providing fun, but he is also making a serious statement about Harding's mind.

Neither of these passages is particularly complicated. They make fairly simple points. But vivid language is not limited to the simple as you can see in the following passage.

It seems to me that there is a historical parallel, in white American history, between the treatment of the land and the treatment of women. The frontier, for instance, was notoriously exploitative of both, and I believe largely for the same reasons. Many of the early farmers seem to have worn out farms and wives with equal regard-lessness, interested in both mainly for what they would produce, crops and dollars, labor and sons; they clambered upon their fields and upon their wives, struggling for an economic foothold, the having and holding that cannot come until both fields and wives are properly cherished. And today there seems to me a distinct connection between our nomadism (our "social mobility") and the nearly universal disintegration of our marriages and families. (Wendell Berry, "Discipline and Hope")

Berry, a naturalist and poet, brings an intriguing and complex point to life.

As you can see, good writing comes in many shapes, sizes, and colors — and can be the result of different intentions. Sometimes we forget that with a little effort we, too, can write a prose that has more flair. Perhaps a few precepts can help to translate what we admire into what we write.

Appeals to the Senses

Earlier in this chapter, in the section entitled "Writing with Precision," we said that the best writing is concrete and specific. Not all concrete and specific descriptions, however, are vivid. Take this one:

> The child played ball on the sidewalk.

The description is both concrete and specific, but it is not particularly vivid. In revising we wanted to create a picture, a mental image, in the reader's mind.

First we visualized the subject: *boy* is more visual than *child*, but we thought harder about the image and tried to picture physical qualities. Then we turned to what the child was doing. We imagined as vividly as we could.

> The gap-toothed little boy with frizzy red hair furiously slashed line drives to himself off the brick wall.

We thought the reader could better see the boy when we described his frizzy hair and missing teeth. *Slashed* conveys a specific action: the sweeping stroke of the boy's arm. *Furiously* indicates the quality of his act. The *brick wall* completes the picture.

According to an ancient Chinese proverb, one picture is worth more than ten thousand words. But by using words, we can create a picture in the reader's imagination, as James Baldwin does here:

> [My father] looked to me, as I grew older, like pictures I had seen of African tribal chieftains: he really should have been naked, with warpaint on and barbaric mementos, standing among spears. (James Baldwin, *Notes of a Native Son*)

By creating an exact image, Baldwin illuminates his father's personality.

Unfortunately, dull language is as hard to fight in writing as crab grass in a lawn. When we get the least bit lazy it springs up. This kind of sentence results.

> Many residential structures were destroyed for redevelopment.

It is a sensible sentence and we understand it. But compare it with this.

> To clear the way for a new glass box, the wreckers sledgehammered the Victorian mansions and reduced them to rubble and dust.

The reader hears the wrecking ball, sees the rubble, and can taste the dust. Only the redeveloper hoping to go unnoticed would be happy with that first version.

All things being equal, we would not recommend additional words. But if you want to appeal to your reader's senses, you may need more words. Brevity is not the only virtue of good writing.

Vivid writing is important for two reasons. First, it makes understanding easier and quicker for the reader. In the "Victorian mansions" example, only the image of rubble and dust could quickly tell the real damage. Second, vivid writing pleases readers. We all like to read about the world of sight and sound and smell and taste and touch.

Figurative Language

One way of adding flair to writing is to use figures of speech, that is, words and expressions not used for their literal sense. Writers make figures of speech by describing one idea or object in language that properly belongs to another. If we say

Doubt crucified the president.

we borrow feelings and ideas the reader has about actual crucifixion to illuminate the idea of painful doubt. By comparing one thing to another this way, we can reveal a new world for our readers and often ourselves.

The three major forms figurative comparisons take are similes, metaphors, and analogies.

Similes. A simile is an explicit comparison of one thing with another: the writer clarifies one idea or thing by claiming it is like another. A simile always includes *like* or *as*. In describing his father, James Baldwin said that people thought him ingrown "like a toenail." This simile conveys the isolated, pained, and disturbing old man. Here are more similes:

During the swing, the golf club bends like a whip.

Seen from a distance, the brightly dressed crowd in the market looked like a basket of summer fruit.

Like a mysterious, fog-enshrouded island approached by explorers, atomic energy fascinated and frightened the scientists.

An apt and nicely shaped simile can not only paint a vivid picture but also illuminate an idea. Shakespeare's work is rife with similes that make pictorial the nonpictorial opinion or abstraction. Near the end of *King Lear*, the Duke of Gloucester expresses his despair at human existence.

Like flies to wanton boys, are we to the gods;
They kill us for their sport.

The successful simile, like that one, is brief and to the point. You shouldn't try to keep a comparison rolling just because you can. It can become silly and tedious if carried too far. But you should occasionally enrich your prose with an apt simile.

Metaphors. A metaphor compares two things without making the comparison explicit: two things, the metaphor suggests, are the same.

A mighty fortress is our God,
A bulwark never failing.

wrote Martin Luther.

Religion . . . is the opium of the people.

said Karl Marx.

Some words once used in a metaphoric way no longer provide a comparison. They have been taken into the language as denotative words and we hardly think about them. Every four years, for example, we have a *race for the presidency.* Every two years congressional candidates *fight* for office. We no longer consider these metaphors, so deeply embedded are they in our language.

"The metaphor is probably the most fertile power possessed by man," said the Spanish philosopher José Ortega y Gasset, relying on metaphor to make his point. A good metaphor lets us think and talk about the world in fresh ways by converting vague ideas into images. Sometimes a longer metaphor can illuminate a complex situation. The following extended metaphor by the historian Barbara Tuchman describes marriage among ruling families of the Middle Ages:

> Marriages were the fabric of international as well as inter-noble relations, the primary source of territory, sovereignty, and alliance, and the major business of medieval diplomacy. The relations of countries and rulers depended not at all on common borders or natural interest but on dynastic connections and fantastic cousinships. . . . At every point of the loom sovereigns were thrusting in their shuttles, carrying the strand of a son or a daughter, and these, whizzing back and forth, wove the artificial fabric that created as many conflicting claims and hostilities as it did bonds. [The leading families of Europe] were all entwined in a crisscrossing network, in the making of which two

things were never considered: the sentiments of the parties to the marriage, and the interest of the populations involved. (Barbara Tuchman, *A Distant Mirror*)

Because of Tuchman's metaphor, her reader is able to understand how tightly connected the various families were and how important these connections were. By representing an abstraction in concrete terms, she achieves the persuasiveness of illustration. Moreover, her metaphor adds energy to ideas and observations that might otherwise have been dry or tedious. Imagine that passage written in abstract, purely analytical language. The metaphor makes the idea dramatic and visual.

Some people dismiss metaphors and similes as too "literary." They need not be, however. Politicians have frequently used them, as Theodore Roosevelt did when he recommended that the United States

Speak softly and carry a big stick.

Franklin Roosevelt spoke metaphorically when he said,

I pledge you, I pledge myself, to a new deal for the American people.

Athletes and sportswriters instinctively use metaphors when nicknaming the greats: Ted Williams is "the Splendid Splinter" and Earvin Johnson is "Magic." Likewise, scientists often find that a simile or metaphor will help explain a difficult concept, as did Loren Eiseley when he titled an essay "The Ghost Continent" and another "The Angry Winter."

You shouldn't force figures of speech — gone wild they will undercut an essay. But make an effort to think of a natural simile or metaphor and then use it. For there are occasions when, despite all the evidence, reasons, or analysis you come up with, your reader is still a step away from understanding your ideas. Then a well-chosen, forceful comparison — simile or metaphor — may clarify and persuade.

Analogies.   An analogy is an extended comparison, drawn point by point, between two things or ideas. Its purpose is generally to explain a complicated or remote phenomenon by reference to a more accessible one. The advantage of an analogy comes from its careful elucidation of an idea.

The Bible is full of analogies. The parable of the prodigal son is an example. In it Jesus discusses God's forgiveness of sinners by suggesting it is like a father's treatment of his wayward son. The remote idea of the deity is made clear by reference to the homely idea of the father.

Sigmund Freud said, "Analogies prove nothing, that is quite true, but they can make one feel more at home." (We discuss the limitations of analogy as proof in Chapter 10.) Because they do make readers feel more at home, they appear everywhere, even in instructions for using a soldering iron.

Soldering is the joining of metal surfaces by a melted metal or metallic alloy. We can compare this roughly with the gluing of two pieces of wood. Instead of wood, the solderer joins two pieces of metal and instead of glue, he or she uses a melted alloy or metal that, like the glue, hardens and forms a bond.

Analogies can be surprising when used to compare things not obviously similar. In the sixteenth century, a band of thieves waylaid a parson and forced him to make a speech praising all thieves. At the height of his oration, he conferred high praise indeed, drawing an analogy between the thieves and Christ.

I marvel that men can despise you thieves, since in all points (almost) you are like Christ himself. For Christ had no dwelling place; neither have you. Christ went from town to town; so do you. Christ was laid wait upon in many places, and so are you. Christ at length was captured; so shall you be. He was brought before the judges; so shall you be. He was condemned; and so shall you be. He was killed; so shall you be. He thereupon went to heaven — and that you shall never do.

That little twist at the end goes to show that even the best analogies should not be pushed too far — no two things are alike in all particulars (or they would be the same thing). The thieves must not have noticed, though, for according to the legend, "they went away well pleased."

TIPS FOR FLAIR

- Take some risks with your writing.
- Write to appeal to your reader's senses; make pictures as vivid as possible.
- Try for an occasional simile, metaphor, or analogy.

EXERCISES FOR FLAIR

1. Write a vivid sentence to describe a specific experience with each of the five senses.

2. Complete each of the following sentences with a simile:
   a. The bird's raucous song was like
   b. The entire team sprawled on the turf, looking like
   c. He hated tap dancing just as . . . hated
   d. For Napoleon, those winter months in Moscow were like
   e. Dealing with inflation is like

3. Make an apt metaphor based on the following ideas:
   a. A bird and a squirrel quarreling
   b. Pollution in the city during a rainstorm
   c. An old woman on a park bench on a cold winter day
   d. The state legislature during a heated debate
   e. The space shuttle taking off

4. Make an analogy for two of the following sets:
   a. The circulatory system and a college or university
   b. A lion and her cub and a teacher and her student
   c. The solar system and a family
   d. Crime in a society and chicken pox
   Remember that you are using the known to explain the unknown.

5. Revise passages in an essay you wrote for an earlier assignment to include a simile, a metaphor, and an analogy.

8 / Style and Tone

*Oh tain't what you do, it's the way
that cha do it. . . . Tain't what
you say, it's the way that cha say it
— That's what gets results.*
> – Sy Oliver (b. 1910) and Trummy
> Young (b. 1912)

Style and tone are what the artist does to the raw material of the art. They are the way the writer or the speaker treats the thought communicated. Every decision you make while writing — the words you select, the construction of sentences, paragraphing — will contribute to your style and tone. In that sense, this book has been discussing style all along, especially in the sections on sentences and words. In this chapter, however, we want to bring all the foregoing elements together to concentrate on the way thatcha say it, the way that *you* present *you*.

STYLE: BEING THERE IN YOUR WRITING

We should not underestimate the importance of style. The way that we say or do something is distinct and makes even the most common thought or gesture our own. We hear a few bars of music and we say, "That's Brahms" or "That's Beethoven." We read a paragraph from a novel, and we probably know it is by Faulkner, Woolf, or Hemingway. We read the inaugural addresses of John Kennedy, Richard Nixon, Jimmy Carter, and Ronald Reagan, and even though the sentiments expressed are pretty much the same, we know whose speech each is. We know by the style. Style is the indelible signature of personality in our speech and our acts.

All saying much the same thing, some very important military commanders presented themselves in these statements:

> There is many a boy here today who looks on war as all glory, but, boys, it is all hell. You can bear this warning voice to generations yet to come. I look upon war with horror. (William Tecumseh Sherman, 1820–1891)
>
> I hate war as only a soldier who has lived it can, only as one who has seen its brutality, its futility, its stupidity. (Dwight D. Eisenhower, 1890–1969)
>
> I know war as few other men now living know it, and nothing to me is more revolting. I have long advocated its complete abolition, as its very destructiveness on both friend and foe has rendered it useless as a method of settling international disputes. (Douglas MacArthur, 1880–1964)
>
> My first wish is to see this plague of mankind, war, banished from the earth. (George Washington, 1732–1799)

These quotations all convey the same thought: war is bad. But the styles of the speakers differ, and so do our responses to them.

Read the quotations again. Which commanders attract you and which put you off? Would you like to know any personally? Which ones would you trust? Imagine for a moment that the statements involved complicated, arguable ideas about matters that affect you directly — say, nuclear armaments or registering for military service. Judging purely by the stye of these quotations, which commander would you be most apt to believe?

We do not want to push this analysis too far — these quotations are taken out of context and are too short to be a fair representation of the person. Nevertheless, they do illustrate our point: behind words we can sense the attitude of the person: sincere, modest, self-important, despairing. Words convey values and feelings as well as thoughts. "Style," said the eighteenth-century French thinker Buffon, "is the man."

Too frequently, people think style is just so much verbiage to be slathered over thought like a rich coat of paint over wood. It isn't. It isn't filigree and curlicue added to substance. It isn't fancy packaging. It isn't decoration at all. Style is an integral part of the message. It is the presence of the writer in the message. When Sherman said, "but, boys, it is all hell," his words in their very bluntness conveyed his personality as well as his attitude toward both subject and audience.

Look closely at Sherman's statement. The abrupt use of commas, representing pauses in his speech, rivets the attention, and then the word *hell* hammers home the simple message. The use of the word *boys* establishes a friendly, though paternalistic, relationship between Sherman and his audience, all former soldiers. By his choice of words, phrasing, and punctuation, Sherman has perfectly matched the language to his meaning. That is style. That is the man William Tecumseh Sherman.

Although some lucky few seem born with a distinctive writing style, most of us must work to develop one. Improving our writing style is at least as hard as improving our guitar-playing style or our tennis-playing style or even our having-a-good-time-at-a-party style. And as with these, improvement results from observation, practice, and imitation. Don't be afraid of imitating — most professional writers imitated other writers they admired before developing their own style. And don't be afraid of trying and failing. You will get better if you are willing to write, rewrite, rewrite again, and perhaps rewrite again. (This chapter has been rewritten four times.)

We cannot set up absolute standards for style. Some very good styles are simple and direct, some are florid, some are sinuous, some are muscular. The following passages, all excellent, demonstrate how varied good style can be:

> To everything there is a season, and a time to every purpose under heaven.
> A time to be born, and a time to die;
> A time to plant, and a time to pluck up that which is planted;
> A time to kill, and a time to heal;
> A time to break down, and a time to build up;
> A time to weep, and a time to laugh;
> A time to mourn and a time to dance . . . (Ecclesiastes 3:1–4, King James Version)

> It is difficult to imagine, with what obstinacy truths which one mind perceives almost by intuition, will be rejected by another; and how many artifices must be practiced, to procure admission for the most evident propositions into understandings frighted by their novelty, or hardened against them by accidental prejudice: it can scarcely

be conceived, how frequently in these extemporaneous controversies, the dull will be subtle, and the acute absurd; how often stupidity will elude the force of argument, by involving itself in its own gloom; and mistaken ingenuity will weave artful fallacies, which reason can scarcely find means to disentangle. (Samuel Johnson, *The Adventurer,* August 28, 1753)

Man, it is well to remember, is the discoverer but not the inventor of fire. Long before this meddling little Prometheus took to experimenting with flints, then matches, and finally (we hope not too finally) hydrogen bombs, fires had burned on this planet. Volcanoes had belched molten lava, lightning had struck in dry grass, winds had rubbed dead branches against each other until they burst into flame. There are evidences of fire in ancient fossil beds that lie deep below the time of man. (Loren Eiseley, "Man the Firemaker")

Well, evolution *is* a theory. It is also a fact. And facts and theories are different things, not rungs in a hierarchy of increasing certainty. Facts are the world's data. Theories are structures of ideas that explain and interpret facts. Facts do not go away when scientists debate rival theories to explain them. Einstein's theory of gravitation replaced Newton's, but apples did not suspend themselves in mid-air pending the outcome. And human beings evolved from apelike ancestors whether they did so by Darwin's proposed mechanism or by some other, yet to be discovered. (Stephen Jay Gould, "Evolution as Fact and Theory")

In the pages that follow, we refer to these passages. For now, we want to point out that these four very different stylists all treat an interesting subject respectfully and put their stamp upon it.

Tone: The Voice from Deep Within

Perhaps the most important ingredient of style is tone, that is, the atmosphere or attitude the words convey. In speech, the way we say something — the tone of our voice — will telegraph our attitude, even if the words are neutral. Our voice indicates whether we are being sincere, bewildered, amused, or any of dozens of other possibilities. To change the tone, we make small changes in pronunciation or pacing. For instance, the sentence *The college newspaper critic said this was the best movie of the year, and so it must be really great* could be sarcastic, pompous, innocent, deadpan, and so on — the difference depending on a subtle adjustment of tone.

Tone in writing is not as unconsciously or automatically achieved as tone in speech. A writer cannot "drip sarcasm" by anything as simple as modulating the voice. In writing, to change "the way thatcha say it," you have to change what you say. Choice of words, length of sentence, rhythm, and punctuation all contribute to the atmosphere in which the ideas exist. They help the writer express an attitude toward the subject.

Too much writing today, unfortunately, sounds as though it issued from a vending machine — cold, detached, nonhuman. Three sentences for a quarter. Some students actively seek tonelessness believing that tone has no business in academia. That notion is mistaken. Tone in writing is a significant part of the message. Reread the first two sentences of the Eiseley passage on page 253 and compare them with this paraphrase:

This planet knew fire before there were human beings.

The paraphrase gets the fact across, but that is all it does. Eiseley's tone illuminates the matter: we human beings are not as great as we think. His words challenge the reader, establish the angle, and prepare the way for the argument he will make.

Not all tones are acceptable in college writing or any kind of writing. Some can be downright unattractive. In this section, we will discuss six tones that you should keep out of your papers.

Flippancy.   When something is flippant, it indicates a disrespectful levity. Here is the opening of an essay on utilitarian philosophy:

Suppose Jesus Christ had truly lived and suppose he had fallen in love with some Egyptian girl who jilted him for a pharaoh. Brokenhearted, he had committed suicide before he had spread his word to the people. Now, by committing suicide, more grief would have been caused, and therefore the utilitarian must say that his act was immoral.

This flippancy is inappropriate both to the audience (an instructor) and the subject, serious and to some people sacred. With such a tone, almost no argument, however cogently reasoned, could salvage the paper. Flippancy can be fun to say or write — maybe fun to hear — but almost never fun to read. To be flippant about a subject indicates that we do not take it seriously. Instructors, and bosses, are unlikely to appreciate that approach.

Sarcasm. Sarcasm is a contemptuous remark or taunt, often couched in words opposite to the speaker's real meaning.

> If only the rest of us misguided students were one-quarter as intelligent as my roommate, what a brilliant student body we would be.

In an essay, sarcasm is even less attractive than flippancy. When you think of that word, don't you picture a sneering, superior look on someone's face? We do, perhaps because when we succumb to sarcasm that is the way we feel. A sarcastic tone may create in the reader's mind that image of the writer.

Sentimentality. Sentimentality means forced or shallow feeling, and it is another tone to avoid. It is good to express feeling in our writing, of course, but only honest — not pumped up — feeling. Excessive sentiment in an essay casts doubt on both the thinking and the sincerity of the writer. When people overstate their feelings, their writing is apt to deteriorate. They begin to dredge up clichés and trite sayings to back up an emotion they don't have.

> Tears spring to my eyes when I think of that helpless little kitten — gone but not forgotten these many years.

We doubt those tears — we even doubt the kitten.

Self-righteousness. Akin to sentimentality is the self-righteous, or holier-than-thou, tone. Some writing seems to suggest that the writer has a special claim to virtue. Often this tone is accidental. The following, from an autobiographical essay, was written by a modest but naive young man:

> The well-being of my mind, body, and spirit is the result of my family life. My parents love and respect life. This love has inspired me to use my gifts to the height of their potential so that I perform at my best throughout my life.

Appreciating one's parents is a virtue, but a recognition that things are not always as they seem and no one is perfect would have added depth to the essay.

Belligerence. The belligerent writer comes right at the reader, chin thrust forward, fists doubled, like the schoolyard bully, threatening to beat up anyone who dares to disagree. We once read a letter to the editor of a college newspaper that began, "I just can't believe how ignorant and stupid some people are regarding nuclear weapons. They just like to protest something in between hits of the old weed." Not many people would want to associate themselves with views expressed that way.

Some ideas are, of course, worth fighting for. It would be absurd not to show feeling about important issues, like hunger in Africa, missing children in America, or the torture of animals. Indeed, honest indignation can contribute to effective argument.

There is a line, however, between belligerence and acceptable indignation, and the line should be carefully observed. State your opinion with a tone of indignation, but back it up with evidence. Do not bully us into agreement but respect us enough to want to persuade us with argument. The tone of the letter writer, on the other hand, offers no evidence of argument but only more bullying: "Take my word for it or else."

Apology.   The opposite of belligerence, and equally inappropriate, is the apologetic tone, what might be called the po'-li'l-me tone. With this, the writer claims that he or she is modest, diffident, and hard working and thus deserves special consideration.

> Even after reading T.S. Eliot's "The Hollow Men" five times, I could not figure it out. I know it is a great poem, and I realize I have not received the education necessary to understanding it.

Professors seldom give A for effort, and they never do when they realize they are being manipulated for a grade. They want ideas, not the writer hat in hand. Imagine Samuel Johnson saying "I know I don't know much, but."

Characteristics of Good Style

Although a good style cannot be defined in a single set of qualities, all good styles share three characteristics: clarity, appropriateness, and interest.

Clarity.   First, a good style is clear. Although some poets and novelists have different aims, the expository writer seeks clarity as the prime virtue. When readers have to work too hard to reconstruct our thought, they are apt to be irritated and give up. Whether we ever develop a great style, we can with care, thought, and practice learn to write clearly.

Reread the Gould quotation — can anyone mistake its message? Or even that of Johnson, though he wrote in a more leisurely and complex style.

Clarity requires that we follow the rules of the English language. Grammar, mechanics, and punctuation all show the reader how to read the prose. When a reader must translate a plural pronoun into a singular one to match up with a verb, or figure out where the commas and periods should go, that reader will miss much of the meaning — and perhaps think you also are befuddled. Mastery of the rules is essential to a clear style. (For more on grammar, see the appendix.)

So is a rich but natural vocabulary. To write six words instead of the single appropriate word weakens prose. Look at the word *artifices* in the passage from Samuel Johnson. It means "skill or ingenuity; a clever expedient; a sly or artful trick." In one word, Johnson brings all these meanings into his sentence. At the same time, if readers must constantly scurry to the dictionary, they may not return to the manuscript. Had Eiseley begun his first sentence with "The tellurian hairless biped . . ." we probably would not have arrived at the verb. (See Chapter 7 for more on this subject.)

Proper organization and emphasis contribute to clarity. The parallelism in the passage from Ecclesiastes, for instance, helps to keep the ideas exactly ordered. Without the parallelism, we might read something like

> We are born at a given time and planting takes place every spring. Although to be perfectly rational about it, some people die by accident and that can hardly be said to be happening at a special or preordained time. In the fall is when farmers and their helpers get up really early in the morning because it's the harvest. Which brings me to hunting, I think. . . .

Clear writing is the writer's courtesy to the reader.

Appropriateness.   A good style must be appropriate to subject, audience, and self. If Sherman had been addressing the U.S. Congress — instead of a reunion of old soldiers who had served under him — he no doubt would have been the same blunt soldier, but he would have couched his message in more sophisticated terms, and he most assuredly would not have called his listeners "boys."

Style must be appropriate to the subject. Samuel Johnson wrote about the complex relations of reading, thinking, and writing, and the subject required complex treatment. The writer of Ecclesiastes treats simple, straightforward ideas in a simple, straightforward way.

Audience also makes demands on style. Had Gould been trying to persuade an audience of fundamentalists, he no doubt would have couched his thought in different language. Had he been addressing a scientific audience, he no doubt would have assumed greater knowledge. But his language was appropriate for readers of *Discover* magazine, where his essay appeared.

Finally, style should fit the writer's personality and situation. We have read essays that sounded — or tried to sound — as if some graybeard had written them. It seems to us appropriate for Samuel Johnson to use a neoclassical style — he lived in that age. Gould, however, is young and American, and his prose appropriately sounds young and American. Style should fit like good shoes.

We are not suggesting, though, that you write exactly as you speak. Your writing style should represent you at your considered best. Stretch to use the most expressive and precise language that you feel comfortable using.

Interest.   That brings us to the third characteristic of good style: it must be interesting. No law says that an academic paper, a personal letter, a law brief, or any other writing must be boring. Nobody — not even the world's greatest pedant — wants to read something written in a dull, uninteresting style.

What makes a style interesting? Colorful imagery. The unexpected twist of a phrase, a startling comparison, an illuminating allusion to any other work. The sentences are rhythmic, vigorous, varied. An interesting style avoids the overblown, the quaint, the pretentious. It is down-to-earth and sincere without being ponderous. It has personality without self-preening. It conveys wit, insight, sensitivity. The most interesting style is the most interesting you that you can get on the page.

THE HIGH INFORMAL STYLE

For work in college, seek to write in what could be called the *high informal style.* This style is high because it shows respect, for the reader and for the subject. It observes the rules of etiquette and of argument. It avoids silliness, breeziness, overfamiliarity, and vulgarity.

Seriousness does not mean "academic writing." As university instructors, we are particularly sensitive to this kind of writing. For decades, perhaps centuries, academics have been pilloried and parodied for being precise to the point of pedantry and pomposity. Whether the reputation was ever deserved, we think it is not now. Some of the best writing in the country comes from academics. Lewis Thomas, Helen Vendler, Marvin Mudrick, and Scott Momaday are only a few of the professors who write with elegance, imagination, and personality. They are well worth imitating.

Some writers, unfortunately, imitate the worst kind of academic writing, the kind that really is pedantic. They insert ten-dollar words when nickel ones would be better. They pile clause on clause, modification on modification until their sentences and paragraphs teeter and collapse. Along the way, they are apt to lose touch with their thought and certainly with themselves. Imagine how baffled the instructor was when she read the following passage:

> If it were in my power to change one aspect of modern living, I would prioritize change in the capitalist ideology that is predominant socially at the present point in time. It is because of this ideology that pursuit of truly valued goals is prevented. Many settle for conditions that create the possibility of generating sufficient income for inordinate materialistic wants. Stifled by the deluding paradigm of materialism, individual hopes and dreams are stillborn, poverty is the norm while the wealthy survive, and many people are forced into molds that will reflect a wealthy life-style.

This sort of writing will "amaze the unlearned and make the learned smile," as the eighteenth-century poet Alexander Pope put it. It is not all the writer's fault, however. She was trying, too hard, to write the way she thought she was expected to write. And so she stumbled over awkward combinations of words, the complex ways of saying simple things, the strained effort to sound intelligent.

The high informal style shifts a little toward informality. It gives the impression of natural speech — without, of course, lapsing into error in form or diction.

In the revision, the writer relaxed and began to sound more like herself and less achingly formal and pretentious:

> If I could change one thing in the world, I would change the emphasis on materialism that I see today. Because of the rush to get rich,

many people cannot pursue what they really find valuable in life, like teaching or farming or social work. Instead, many settle for being doctors, lawyers, bankers, not because these careers interest them, but because the salaries will provide material rewards. It is very sad to see the dreams and aspirations of so many people destroyed by the search for money. But perhaps we cannot expect anything else in a world where the poor struggle or perish and the wealthy have much more than enough.

Writing like this preserves the high aspect of style — the need for respect and seriousness — and adds the informal, the personal, the sense that someone is talking. We know full well what that writer believes and cherishes. In the examples she uses, she puts her stamp on the thought. An appropriate style is always a personal style. It should include not only your values but also your humor, your tolerance, your quirky way of viewing the world.

Be as fine a stylist as you can be. Don't settle for the first sentence that emerges. Work in an occasional metaphor or analogy. Notice what writers you admire do in their writing and try it on for size. Just as you may experiment with different styles of clothing, experiment with different styles of writing. Challenge yourself. Stretch for a fine style.

TIPS FOR STYLE AND TONE

- Keep in mind that your style is the you that you present to your reader.
- Read your work critically so that you can evaluate whether your tone is the one you want to convey.
- Avoid flippancy, sarcasm, sentimentality, self-righteousness, belligerence, and apology.
- Think about the qualities and techniques that make a style clear, appropriate, and interesting.
- Seek the high informal style, a mixture of respect, reserve, and informality.
- To learn how to get yourself across in your style, observe and imitate what good writers do, and practice.

EXERCISES FOR STYLE AND TONE

1. Here are passages by three professional writers. What kind of person do you think each writer is? Analyze the texts to support your opinion.

The world has heaped contumely on my people, even on the one of us who is President [Jimmy Carter]. But do we try to make people feel guilty for the misunderstanding? No. Do we file anti-defamation suits? No. That ain't my people's way. We don't even like to *wear* suits. (Roy Blount, Jr., *Crackers*)

Many years ago, as a solitary youth much given to wandering, I set forth on a sullen November day for a long walk that would end among the fallen stones of a forgotten pioneer cemetery on the High Plains. The weather was threatening, and only an unusual restlessness drove me into the endeavor. Snow was on the ground and deepening by the hour. There was a rising wind of blizzard proportions sweeping across the land. (Loren Eiseley, *The Unexpected Universe*)

The emphasis on skills was a response to what had been the major weakness of Peace Corps programs in the 1960s. There has always been a debate within the agency about whether its emphasis should be on socioeconomic development or cross-cultural exchange. In theory, one goal is as important as the other. In the 1960s, however, too many projects tended to focus on the second goal of the Peace Corps Act (the people-to-people aspect) and neglected the first goal (the supply of *trained* manpower). (Gerard T. Rice, *Twenty Years of Peace Corps*)

2. Describe the tones of the following passages:
   a. Abortion is a vicious crime and any person who encourages another person to have one is an accomplice in a murder and should be prosecuted to the fullest extent of the law.
   b. Males are so honorable by nature that they would naturally take the high moral position on this issue of abortion because of course it affects them so greatly and they have so much to lose if abortion is recriminalized.
   c. I don't care about the issue — what's one more aborted fetus or one more unwanted baby? People have always had abortions and people have always hated their children. The thing that amuses me is how excited people who are centuries past the childbearing years can get about this. Now that is worth pondering.

3. Revise the three statements in Exercise 2 to remove the offending tones. Write the passages in the high informal style.

4. Resurrect the oldest essay of yours that you still have. Analyze it for the various aspects of style. Revise it. Describe the differences between the two versions.

part four

The Critical Moment:
Persuasion
and Argument

9 / Writing to Persuade

> *Reason is God's crowning gift to man.*
>
> – Sophocles (c. 495–406 B.C.)
> Greek dramatist

> *We reason deeply when we forcibly feel.*
>
> – Mary Wollstonecraft (1759–1797)
> English writer and feminist

We are always trying to get people to do something, say something, or believe something that we tell them. *Pick up your room or I will spank you. Smith will make the best mayor because he is an honest, efficient administrator. I've never seen* Gone with the Wind — *please go with me tonight. Pass the salt.*

Much of the writing you will do in college will also try to get people to see things your way. In a political science class, you may want to persuade your instructor that voting patterns changed in 1980 because of increased affluence. In an American literature class, you may want to prove that the three major characters in Melville's *Billy Budd* represent the three main American national character types. In a history class, you may want to claim that America's participation in the Korean War of 1950–1953 was, or was not, imperialistic.

To support your ideas, you will need to call on all the skills you have learned in this book. You will state a thesis that you must prove, and you will develop your evidence to prove it. You will organize your thoughts, draft strong paragraphs and sentences that support your view, and revise to make your essay stronger. And you will always bear in mind your purpose: to convince your reader that your views on the subject make sense.

This process is called *argument*. When used to describe a kind of writing, argument does not refer to violent disagreement often leading to anger and perhaps a confrontation with your opponent out in the alley. It means presenting a case so carefully that reasonable people will agree with it.

In this chapter we discuss how to argue as correctly, clearly, and convincingly as you can.

THE COMPONENTS OF ARGUMENT

In *The Uses of Argument*, the philosopher Stephen Toulmin described the components of a good argument. He called the three basic components *claim, evidence,* and *warrant*.

Suppose you look out the window and say,

It's going to rain today. Those clouds look pretty dark, and around here, dark clouds mean rain.

You have put forth an argument containing a claim (It's going to rain), evidence (Those clouds look pretty dark), and a warrant (around here, dark clouds mean rain) in that order. The claim states what you will be proving; the evidence supports it; the warrant explains the connection between claim and evidence. Bearing this threesome in mind can help you build good arguments.

Claim

The claim is the idea or statement the argument will back up. All these are claims:

Capital punishment should be outlawed.
When volatized, bromine is irritating to mucous membranes.
Star Wars is the greatest movie ever made.
Lower taxes will lead to greater federal revenues.
Arthur killed Daphne in self-defense.

On the essay level, your thesis statement is the claim your essay will argue. On the paragraph level, your topic sentence is the claim your paragraph will argue.

Claims have two parts: the topic and the assertion. The topic is the subject you will discuss; the assertion is what you are saying about the topic.

Topic	*Assertion*
Capital punishment	should be outlawed
Star Wars	is the greatest movie ever made
Arthur	killed Daphne in self-defense

In your thesis statement and your topic sentence, you must clearly state both topic and assertion so that your reader can understand the claim you are making. Confused or obscure claims can ruin an argument.

Writers make two kinds of claims: claims of fact and claims of value. A claim of fact seeks to portray or establish what was, is, or will be.

When volatized, bromine is irritating to mucous membranes.
Lower taxes will lead to greater federal revenues.
Arthur killed Daphne in self-defense.

The argument in a claim of fact rests on information. To check the claim that *When volatized, bromine is irritating to mucous membranes*, for instance, scientists could run a simple experiment on mucous membranes. Because the validity of a claim like *Lower taxes will lead to greater federal revenues* depends on future events, economists making this claim would have to rely for support on mathematical models that can predict the future. Later, we can compare actual revenues with the economists' predictions. To prove that *Arthur killed Daphne in self-defense*, Arthur's lawyer must try to uncover facts. He or she would probably interview all witnesses, check out ownership of the gun, investigate various motives. If the facts support the claim, the jury will acquit Arthur.

The second kind of claim is the claim of value. We make a claim of value when we say that a thing or action is good or bad, that a person should or should not do something, that something is worthwhile or worthless. Claims of value rest not on information but on norms, a sense of what is right or good. The writer seeks to persuade the reader of what ought to be. No investigation, no experiment, no mathematical model could prove these claims of value:

Capital punishment should be outlawed.
Star Wars is the greatest movie ever made.
Chocolate ice cream is better than vanilla.

Sometimes claims of value depend on claims of fact. In arguing against capital punishment, for instance, a writer may claim that many innocent people have been executed, a claim of fact; another writer might claim that capital punishment has deterred crime, also a claim of fact. But claims of value cannot be directly proven, for in the last analysis they rest on personal interests and considerations and often highly emotional beliefs. This does not mean that you should dismiss claims of value — they involve the most important issues of our lives. But it does mean that you should be clear about what kind of claim you are making in order to amass the proper evidence.

Evidence

Evidence is any support for your claim that your audience will accept without further proof: the specific example, the statistic, the next logical step, the quotation, the shared belief about what is right or good. Each piece of evidence is a foundation stone for your claim. Once you have accumulated enough of these stones, your claim is firmly based.

Consider the lawyer's argument in Arthur's murder trial.

Arthur does not deny that he killed Daphne. In fact, several witnesses say they saw the two of them struggling, saw Daphne fall, and saw the gun in Arthur's hand. But it was clearly self-defense. Daphne was out to kill Arthur, and he had to protect himself. Daphne's friend Louella testified that Daphne admitted hating Arthur and said he ought to be done away with. Louella quoted Daphne as saying, "If no one else will do it, I will." And the deed was done with Daphne's gun.

A pretty good case. Each piece of evidence supports the claim: the struggle, the killing, Daphne's statement of her motive, the ownership of the gun. The jury would probably begin to think that, yes, the claim of self-defense is upheld by the evidence.

Arthur's lawyer knows, however, that the prosecutor may question whether the gun was actually Daphne's, and that might undermine the defense argument. So the lawyer constructs a subargument to support the subclaim that the gun was Daphne's.

> The gun, as I say, belonged to Daphne. It had been purchased by her two days before her death. The police found in her handbag a receipt indicating she had charged the gun on her credit card. Furthermore, the salesclerk identified Daphne's picture as that of the woman who purchased the gun.

If the prosecutor challenges the signature on the charge receipt or the identification by the salesclerk, the defense lawyer would have to construct another subargument regarding the signature and the identification. Could this go on forever? It could, until the evidence has become so detailed that no further proof is necessary to convince the jurors.

Writing a college paper bears a close resemblance to arguing in a court of law, for it also requires a claim supported with evidence. Suppose you were writing an essay on the poet Robert Frost and you devised this claim:

> Robert Frost's character had two sides. He was extremely ambitious and competitive, but he responded to kindness, and he was generous to students and loving to old friends.

To prove that claim, you would divide it into parts, each of which would become a subclaim in the form of a topic sentence.

1. Frost was extremely ambitious for fame and admiration.
2. He was highly competitive with other poets of his time.
3. But he responded to kindness.
4. Despite his often unpleasant attitude toward peers, he could be generous to students and loving to old friends.

You would now need to develop evidence for each topic sentence, just as Arthur's lawyer developed evidence for each point in Arthur's case. You might, for instance, support the second topic sentence this way:

> He was highly competitive with other poets of his time. Edwin Arlington Robinson seemed to give him the most trouble, for time and again Frost expressed a deep-seated jealousy of him. Perhaps he thought Robinson's fame was greater than his. Even the poet Archibald MacLeish, seldom considered as good as either Frost or Robinson, came in for attack. At a testimonial dinner, Frost so upstaged MacLeish that the audience became restive. Frost did not hesitate to

show disdain even for those whom some consider the most important poets of the era, Ezra Pound and Wallace Stevens. Frost made open fun of Pound and had several heated arguments with Stevens. He seemed unable to accept the success of his peers.

With such evidence, you gradually persuade the reader to accept your claim. (In Chapter 10, we discuss kinds of evidence.)

Warrant

A warrant is the glue that holds an argument together. It links the evidence to the claim. It says something like "This evidence supports this claim because . . . "

> Based on the evidence that those clouds look pretty dark, I can claim it is going to rain today because around here when clouds are dark like that, it means rain.

Here is how we might diagram this argument:

Claim	It's going to rain today.
Evidence	Those clouds look pretty dark.
Warrant	Around here when clouds are dark like that, it means rain.

Although an argument can be presented in any order, most start with the claim, go straight to the evidence, and state the warrant later.

Sometimes the connection between the claim and the evidence is so obvious that the writer does not need to state it. Baby Bear says,

> Someone has been eating my porridge. It's all eaten up.

A warrant would supply the connection.

> When my porridge is gone and I didn't eat it, I assume someone else did.

But not even the bears needed to spell that out.

> Let's go back to Arthur's murder trial.

> The gun belonged to Daphne. It had been purchased by her two days before her death. The police found a receipt in her handbag indicating she had charged the gun on her credit card. They verified that it was her signature on the receipt.

The lawyer pauses. Is the connection clear? If stated, the warrant would be

Charge receipts are reliable proofs of purchase when the signatures on them have been verified.

Deciding not to insult the jury's intelligence, the lawyer moves to the next point. If you make every single warrant explicit, your audience may think you are talking down to them.

Frequently, however, people leave out warrants that are essential for understanding the argument, as in this pair of conflicting arguments.

First Fan:

Claim	Ty Cobb is the best hitter in baseball history.
Evidence	He had a lifetime batting average of .367.

Second fan:

Claim	Hank Aaron is the best hitter in baseball history.
Evidence	He had more total homers, runs batted in, and extra base hits than any other player.

In both arguments the evidence is correct, yet the claims differ. So what is wrong? To get at the disagreement, we need those warrants.

First fan:

Claim	Ty Cobb is the best hitter in baseball history.
Evidence	He had a lifetime batting average of .367.
Warrant	Lifetime average is the best way to assess a hitter.

Second Fan:

Claim	Hank Aaron is the best hitter in baseball history.
Evidence	He had more total homers, runs batted in, and extra base hits than any other player.
Warrant	Power statistics are the best way to assess a hitter.

If these two fans are to resolve their dispute, they will have to argue the validity of the warrants. The warrants would become subclaims, and the two fans would have to provide evidence to support them. If the fans cannot resolve their differing criteria for the best hitter, they will have to agree to disagree. In the meantime, by presenting their warrants they at least identify the real argument.

Baseball fans would probably infer the warrants in these two arguments. But sometimes if you do not explain why evidence suits the claim, your audience will lose the thread and you may lose your audience. Because the following example lacks a warrant, the argument is impossible to follow.

> The most popular soap opera on American television is *Wild Wet Winds of Love*. Fully 76 percent of the viewing public of Wadkins, Florida, watches this program.

What does that prove? the reader wants to know. Who cares about some little town in Florida? Warrant needed:

> And the viewing public in Wadkins, Florida, is a cross section of viewers much like those in the rest of the United States. Thus, a show's popularity there indicates its popularity throughout the land.

Now we have the missing link in the chain of reasoning. We may or may not accept the warrant, but at least we know how the writer reasoned.

When should warrants be stated and when can they be implicit? When the evidence obviously illustrates the claim, the writer does not need a warrant. When, however, the connection is unclear or complicated, you need a warrant. It is, of course, a matter of judgment. In this, as in all aspects of expository writing, err on the side of too much clarity rather than too little.

PUTTING THE COMPONENTS TOGETHER

. So far we have looked at claim, evidence, and warrant as separate building blocks. In an argument, however, they form a unit of continuous thought. The following is a passage from an essay whose thesis is "Computer-aided instruction can be extremely valuable in teaching writing":

> Computers have many advantages over human teachers when   1
> it comes to giving the repetitive drills needed to teach writing. Computers are more patient and can run the same drill over and over until
> the student masters it, something few teachers can endure. Computers can provide instant feedback, which busy teachers often cannot do. Where large classes make it difficult for teachers to gear their
> instruction to the needs of individual students, computer programs

are entirely adaptable to each student's pace. Best of all, they cost almost nothing to operate.

A computer really is a video textbook. It presents information on screens rather than on sheets of paper. Students press buttons instead of turning pages or writing down answers. Quizzes appear every few screens to ensure that students are getting the point. If they pass these quizzes, students can go on; otherwise, they must go back, review the material, and take the quiz over. Video textbooks can do anything regular textbooks can do, from drills to the actual teaching of writing.   2

In sum, the computer can engage students' attention and guide their progress without involving a teacher. Thus, it is preferable to today's expensive and often ineffective methods of teaching writing.   3

Each paragraph is composed of a claim, evidence, and warrants. The claim in the first paragraph is in the first sentence. The rest of the paragraph is bits of evidence and warrants connecting the evidence to the claim. For example, the first piece of evidence is that computers "can run the same drill over and over until the student masters it," and the warrant for that is "something few teachers can endure." The second piece of evidence is that computers "can provide instant feedback," and the warrant is "which busy teachers often cannot do." We might call the concluding sentence a *reinforcing warrant*. It treats as a unit all the evidence and other warrants and connects that unit to the claim.

The same process is at work in the second paragraph. The topic sentence states a claim. The other sentences contain bits of evidence and warrants that connect the evidence to the topic sentence. The concluding sentence is a reinforcing warrant.

As we pointed out in Chapter 3, once you prove your claim in a paragraph, it becomes evidence for the thesis of the essay. The third paragraph clearly links the preceding two paragraphs to the thesis of the essay. It, then, acts as a *final warrant* for this part of the essay.

CONSIDERING THE OPPOSITION

The claim-evidence-warrant model is fine if you think your audience is open to your line of argument. Careful writers, however, assume skeptical readers who wait to be convinced. Skeptical readers ask hard questions, demand more evidence if they are not satisfied, and attack weak places in the argument. Writing for a skeptical reader demands three further tools: backing, rebuttal, and concession/qualification.

Backing

Backing shores up a warrant. When you cannot assume your audience will accept your warrant, you need to prove it. To do this, you treat the warrant as a claim that needs evidence.

Suppose you were sick of living in a sloppy dormitory, so you made the following argument in a meeting with college administrators:

> The college should provide janitorial service for the dorms. The dorms are falling apart, and it is costing the college a great deal of money to maintain them. *This high cost of maintenance justifies hiring janitors.*

Skeptical administrators might ask, what have maintenance costs to do with the janitors?

You would need to respond by building an argument around the warrant, italicized in the following paragraph:

> *The high cost of maintenance justifies hiring janitors.* Because of yearlong neglect, dorm rooms are in such serious disrepair that they must be painted and refurbished at the end of the spring term, and this costs nearly $1 million per year. If the college had routine janitorial service, we would not need annual painting and refurbishing.

The administrators might question the warrant of this argument as well: Why would routine janitorial service make annual painting and refurbishing unnecessary?

You would answer with still more backing.

> *Routine janitorial service would make annual painting and refurbishing unnecessary.* If walls were washed regularly, they would not need painting every year. If floors were swept and carpets vacuumed regularly, they would last much longer.

Backing clarifies and supports weak or unclear connections.

When you use backing you are not assuming that your audience disagrees with you, only that they hold an understandable skepticism. Rebuttal and concession/qualification, however, presume a doubting or even antagonistic audience. Anyone who wants to convince such an audience — a very common kind — must address their contrary beliefs or opinions.

Rebuttal

Rebuttal is the process of refuting the opposing view. In essence, it says, "People who say X are wrong because . . ." Rebuttal demands a great deal of tact because it is aggressive. You want to confront the differing opinion without alienating readers so that they refuse to hear what you say. If you imply that a reader is a fool or a knave, as in these openings, you will fail to persuade:

Ignorant people would perhaps think . . .
People with bad judgment or ulterior motives would claim . . .

Writers sometimes begin their rebuttals by attributing the erroneous view to some hypothetical group.

Some people may think . . .
There is a widely held but false view that . . .

More diplomatic writers might go even further.

Many reasonable people do hold this opinion, even though it has turned out to be mistaken.

Once you have found the right tactful entry into your rebuttal, you must face the real work. You must fairly present the opposing claim and then show why it is invalid.

Suppose that in the argument about janitors, the administration has asked you to put your proposal in writing for the board of trustees. In writing the report, you anticipate that the trustees will say something like

College kids can clean up after themselves. They never had janitors at home — why should they have them in college?

You rebut this point by fairly paraphrasing the opposing claim and acknowledging the evidence on which it rests. If you distort the claim or ignore the evidence, your audience will lose confidence in you. (We have more to say about the ethics of argument in Chapter 11.)

Many people may think that students can be made to care properly for their rooms themselves. Certainly, these people argue, the students never had a janitor at home.

Now it is time to erect your counterclaim.

> Our experience, however, indicates that students will not take care of their dorm rooms, no matter how they behaved at home. Three years ago, the college instituted a program of weekly inspections. After one semester, the administration abandoned the program as a failure. There was no good effect, and in fact students, their parents, and faculty complained. Last year the college tried again, providing housekeeping equipment and supplies to each wing of every dormitory. The students agreed to keep their particular wings clean. In one wing the original bottle of cleanser was three-quarters full at year's end. In another, students used the broom to prop open a window. Apparently, whatever action the college takes, the problem persists.

Because the evidence is sufficient, the argument effectively refutes the opposition.

Concession/Qualification

At times all of us have to make concessions. When you cannot find a way to refute the opposition, there is nothing to do but admit it: "You have a good point — I'll give you that one." It would be counterproductive to deny a solid claim just because the opposition has made it. It would be equally useless to hold tenaciously to an untenable position. Just concede the good point and qualify your own claim accordingly: that is, redefine it so that it no longer conflicts with the valid claim the opposition made.

In response to your report about the need for janitors in the dorms, suppose the trustees say

> Students are, after all, adults and should be fully capable of taking care of their living accommodations. They should be trained to do so.

Now that is a good point. Who would want to argue that students are not adults or are not capable of taking care of their rooms? You'll have to concede these opposing claims and then find a way around them.

> Of course, students ought to be more responsible than they have shown themselves in this matter, but that is a problem for society, not for the school. The issue here is whether janitorial service makes good economic sense.

You acknowledge that students should be responsible enough to take care of their rooms and then qualify your claim by limiting it to a point the trustees will accept: dollars and cents.

An argument using the model we have just outlined would read this way:

> I have evidence that warrants a claim. Because I anticipate skepticism from my audience, I will provide additional backing for warrants, rebut any conflicting arguments that I can, concede opposing arguments I cannot rebut, and qualify my original claim to account for the concession.

Mastering this form can help you conduct a persuasive argument.

CASE STUDY: ARGUMENT IN ACTION

Earlier in this chapter we presented a piece of an essay arguing that "computer-aided instruction can be extremely valuable in teaching writing." That essay was directed toward persuading teachers in writing programs. After he drafted the essay, the writer realized he had not considered the possible opposition. He went back and brainstormed the concerns, objections, and contrary opinions his audience might have. After combining and arranging what he had generated, he came up with these points:

1. Computers are bad for the soul, and I don't want to use them.
2. Writing is a vital process that can't be taught by computers.
3. Computer instruction would be simple-minded and distracting.
4. I don't have time to learn the new technology, and I'm too old to bother.
5. Existing programs wouldn't fit the exercises the teacher creates.
6. Available software probably won't run on our school computers.
7. Computers will be costly and take money from other projects.

Now the writer had a good idea of what the opposition thought, and he was ready to use backing, rebuttal, and concession/qualification.

He wrote the following addition to his argument:

> Computers are not for everybody, especially not for people who 1
> simply can't stand them. No writing program should *require* that
> teachers use computers. And, of course, no one would argue that
> computers should, or could, replace teachers. The teaching of writ-

ing demands an individual, balanced, thoughtful, and human response — something the most advanced computer cannot provide. Actually, the point of the computer is to give the teachers free time so that they can devote their attention to just these necessities. On a voluntary basis and limited to what they can do well, however, computers can be extremely helpful.

Many ideas about computer-aided instruction are no longer 2 soundly based. Admittedly, the very first programs were crude and simpleminded, and some were so difficult to operate that they interfered with the learning process. But times have changed. Today, programs are sophisticated and effective. Educational software is even being produced by major publishers — the very ones that publish the finest textbooks. And while they have grown in complexity, the machines are much simpler to operate. This has come about because the large computer firms have invested so much time and money in making their machines "user friendly."

Computer-aided instruction has become more attractive in other 3 ways as well. Programs are more flexible. Software is now available that lets you modify exercises and lessons and even create your own, from scratch. All you have to do is respond to a series of questions and prompts from the computer. Even if you are a beginner, you need learn no new technology — no more, at any rate, than you would need to drive a new car. With the advancing technology, the machines are becoming more and more useful in the classroom.

If the state-of-the-art software will not operate on your school's 4 machines, you should consult one of the computer companies. Both IBM and Apple have donated or heavily discounted machines for schools and teachers. You may be able to arrange for at least a pilot program for your school. Virtually all educational software is written for computers made by one or the other, so you would probably have no compatibility problem. You will be pleasantly surprised by how little the computers will cost your school and yet how helpful they will be to you.

The first paragraph is almost all concession and qualification. The writer realized he would have no chance of overcoming hard-line prejudice, and so in the first sentence he conceded that some people will never like computers. With this concession, he singled out the part of the audience that most wanted to argue and said, diplomatically, "I'm not going to argue with you, at least not on these grounds." In this paragraph he also conceded that computers would not replace human teachers.

He made another concession in the second paragraph when he admitted that computers were once crude. At this juncture, he knew he had to take a stand and he shifted to rebuttal. He pointed out that educational computer programs are now much more sophisticated. To emphasize their credibility, he noted that textbook publishers now produce software. In further rebuttal, he pointed out that computers are now easy to operate.

In the third paragraph, he continued the rebuttal. In responding to teachers who fear the computer will dominate the classroom, he said that they themselves can dominate the computer by modifying, even creating, programs. He backed his rebuttal by providing explicit information on how simple it is to change programs.

In the final paragraph, he rebutted the idea that the machines will be expensive. He offered ways to save money and pointed out that the school would probably not encounter compatibility problems. He wrapped up his argument by saying that the audience would be pleasantly surprised, a final warrant that backed all his other points.

TIPS FOR WRITING TO PERSUADE

- Make your claims clear and unambiguous.
- Distinguish between claims of fact and claims of value so that you will know what kind of support to provide.
- Be sure you have sufficient evidence to support all parts of the claim.
- When the connection between the claim and the evidence is unclear or complicated, provide the warrant.
- If a connection seems weak, supplement it with backing.
- Anticipate the opposing arguments and provide rebuttal.
- When an opposing idea is too strong to be denied, concede the point and qualify your argument accordingly.
- After completing a draft, check to be sure you have used claim, evidence, warrant, backing, rebuttal, and concession or qualification.

EXERCISES FOR WRITING TO PERSUADE

1. Which of the following are claims of fact and which are claims of value? Explain why you made the identifications you did.

If you see a situation in which something is wrong and you could rectify it and yet do nothing, then you are also responsible for that situation.

Meat eaters have a much higher chance of developing cancer of the digestive tract than do vegetarians.

Watching television makes a child less sensitive to violence, and it makes an adult more indifferent to the actual violence in the world.

Smoking marijuana and smoking cigarettes are equally dangerous.

Briefly indicate how you would go about supporting each of these claims.

2. You can do this either alone or with a partner. Choose either the affirmative or the negative of the following claims.
   a. Creationism should be taught along with evolution.
   b. Pay television should not be censored.
   c. Congress should decriminalize possession of marijuana.
   d. The state should help finance parochial schools.

   List points of evidence to support your position. Now list all the opposing points you can think of and see if you can rebut each point on one list with a point on the other. Write a paragraph accounting for any discrepancies. With these opposing ideas in mind, qualify your claim.

3. Here is a list of claims, each of which is paired with a piece of evidence.
   a. Dolphins should be considered equal to human beings. They have their own language.
   b. Shakespeare must not have been interested in women. His female characters are not drawn in detail.
   c. The Beatles were better musicians than Elvis Presley. They sold more records than Elvis did.
   d. We must all start learning Chinese. Otherwise we cannot hope to understand China.
   e. Women should not wear the same clothes as men. If both sexes dress alike, we won't be able to tell them apart.

   What is the implied warrant for each argument? Is it persuasive? If the warrant needs backing, provide it.

4. Here is a claim followed by seven statements. Which statements would a reader accept as evidence and which require further proof? Explain.

   Claim: This institution should discontinue participation in intercollegiate football.

Evidence:

 a. Football is brutalizing, and the school should not give even tacit approval to such a sport.

 b. Intercollegiate football creates antiintellectualism.

 c. Although football may build character, only the players benefit.

 d. Studying Western civilization is also good for building character.

 e. Basketball has become a dangerous contact sport and should also be banned.

 f. Both playing and watching games distract students from more important intellectual pursuits.

 g. Playing football is dangerous, and the school may be liable for injuries during practice sessions and games.

Explain your decisions.

5. From the following list of topics, choose one that you and a partner disagree about.

 All students should be required to take computer science.

 All students should be required to take a foreign language.

 Playing radios and stereos should be forbidden every evening between seven and ten o'clock and after midnight.

 Automobiles should be excluded from campus.

Write an essay stating your belief and providing an argument. Try to anticipate what your partner will say. Exchange essays. Now revise your essay, backing, rebutting, and conceding or qualifying on the basis of what your partner wrote.

6. Write an essay in which you argue for one side of one of the following controversies. Provide three reasons why you think the way you do; provide an example for each reason. These reasons will now become the main supporting points for your chosen thesis. For each reason, provide at least one claim of fact and one claim of value that will support that reason. Accompany these claims with one sentence each of further explanation.

 A terminally ill patient should/should not be allowed to end his or her life.

 Taxpayers should/should not be able to withhold part of their taxes when they are dissatisfied with government actions.

 Female reporters should/should not be allowed access to male locker rooms following sports events.

7. Here is a passage of argumentative writing. Read it closely and analyze the structure of the argument. Then write an essay in which you identify the passage's main claim, evaluate the evidence it puts forward, and discuss the warrants that tie the claim to the evidence — remember, some of the warrants may be implicit, and you will need to put them in your own words. In your conclusion, evaluate the argument as a whole. Do you agree or disagree? Which pieces of evidence are especially convincing or especially weak? Which warrants are especially strong or especially questionable?

Photographing is essentially an act of nonintervention. Part of the horror of such memorable coups of contemporary photojournalism as the pictures of a Vietnamese bonze reaching for the gasoline can, of a Bengali guerilla in the act of bayoneting a trussed-up collaborator, comes from the awareness of how plausible it has become, in situations where the photographer has the choice between a photograph and a life, to choose the photograph. The person who intervenes cannot record; the person who is recording cannot intervene. Dziga Vertov's great film, *Man with a Movie Camera* (1929), gives the ideal image of the photographer as someone in perpetual movement, someone moving through a panorama of disparate events with such agility and speed that any intervention is out of the question. Hitchcock's *Rear Window* (1954) gives the complementary image: the photographer played by James Stewart has an intensified relation to one event, through his camera, precisely because he has a broken leg and is confined to a wheelchair; being temporarily immobilized prevents him from acting on what he sees, and makes it even more important to take pictures. Even if incompatible with intervention in a physical sense, using a camera is still a form of participation. Although the camera is an observation station, the act of photographing is more than passive observing. Like sexual voyeurism, it is a way of at least tacitly, often explicitly, encouraging whatever is going on to keep on happening. To take a picture is to have an interest in things as they are, in the status quo remaining unchanged (at least for as long as it takes to get a "good" picture), to be in complicity with whatever makes a subject interesting, worth photographing — including, when that is the interest, another person's pain or misfortune. (Susan Sontag, *On Photography*)

10 / *Using Evidence*

> *Some circumstantial evidence is very strong, as when you find a trout in the milk.*
>
> *– Henry David Thoreau (1817–1862)*
> *American writer and naturalist*

Although we discussed evidence as part of an argument in Chapter 9, we are now going to examine evidence more closely in its own chapter. We have three reasons for this special treatment. First, evidence will take up the bulk of your argument essays. For a single claim, you may need to present two, three, or perhaps four pieces of evidence. Second, handling evidence well is essential. The processes of gathering, evaluating, interpreting, and defending evidence are major parts of any college work. Third, evidence is extremely varied and therefore complicated. In an essay on the effect of pollution on southern California's ecology, for instance, you would certainly call on expert testimony to analyze the situation, statistics to indicate the rate of increase in pollution, examples of damage, and perhaps other kinds of evidence as well. What evidence you use will depend on what you are trying to prove and to whom.

In the following pages, we discuss seven kinds of evidence available and how to use them.

EXPERT TESTIMONY:
LEARNING FROM THOSE WHO KNOW

Learning to evaluate experts and what they have to say is one of the most important goals of education. All our lives, our opinions and even our values and actions are shaped by experts — the doctor, the lawyer, the engineer, the secretaries of the treasury, state, defense. These experts will not always agree with one another. One lawyer may advise suing, another negotiating. One foreign policy expert says we should send financial aid to Country Y, another says absolutely not. Most of us have not had legal training, and few will know much about Country Y. We have to rely on experts.

What is an expert? An expert is someone who has special skill and knowledge based on careful study and wide experience in a certain area. More than that, an expert has tested his or her skill and knowledge in a public forum — through books, articles, performances, lectures, debates — where other experts can challenge his or her opinion. Expertise must be able to survive public scrutiny. Clearly, the testimony of self-style experts carries little weight. Albert Einstein did not achieve the status of authority until other scientists found evidence for his theory of relativity in their own calculations and experiments. Gregory Bateson became an expert in anthropology by first doing fieldwork and then publishing his findings so that other anthropologists could examine them.

Many assignments in college will test your ability to use expert testimony. An economics instructor could ask you to write an essay on monetary theorists. An Asian history instructor could assign a study of the various interpretations of the 1899–1900 Boxer Rebellion in China. They will want you not merely to condense and repeat what the experts say but to evaluate it and then use it to help you form your own opinion. Once your opinion is firm, you can use expert testimony to support it. To use expert testimony wisely, be both respectful and critical.

You will need to differentiate among three kinds of evidence that experts provide. The first is *facts*. Facts are incontrovertible: anyone investigating a subject would come up with the same facts, the same numbers, the same report.

The United States has experienced inflation almost steadily since 1776.

Until recently, bacteria were a genuine household threat.

If you use only recognized experts, you can rely on the validity of the factual evidence they supply.

Experts become experts not only by knowing facts but also by developing *informed opinions* about them; this is the second kind of evidence they provide. Facts need the play of the human intellect to give them significance. Careful experts constantly bring facts together and interpret them. When a scholar or professional concludes that the facts justify a particular generalization, you can use that generalization as support for your claim. It is not quite a matter of "If Professor X thinks so, it must be so" — Professor Z, also an expert, may disagree. But if Professor X thinks so, then that does carry some weight. For instance, the historian A. J. P. Taylor's opinion that the major factor leading to the end of World War I was a revolution in Germany lends considerable, if controversial, strength to any argument advancing the same point.

The third kind of evidence experts offer can be dangerous for the unwary to use. It is *speculation* neither contradicted nor adequately supported by the facts. As do the rest of us, experts like to project their ideas beyond provable limits. Often this imagining opens up new areas for research and study and may give rise to new facts. But speculation is only what one person, albeit an expert, thinks is plausible. It should be treated as merely a suggestion, a hypothesis, something that *could* be true.

When experts speculate, they qualify their hypotheses with words and phrases like *perhaps, seems, may be, conceivable, possibly*. It is up to the reader to notice those qualifiers and to use the statement accordingly, that is, not as a claim or as an interpretation but as a conjecture.

Check the credentials of any authority you cite. Find out the background and the source of his or her expertise. Assess the range and breadth of any bibliographies provided at the end of articles or books. Check for possible bias — a scientist employed in industry may be slow to find harm in his or her company's products, and a scholar holding a government post may have lost some objectivity. Be aware, too, that their opponents could be equally biased. Be particularly careful with eyewitness accounts in which the observer has a stake in what happened. For example, you should check the official account of the 1966–1976 Cultural Revolution in China against the descriptions by experts with other political and cultural view-points. The same goes for the CIA account of its activities in foreign countries.

STATISTICS AND SAMPLES: THE MAGIC OF NUMBERS

Whether they are raw data or translated into charts and figures, numbers are powerful evidence. Properly used, they can prove a claim rapidly and conclusively. Understanding numbers has become essential to a college education. It is basic to the sciences and the social sciences and is increasingly important to disciplines like history.

Statistics are numerical data gathered and tabulated to yield significant information. Statistical data can be used in many ways. An investigator who had collected a mass of data on grades in a chemistry class, for instance, could construct from it a graph in the form of a curve. At one end of the curve would be the highest grade and at the other end the lowest. If the curve is a bell curve, a gradual increase of numbers would appear from the lowest grade to the middle grade and then a gradual decrease to the highest. Most students, that is, would fall in the middle. Or the investigator could compare each individual's performance with that of the rest of the class by placing him or her at the appropriate place on the curve.

The investigator could also determine the performance of the statistically average student. There are three ways to do this. To compute the *mean*, you add all the grades and divide the total by the number of students. To compute the *median*, you find the grade in the exact middle of the range from highest to lowest. Half the grades would be above the median, half would be below. To compute the *mode*, you determine what grade the greatest number of students achieved. When dealing with averages, pay close attention to which of these methods is used, for computing the mean, median, and mode will render different results.

Scientists often use the technique called *sampling* to discover the typical acts or beliefs of a very large population. Rather than trying to interview or test each individual, the investigator studies a representative number in a group. This is the technique used by Gallup polls. To discover what the American public thinks about an issue,

Gallup poll-takers interview a small representative group of Americans.

The problem arises in selecting the group to be interviewed because it must truly represent the whole. The findings of a study on what Americans think about pornography on cable television, for example, would be distorted if the proportion of pornography watchers in the group studied was higher than in the general population. The result would almost certainly indicate a higher percentage of approval than was the case. Be sure any sampling data you use comes from a representative group.

Numbers can mislead the unwary. Say you are going to write an essay on unemployment. In your research you find a graph in a reputable journal indicating that X million Americans are presently employed, the largest number of workers in America's history. You would perhaps conclude from this that unemployment is not a problem. But then you read in another reputable journal that Y percent of Americans are presently out of work, the largest percentage since 1940. Based on this evidence, you would perhaps conclude that unemployment is in fact a serious problem. Both journals are correct. The problem is that different ways of calculating the numbers tell different stories.

Deep down, we still believe in the magic of numbers. We trust them. But alas, nothing obscures the truth more effectively than numbers misused. Fifty million Frenchmen can't be wrong, says the song. If polls say Senator Smith will be defeated, why bother to vote? Cite numbers, yes, but handle with care.

EXAMPLES: BEING SPECIFIC

Every day of your life you use examples as evidence for your claims. You might say, "*King Kong* has some marvelous scenes. In one scene, Kong is on top of the Empire State Building and the whole thing is swaying." Or you might write to your parents, "Sorry I haven't written much but I've been very busy. I spent last week in the library, bent over the books studying for two midterms." In each case, you establish your claim ("*King Kong* has some marvelous scenes," "I've been very busy") and you back it up with a specific example.

Examples serve three purposes. First, they clarify meaning. Your parents may not know exactly what you mean by *busy* until you show them. Second, examples demonstrate why, at least in one instance, you are justified in making your claim. Two midterms does sound busy. Third, examples make for entertaining reading. Abstractions are dry. Claiming that you are busy isn't very interesting. But the image of you bent intently over a book probably pleases your parents, who may now forgive you for not writing.

We wish we could offer a rule about how many examples you need to prove what, but of course the number varies. The best we can say is, err on the side of abundance, but don't exhaust your reader.

PERSONAL EXPERIENCE: WHAT YOU KNOW ON YOUR OWN

If we actually experience something directly, we don't need experts or statistics to back us up. We saw the robber running from the scene of the crime. We know people lose contact with high school friends. Although we know that our experience is not totally reliable — the robber turned out to be a cocker spaniel — until proven wrong, we trust our senses and our ability to understand our personal experience.

In complex matters, however, beware of jumping to conclusions based on limited personal experience. One occurrence does not make an immutable law. Your experience may help to explain, but it cannot prove a more general thesis. Knowing someone who cheats on her income tax does not prove that the problem with income tax cheaters is pervasive. Even if you know five or ten or twenty cheaters, all that proves is that you are unlucky in your acquaintances. For such a complex subject, you need more than personal experience. You need statistics and expert interpretation.

Personal observation can be useful, nonetheless. In an essay opening it may sharply focus your argument. In a conclusion it may sum up points more emphatically than further exposition. Throughout an essay it may powerfully illuminate facts and figures. Personal experience may not prove much, but it makes for lively reading.

ANALOGY: SHOWING HOW THINGS ARE SIMILAR

An analogy, as we discussed in Chapter 7, is a comparison of apparently dissimilar things, and its purpose is to illuminate one thing by showing how it is like and not like the other. To the extent that analogies make a point easy to see, they are evidence. But they don't prove the point — they can never be sufficient evidence for a complex idea. A student wrote an essay on World War II in which she wanted to suggest that General Eisenhower functioned as coordinator of the armies in the European theater rather than as strategist, tactician, or field commander. She constructed this analogy:

> Eisenhower served as the conductor of the invasion of Europe. He did not write the music or play an instrument, but he selected the music and the musicians, determined the interpretation, kept the beat, and then evaluated the whole performance.

Although this analogy does not prove that Eisenhower was only the coordinator, it clarifies what the student wanted to say. Because she had other powerful evidence, the analogy drove the point home. For a discussion of false analogy, see Chapter 11.

KNOWN FACTS AND SHARED BELIEFS: WHAT WE ALL HAVE IN COMMON

When writing, you can safely assume that you and your reader share a vast body of facts and beliefs. You do not need to provide evidence for things your reader already knows or believes. You do not need to point out that Columbus arrived in America in 1492, that Theodore Roosevelt was once president, that fascism is evil. No one wants to waste time and eyesight reading that sort of thing.

But generally known facts can be effective when used in a surprising context:

> Columbus presumably brought civilization to the Western hemisphere in 1492, but the Mayans knew mathematics and astronomy and practiced urban planning long before that.

Juxtaposing this generally known fact with less familiar information about the Mayans can underscore our cultural bias. Or you might write:

We all believe fascism is evil, but what do we believe about social programs that incarcerate unwilling bag ladies in overnight shelters?

Here, reference to the truism about fascism aggressively questions some elements of our liberal, democratic tradition. When we appeal to known facts and shared beliefs, we strengthen our point.

REASONING AND LOGIC: THINKING IT THROUGH

Sometimes the only evidence you bring to bear is your ability to reason and employ logic. If, say, your instructor asked you to respond to Plato's *Apology* or John Stuart Mill's *On Liberty*, he or she would want to know how you think, not what some professional philosopher wrote about these works. The only relevant evidence would be your reasoning. In Chapter 11, we discuss the basic ways of reasoning. Here, we just want to point out that in your arsenal of evidence, thinking itself is a very powerful weapon.

CRITERIA FOR GOOD EVIDENCE: MAKING SURE

Solid evidence of every variety exhibits the following five qualities.

Relevance

Good evidence speaks directly and unequivocally to the point. You should select a particular piece of evidence because it supports the point, not because it is novel or comic or elegant. In discussing similarities between the foreign policies of Presidents Nixon and Carter, for instance, describe their attitudes toward Israel, for they are relevant. Don't present evidence that the two men are sixth cousins — even though a genealogist claims they are. Their possible kinship is irrelevant. Be sure your evidence speaks to the topic.

Representativeness

Evidence should fairly represent its source or the situation it describes. Sometimes writers ignore large segments of relevant information in order to make a point, as this one did.

> The people of California enjoy an incredibly high standard of living. Malibu has one of the highest concentrations of wealth in the world.

The writer misrepresents the situation by ignoring the much poorer cities like East Palo Alto, San Jose, and Fresno. Be sure you let your reader know the full context of any material you use.

Accuracy

The writer is always responsible for the accuracy of all evidence he or she uses. Even if evidence appears to be from a bias-free source, cross-check it with other sources. In writing a paper about America's economic condition, don't rely only on *Time* or the *New Republic* or *National Review* or *Partisan Review* or even the *New York Times* or the *Los Angeles Times*. Verify the facts.

Detail

The closer your evidence is to the concrete — facts, numbers, quotations from a text — the more believable and acceptable it is. If, for instance, you were describing the ill effects of working around asbestos, you might write,

> Of hundreds of asbestos workers studied in the 1970s, more than a third were dying of cancer.

But how much more potent to do what Paul Brodeur did in "The Asbestos Industry on Trial":

> Dr. Selikoff and his colleagues at Mount Sinai had continued to observe the cause of death among an original group of six hundred and thirty-two asbestos insulators they were studying, and by 1976 a broad picture of the asbestos-disease toll among them had become tragically clear. Nineteen percent of them were dying of lung-cancer;

nine percent were dying of gastro-intestinal cancer; eight percent were succumbing to mesothelioma; and nine percent were being killed by asbestosis and other noninfectious lung diseases.

This direct quotation is more effective than paraphrase or summary. Except where space dictates otherwise, provide the poet's own words, the pollster's charts, the Health Department's statistics. And then interpret them.

Adequacy

No one can state a general rule for the appropriate quantity of evidence. We think lavishness is preferable to stinginess. But choose your places to be lavish. Your supporting points that most importantly support your thesis deserve the most detailed and concrete substantiation. Your second-level points need evidence, too, but don't let them overshadow more important ideas. Your third-level points are lucky to be there at all. And don't be sentimental: if you can't make the evidence fit the idea, let the idea go. In the end, the best way to determine whether or not you have enough evidence is to ask a familiar question: Would a reasonable member of my intended audience be convinced? Once again, put yourself in the reader's place.

TIPS FOR USING EVIDENCE

- When examining what experts say, distinguish facts from interpretation and speculation.
- Be careful when using statistics: they can be dangerous.
- Use examples to clarify meaning, demonstrate why, or entertain your reader.
- Use personal experience sparingly; it carries little weight.
- Remember that though they can clarify a point, analogies cannot prove anything by themselves.
- Remember that reasoning can provide powerful evidence.
- Be sure your evidence exhibits relevance, representativeness, accuracy, detail, and adequacy.

EXERCISES FOR USING EVIDENCE

1. Read the following paragraph.

> I suspect that any new religions that appear in the '80s and '90s will have the computer figuring prominently in them, just as some of the religions of the '60s and '70s have been built around the image of the flying saucer. In some it will play a Satanic role, and it is conceivable that any anti-computer movements of the future will have a mystical — and therefore particularly dangerous — thread running through them. Once again there are straws in the wind. The "down with Western technology" and "back to the fundamental religion" movements which are at this time of writing wracking Iran, Turkey, and Pakistan seem to be manifestations of a more general disquiet but perhaps, unconsciously, *all* human beings deeply resent the advance of science and the inhospitable view of the universe that it is painting, and yearn for a more primitive view of things. These feelings of resentment are only surfacing at the moment in countries where technology is a recent import, but they may in due course surface in the heavily mechanized West, in which case the '90s could turn out to be unexpectedly turbulent. But there also remains the real chance that computers will be seen as deities, and if they evolve into Ultra-Intelligent machines, there may even be an element of truth in the belief. (Christopher Evans, *The Micro Millennium*)

How much credence would you give each kind of evidence the author brings forward? Which elements are fact? interpretation? speculation? Write a paragraph about the passage in which you evaluate the persuasiveness of its evidence.

2. Write an essay in which you interpret the following examples and statistics concerning the crime rate in Bodie, California, a frontier town that boomed in the late 1870s and early 1880s.

> Fistfights and gunfights were regular events.
>
> Stagecoach holdups were not unusual.
>
> The old, the young, the weak, and the female were generally not harmed.
>
> In modern American cities, the old, the young, the weak, and the female are often the objects of crime.
>
> There were eleven stagecoach robberies in Bodie between 1878 and 1882, and in two instances passengers were robbed. Highway robbers usually took only the cashbox carried on the coach.

There were only ten robberies and three attempted robberies of individuals in Bodie from 1878 to 1882.

Bodie's total of 21 robberies over a five-year period converts to the
rate of 84 robberies per 100,000 inhabitants per year.

New York City's robbery rate in 1980 was 1,140 per 100,000 people; Miami's was 995; and Los Angeles's was 628.

The rate for the United States as a whole in 1980 was 243 per
100,000 people.

Between 1878 and 1882 there were 32 burglaries in Bodie; seven-
teen were of homes and fifteen of businesses.

At least six of these burglaries were thwarted by the presence of
armed citizens.

Bodie's burglary rate for those five years was 128 per 100,000 inhabitants.

Miami's burglary rate in 1980 was 3,282 per 100,000 people; New
York's was 2,661; Los Angeles's was 2,602.

The rate for the United States as a whole in 1980 was 1,668 per
100,000 people.

In the relevant period in Bodie, only one woman, a prostitute, was
robbed; there were no rapes.

Thirty-one people in Bodie were shot, stabbed, or beaten to death
from 1878 to 1882.

The homicide rate was 116 per 100,000 inhabitants per year.

In 1980, Miami led the nation with a homicide rate of 32.7 per
100,000 people; Las Vegas was second with 23.4.

The homicide rate for the United States in 1980 was 10.2 per
100,000 people.

The majority of Bodie's residents were young, single males.

Courage was the most admired characteristic.

Alcohol was heavily imbibed.

Most of the young men carried guns.

Most of the shootings in Bodie between 1878 and 1882 involved
willing combatants. (Based on Roger D. McGrath, ''The Heritage of the Frontier.'')

3. What kinds of evidence are represented by the following?

If the efficiency of the car had improved at the same rate as that of
the computer over the last two decades, a Rolls-Royce would
cost about three dollars, would get 3 million miles per gallon of
gas, and would deliver enough power to propel an ocean liner.

The notion that the best way to avoid war is to destroy nuclear
weapons goes against common sense.

A baby chimpanzee far outstrips a human infant in the rate of development of its motor ability, reflexes, and physical coordination.

> We once lived next door to some Somalis. Their house was, of course, always dirty.

Evaluate the quality of the evidence. Write a statement that each item could be used to illustrate. Now decide if you would need another illustration to make the point. If so, provide it (make it up if you must). Make the whole into a paragraph.

4. Find the answer to three of these questions.

> What is the dollar-and-cents value of the human body?
>
> What were the numbers and national origins of immigrants to America between 1900 and 1910?
>
> In which countries is French the official language, and how was it established in each?
>
> What area in the United States had the highest cost of living in 1980, and what area had the lowest? (Be sure to explain how the term *cost of living* is defined.)
>
> What professional basketball team's players received the highest average salaries in 1981, and how did their salaries compare with the average salaries of players on the best-paying teams in football and baseball?

Describe how the statistics or facts in your answers were arrived at. Explain and define any statistical concepts you came across in your research. (This may require some further investigation.)

5. Write an essay in which you use personal experience to support or attack one of the following statements.

> Americans allow their children's adolescence to continue too long.
>
> Memory is a crucial social asset.
>
> Most people pay more attention to their bodies than to their brains.
>
> A high-school education has no practical value and is only a way of keeping young people off the street and out of the job market.

Be sure you tie your experience directly to your thesis statement. In a separate paragraph, indicate how much credence you believe the experience deserves. If the statement needs further evidence, what kind should it be and where would you find it?

6. Using as many different kinds of evidence as you can, write an essay about your family. If you have the information, go back three generations. Include date and place of birth, age, sex, national origin, and occupation for each family member mentioned. In your last two paragraphs, speculate on the future you see for the family as a whole. Base your speculation on the evidence presented in the essay.

11 / *The Critical Consumer of Persuasion*

> *The critical sense is so far from*
> *frequent that it is absolutely rare,*
> *and the possession of the cluster of*
> *qualities that minister to it is one*
> *of the highest distinctions.*
>
> *– Henry James (1843–1916)*
> *American novelist and essayist*

Just as we are trying to sell our ideas when we write, so almost everyone we read is trying to sell us something. They want us to believe what they believe or do what they tell us to. Good consumers of persuasion, however, refuse to buy whatever happens to be on the market. They slow the writer down, look over the product, kick the tires. Only when satisfied about the overall quality will critical consumers buy.

Unless we are willing to sell shoddy goods, and probably get caught in the act, we should be as critical of what we write as of what we read. The writer about whom few are critical enough is the writer within. When we have written something down, we figure we have proven the point when in fact we may need more evidence or a clearer warrant.

Try to become your own audience. Assume the reader's vantage point, and take a hard look at what you have written. Be the critical consumer not only of the work of others but also of your own work.

In the following pages, we discuss the fine points of the logic of argument and the ethics of persuasion. We hope this discussion will help you to know which spark plug isn't firing and to discover the source of the rattles, even in your own chassis.

THE LOGIC OF ARGUMENT: THINKING STRAIGHT

Logic is the study of valid reasoning. It describes the relation between facts and meanings, between evidence and claims. When an argument is "logical," the conclusions based on it are sound. Logic can take the form of either induction or deduction.

Induction

Induction is the act of reasoning from individual facts or cases to a general conclusion. When we reason inductively, we start with particular pieces of evidence and follow them where they lead. We keep amassing evidence until, when we think we have enough, we can make a claim and with the warrant show how the claim is based on the evidence. Here is an example.

> My family was out of town that night. I was reading and I heard a sound. The curtain moved. The shrimp on the kitchen table were missing. I saw the shadow of a human being in the darkened kitchen. Because all these things indicated that a stranger was in the house, I was frightened. I was justified in calling the police.

Claims based on induction are only as good as the strength and breadth of their facts and the strength and relevance of their warrants. In this example, the speaker has a good case for the claim. Drop a few facts, however, and you get this:

> I heard a sound. I was justified in calling the police.

Here, the speaker has leaped to an improbable conclusion. We can test this by articulating the implied warrant.

> Whenever I hear a sound, I should call the police.

With the warrant in place, we can see how unreasonable the argument is

Because we can seldom know every relevant fact, inductive arguments are not apt to be absolutely certain or inevitable. In the very best case, the facts make the claim only *probable*. The more facts, the more probable the claim. A careful writer will indicate the degree of proof by inserting words like *conceivably, possibly, likely,* or *almost certainly*. When a claim should be qualified but these qualifying words are missing, you should refuse to be persuaded.

Deduction

In a deductive argument, we reason from a general statement to an inevitable conclusion. In the very best case, when the premises are true and the reasoning valid, the conclusion is *certainly* true. The most famous example is

> All men are mortal.
> Socrates is a man.
> Therefore, Socrates is mortal.

This form of argument is what logicians call a *syllogism*. It contains two statements and a conclusion. The first statement makes a general assertion, called the *major premise*. This assertion is the foundation of the argument. For the argument to proceed, the reader must accept that *All men are mortal*. The second statement, called the *minor premise*, provides a specific instance of the major premise. It is the link between the major premise and the last statement, which is the claim. The minor premise can be thought of as a warrant. It "warrants" making the claim. Without the warrant, we would have

> All men are mortal. Socrates is mortal.

The reader may ask, What is the thing called Socrates?

> Socrates is a man.

Reasoning from those two premises, the writer arrives at the claim, also called the *conclusion*.

We frequently use this form of reasoning in everyday life, as in this series of statements.

> I always enjoy movies starring Kevin Kline. I am going to see him in his new movie. I will no doubt enjoy it.

Scientists and physicians also think this way.

> White blood cells multiply to combat infection. This blood sample indicates a rapid increase in the white count. There must be an infection.

As in inductive arguments, sometimes the warrant in deductive arguments is assumed.

> As a naval officer and engineer, Jimmy Carter worked with Admiral Rickover on nuclear submarines. Carter must be an expert on nuclear submarines.

Missing from that syllogism is the minor premise, or warrant.

Anyone who worked with Admiral Rickover would become an expert on nuclear submarines.

The validity of a deductive argument depends on both the truth of the premises and the reasoning from the premises to the conclusion.

If either premise is doubtful, then the conclusion is doubtful, as in this syllogism:

All my friends are brilliant.
Conrad is my friend.
Therefore, Conrad is brilliant.

We have to wonder about the truth of the premises. Surely everyone has at least one friend who is not brilliant. That first premise is hard to accept, and therefore the conclusion is doubtful. Conrad may indeed be brilliant, but this argument does not prove it.

Likewise, the reasoning from premises to the conclusion must be valid for the conclusion to be correct. Here is a syllogism that is invalid because of its reasoning.

The state punishes embezzlers.
The state punished Frank.
Therefore, Frank is an embezzler.

The facts are correct: the state does punish embezzlers, and the state did punish Frank. But the reasoning is invalid because the syllogism is incorrectly formulated. The state punishes other criminals besides embezzlers. If the major premise had said, "The state punishes only embezzlers," the reasoning would have been valid. (The technical term for this error is *affirming the consequent*.)

Very few arguments are genuinely deductive. Most are based on some prior induction. In the case of the argument about white blood cells, for example, the first statement — that white cells multiply to combat infection — is a product of an inductive process. When you see a deductive argument, you should also evaluate the inductive argument on which it probably rests.

Logical Fallacies

Errors in induction or deduction are called logical fallacies. These are patterns of reasoning that are at worst completely invalid and at best weaker than they appear to the unwary. Human beings have invented so many logical fallacies that we could never name every possible one. The following eight types, however, are the ones you will encounter most often.

Oversimplification. Most of us take the easy way around complexities whenever possible. When we reason inductively, we are tempted to oversimplify, to ignore some relevant facts. If we are arguing cause and effect, we are tempted to find the *one* cause; if we are trying to make a decison, we look only for easy benefits and clear dangers. Here are five kinds of weak reasoning resulting from such oversimplification.

1. *No choice*: Sometimes writers claim that a question has only one side. *If we want to improve education, we have no choice but to eliminate electives from the high school curriculum.* Almost every question has two, probably more, sides. We have other ways to improve education: cut a few electives, limit extracurricular activities, pay higher salaries to get better teachers, and so on.

2. *Either/or*: Occasionally writers present a false either/or dilemma. *You are either for me or against me.* Not so. I might not care. I might not even know you. *Either we cut off all trade with South Africa or we risk being discredited in the eyes of the world.* If we cut off some trade or exercise other kinds of pressure, chances are other nations will still respect us. A complex question has complex answers.

3. *Nothing but benefits*: Writers sometimes consider only the positive side of a proposition, ignoring the negative or harmful effects. *We should disband the CIA so that our reputation will improve.* Actually, the CIA, for all its problems, helps us in many ways; if we disband it, we will lose those benefits.

4. *The end justifies the means*: Writers sometimes argue that a certain goal is so desirable that it does not matter how we achieve it. They might, for instance, claim, *Restraints on police behavior should be removed because they interfere with apprehending criminals.* Apprehending criminals is certainly desirable, but removing restraints on police behavior could lead to dangers — excessive force, lack of accountability. When you encounter an argument of this type, examine the means of attaining the proposed end at least as closely as you examine the goal itself.

5. *The sole reason*: Occasionally a writer assumes that one reason alone will justify a conclusion and that our task is to find the reason. *We would never have had a drug problem in the United States had it not been for rock and roll music.* There are other reasons for drug abuse, if indeed rock and roll is one.

Hasty Generalization.   Many of us like to leap over all the obstacles in our path and rush to conclusions. But whenever writers, like this one, draw broad conclusions from little evidence, they are guilty of hasty generalization.

> Abraham Lincoln did not start pushing the Emancipation Proclamation until 1863. He really did not care about the problem of slavery.

A writer simply cannot base a sweeping statement like that on one fact. What were the other reasons for the delay, and isn't there evidence that Lincoln cared deeply about the enslaved?

Sometimes writers jump from a small or biased sample to a large general conclusion.

> Senator X never went back to his home district after he left the Senate. Senators would rather live in Washington.

The writer cannot assume that Senator X is typical and that what he does reflects what all senators do. No writer can make an absolute assertion based on one case, or even twenty-five cases. Another twenty-five former senators might have gone home. When writing or reading, be sure every generalization has a broad base. When a general claim is not proved absolutely, the writer should qualify that claim accordingly.

> If the experience of twenty-five senators is typical, then many senators remain in Washington after they leave the Senate.

Non sequitur.   The Latin words *non sequitur* mean "it does not follow." They apply to any argument whose conclusion does not follow from its premises.

> Ralph Warfield will make an excellent governor because he was an excellent captain of his college football team.

This is a deductive argument, but the warrant is not correct. Football prowess has little relevance to political know-how.

Commercials specialize in non sequiturs. If we see a handsome man, a beautiful woman, a lithe cat, and a desert landscape, does it follow that we should want to buy that car?

A second kind of non sequitur occurs when a writer has in mind a connection between two seemingly disparate statements but fails to make that connection clear.

> You should exercise daily because blood lactates are responsible for mental dullness and lethargy.

The missing link might be

> Exercise lowers the quantity of blood lactates.

The writer needs to provide the intervening steps.

Weak, Unclear, or False Analogy.   As we saw in Chapter 10, writers use analogies as evidence for their arguments. Problems arise, however, when they either ignore or suppress differences that invalidate the analogy. Analogies can be weak, unclear, or false depending on how damaging the differences are.

> We can view the African practice of sister-trading to be exactly analogous to conversation, the trading of words.

The analogy is false: conversation is portable and repeatable in a way a sister is not and has no inherent right to be treated with dignity and consideration.

Sometimes a writer uses an analogy indirectly to argue a point the reader would not otherwise agree with, as here:

> Human beings in society are like the bees in a hive. Each person's identity is determined by his or her function and place in the overall system. Like drones, no one has any identity apart from the work he or she does. If people do not work or refuse to conform to the role the system has assigned them, they, like weak or unfit bees, should be thrown out of the system to live or die on their own.

Hey, wait a minute. Analogies are valid only when the two things compared are clearly similar, which beehives and human society are not. The difference between bees and human beings is too great. Think of dissimilarities, and keep your eye on where an analogy will lead you.

Ipse dixit.   The Latin phrase *ipse dixit* means "he himself has spoken." Writers commit this blunder when they appeal to unqualified "experts." Whether as coach or broadcaster, John Madden speaks as an expert on football and could give an authoritative opinion on the right choice for most valuable player, but his background and experience do not qualify him as an authority on politics, beer, or steel-belted radials. No more does Linus Pauling's or Edward Teller's expertise as a scientist mean expertise in politics.

Post hoc, ergo propter hoc. Also from the Latin, the phrase *post hoc, ergo propter hoc* means "after this, therefore because of this." We commit this fallacy when we argue that because x occurred before y, x caused y.

> Herbert Hoover was inaugurated as president in the spring of 1929, and that autumn the stock market crashed. Hoover must have caused the crash.

The causes of the stock market crash go much further back than the spring of 1929 and the actions of a single individual.

A variant of the *post hoc* fallacy is the argument that because A helped bring B about, we will eliminate B by getting rid of A.

> Prime Minister Chamberlain's negotiation with Hitler allowed Germany time to rearm and increased its ability to make war in the 1930s. We should never negotiate.

It may not have been wise to negotiate with Hitler, but this does not mean that negotiation is always unwise. Examine the connection between things that are claimed as causes and their effects.

Circular Reasoning. An argument is circular when it assumes as evidence what it sets out to prove; this is also known as *begging the question*.

> Freud's investigations were truly scientific because they were based on Freud's own clinical research.

Compare the conclusion and the evidence. If they are the same thought but expressed in different words, the reasoning is circular.

Another form of circular reasoning is the *tautology*, that is, an idea repeated in different words.

> We must preserve the American way of life because without it we
> won't be able to live the way Americans should.
> This car doesn't work because something's wrong with it.

These are tautologies because they are tautological.

Ad hominem. The Latin words *ad hominem* mean an argument "to the man," that is, the person making the argument. A writer guilty of this fallacy argues against a claim by presenting irrelevant statements — usually character slurs — about the person who made the claim.

> Ralph Nader's attacks on environmental laws don't amount to a hill of beans. He is conceited and self-righteous.

Maybe he is, but his *opinion* is the point, not his character; he may still have important claims to make about environmental laws.

Ridicule is a particularly effective ad hominem argument because it is based on humor. Once when he saw Sir Stafford Cripps, an old opponent with a reputation for arrogance, Winston Churchill said, "There but for the grace of God goes God." Nevertheless, Churchill had finally to debate the merits of Cripps's proposals.

When reading or constructing an argument, closely examine the logic being used. Remember that between the world of claim and the world of proof yawns a chasm of error.

ETHICS: BEING FAIR

Problems can arise in the ethics of argument as well as in the logic. Ridicule, for instance, easily degenerates into unacceptable ethics. Any trick or slant that tries to pull the wool over the reader's eyes, any disguised or false emotional appeal, anything that denies the reader the chance to make his or her own informed judgment is, purely and simply, unethical. The rest of this chapter outlines the most common unethical methods of argumentation.

Forms of Deception

You need to watch for these four forms of deception in argument.

Intentional Obscurity. We frequently read something that is so vague or ambiguous that we have to assume the writer either was being intentionally obscure or didn't care whether anyone understood. A report on a plan to build a dam included this passage:

Finalization of the project may involve relocation logistics for residents of the area.

That sentence is obscure double-talk for this one:

Before the dam is built, homeowners in the valley will have to move.

Writers tend to use double-talk to gloss over weak, unfair, or unpopular points in their arguments. We sometimes hear indirect slurs in politics.

I'm not judging guilt or innocence, but Representative X could lose his credibility if his alleged involvement with clandestine foreign interests ever comes to light.

Some ideas really are difficult, and obscurity may arise inevitably — for instance, when arguing for a particular interpretation of quarks and quasars. Some subjects even in their simplest form call for difficult language. But good, ethical writers refrain from hiding vulnerable or controversial points in foggy wording.

Rumors and Grapevine Beliefs.   In their desire to have something relevant or interesting to say, writers sometimes pass on as fact thoughts or ideas they do not know to be false — but have no concrete reason to believe true.

It is said that many top Vatican officials are impatient with the conservatism of Pope John Paul II.

We want to know who said it and where the information appeared.

In this passage the writer craftily moves from rumor-as-rumor to rumor-as-fact.

In the years just after the war, reports indicated that De Filippo was apparently under the protection of rebel leaders of the island. He was in hiding with fanatic monks in a small monastery in a secret colony in the Kabbur Mountains.

Notice the shift from the qualified phrases *reports indicated* and *was apparently* to the plain statement *He was in hiding*. This kind of writing can lead to misunderstanding and even serious trouble. Try to distinguish speculation from substantiated fact; it is not always easy, but it is worthwhile.

Phony Fronts.   Writers usually give us a picture of themselves, their attitudes toward the audience, their concern with the subject. Occasionally these portraits may be false or misleading. The writer puts his or her arm around the reader's shoulder and then tries to sell the lemon on the car lot. The following exemplifies a fairly common practice:

> Our company is deeply concerned with clean water and a healthy environment. You can be sure we would not dump this waste in the river if it would in any way harm the water.

Maybe. Or maybe the initial avowal of concern for clean water is only a smoke screen. Try to separate the author's self-portrayal from the merits of what he or she says.

Hidden Ends, Ulterior Motives.   All writers have ends and motives. Most are apparent, but some are not. A manufacturer of computers who argues that relaxed trade restrictions with Communist countries will promote worldwide understanding may only want wider markets for computers. Nothing is wrong with wanting to sell computers, but a reader ought to be aware of the motive. Try to learn or deduce as much as possible about writers, their philosophies, their politics, and their previous views on the subject. Critical readers are informed readers.

Infringing the Rights of Others

In addition to obscuring or deflecting the issue, an unethical writer may also infringe on the rights of others by using and abusing their intellectual property. These tricks are often hard to spot, but they are not as uncommon as we wish they were.

Plagiarism.   Whenever writers state or imply that the language or the ideas in their work are original when in fact they are not, that is plagiarism, literary theft. The writer has passed off as his or her own what is in actuality another's.

Virtually all writers build on what they read. They base their studies on the findings of others or use expert opinions to bolster their arguments. The problem emerges if they do not acknowledge the debt. Everything that a writer gets from some other writer should be acknowledged: an apt phrase, a quotation, a line of argument.

We have more to say on this subject in "Documenting Your Sources" in Chapter 12 — please read it carefully. No quality is more essential for ethical argument than giving credit where credit is due.

Distortion of Quotations.   When quoting or referring to what others have written, a writer must, out of common decency, treat what was said in its proper context and respect its intended meaning. Distorted, any statement could look bad.

Let's look at three ways a writer might distort the following passage:

> Our society has failed utterly to treat women, blacks, and other minorities as equal to the dominant white male. If we can do no better than we have, then totalitarianism and fascism, where all are equals for better or for worse, in this respect are preferable to the democratic way of life.

The language is strong and the point clear, but suppose another writer wished to put the author of this passage in a bad light. She might simply misquote.

> The author has called for "totalitarianism in place of democracy."

This is a flagrant case of misquotation, and many readers would probably detect it. To make the smear campaign a little subtler, however, our unethical writer could quote exact words but out of context.

> The author is on record as saying that "totalitarianism and fascism . . . are preferable to the democratic way of life."

From this example you can see how those little dots, called ellipses, can wholly distort a statement.

A third shady maneuver is to bend the author's meaning, willfully to misunderstand it. This has the slimy beauty of being hard to trace.

> What the author wants is the abolition of all democratic institutions and the forcible establishment of equality, by an authoritarian state if necessary.

Whenever you see another writer use a quotation, look out for scanty discussion of context, ellipses, or interpretations that seem extreme or surprising. If you can, compare the quoted version with the full passage in the original work. And in your own writing, don't misquote, quote out of context, or bend another writer's words.

Insincere Appeals to Emotion

Writers do not persuade readers through logic alone; they also appeal to their readers' emotions. *Pick up your room or I will spank you* probably appeals to the emotion of fear. *I've never seen* Gone with the Wind — *please go with me tonight* appeals to both emotion and reason: it provides a good explanation but also arouses the other person's affection. Although it contains no explicit appeal, *Please pass the salt* possesses implicit appeals to both emotion and reason. The desire to please appeals to emotion, and complying with a reasonable request appeals to reason.

Used sincerely and honestly, emotional appeals have a place in argument. Honest writers use emotion to guide their audience and to bring about a deeper commitment to the ideas expressed. They also quite candidly express their own feelings. In many situations it would be impossible, even foolish, to pretend that reason alone was operating, that the writer did not care one way or the other.

The following passage shows a writer using strong emotional appeals to make his point more convincing.

> Burn down your cities and leave your farms, and your cities will spring up again as if by magic; but destroy our farms, and the grass will grow in the streets of every city in the country. (William Jennings Bryan, Speech to the National Democratic Convention, 1896)

The shape and rhythm of the clauses, the pictures of violent destruction, magical growth, and grass growing in the streets — all make a strong appeal to our respect for the farms and our fear of their collapse. Bryan's appeals mirror his own emotions and thus are honest and ethical.

When a writer uses emotional appeals to mask the logical or moral weaknesses of an argument, however, that writer is being unethical. Some writers try to arouse emotion in order to distort, not support, the reasoning process. They calculate appeals that will stampede or bully the audience. They express emotion not because they feel it but because they want the audience to feel it and to be overcome by it. Here are seven common danger areas.

Appeal to Pride or Vanity

Any intelligent person would agree that we need a proctoring system at this school because only a small proportion of students have the inner strength and character to resist cheating.

Appeal to Fear

Rock music is harmful because it is turning our youth into enervated zombies, sapping the strength of the American character from within, and exposing us to takeover by our enemies.

Appeal to Hatred or Prejudice

Unless we want our children growing up working for the Japanese, we should not allow foreign cars into this country.

Appeal to Pity

We really should not send felons to work camps. A cousin of mine was so broken physically and emotionally after serving time that his little sister had to support him.

Appeal to Patriotism

Gun control legislation would undermine the very fiber of this nation and destroy what makes us great.

Appeal to Conformism or the Bandwagon Instinct

Try some of this stuff — everybody else is doing it.

Appeal to Greed

If the administration did away with student aid, it could lower tuition, and we would all have more money.

Each of these appeals goes right to heart of a basic human emotion. We could add appeals to sloth, lust, and all the rest of the sins, deadly or venial. Unfortunately, some writers use these to deflect attention from their claims and befuddle our reason. Whenever you sense that an argument is pulling heartstrings rather than proving claims, be wary.

TIPS FOR THE CRITICAL CONSUMER

- Remember that even in the best case, a conclusion from induction is only *probable*.
- Remember that only when facts are correct and reasoning valid does deduction provide a certain conclusion.
- Avoid the most common logical fallacies: oversimplification;

hasty generalization; non sequitur; weak, unclear, or false analogy; *ipse dixit*; *post hoc, ergo propter hoc*; circular reasoning; and ad hominem. Watch how other writers reason.

- Do not deceive your reader with intentional obscurity, rumors and grapevine beliefs, phony fronts, or hidden ends and ulterior motives. Watch for such tactics in what you read.
- Respect the rights of others — do not plagiarize or distort quotations. Watch how other writers treat quotations.
- Avoid insincere appeals to emotion, especially pride or vanity, fear, hatred or prejudice, pity, patriotism, the conformism or bandwagon instinct, and greed. Question how other writers use appeals to emotion in their arguments.

EXERCISES FOR THE CRITICAL CONSUMER

1. Read the following statements and spot any problems in their reasoning.
   a. The health commissioner just ordered all child-care centers closed. That's exactly what you would expect him to do — he's a rich doctor and has no children.
   b. Right after Carl started using Mr. Good deodorant, Wanda said she would go dancing with him. Mr. Good does it again!
   c. Grandfather lived to be a hundred. That means there is something special in my genes.
   d. My son went to Yale, and now he doesn't want to go to medical school. I want my daughter to be a doctor, and so I won't send her to Yale.
   e. Drug abusers are mentally ill. My mother is a lawyer and has defended a lot of them, and she says so.
   f. We should close the student union so that there will be more money for scholarships.
   g. There is nothing for us to do but capitulate to the terrorists' demands.
   h. It was a mistake to make this a coed dorm. Ever since they allowed males to live here, we've had an increase in thefts.
   i. We should bring back grading on a curve. That would stop grade inflation.
   j. Because the English don't arrest drug addicts but instead have government clinics, they have fewer addicts than we do.
   k. Letting students have a say in what goes on at this school is like letting the inmates run the asylum.
   l. The president should have the right to make decisions about national security without media criticism.

m. Marijuana is evil because of its harmful effects.

n. We must make absolutely certain that no homosexuals teach in the schools. Otherwise, our national values will crumble.

o. I really don't care that I lost the election. I just thank God that we live in a democracy.

p. Those who oppose a Western civilization requirement must believe that ideas are not important.

q. The instructor gave me a C because he didn't like me.

r. People who argue for increased defense spending want to turn the country into a military state.

s. People who argue against increased defense spending have IQs as high as their ages.

2. Here is a letter to the editor.

Dear Editor:

For the very reason the minimum wage should be lowered for teenagers, it should be abolished for everyone. Just as shoppers at my grocery store buy more blueberries at a lower price, employers will hire more labor at a lower wage. That, of course, would mean less unemployment, and less unemployment would mean less welfare, and that would mean lower taxes. If people did not have to pay so much money in taxes, they would have increased purchasing power. And that in turn would make for more workers being employed. We would be far along in solving our economic problems. If we don't get rid of the minimum wage, we might as well give up pretending we have a free enterprise system.

Analyze this letter sentence by sentence. Evaluate the use of facts. Identify all logical fallacies and any ethical failures. Assess the writer's objectivity. Now brainstorm the same issue and come up with either a revision or a rebuttal.

3. Try your hand at some illogical and unethical writing. Write a paragraph about one of the following subjects:

No one over age eighty should serve in the U.S. Senate.

Anyone who has imbibed any alcohol within ten hours of driving should receive an automatic jail sentence.

Zoos should be outlawed.

College students are incapable of deciding their course of study; this should be done by the school officials.

Be sure you have at least one problem — logical or ethical — in each sentence. Then rewrite the paragraph, keeping the main idea but removing all the problems.

4. From this list choose someone you have never heard of, and then go to the library and find something that person has written.

Betty Friedan	Norman Podhoretz	Patrick Buchanan
Phyllis Schlafly	George F. Will	Roy Wilkins
Hunter Thompson	Irving Howe	Richard Rodriguez
Angela Davis	Edward Said	Helen Caldicott

Do not read anything about the person, even if it prefaces his or her work. Based solely on what the person wrote, write a short biography of him or her. Include age, occupation, and, most important, values and politics. What issues would the person be most likely to write about? What stands would he or she take? All of this you will, of course, have to invent based on what you read. Now go to some biographical source and find out about the person. Were you more or less correct? If you were far off the mark, go back to the reading you did and analyze what about it gave you a wrong impression. Write a report about your findings. Be as objective as you can.

/part five

Putting It
All Together:
College Writing

12 / Writing Research

> My library
> Was dukedom large enough.
> – William Shakespeare
> The Tempest, 1.2.109–110

Somewhere along the way it is going to happen. A teacher, an employer, or a colleague will ask you to study a topic thoroughly, gather information, and write a paper that communicates your research in an accessible form. A time-honored response is to wait until the last moment, then whirl in a frenzy to the library for two days, thence to the typewriter and correction fluid, pencils, erasers, and coffee, to bash out an overnight wonder. This method has a world of drawbacks. The results are almost always shabby. Worst of all, last-minute researchers waste a real opportunity to do something challenging and significant.

Research gives us an excellent chance to pull together what we have learned in a course and to learn a great deal on our own about an important topic. If researched haphazardly and written carelessly, a research paper can be a tedious, sloppy mess; if treated with care and consideration, it can be a source of pride.

Modern researchers have a powerful arsenal of tools and techniques. The most powerful is still the mind, its interests, its way of seeing things. Research tells you almost as much about yourself as about your topic. That may be why so many people like doing it. Research has its own suspense, its close calls, its mystery trails, its revelations. Enjoy it.

No research project happens all at once. Like any writing project, it emerges out of a process. We will divide that process into ten stages and then look at each.

Choosing a General Subject
Compiling a Working Bibliography
Limiting Your Area of Research
Formulating a Tentative Thesis
Reading and Taking Notes
Restating Your Thesis
Preparing an Outline
Writing a First Draft
Documenting Your Sources
Revising, and Writing the Final Draft

If these stages sound like repetitions of much of our book, all the better: a research paper requires us to combine all our critical and analytical skills with all our writing skills, from drafting and inventing to choosing words.

The order of these stages varies from project to project, but no research paper is written without involving all of them. Some stages repeat themselves; research is a recursive rather than a linear process. Be ready to restate your thesis many times, to return to the library again and again, to go back over steps you thought you had left behind. To leave any of the steps out is to court mediocrity.

CHOOSING A GENERAL SUBJECT

A research paper has to be about something. That seems perfectly obvious, but, strangely enough, some writers neglect this essential requirement. They circle a possible topic page after page, switch to another one, and perhaps somewhere near the end, discover what it was they should have been discussing all along. By then, of course, it is too late. The first step in writing a research paper is to choose the general subject you will study.

Research topics will come to you along different paths. Your instructor may explicitly define the topic or leave it as broad as possible.

Working with an Assigned Topic

When you are given a topic for writing, read the assignment carefully. You will want to stay within its limits. Look carefully at the questions or statements your instructor provides. You may find clues in them to direct you. Here, for instance, is a research assignment for an African studies class.

Examine studies done by Warner, Junker, Adams, and Edwards. Compare their thinking about black group stability on the basis of class, economics, and social structure.

Go straight to the command words, *examine* and *compare.* They lead to both the sources (the various studies) and the subject (*their thinking about black group stability*). The assignment even provides subheadings (*class, economics, and social structure*) that could help you organize your paper.

Here an instructor limits the topic in a different way.

What in your opinion were the main causes of the Johnson administration's "failure" in Vietnam in 1964–1967? Argue with references to documents, debates in the press, and major scholarly interpretations.

Rather than asking for an analysis of what scholars have written, this instructor wants you to defend an opinion. He has been unusually kind, providing not only the topic and a suitable strategy (cause and effect) but also a possible theme: "failure." Those quotation marks are asking you to define the term, perhaps even to disagree with the verdict that the administration's policy *was* a failure. The assignment also specifies a time frame (1964–1967) and three broad kinds of sources. It will be up to you to limit the topic further in your research paper. But again, the way the question is phrased has given some idea of how to begin.

Discovering Your Own Topic

Frequently you will have free rein to do research on any aspect of a course. You will find your own topic. You might discover a topic in the form of a surprise in the course. In the assigned reading for a course on architecture, for instance, you might come upon this sentence:

> Now Jefferson's plan [for Monticello] prefigures that by Frank Lloyd Wright of the Ward Willits House of 1902.

If you had never thought of Thomas Jefferson as an important architect, that might lead you to consider whether other architects were deeply influenced by him. Your research project would be your opportunity to find out. Or in a psychology class your lecturer may comment in passing that

> Communist governments have been especially critical of Freudian forms of therapy.

If you want to know why, you may have a research topic.

Take pains to choose a subject area large enough to offer you interesting research but small enough to allow you to treat it fully. No single paper can cover the whole field of Soviet-American relations or American fiction in the twentieth century. Researcning a large, amorphous subject can be like trying to serve Jell-O with your fingers.

Begin thinking about your subject early. Go over your textbooks, notes, and assigned readings. Think over the possibilities. Brainstorm. Free-write. Question yourself and the subject systematically. Write out a few ideas. Let your ideas ripen.

You may have trouble brainstorming if you don't know much about a topic. In that case, off to the library immediately: crack open some encyclopedias and other general reference works on the subject. Get some background. Talk to your instructor. See how the subject looks before trying to narrow it.

When you have found a subject, you will need to start narrowing it to a manageable size. Here are ways of narrowing the two broad subjects we mentioned earlier.

Soviet-American relations
   Soviet-American relations and human rights
      Soviet-American relations and Russian dissidents

American fiction in the twentieth century
   American short fiction in the twentieth century
      American short fiction in the 1920s

These topics are still too broad to write on, but they are a proper size for starting a research project.

Christina Gerke, who wrote the paper reproduced at the end of this chapter, had complete freedom in her freshman composition class to choose her research topic. She was also taking a course entitled Contemporary American Society, which had made her interested in the changes taking place in America. She knew that this topic was far too broad for a research project, so she began to whittle it down.

Recent changes in American society
   Minorities and recent changes in American society
      Minorities and the educational system

Now she still had a broad subject, but she had enough direction to make her first sweep of the library.

COMPILING A WORKING BIBLIOGRAPHY

Once you have chosen a general subject, it is time to begin your library work. Notice that this is the groundwork for more extensive research later. You are scouting ahead, getting the lay of the land, so that when the time comes for the real journey to begin, you will know where everything is.

Your main aim during this first sweep, which will take a number of visits to the library, is to compile a working bibliography, or a list of the books, articles, and other sources to be consulted in your research. The working bibliography will help you come up with the list of works cited in your final paper. Many instructors also require that you submit a preliminary bibliography at some early point in the research process, and this stage will help you compile one.

You will find titles of and leads to sources in many of the places we discuss in this section; you will also find them in the bibliographies of the books and articles you consult. Each source will send you to more sources, and so your working bibliography will grow. Make your list using notecards — they are the neatest and easiest way (see a system for note taking in the next section). Add to and delete from your working bibliography as you extend your research.

Time Management

You will want to use your research time as efficiently as possible. Here are five hints on how to do so.

1. Start early on all projects. As we suggested in Chapter 1, a good rule of thumb is to start writing about halfway between the time you receive the assignment and the deadline. That means that your research should have been started well before then—certainly before a third of the time has passed. Remember that every step will take half again as long as you think it will. Do not rely on the pressure of an advancing deadline to squeeze a project out of you.

2. Make frequent two- or three-hour visits to the library. This method usually works much better than marathon sessions. First, it gives you more time to ponder what you find. Second, you will remember and understand more in shorter sessions than when you are fatigued, hungry, and under pressure — for instance, frantically researching at three o'clock in the morning during the last week of the term.

3. Since few of us are at tip-top form all day, do your most challenging and creative work at your best time, whether that is early morning or late evening. Search, read, and take notes then; review notes and drafts when you begin to run down.

4. Schedule your research visits for the same time every day, if possible. Like you, your brain likes habits.

5. Find a place free of distraction for your work. If your dorm room is a popular conversation spot, avoid it. If the library is a social center, check out the books and flee. Take frequent short breaks; get a drink or just gaze out the window. But make the breaks short; don't steal time from yourself.

Using Notecards

Here you are, in the optimal place at the best time, notecards and sources at hand. Yes, notecards. Even at this early juncture, you will want to retain what you read. Do not rely on memory. Take careful notes.

For each source you plan to consult in detail, make a *main entry card*. This card will contain all the vital information about the source. Put down the author's last and first names, the title, the jour-

Figure 12.1   Main Entry Notecard

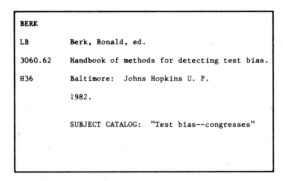

```
BERK

LB          Berk, Ronald, ed.

3060.62     Handbook of methods for detecting test bias.

H36         Baltimore:   Johns Hopkins U. P.

            1982.


            SUBJECT CATALOG:   "Test bias--congresses"
```

nal name (for articles), and all publication information (place, publisher, date). Be sure you include the library call number. And in case you need to return to it, write down where you found the source mentioned — what list, bibliography, or subject heading. Put the author's last name in capital letters in the upper-left corner of the card. Losing or garbling any bibliographic information could cost you time later — or even the ability to cite a promising source.

Figure 12.1 shows a main entry card that Christina Gerke made during her research.

We will discuss note taking in more detail in "Taking Notes" on page 340. Here we want to emphasize that you should always make a complete record of every source that you expect to consult in any extensive way.

The Modern Library

Although most research will rely on the written word, college and university libraries house not only stacks of books. Researchers now must know more than how to look up an article or a book title. Computer data bases, record collections, audio- and videotape collections, motion picture catalogs, and interlibrary loan services are among the resources available to you. Few libraries have all these, but most now offer many of them.

If a researcher was studying "The Treatment of Japanese-American Servicemen during the Second World War," the traditional and necessary first approach would be to amass the titles of relevant books and articles. But it is not hard to think of materials that would augment the information in printed sources: newsreels and photographs, audio- and videotapes of interviews with Japanese veterans, even memorabilia in a university collection. This kind of research can aid the traditional kind in creating a fully rounded and persuasive project.

Therefore, *know your library*.

As early as possible in your education, take a tour of your school's main library and learn the locations of any other libraries on or near campus. If your school offers guided library tours, take one. If your library offers informational pamphlets, read them. Detailed knowledge of a college or university library system would take a research project in itself, but you will find it useful to develop a general idea of what materials are where. You might not have planned to step into the campus geology library, for instance, but you may find it useful if you do a report on the San Francisco earthquake of 1906. Also, learn about other institutions affiliated with yours. Become familiar with your school's information network.

Oh, yes — know the hours the libraries keep. Save yourself disappointment later.

Finally, get to know the librarians. People are often a library's most valuable resource. Librarians have been trained to know their collections and other available resources and to help those who do not know them as well. Reference librarians are paid to answer your questions, so ask them. And circulation librarians can help you locate a book if you cannot find it on the shelf; if you need it badly, they can even call it back for you.

Primary and Secondary Sources

In the library you will find two kinds of material: primary and secondary sources. You will probably use both, but it is important to distinguish between the two.

Primary sources are the contemporaneous documents relating to a subject: letters, interviews, polls, eyewitness accounts, experiments, speeches, and surveys. To write an essay on the battle of Vicksburg during the Civil War, you could consult *The Official Records of the War of the Rebellion between the Armies of the United States and the Armies of the Confederacy*, which contains primary documents, including military orders. Most instructors want you to examine available primary sources at some stage in your research. You can even create your own primary sources when you conduct interviews or take polls. For a discussion of this topic, see "Being Your Own Source," page 333.

Secondary sources are what other investigators have said about a subject. Douglas Southall Freeman's great tome *Lee's Lieutenants*, a scholar's informed study of the decision makers in Lee's army, is a highly useful secondary source on the battles of the Civil War. (For a discussion of how to evaluate and use the expert evidence that secondary sources represent, see Chapter 10, Using Evidence.)

Most instructors want you to consult whatever primary documents are involved with your topic along with reliable secondary sources. Strike the proper balance between the two in your research: do not neglect primary sources, but do not ignore the helpful insights that secondary sources represent.

The Reference Section

The main library will probably be your research center, and its reference section will be an early stop. Here you will find overviews of virtually every subject and guides to getting right to the more detailed information. Start big. Consult general surveys of your topic. Once you get an overview, you will know much better what aspect you want to pursue. Encyclopedias are especially good for background reading; they can provide you with the main terms, controversies, and people in your subject. Even if you do not have a subject yet, you may find one while looking through general reference works. Among the many types of resources available in the reference section, we will describe eight that you will find especially helpful.

General Encyclopedias. General encyclopedias offer broad overviews of a variety of topics. Indeed, they are a library in themselves. Consulting them is a sensible first step: what you find under the entry for your subject can provide a capsule survey, including a list of books for further reading. Christina Gerke consulted encyclopedia entries for "Intelligence" and "Education" as a first step in her research. Among the best general encyclopedias are *Collier's Encyclo-*

pedia, Encyclopedia Americana, Encyclopaedia Britannica, and *New Encyclopaedia Britannica.*

Specialized Encyclopedias. After consulting a general encyclopedia, you will probably want to follow up your leads by looking at a specialized one. Almost all fields have their own encyclopedias. They can help you with definitions of special terms and recurrent themes within a subject. Christina Gerke, for instance, looked in *The Encyclopedia of Education* for a discussion of educational testing. Here are some other specialized encyclopedias:

> *Encyclopaedia of Religion and Ethics*
> *Encyclopedia of World Art*
> *International Encyclopedia of Film*
> *International Encyclopedia of the Social Sciences*
> *McGraw-Hill Encyclopedia of Science and Technology*
> *Oxford Companion to English Literature*

Dictionaries. Dictionaries offer not only spellings, etymologies, and histories of words but also rules of punctuation, indexes of foreign phrases, and lists of famous people and places. Dictionaries become important at many points in research. When Christina Gerke needed a good, solid definition of *intelligence*, she consulted the dictionary, where she discovered that the word refers not to one thing, but to many, including understanding, quickness, and wisdom. She realized that measuring intelligence would not be an easy task. The dictionary she consulted is generally viewed as the most comprehensive and scholarly in English, the *Oxford English Dictionary.* Also among the most wide ranging and thorough is *Webster's Third New International Dictionary of the English Language.* (For more on dictionaries, see the discussion in Chapter 7, Working with Words, page 208.)

Biographical Works. Biographical works contain brief, informative entries on prominent people, detailing their lives and achievements. Such directories exist for people living and dead, for different countries, and for various fields. Some are periodicals, and some are updated every few years. Consult them if you want to know more about the people in your study, or if you wish to follow up on unfamiliar names. Christina Gerke consulted *Who Was Who* to learn more about Alfred Binet, and *Who's Who in America* for more on Arthur Jensen, both influential figures in educational testing. Other valuable biographical works include

> *American Men and Women of Science*
> *Biography and Genealogy Master Index*
> *Biography Index*
> *Current Biography*
> *Dictionary of American Biography*
> *Dictionary of National Biography* (British)
> *International Who's Who*
> *Notable American Women*

Guides to Books.   Guides to books can tell you what is currently being published in your field. Two general guides are *Books in Print*, yearly lists of books by author, title, and subject, and *Book Review Digest*, which offers summaries of book contents and reviews.

Atlases.   Atlases contain more than maps. They can help you locate unfamiliar place names and also give you extremely useful facts and statistics about topology, population, economics, and forms of government. There are atlases for the whole world, for single countries, for specific regions, for the oceans, and for the heavens. There are atlases for the modern world and for the ancient world. Here is a small sampling: *Historical Atlas of the World, National Atlas of the United States of America,* and *The Times Atlas of the World.*

Yearbooks.   Yearbooks summarize the issues, events, and statistics of a given year. Many are connected with encyclopedias. They chronicle a year's major events. A few examples are *Americana Annual, Britannica Book of the Year*, and *Facts on File Yearbook.*

Almanacs and Gazetteers.   Almanacs, such as *The World Almanac and Book of Facts,* can be either compendia of broad, general information arranged by the days of the year or annual general reviews of statistics and facts of all kinds. Gazetteers, such as the *Columbia Lippincott Gazetteer of the World,* are geographic dictionaries. Both contain useful information. If you cannot find the reference works you need, ask your reference librarian.

Book Files and Catalogs

If you spend some time doing patient and alert reading in the reference section, you will emerge with a list of authors and titles of books. You may well return to the reference section later as you learn more about your subject. But now you need to know which of these books the library has. The library's book files and catalogs are your next stop.

If you are not familiar with the following files and catalogs, take time to learn their location and their use. Many libraries now have catalogs in different forms, including bound books, microfilm or microfiche, and computer searches. The most familiar form is the card catalog, which lists each book the library owns on a separate card. The cards are arranged alphabetically by author, by title, and by subject heading. Some libraries house these catalogs separately, and some combine them in a central card catalog. Each card provides the call number by which you can locate a book on the shelves.

In a bibliography on educational testing, Christina Gerke had discovered a listing for "Austin, G., and H. Gardner, *The Rise and Fall of National Test Scores*." Figure 12.2 shows the *author card* she

Figure 12.2   *Main Entry Library Card*

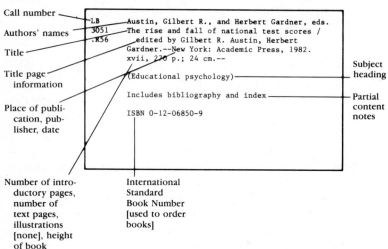

Call number

Authors' names

Title

Title page information

Place of publication, publisher, date

```
 ┌LB        Austin, Gilbert R., and Herbert Gardner, eds.
   3051      The rise and fall of national test scores /
  .K56        edited by Gilbert R. Austin, Herbert
             Gardner.--New York: Academic Press, 1982.
             xvii, 270 p.; 24 cm.--

             (Educational psychology)

             Includes bibliography and index

             ISBN 0-12-06850-9
```

Subject heading

Partial content notes

Number of introductory pages, number of text pages, illustrations [none], height of book

International Standard Book Number [used to order books]

Figure 12.3 *Sample Title and Subject Library Cards*

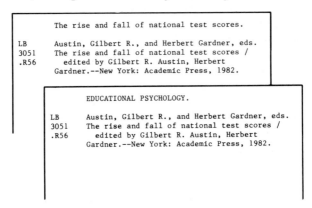

```
        The rise and fall of national test scores.

LB      Austin, Gilbert R., and Herbert Gardner, eds.
3051    The rise and fall of national test scores /
.R56       edited by Gilbert R. Austin, Herbert
        Gardner.--New York: Academic Press, 1982.

        EDUCATIONAL PSYCHOLOGY.

LB      Austin, Gilbert R., and Herbert Gardner, eds.
3051    The rise and fall of national test scores /
.R56       edited by Gilbert R. Austin, Herbert
        Gardner.--New York: Academic Press, 1982.
```

found for that book under *A* for Austin in her library's author-title catalog. The call number in the upper-left corner led Gerke to the right floor of the library, then to the right shelf, then to the right book.

The *title card* (see the Austin and Gardner example in Figure 12.3) is exactly the same as the author card, except that it has the title at the top and is filed alphabetically by the first word of the title, not counting *a, an,* and *the.*

The *subject card* lists the work alphabetically under the subject heading or headings shown on the title card. The subject card for Austin and Gardner, under *Educational psychology,* appears in Figure 12.3

Subject headings can be a good lead in your research and can be used to locate books classified under both the Library of Congress and Dewey Decimal systems. Your library reference desk will have books called the *Library of Congress Subject Headings,* which list all the subject headings most library catalogs use. Consult them to see the range of headings that may apply to your subject. If your library uses the Dewey Decimal Classification System, consult the *Dewey Decimal Classification and Relative Index* for a directory of subjects. Once you have the headings, you can examine the card catalog to learn what your library has on the subject. Christina Gerke first searched under the heading *Educational psychology*; a cross-reference sent her to *Educational tests and measurements*, under which she found this list of other possible headings:

Ability — testing
Character tests
Examinations
Grading and marking (students)
High school placement test
Iowa tests of educational development

The subject heading directories cannot tell you which headings will fit your subject and which will not — you must determine that. Since most of us start off as novices in our subject, we must use our imaginations to decide which leads to follow. *Ability testing* and *High school placement tests* were closer to Gerke's interest; *Character tests* and *Grading and marking (students)* did not seem relevant. She could now return to the card catalog and see what books the library had under the headings she had chosen. More and more, she gravitated to tests and their effect on minorities. The process of going from reference works to catalogs to subject headings, and deciding which titles and subjects to follow and which not, can help narrow a subject.

When using the files and catalogs, be a sleuth. Follow leads. Trace connections between ideas. When you know a few names, check under the authors' listings to see if they have written other books on the subject. Check subject headings under major key words you find in your study — *testing, educational psychology*. And do not forget to complement your search for books with an equally vigorous search for articles in periodicals.

Periodical Catalogs and Guides

The library's periodical catalog lists all the newspapers, newsletters, magazines, journals, and other periodicals the library owns. College writers sometimes avoid periodicals, probably because the process of finding books seems more familiar and less complicated. Locating an article is occasionally more difficult than tracking down a book, but the rewards can be worth the effort. Periodicals are rich, varied research sources. They carry the latest scholarship and debate: you cannot ignore them if you want to know what people are thinking or learning *now*.

You can locate the issues you want in a general or specialized periodical index. Recent issues will be out on the shelves in what is often called the Periodical Room. Older issues are usually bound and located in a special section of the library. Many libraries are now putting older periodicals on microfilm. Using material stored on microfilm is just as easy as turning pages.

General Periodical Indexes. General periodical indexes are invaluable directories to articles. They are organized in different ways, alphabetically or chronologically, but it will only take a moment to figure out the organization. Four extremely helpful general indexes are the *Essay and General Literature Index,* the *Newspaper Index,* the *New York Times Index*, and the *Readers' Guide to Periodical Literature.*

The New York Times Index is a traditional source for many research projects on current events or recent history. In the 1975 volume of the index, Gerke found one of her sources (see Figure 12.4). At first she had looked under the heading *Scholastic Aptitude Test,* which referred her to the heading *Colleges and Universities — United States — Grading of Students.* One article listed there sounded promising. To find it she went to the microfilm room of the library, got the spool that included the May 4, 1975 issue of the *New York Times*, located the proper section, and read the article. She thought the information well worth her search.

The *Readers' Guide* is also a good starting point for research. It indexes articles in popular periodicals by year, by quarter, and by month, and it lists articles by author and by subject. Be careful with it, though — not all the periodicals it covers are authoritative. Check the title of the journal and the author's credentials.

Gerke consulted the *Readers' Guide* to look for up-to-date entries on standardized testing. In the March 1982–February 1983 volume, for example, she found a source (see Figure 12.5). First she looked under the heading *Aptitude tests*, which referred her to the heading *Educational tests and measurements*, and there she saw an article with a possibly relevant title. Her next step was to locate where older issues of *New Republic* magazine were shelved in the library and look for the December 20, 1982 issue.

Figure 12.4 *Entry from the* New York Times Index

Main subject heading —————— **COLLEGES and Universities – United States – Finances – Cont**

Nathan Kolodney disagrees with Prof Richard Gambino's remarks on Jews in Dec 8 article on high cost of coll educ, Ir, D 20,26:5

NY Times survey of NYC's fiscal crisis notes leading social scientists see parallel between that plight and plight of univ; notes costs have spiraled for colls, and tuition often exceeds means of students, while full-time teaching load is 6-8 hours per week in many insts, with 4-month vacations; Yale Univ Prof Douglas Yates cites 'unconscious acceptance of past practice' (M), D 29,50:7

Subheadings and —————— •*Foreign Students.* **See** subhead Foreign Study
list of other relevant •*Fraternities and Sororities.* **See also** names
subheadings

Pres Ford on Dec 31 signs bill containing amendment following up regulation on sex discrimination in educ activities issued by HEW; measure exempts from provisions membership practices of tax-exempt social fraternities and sororities (S), Ja 1,36:4

•*Grading of Students.* **See also** subhead US – Adult Education, Ag 3. Subhead US – Equal Educ, Ja 16. Subhead US – Student Activities, My 18

Jackson never graduated from hs; NCAA official Bill Hunt
Author's name —————— comments on increased violation of acad rules; King illus (M), F 7,22:3; Diane Ravitch article explores history,
Detailed summary —————— theory, purpose, value and other aspects of Scholastic Aptitude Test (SAT), which will be given this yr to some 1.5-million hs srs seeking to enter coll; notes supporters of tests view them as reliable indicators for predicting coll performance, while critics contend tests are racially and culturally biased; some educators concede tests may be culturally biased to extent that reading is culturally linked; many colls are now giving weight to other factors, such as depth of preparation and unusual personal qualities, in admitting students; modifications expected in some aspects of tests but prospects for future is that testing, evaluation and assessment on national basis will be a regular and
Date, section of the paper, pervasive aspect of educ policy; samples of typical
and page on which the questions from SAT exams; student taking exam illus (L),
article begins. Note: you My 4,VI,p12; Mrs Charles M Apt Ir on Diane Ravitch May
must consult the article 4 article on College Entrance Examination Bd holds
itself for the title and manner in which exam dates are set militates against public
pagination. school students; Ravitch replies; illus, Je 8,VI,p54; efforts on some coll campuses to do away with grade inflation, by

Specialized Periodical Indexes and Bibliographies.

Specialized periodical indexes and bibliographies list articles and books in specific fields. They are a natural resource as your subject focus narrows and you need more specific information. After using the general indexes, Gerke consulted the *Social Sciences Index* and the *Education Index*, both of which yielded further leads. Almost every field has an index; here are a few.

Applied Science and Technology Index
Art Index
Business Periodicals Index

Figure 12.5   *Entry from the* Readers' Guide to Periodical Literature

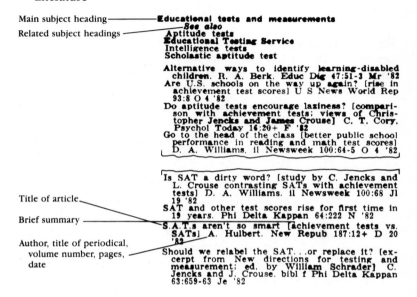

Main subject heading

Related subject headings

Title of article

Brief summary

Author, title of periodical,
   volume number, pages,
   date

Education Index
General Science Index
Humanities Index
MLA International Bibliography
Social Sciences Index
Guide to U.S. Government Publications

Abstracts.   Abstracts list journal articles in specific fields and offer brief article summaries. The summaries do not take the place of reading the article, but they do tell you whether an article is what you want. *Abstracts in Anthropology, Historical Abstracts, Psychological Abstracts,* and *Science Abstracts* are among the abstracts you may find helpful.

Other Library Resources

We have been discussing the main reference works your library offers. These will doubtless be somewhere on your itinerary, but they do not exhaust the library's resources. Depending on your research, you may have many other places to visit, including the following five.

Recent Acquisitions List.   Listings for recently purchased books and periodicals take a while to get into the library's catalogs. Thus, most libraries have separate up-to-date lists of relatively new materials, usually on computer printouts or microfiche. Consult these lists especially if your topic concerns very recent events.

Microfilm Holdings.   More and more libraries now own microfilm copies of old and rare books, newspapers, and public and private documents. Many, for example, own microfilms of books printed in English before 1640. Usually, the card in the author-title catalog will tell you if a work is on microfilm.

Special Collections.   Because some library collections are marked *special*, you may be intimidated. Don't be. The books are there to serve you, and some of them can be quite helpful. For instance, in writing a paper about the history of Boston, you may find that one of your library's special collections includes a privately printed booklet about one of the city's earliest merchant families. Materials in special collections may be listed either in the author-title catalog or in separate catalogs.

Government Documents.   Many libraries have a special area in which they house government documents, that is, publications by various federal, state, and foreign governments. These documents are not as dry or narrowly focused as they sound. The U.S. government, for example, publishes material on everything from international arms negotiations to how to collect honey from bees. The *Congressional Record* is an unsurpassed primary source for what goes on in the U.S. Congress. The government documents area is definitely worth a detour.

Computer Searches.   Many libraries also have computers that can help you in your research. Some can tell you whether what you seek is on the shelves, suggest other books and articles on the same or a related subject, give you cross-references along with related subject listings, and even tell you the nearest place that owns the book or article you need if your library does not. There may also be data bases you can peruse for more information on your subject. (For more information on data bases, see page 345.) Computers are very user-friendly, so learn what kind your library has and how to use it.

Being Your Own Source

You need not limit yourself to material you can find in libraries. You can also generate your own primary source information, and some of it can be quite exciting. Here are some examples.

Interviews.   You can interview people involved with your subject. Ask them about their experiences and what they know. One report on the social organization of a local Quaker congregation included interviews with elders and newer members. When you conduct an interview, do not waste time; have your line of questioning written out in advance.

Correspondence.   You often can get helpful information by writing to people involved with your topic, such as congressional representatives, your governor or mayor, or people in business, sports, or entertainment. If you write a respectful, serious letter, the results can be surprising. One memorable research project on the Mercury astronauts was based in part on correspondence with John Glenn, Wally Schirra, and Alan Shepard. Be sure to leave ample time for an answer.

Polls.   One of our favorite essays included polls measuring audience response to three different performances of Henrik Ibsen's play *Hedda Gabler*. Unfortunately, though, polls are easy to get wrong. If you do not have experience with them, consult a friend or teacher who does. The better the instrument, the better the data. (For a brief discussion of polling, see Chapter 10, Using Evidence.)

Fieldwork.   Some researchers can go right out into the field to collect information. For a research paper on Indian burial grounds in the San Francisco Bay area, one student visited an archeological excavation on the site of a planned subway station. Eventually, he started digging himself.

Experiments. Much writing in the natural and social sciences is based on experiments the writer has conducted. To test extrasensory perception, a student designed a set of cards and then asked all the students on his dorm floor to identify what was on the hidden side of each card. He analyzed the responses, and then, disappointed to learn that only chance was operating, he valiantly wrote up the experiment anyway.

Other Personal Experiences. You can do research on your own experience or background. Did your family name change when your ancestors came to America? You could discuss when and how it changed in a paper on immigration history. Have you ever had to testify in court? Your experience could contribute to a paper on the legal system.

Personal experience has both its own authority and its own limitations. When using it, work especially hard for objectivity and relevance. You should be at least as careful when you are your own source as when you use library research. For a brief discussion of personal experience as evidence, see Chapter 10.

LIMITING YOUR AREA OF RESEARCH

As you learn more and more about your subject, you will begin to see how it divides into parts. This will suggest ways to narrow the subject to exactly what you want to research.

One of the leading killers of research projects is an overly large topic. If you take on too much, you will not be able to shape your material effectively, If you neglect the research necessary to cover the topic, your ideas will lack the background or support they need. Your paper will be as deep as a teacup. You should aim to work on a topic *small enough to cover well but challenging enough to be worth covering.*

After Christina Gerke had scouted the reference books, the card catalog, and the periodical indexes, she saw that her topic, *Minorities and the Educational System*, was far too broad. She decided to list some of the parts of the subject that attracted her.

Affirmative action in colleges
Busing
Changing populations in city schools

Supreme Court decisions on minorities in education
Incorporating minority views into history
The effects of standardized testing

She paused there. While compiling her working bibliography, she had discovered that standardized tests were a hot issue. People argued about what the tests measured, how they were designed, and what effects they had on future careers. There was obviously a good deal more to learn about testing, particularly about its effects on minorities.

By eliminating some possibilities and focusing more intently on others, Gerke narrowed her topic this way.

Recent changes in American society
Minorities and recent changes in American society
Minorities and the educational system
Standardized tests and their effects on minorities

Cutting subjects down to a workable size is essential. Let's return to our examples from early in the chapter and hone them further.

Soviet-American relations and Russian dissidents
Andrey Sakharov's influence on Soviet-American relations
Sakharov's exile and its effect on Soviet-American relations

American Short Fiction in the 1920s
Women and American short fiction in the 1920s
Women writers of short fiction and the American magazine industry in the 1920s

These topics are now limited to a manageable size for a research project.

As you read more and narrow your subject further, you no doubt will begin to identify controversies to be settled, causes to be traced, patterns to be explained, questions to be answered. While you consider the possibilities, ask yourself a series of questions about your direction and focus.

Do I like this topic?
Do I feel in control of it?
Do I have enough time to do thorough research on it?
Will I be able to find out enough about it in the sources available to me?
Will I find adequate support for my ideas?
Is the topic appropriate for the assigned length?

Is it too elementary?
Is it too technical?
It it worth my while?
Will it interest my audience?

Know the answers to these questions before you write. Early in the project, your instructor may advise you on some of them.

FORMULATING A TENTATIVE THESIS

At this point, a tentative thesis can help you organize your thoughts and direct your research. A tentative thesis in a research project is like a working hypothesis in a scientific experiment. It is the "idea" the research will examine, so it serves as the basis for further investigation.

You may find it helpful to express your topic in the form of a question and your position as an answer. That answer can often be your tentative thesis. This is what Christina Gerke wrote.

Question: In light of the effects of standardized tests on the careers of minority students, should educators continue to use the tests?

Answer: We should do away with standardized tests because they perpetuate prejudice against minorities.

Gerke was fully aware that her ideas might change. Her thesis was truly tentative; by the end of the research process, she would very likely discard, change, or modify it.

Stating a narrowed topic as a question will often produce a workable tentative thesis statement, as it could for the Soviet-American relations and twentieth-century American fiction projects.

Question: Has the exile of Andrey Sakharov affected Soviet-American relations?

Answer: Sakharov has been conveniently forgotten by American policymakers.

Question: Was short fiction by women an important factor in the American magazine industry in the 1920s?

Answer: Short fiction by women did not greatly influence the economics of the American magazine industry in the 1920s.

At this stage, don't lock yourself into a set proposition. The intensive search you are about to undertake may — probably will — uncover facts and opinions that will make you change your ideas. Further research would show, for instance, that women writers were economically important to the American magazine industry in the 1920s. Welcome the opportunity to change your thesis as the material guides you.

We have so far been discussing the tentative thesis with an argumentative edge. Some research assignments, however, only want you to gather information and report it. Your paper will still need an organizing principle or thesis to give shape to your research. Without this thesis, you would have just a shapeless pile of data. (See "Subject and Thesis" in Chapter 1.)

Here are three of the most common ways of finding a shape for a report without an argumentative edge.

Chronology. When you are surveying events that happen over time, you may want to organize your subject chronologically. A report on American soldiers listed as "Missing in Action" (MIA) during the Vietnam War, for instance, has this statement as its thesis:

> The situation of the American MIAs has changed dramatically as relations between the United States and Vietnam have developed over the past fifteen years.

The writer then surveyed how relations changed over time and how they affected the situation of MIAs.

Division and Classification. You can often break down a large topic into smaller parts and treat them one at a time. (See "Classification and Division" in Chapter 5 for more on this method.) A report on the nutritional value of the American diet had this as its thesis statement:

> The value of the average American's diet depends on a balanced consumption of three essential nutrients — proteins, fats, and carbohydrates.

The writer then went on to identify the nutrients present in favorite American foods from potato chips to enchiladas.

Recurrent Themes. As you study a topic, you will notice themes that arise again and again. Such recurrent themes can help you organize your report. In studying disputes over gun control laws, for example, a student found that these themes kept popping up:

> The constitutional guarantee of the right to bear arms
> The necessity for owning guns in some parts of the country
> How easy it is for anyone, including criminals, to get guns
> The (disputed) relation between the crime rate and ownership of guns

The writer then started the report with this statement:

> The main clash over gun laws is between those who defend the right to bear arms and those who worry over the availability of guns.

Having chosen this main theme, the writer then went on to review the others in connection with it. Recurrent themes can both guide you in your research and help suggest a natural shape for your discussion.

Whether argumentative or not, your tentative thesis organizes and directs the rest of your research.

READING AND TAKING NOTES

Back to the library, thesis in mind.

Here among the stacks, you will now read more intensively, gathering evidence to support, or correct, your tentative thesis. Don't stint on gathering information. Browse the stacks. Page through a few books and evaluate them. Follow interesting leads. Chase ideas through periodicals. Collect the details of your subject, the uncommon facts, other people's theories about it. Whenever possible, trace all references back to their original sources. You probably will not use everything you amass, but the more you know, the more confidence you can have when you sit down to write.

Recognizing Good Sources

A kind of reasonable panic may set in at this point. "I'm going to have 3000 notecards! It could take weeks just to write everything down. How can I decide which materials are authoritative and which I can leave alone?"

Excellent question. Not all your sources are going to be good ones. Some will be popularizations, summaries, quick-and-easy presentations of topics you need to read about in depth. To sort out the useful from the fallible, test each book or article you find in these five ways.

Reliability of the Author. Ask yourself whether you have seen the author's name in other references. Check his or her background in a biographical or bibliographic index. Consult the *Book Review Digest* for reactions to his or her writings. Ask the reference librarian or your instructor for help.

Quality of the Periodical or Publishing House. Try to get a sense of which periodicals are truly authoritative for your topic. *Time* magazine offers mostly glossy and simplified versions of events. A *Time* account of recent heart transplant techniques would not be nearly as detailed and reliable as one in the *New England Journal of Medicine*. *Scientific American* is a respected science magazine, but it is hardly as authoritative as the more scholarly *Nature*. For books, assess the publishing house. Is it a university press or one of the well-established trade houses? Have you heard of it before? Have you seen it in other references? Again, ask your reference librarian or your instructor.

Currency of the Material. Check dates of all sources. With most topics, especially current issues, you will want sources as up-to-date as you can find. Suppose your topic is the economy of Pakistan. Pakistani politics and external relations are changing so rapidly, few books more than five years old will be authoritative. Some topics, of course, have standard references that are quite old. Sir James Frazer's *The Golden Bough*, for instance, is still a classic source in anthropology, although it was first published in 1907. But even in a relatively established field, like Elizabethan drama, most authoritative studies are less than thirty years old. If a source seems out of date, look for newer material.

Completeness of the Presentation. Look for both detail and comprehensiveness. Do not rely wholly on summaries. Prefer Professor Y's original journal article to a brief excerpt from her informal talk to high-school students. For clues to the completeness of a book or article, check the title and subtitles, the length, the table of contents, chapter headings and subheadings, the bibliography, and the index.

Slant or Bias. Some sources have a bias arising from politics, nationality, the methods of research used, or the sponsors of the study. Books or articles out of the conservative Hoover Institution or the Heritage Foundation may have a different slant from those out of the liberal Brookings Institution or Common Cause. We are not suggesting that you should ignore works from these organizations. That would be foolish, for they can be useful and scholarly. But whatever you consult, be alert to bias. Read prefatory chapters carefully: authors sometimes bring their affiliations and their prejudices to light at the beginning of a work. Notice the tone: does it seem judicious? Look also for a balance between opinion and substantiation. Is opinion clearly and consistently distinguished from fact? If so, the source may be a responsible one; if not, you should have your doubts.

Taking Notes

Never sit down with any source unless you are prepared to take notes. Taking notes on what you read serves two purposes: it helps you store information for easy recall, and it helps you organize your essay. You will reap these benefits only if you gather and arrange your notes carefully. Review Chapter 2, The Reading Process, and apply the principles there to any source on which you take notes. As always, read critically.

We all have our own ways of taking notes, and no system in this or any other book can guarantee brilliant results. The following suggestions, however, have worked well for many people.

Take notes on notecards. Although some people use sheets of paper when they take notes, we think notecards are the most efficient way to store information. They are flexible: you can move them around in a pack as you wish, and, as you will see, you can group them to help you shape your essay. Unlike main entry cards, which contain bibliographic information, notecards remind you of the content of sources.

Figure 12.6 *Key Phrase Notecard*

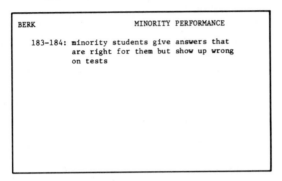

```
BERK                        MINORITY PERFORMANCE

   183-184: minority students give answers that
            are right for them but show up wrong
            on tests
```

Whenever you find something interesting or significant relating to your topic — a quotation, an idea, a piece of information, a reference, a picture, a statistic, a graph — make a note of it on a notecard. Develop notecards on all the books and articles you consult in any depth.

Use one card for each major point. Avoid covering cards with too many notes; if you do, you will not be able to file them efficiently. It is much better to make a separate notecard for each point. In the upper left corner, write the author's name. In the upper right corner, write the topic of the note in a key word or short phrase. Never forget to write down the *exact* page numbers on which the noted material appears: you may well need to find your way back to important information, and you will need page numbers for documentation later. In the notecard in Figure 12.6, Christina Gerke used the key phrase *minority performance.*

File each notecard under the key word or phrase. As you accrue notes, you will be compiling stacks of cards on the various aspects of your subject. They will all be together when you need them. Under each key word or phrase, alphabetize your notecards by the author's last name. If the author is anonymous, use the first word of the title of the source. This will be helpful later when you want quick access to specific points; you can go directly to the exact spot in the stack.

Keep your cards grouped together with rubber bands. You may want to use different colors or sizes to keep notecards separate from main entry cards. 3-by-5-inch cards will be adequate for main entries, but use 4-by-6-inch cards for notes because they have more room. Edit your notes frequently.

There is no rule for how many notecards are enough, though you can usually tell when your research is skimpy. An old high-school rule of thumb says, with some reason, that forty is a lower limit for a ten-page paper. It is not unusual, however, to get into the hundreds. Do not be afraid of a rich supply.

What kind of notes should you take? You have three choices — quotation, paraphrase, and summary — and you should probably use them all.

Quotation. Sometimes an author makes a point with such authority or eloquence that you will want to write down his or her exact words. Copy the source carefully; you may want to use these words in your paper, and you do not want to misquote them. Put all quoted material in quotation marks, and be sure you note precisely where you found it. Spell and punctuate exactly as the author did. After you complete the transcription, go back and check your card against the text. This may seem slow, but it will save you grief later.

Gerke found that a passage from an article by George F. Madaus expressed fears similar to her own about standardized tests.

> The more one knows about the technology of testing, the more one realizes the potential for harm when a test score is used as the sole or primary criterion on which to make an important decision affecting an individual's future.

She already had a main entry card for Madaus, so now she made a notecard on which she quoted this passage exactly (see Figure 12.7).

If the material you are quoting is lengthy, think about photocopying it. Photocopying can save you hours of copying by hand, especially passages from noncirculating journals, reference books, and special collections materials. Two drawbacks exist, however. First, the cost of photocopying can add up. Second, copyright laws govern the amount of material you may photocopy and the purpose for which you may use it. The library staff should know the laws and be able to advise you.

Paraphrase. If the ideas expressed in a book or article look important but the exact wording is not essential, you may paraphrase. When you paraphrase, you follow the writer's thought closely, but

Figure 12.7 *Quoted Passage Notecard*

```
MADAUS                              EFFECTS OF TESTS

    93:  "The more one knows about the technology of
    testing, the more one realizes the potential for
    harm when a test score is used as the sole or
    primary criterion on which to make an important
    decision affecting an individual's future.
```

you put it in your own words. Paraphrasing a passage is a good way to get a hold on the material. Just as a quotation is faithful to the exact words, so a paraphrase should be faithful to the meaning. But be sure you have recast the thought in completely original language. Do not let the author's words bleed into the paraphrase. Figure 12.8 shows how the notecard might look if Gerke had decided to paraphrase instead of quote the Madaus passage we just discussed.

Summary. When we summarize, we do not closely follow and reproduce the details of a writer's argument. In fact, a summary may condense a whole paragraph, even a page or a section, into one or

Figure 12.8 *Paraphrased Passage Notecard*

```
    Test scores have the potential to hurt students
    when educators use the scores as the only or the
    most important basis for making decisions that
    can influence the students' futures.
```

Figure 12.9   Summary Notecard

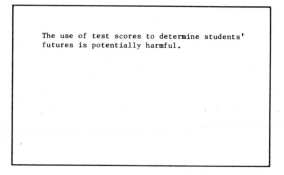

two sentences. The purpose of a summary is to preserve the general idea. But you still must acknowledge your source. Indicate exactly where you got the summarized material. Figure 12.9 shows how the notecard might look if Gerke had summarized the section of Madaus's article about use of test scores.

We will discuss plagiarism in more detail under "Documenting Your Sources." Here we want to point out that good notes can protect you from that worst of academic problems. Put quotation marks around *any* words directly from the source. Identify whatever you paraphrase or summarize. Record all information accurately. If you get an idea about something you have noted, write the idea on the same notecard. But put your idea in brackets or write it out in a different color pencil.

Using the Computer

This section is for those of you who have access to word processors or word-processing programs for computers. We know we cannot cover everything computers do, but our students have taught us that these lovely machines can be very useful tools for research. Although they will be most important when you start writing, they can come into play at almost every stage of research.

Storing Notes.   Computers are excellent places to keep your notes. Some can alphabetize for you, and some can find your note in a split second when you give them a key word. They can also store important passages and your reactions to them. If you get more ideas later, you can always insert them. You can also highlight key words, concepts, or phrases that you think important or want to use later. And typing, unlike handwriting, is rarely illegible. Smearing and destruction by fingers and food are hazards foreign to the computer screen.

Of course, computers can't replace cards in all respects — especially if your instructor requires that notecards be handed in along with the completed paper. Still, if you own a computer, it can save you a great deal of work.

Documentation.   You can also build your list of works cited on the computer. Each time you use a source extensively, make a complete entry for it in a file named, let us say, LIST; put the entry at the correct alphabetical position. By the time you have finished your research, the file should contain a fairly complete version of your list of works cited. Make sure to print out a draft to check it for completeness and accuracy — most researchers forget to enter one or two sources. Then you can either add your list of works cited to the end of the file that contains your paper or print it out separately.

If you use footnotes or endnotes (see "Documenting Your Sources"), some word-processing programs can be a great help. They can make both types of notes automatically. Make sure you know what features your program has for handling notes.

Data Bases.   Some university and college libraries now offer services that allow students to hook a computer up to a number of useful data bases, including bibliographies, indexes, and biographical materials. A few offer computer access to their catalogs, so you can make a preliminary search before traveling to the library. This search, of course, remains preliminary: nothing takes the place of browsing through the stacks, paging through books, and scanning periodicals. Check with your librarian about the services available to you.

And do we need to remind anyone of the three cardinal rules of word processing?

1. Save your work often, every fifteen to twenty minutes. This is an extremely useful superstition.
2. Make backup copies of your work on a separate disk.
3. Never forget to do Steps 1 and 2.

RESTATING YOUR THESIS

Now you are back from the stacks with plenty of notes and a much better understanding of your topic. You should be able to tell at this point whether your tentative thesis needs modifying. The temptation will be strong to ignore contrary or qualifying evidence and start writing immediately. Beware: do not defend a thesis that should be changed. Instead, interrogate it in the light of your research.

Do you still believe it?
Does your research amply support it?
Should you modify it in any way?

In the light of her research, Christina Gerke had begun to question her tentative thesis, which had been

We should do away with standardized tests because they perpetuate prejudice against minorities.

This statement now seemed to her too extreme. Her research did not fully support it. After her reading she thought that some tests had value and that the bias in them was often accidental. During her research, she had asked herself more probing questions, like *Why* are the tests harmful to minorities? And from her reading she had developed an answer: they are harmful because a low score on a test can determine much of a person's future. Her revised thesis shows how research had refined her ideas.

Standardized tests often shape the course of people's lives, not to mention their self-image and their society's image of them. Until we know more about this crucial yet controversial subject, educators and employers should continue to use the tests but should de-emphasize them.

Gerke had gone from an ill-defined general feeling to a refined and arguable thesis, one that mattered to her and would guide a rich essay.

Examine your thesis, write it out, and be sure it is clear. If you are in doubt, state it to someone else. The response should tell you a great deal. Be sure it is worth arguing. Be sure you have time and space to do it justice. Take time to reconsider the thesis at least once during each day of work.

PREPARING AN OUTLINE

You and your project are still together after all these trials. Now you have a thesis and a mass of research to mold into some shape. A first step toward that goal is to make an outline. This will help you in three ways.

It will put your argument or exposition down on paper for the first time.
It will force you to organize and develop your material.
It will carry you a long way toward your completed essay.

Think of your outline as an opportunity to combine each of your ideas with relevant evidence or background and to place each idea in its proper relation to your other points.

To devise an effective outline, you should have completed your research and have your notecards stacked in order, your authorities and accurate quotations at your elbow. Now is the time to think carefully about your approach to the subject.

First, go through all your notecards. Note which topics have grown largest. Make a scratch list of the main points you want to make. Try arranging your notes into piles according to these important topics. Is there a natural form for your discussion? Look for one. If the organization "wants" to go in a certain direction, follow it and see how it works. Think about where you might employ different strategies: description, process analysis, cause and effect, comparison and contrast, definition. Consider what will be the crucial parts of your paper. Write out a few trial outlines.

Christina Gerke decided to begin her paper with general background on standardized tests, move to an overview of the controversy, and then present her thesis. Later, she could treat the debate in more detail and present one test — the Scholastic Aptitude Test — as a case study. Her outline, which appears just before her paper at the end of this chapter, reflects these decisions.

For an assignment as large as a research paper, no rough list of points will help you keep your information in order. We recommend, therefore, that you make a formal outline — that is, an outline that presents the shape and direction of your paper as exactly as possible. You may choose either a phrase outline that identifies in short phrases the topics your paper will cover, or a sentence outline that makes a statement in a complete sentence about each topic. Many instructors require that students submit an outline at some stage of research, so be sure you know what is expected. Even if your outline is less formal, be sure you

Connect all points in intelligible order
Distinguish major points from minor ones and emphasize them appropriately
Gather evidence adequate to support each point or background sufficient to explain it
Assemble enough material overall to support your whole thesis

Once you have made your outline, go back to your notecards. Working by the topic key words and phrases, organize your cards according to the outline. If a note pertains to your conclusion, it belongs on the bottom of the pile; if it pertains to your introduction, it belongs near the top. Once you have your notes in order, reading through them ought to be like surveying a compressed version of your paper. Do not worry about having too much material. As writing proceeds, you can decide which pieces of support you need most. It is far easier to cut excess material than it is to search for new sources at the last moment.

The research project's most important elements — organization, argument, evidence — should all be there when you finish a good outline. Even now, much about your outline may be provisional. Problems may stick out. You may see that one part needs more work or that one of your main points is out of place. Many writers find it painful to sit down, bash out the shape of the argument, and arrange all the evidence without writing the paper at the same time. But correcting problems in an outline is more efficient than trying to fix a finished product. A little work ahead of time will make things easier later. (For more information on outlines, see "Organizing," page 34.)

WRITING A FIRST DRAFT

Once you have an outline and notecard order that seem to work, you are ready to begin writing your first draft. With something as complex as a research paper, you won't get everything right — ideas, references, commas — the first time. The whole point of the first draft is to be flexible. You may find, for example, that your outline, so painstakingly thought out, doesn't work in all parts. Some of your most cherished ideas may go up in smoke. Some may require more research. You may even need a different thesis, a whole new approach. Take all such discoveries with good humor: the purpose of a first draft is to help you figure out what you want and need to say. Nothing characterizes research more than global revisions at every stage, down to the last minute.

Two issues will be especially important to you at this stage: using your evidence and integrating different sources.

Using Your Evidence

In an argumentative project, your ideas make your paper go; they make it new and worth reading. But assertion of opinion — no matter how brilliantly phrased or original — is not enough. You must show the reader how you arrived at your ideas, or how you justify them. That is why you did all that research. When you provide evidence, you allow your reader to make an educated decision about the validity of your argument.

Let your reader review all the evidence. Don't suppress information contrary to your thesis. Presenting the opposition and responding to it can only strengthen your argument. (For a discussion of how to construct a complete argument, refer to Chapter 9, Writing to Persuade.)

In Chapter 10, Using Evidence, we discussed the various kinds of evidence. But we want to say a special word here about quotations.

Almost all research contains quoted material because it is such good evidence. For example, quotations can help you amplify or clarify a point, as this one does.

> Baseball players have an unusual approach to language, as in Yogi Berra's famous line, "The game isn't over till it's over" (Bartlett 903).

In the examples given here, the parenthetical reference after the quotation follows the Modern Language Association's system for documenting sources, one of three methods that are described later in this chapter.

Or quotations can prove a specific point or attach weight to a theory or opinion, as this one does.

As the complexities of nuclear policy grow, it becomes more and more difficult to decide which information is good and which is propaganda. As one student of international politics wrote, "Reality in the nuclear age tends to become what people whose voices carry say it is" (Newhouse 41).

If you are using a short quotation, you can include it in the text, enclosed in quotation marks.

Perhaps it would be best for everyone to follow William Least Heat Moon's advice and "Beware thoughts that come in the night" (3).

If you only wish to use part of a passage, you can excerpt from it, though you must indicate with ellipses, or spaced periods, where you have left out material.

According to Morris Bishop, during his apprenticeship to the family business, St. Francis "was bored by the drudgery . . . and suffered the reproofs of his father and brother" (13). Though called a good businessman, he had other interests.

Use three spaced periods to indicate material omitted from the middle of a sentence. Use four if the omission coincides with the end of your sentence, or if you have left out a complete sentence or more.

As long as you do it gracefully and grammatically, you can interrupt quotations for effect.

"My father," said John Stuart Mill in explaining his remarkable education, "never permitted anything which I learnt, to degenerate into a mere exercise of memory" (20).

When you have quotations of more than four lines, make them easier to read by setting them off from the text, indented ten spaces from the left margin, double-spaced, and without quotation marks, as in this passage.

Joseph Heller apparently did not care for the world surrounding the traveler:

> It is easily demonstrated, I believe, that with the exception of paintings, three statues by Michelangelo and the city of Florence, everything looks better on picture postcards than in reality, and I can no longer understand why people who do not relish confusion and physical discomfort will travel long distances to gape at something more easily viewed in a magazine or newspaper travel supplement (Heller 38).

Most travelers, even novelists who live in the world of the imagination, would name many more than three things worth traveling to see.

Do not sprinkle your work with unexplained quotations; show the reader the reason for your reference. Make clear how the quotation supports your opinion, as Christina Gerke did in this passage.

Furthermore, a test item designed to measure one ability may actually test different abilities in different people. This accidental shifting can occur in something as simple as a spelling test.

> Asking for the spelling of a given word may require a student who was previously drilled on the word merely to recite from rote memory a string of letters but require a student who was not taught this word to analyze it into syllables and phonemes and then to apply his phonics knowledge to the task. (Bormuth 23)

Consequently, a test item aimed at a specific ability (phonics knowledge) tested something quite different (ability to memorize).

Your instructor wants to know how you think, not just what writers and writing you admire. So limit both the number and the length of quotations. A long series of quotations can suggest you are simply stringing together other people's ideas. A great hunk of quotation can seem like an undigested lump of dough. Remember that a quotation supplements but can never replace your work.

Be sure you carefully document all quotations and paraphrases. To guide you in forms of documentation, your instructor may recommend a particular manual of style, such as the *MLA Handbook for Writers of Research Papers* or the University of Chicago Press's *Chicago Manual of Style*. Later in this chapter we will describe three methods of documenting sources.

Integrating Different Sources

As you write, you may be pullng information from books, articles, and other sources much separated in time and different in style and point of view. One of the most delicate tasks in writing your first draft is that of weaving these various sources into your argument. Here are three tips on this process.

1. Make sure your sources exactly support your claim. One student paper had the following passage:

> Many researchers are in favor of teachers retiring when they reach age sixty-five. According to the National Bureau of Statistics, there are no teachers over eighty-five now active in the United States (123).

Interesting fact, but it does not really fit the claim. Putting the two together will confuse the reader. Resist the temptation to plug in a reference because it is "close" to your own thought. Close gets no cigar.

2. When you use more than one reference to back up a point, compare the references closely to make sure they truly agree.

In her first draft, Christina Gerke wrote this passage:

> Another challenge points to the difficulty of ascertaining exactly what qualities the various standardized tests actually measure. Scientists do not yet agree on a single definition of the word *intelligence*, for example, and, as the meaning of the word changes, so do the tests that try to measure it ("Brave New World"). H. J. Eysenck, a prominent expert in the field of human intelligence, suggests that since we lack a better definition, intelligence is what is measured in IQ tests (Eysenck 78). It is also possible that a test item designed to measure one ability will in reality test different abilities in different people.

Her first reference was indeed appropriate, but her second did not really agree with it. The paragraph treats the problem of "ascertaining exactly what qualities" the tests measure. Eysenck's quotation threatens to derail the paragraph into a discussion of how *intelligence* is defined. In the end Gerke decided to drop it, much as she wanted this expert to appear in her paper.

Some writers put in references out of desperation or the desire to appear informed. But you should never use a reference you don't need. Every reference should push your point forward, not merely add to what you have already established. Your instructor will be able to determine the quality of your research without padding.

3. Be sensitive to the way passages are worded, to the context from which you have taken material, and to the background and point of view of the author. If you weave together uneasy companions, the result will be a strange paragraph, one that may confuse the reader because its pieces of evidence do not follow directly from one another.

The following three suggestions should help you pick and choose among your sources:

Prefer the concrete — facts, statistics — to the general.
Choose firsthand accounts over second- and third-hand ones.
Prefer recent sources to older ones.

As you add body and detail to the skeleton of your outline in your first draft, you may very well find — no surprises here — that you need to make further modifications. Enjoy your first draft but treat it as the first version of what will be a solid, polished piece of writing.

DOCUMENTING YOUR SOURCES

Documentation is an essential part of presenting evidence. You must identify the source of every quotation, fact, statistic, graph, or opinion about your subject that you include in your research paper. You must tell your reader exactly where you got every bit of information that you use. Further, you must list for your reader every relevant source you consulted. In short, you must thoroughly document your research.

You must do this for three reasons:

Documentation provides a guide for any reader who wants to study your subject.
It indicates the extent of your research.
It gives credit where credit is due.

If writers document their sources sloppily or not at all, they disappoint curious readers and undermine confidence in the quality of the research. Worse, they run the risk of plagiarism.

Plagiarism

Plagiarism is the use without due acknowledgment of the thoughts, writing, scholarship, or inventions of another. In college and university writing, as in most other walks of life, people put a great value on knowing what is yours and what belongs to someone else. Therefore, plagiarism is a serious moral issue.

Plagiarism is often the result of carelessness or ignorance: sometimes a student does not fully understand the importance of the issue or does not know the right way to acknowledge sources. The remedy is to learn. Sometimes, however, people in full awareness submit as their own the ideas or work of someone else. Compare this passage from an original source on fifteenth-century art with the next passage on the same subject:

Source

The diminishing role of gold in paintings is part of a general movement in western Europe at this time towards a kind of selective inhibition about display, and this shows itself in many other kinds of behaviour too. It was just as conspicuous in the client's clothes, for instance, which were abandoning gilt fabrics and gaudy hues for the restrained black of Burgundy. This was a fashion with elusive moral overtones. (Michael Baxandall, *Painting and Experience in Fifteenth Century Italy*)

Use

At this time, western Europe was moving toward inhibition of display, which shows up in the diminishing role of gold in paintings as well as in many other kinds of behavior, including the abandoning of gilt fabrics and gaudy hues in clothing. This fashion had moral overtones, though elusive.

In this case the writer has obviously used material belonging to another without crediting the source. He or she has used the same words and phrases, in only slightly altered form. This is plagiarism.

Even if you do not quote any of the words of a source, borrowing ideas can also be plagiarism. Compare this passage from an original source with its use in a paper called "The Psychology of Children's Play."

Source

Just as for its growth an organ needs nourishment in proportion to its functioning, so each mental activity, from the most elementary to the highest, needs for its development to be fed from without by a continuous flow, which [in the case of children's play] is purely functional, not material. (Jean Piaget, *Play, Dreams, and Imitation in Childhood*)

Use

Children play as part of the normal process of growing and developing. Like any bodily organ, the mind needs constant nourishment and exercise as it grows. When children play, they exercise and nourish the mind and assist it in its growth.

These ideas may be in the writer's own language, but he or she has borrowed them from the source without acknowledgment. If the writer did this knowingly and deliberately concealed the source, it is a kind of theft.

Here is the general rule for avoiding plagiarism and providing appropriate documentation: give enough information so that a reader can examine the sources you have used.

Now, here are seven guidelines for applying the general rule.

1. When you incorporate into your paper sentences, paragraphs, or apt phrases from the work of another, you must use quotation marks around the borrowed words — or indent passages longer than four lines — and you must identify the source. In the case of Baxandall's material about fifteenth-century painting, the writer should have credited the source and put borrowed phrases inside quotation marks, like this.

> According to Michael Baxandall, at this time western Europe was moving toward "inhibition about display," which shows up in "the diminishing role of gold in paintings" as well as in other kinds of behavior, including "abandoning gilt fabrics and gaudy hues" in clothing. As Baxandall says, "This was a fashion with elusive moral overtones" (14).

2. When you rely on another person's ideas or train of thought but change the actual words used or the order of the ideas — that is, when you paraphrase — you still must acknowledge your source. To avoid plagiarism, the writer who borrowed from Piaget should have written this:

> Jean Piaget claims that children play as part of the normal process of growing and developing. Like any bodily organ, the mind needs constant nourishment and exercise as it grows. He goes on to say that when children play, they exercise and nourish the mind and assist in its growth (87).

Notice that Piaget is named in the text, not merely in a note. The material was Piaget's own, and he should receive clear and obvious credit. An opinion or an original interpretation of the facts — whether quoted, paraphrased, or summarized — should be part of the text; otherwise, it might appear that the writer doing the quoting is claiming the opinion.

3. When the material you use is widely known and generally available, however, you can acknowledge the source simply in a reference. Christina Gerke acknowledges the sources of some facts in this way:

> The French psychologist Alfred Binet originally formulated his Binet scale of intelligence in 1905 to place advanced and handicapped children in special schools (Wardrop 8; Jensen 141–143).

4. When your ideas or opinions have been influenced in a general way by material you have read or lectures you have heard, you must also acknowledge your debt. In a paper on modern linguistics, a writer indicated the source of a borrowed idea in this fashion.

> Paradoxically, linguists can no longer confine themselves to language to understand how language works. They must now take into account the time, the place, the speaker, the listener, and the actual situation of each single utterance. Mikhail Bakhtin's analysis of these sociolinguistic elements is exceptionally insightful (383).

5. When you rely on factual material gathered by another person, you must state this as well.

> My discussion of Samoan marriage ceremonies will draw heavily on Margaret Mead's *Letters from the Field*.

6. When you have benefited from another person's way of organizing common material, you must acknowledge.

> When researching the movies of Preston Sturges, I found Simonson's *History of American Film* extremely helpful.

7. Finally, when you employ another writer's method of analyzing material, you must give credit where it is due.

> If we agree with David Riesman's view of American society in *The Lonely Crowd*, we can see that . . .

There are practical exceptions to the general rule. Some things it would be nearly impossible to acknowledge. For instance, you need not identify a source for knowledge everyone possesses or could easily acquire and that no one needs to prove.

> Columbus sailed to America in 1492.
> The chemical symbol of water is H_2O.

How could we ever remember where we learned those things? Nor do you need to provide a source for an idea expressed by many people.

Hamlet is one of Shakespeare's greatest tragedies.

Hostility has existed between Israel and the Arab nations since Israel became a nation.

Err on the side of overacknowledgment, however. Be generous and open in giving credit for any source of help.

Every discipline has its own way of documenting sources. Many humanities researchers use the Modern Language Association (MLA) system; social scientists often use the system advocated by the American Psychological Association (APA); the natural sciences use a number system. Indeed, methods of documentation will vary somewhat from course to course. Some instructors will require footnotes; others, endnotes. We will cover the MLA system of parenthetical references most fully in this section. You can read about this system in more detail in Joseph Gibaldi and Walter S. Achtert, *MLA Handbook for Writers of Research Papers*, 2nd ed. (New York: MLA, 1984), widely considered by English instructors as the arbiter on such matters. We will also cover the MLA format for the standard system that uses notes and bibliography. Finally, we will demonstrate the author/year or APA style.

The MLA Parenthetical References and List of Works Cited Format

The preferred MLA format uses parenthetical references that generally give the author's name and the page number after the quoted material. If readers want to know more, they can refer to a list of works cited at the back of the paper. We'll look first at how to present the list of works cited and then discuss how to handle references to these works in the text.

List of Works Cited.   Type your list of works cited on a separate sheet at the end of your paper. This list will include only books you actually cite in your paper, not all the books you consulted in your research. Center the words *Works Cited* one inch from the top of the page and two lines above your first entry. Double-space all entries; arrange them alphabetically by author's last name or, when there is no author, by title.

In each entry you will give the author's or authors' names (last name first), the title of the book or article, and then the necessary publication information: city, publisher, and year of publication for books; name of periodical, volume number and/or date, and page numbers for articles. For each entry, indent all lines after the first one five spaces. Skip two spaces after each period. Whenever italics are called for (as with book titles, for instance), you should underline. Finally, continue to number your pages all the way through the list. See Christina Gerke's list of works cited at the end of her paper for a model (page 404).

Sample Entries

In the following pages you will find examples of the kinds of references you will be most likely to use.

Books by One Author.

Nesbitt, Farah. *The American Press and the American People*. New York: Vincent, 1976.

Note the periods after the author's name, the title, and the date.

Articles in Journals.

Put the title of a journal article in quotation marks. Follow the title with the underlined title of the journal, the volume number (if there is one), the year of publication in parentheses, a colon, then the page numbers.

Barnet, Sylvan. "Some Limitations on a Christian Approach to Shakespeare." *English Literary History* 22 (1955): 81–92.

Articles in Other Periodicals.

For articles in periodicals that come out daily, weekly, or monthly — including most newspapers and magazines — you need not give the volume number. Instead, give the exact date of publication, a colon, and then the page number followed by a period.

"The Bogus Order of Merit." *New Republic* 2 Apr. 1977: 6.

Notice that the date appears as day, month, and year with no commas. Abbreviate the names of all months except May, June, and July. Give all the page numbers on which the article appears. If the article is not on consecutive pages, put a + after the first page number to indicate continuation on a later page.

> Goleman, Daniel. "New Insights into Freud from Letters to a Friend." *New York Times Magazine* 17 Mar. 1985: 31 + .

Multiple Works by the Same Author.   When you have two or more entries for the same author, don't repeat the name, but type three hyphens and a period and complete the reference. List the author's works alphabetically by title.

> Derrida, Jacques. "La Double Séance." *La Dissémination*. Paris: Seuil, 1972. 199–317.
> ---. *Of Grammatology*. Baltimore: Johns Hopkins UP, 1976.

Notice that the first entry is an essay and the second a book, both by Derrida.

Works by More Than One Author.   When you are citing a work by two or more authors, list the authors' names in the order in which they appear on the title page; this may or may not be alphabetical. Reverse only the first author's name, and type the rest out normally, separating names with commas.

> Gibaldi, Joseph, and Walter S. Achtert. *MLA Handbook for Writers of Research Papers*. 2nd ed. New York: Modern Language Association, 1984.

If there are more than three authors, give only the first name that appears on the title page and follow it with *et al.*, two Latin words that mean "and others." Do not underline *et al.* For the following work, the names on the title page were Elizabeth Waldeman, Allyson S. Grossman, Howard Hayghe, and Beverly Johnson.

> Waldeman, Elizabeth, et al. "Working Mothers in the 1970's: A Look at the Statistics." *Monthly Labor Review* Oct. 1979: 39–45.

Anonymous Works.   Sometimes the author of a work is not identified. For a book:

> *Swimmers for Life*. Huntington Beach: Nereid, 1984.

For an article:

> "The Bogus Order of Merit." *New Republic* 2 Apr. 1977: 6.

Works with Editors, Translators, and Compilers. Follow the editor's, translator's, or compiler's name with a comma and the standard abbreviation — ed., trans., comp. — for their relation to the work. Use these abbreviations only in the list, not in your references. Donald Rooney is the editor and the translator for this book.

> Rooney, Donald, ed. and trans. *Tribal Music of Africa and America.* Atlanta: Feldspar, 1921.

Works in Anthologies or Collections. For works in anthologies or collections, give the name of the author of the anthologized work, the work's title, then the title of the anthology or collection. Then give the name of the editor or compiler — but *precede* his or her name with *Ed.* or *Comp.*, capitalized. After the place, publisher, and date of publication, given the page numbers on which the work appears.

> Milton, John. *Paradise Lost. John Milton: Complete Poems and Major Prose.* Ed. Merritt Y. Hughes. Seattle: Odyssey, 1957. 206–469.

Multivolume Works. For works of more than one volume, put the number of volumes after the title, using the abbreviation *"vols."*

> Scherrol, Lydia. *Russian Writers, 1766–1985.* 3 vols. Washington: Novy Mir Press, 1985.

Works by Corporate Authors. Many publications — especially government documents — have no individual author but are of group or corporate origin. In such a case, enter the name of the originating body as the author's name.

> National Congress of Independent Beekeepers. *The Backyard Apiary.* Taos: Natl. Cong. of Independent Beekeepers, 1984.

If a name also appears as publisher, abbreviate it the second time.

Encyclopedias and Other Reference Works. Include articles in dictionaries, encyclopedias, and other reference works in your list if you used them in your paper. If the article is signed, enter it under the author's name; if not, alphabetize it by the title of the article. Af-

ter either one, cite the title of the reference work. If the work ar-
ranges its entries alphabetically, omit the volume and page number.
If the reference work is well known, you need cite only the date of
the edition. For a dictionary:

> "Cytodifferentiation." *Webster's Ninth New Collegiate Dictionary.*
> 1984 ed.

For an encyclopedia:

> Ulrich, Homer. "Music: Western Music." *Encyclopedia Americana.*
> 1985 ed.

Using References in Your Text

To follow the MLA format, document sources in your text by inserting a short acknowledgment in parentheses. Usually, the author's
last name and a page number are enough. We are basing this section
on the *MLA Handbook*, especially on page 136 of that book, so a reference is in order (Gibaldi and Achtert 136).

We just gave it. Notice that there is no comma between the authors' last names and the page number. Close the parentheses before
a period or comma. If you are crediting a longer, indented quotation,
skip two spaces after the concluding punctuation mark and give the
reference. Christina Gerke does this in this passage from her paper.

> Educator George F. Madaus writes,

> > The more one knows about the technology of testing, the more
> > one realizes the potential for harm when a test score is used as
> > the sole or primary criterion on which to make an important
> > decision affecting an individual's future. (93)

If her readers wanted to know more, they could refer to her list of
works cited; there they would find

> Madaus, George F. "NIE Clarification Hearing: The Negative Team's
> Case." *Phi Delta Kappan* Oct. 1981: 92–94.

Whenever Gerke refers to Madaus, she simply uses the brief parenthetical reference and the appropriate page number.

Place such references at natural pauses in your sentences — usually at the end of the sentence, or the end of the phrase or clause that
contains the cited material — and as close to the material as possible.

If the names of the authors of your sources already appear in your text, you need only give the page number in your reference. Here is another example from Gerke's paper.

> Robert L. Green and Robert J. Griffore write, "The negative aspects of testing procedures are especially apparent with respect to racial minorities" (25).

Your readers can find the names of the authors in the text, and complete information is always waiting for them in your list of works cited.

Other systems of documentation have used Latin words and abbreviations, such as *loc. cit.* (*loco citato*, "in the place [previously] cited"), *op. cit.* (*opere citato*, "in the work [previously] cited"), and *ibid.* (*ibidem*, or "in the same place"). Because parenthetical references always cite the page number, even if it is the same as that in a previous citation, the MLA system does not use these abbreviations.

Common Kinds of References

Works by One Author.

> Play, after all, is the way the growing mind gets nourishment (Piaget 87).

Works by More Than One Author. For sources with two or three authors, give the last names of each in the same order as on the title page of the book.

> Platypuses are bizarre holdovers from ancient animal forms (Stein and Ahmad 223).

For sources with more than three authors, give the first author's name as it appears on the title page, then write *et al.* and give the page number. Thus, for the work with four authors that we cited in the section "List of Works Cited," the text citation would be

> As of March 1978 one of every five families with children under the age of eighteen was maintained by a parent who was separated, divorced, widowed, or never married (Waldeman et al. 45).

Notice we kept only Waldeman. If you use a single name as a reference to a multiauthoried source, use it also in your list of works cited.

Anonymous Works.   If the work lists no author, simply give a short title — usually the first main word of the title — in the reference. If your source is a book, underline the word or words from the title.

> Today's lifeguards not only must know how to swim but must be able to differentiate among many different kinds of suntan lotion (*Swimmers* 56).

If your anonymous source is an article, put the title in quotation marks.

> In short, a diet of cotton candy is detrimental to the health of most rodents ("Effect of Cotton Candy").

Multiple Works by the Same Author.   If you refer to more than one work by the same author, simply give the author's name, a short title of the work referred to, and page number.

> Meaning is often lost in transit (Derrida, "Séance" 203). Our final destination is often displaced in the search for something else (Derrida, *Grammatology* 99).

The first reference is to an essay and the second to a book, both by Derrida. For clarity we separate the author's name from the title of the work with a comma.

Multiple Works in a Single Reference.   If you want to support a point by referring to more than one work, separate the references by a semicolon within the parentheses.

> Like the hippies of the 1960s, the yuppies of the 1980s are largely a creation of the press ("Bogus Order"; Nesbitt 6–18).

If you need to refer to three or more sources, use a footnote or endnote in the text of your paper.

> American teenagers now reach puberty at an average age of 11.5 years, much earlier than at any time in this century.[1]

The corresponding note would look like this.

> [1]Delahay 42; Crossbeck 178; Montemayor 788.

Place these notes on a sheet of paper before your list of works cited. Use such notes sparingly. See the two sample endnotes in Christina Gerke's paper, page 402.

Multivolume Works.   For a text reference to a multivolume work, show the volume number with an arabic numeral followed by a colon and the page number.

> Though the two never met, Tolstoy admired Dostoyevski (Scherrol 2: 77).

Works with Editors, Translators, and Compilers.   Do not include titles like *ed., trans., or comp.* in your references. Use only a name, and save any other information for your list of works cited. For example, Donald Rooney is the editor and translator of the book cited in this sentence.

> Tribal music from West Africa eventually reached Indian tribes in America via freed slaves and runaways who settled with native Americans (Rooney 35).

Works by Corporate Authors.   Some publications have a corporate author whose name is quite long. You may put that name in parentheses, but it is better to cite the title of the work and the name of the originating body in your text followed by the page number in parentheses.

> In its newsletter, *The Backyard Apiary*, the National Congress of Independent Beekeepers reported a slight rise in the number of neighbors who sued members over bee stings (44).

Literary References.   Most college papers on literature treat a single work. In this case, establish the author and title of the work you are discussing early and then simply give page, chapter, act, or line numbers in your references. If you are writing about more than one work, give the author's last name and page number in your references as we just described, unless you mention the author or title in your text. In your list of works cited, give a complete entry for the edition you use of each work.

1. Novels. For novels, put the page first, then the chapter, in case your reader has an edition with different page numbers.

> When Jo in Charles Dickens's *Bleak House* is asked where his parents are, he replies, "I never know'd nothink about 'em" (372; Ch. 25).

2. Plays. Cite quotations from plays not by page number but by the division of the play — act, scene, line — in which the quotation

appears. Give these divisions in arabic numerals. If you mention the name of the play in the text, you may omit it in the reference.

> In *Hamlet*, the protagonist's most intense insight occurs when he accepts his fate: "If it be now, 'tis not to come; if it be not to come, it will be now" (5.2.76–77).

Some instructors may prefer roman numerals for acts and scenes (V.ii.76–77). Follow your instructor's preference.

3. Poems. For a poem, give line numbers cited in parentheses. Use the word *line* or *lines* in your first citations; once you have established that the numbers will indicate lines, use the numbers by themselves.

> In John Donne's "The Good-Morrow," the speaker muses to the loved one, "I wonder by my troth, what thou, and I/ Did, till we lov'd?" (lines 1–2). Later, the poet says that any idea he had of beauty before meeting his love was only "a dream of thee" (7).

If you quote two or three lines of poetry, use slashes to separate them in the text. If you quote more than three lines, begin the quotation on a new line, indented ten spaces from the left margin. Break the lines exactly as they appear in the original.

If there are divisions (cantos, books, parts) in the poem you are quoting, give the division number before the line numbers.

> When he sees what he has done, Milton's Adam gives one of the most moving laments in *Paradise Lost*: "The more I see/Pleasures about me, so much more I feel/Torment within me" (9.119–121).

Entire Works.   The best way to cite an entire work is to do so in your text.

> The furthest development of the Russian novel is still represented by Tolstoy's *War and Peace*.

Give a complete entry in your list of works cited for any entire works you cite.

Indirect Sources.   As we mentioned in "Primary and Secondary Sources," you should prefer firsthand sources to all others. Sometimes, however, you may only be able to find an indirect source, such as someone quoting someone else. If you quote or paraphrase material quoted in another source, put the abbreviation *qtd. in* (for "quoted in") before the indirect reference you cite in parentheses.

Even a compulsive worker like Harry Truman was heard to mutter, "Even I need a day off once in a while" (qtd. in Giuseppe 55).

Then cite the indirect source in your list of works cited.

Giuseppe, Raphael. *Type A Personalities in American History.* Seattle: Workplace, 1981.

The MLA Notes and Bibliography System

If, like us, you were brought up with notes and bibliographies, you may be in an elegiac mood after reading the preceding section. But do not be sad. Many college writers and instructors still use this method of documentation. Practicality therefore dictates that we review footnotes, endnotes, and bibliography. Instead of citations in the text, in this system you use raised numerals to direct your reader to references located either at the bottom of the page or on a separate page at the end of your paper.

To indicate a reference, put an arabic numeral half a space up after the final punctuation of your sentence. Number your notes consecutively throughout the paper. If you prefer (or if your instructor requires) endnotes, list them on a separate sheet of paper just before the bibliography. If you use footnotes, be sure to leave enough space at the bottom of the page on which your reference occurs. Skip four lines after the last line of text; indent five spaces; type in the appropriate number and information.

Here are the note forms you will most often need.

Books by One Author.

[1]David M. Potter, *The South and the Sectional Conflict* (Baton Rouge: Louisiana State UP, 1968) 12.

Books by More Than One Author.
Give the first and last name of each author in the same order as on the title page of the book, and then proceed with the entry.

[2]Alexei Abramowitz, Clarrisa Veer, and Thomas Kaplan, *Cartels* (New York: International Library, 1977) 22.

For books with more than three authors, give the first author's name, followed by *et al.* or *and others*, and proceed.

³Florence Sagforth et al., *Canyon Years* (Santa Fe: Illusions, 1982) 112.

Articles in Journals.

⁴Clair Schulz, "The Seat of Our Affections," *Verbatim* 4 (1977): 3.

Articles in Other Periodicals.   For daily, weekly, or monthly periodicals (most newspapers and magazines), follow this form. Our model is from a newspaper, so it uses the newspaper's page number form.

⁵Anthony Lewis, "White Man's Lawyer," *New York Times* 6 June 1985: A27.

Repeated References to a Source.   If you have already referred to a source, do not repeat all the information in subsequent citations. Give the usual full information the first time.

⁶Jacques Derrida, *Of Grammatology* (Baltimore: Johns Hopkins UP, 1976) 95.

Thereafter, simply give the author's name and page number.

⁷Derrida 477.

If there are two works by the same author, give the author's name, a short title of the work, and page number.

⁸Derrida, *Grammatology* 351.

⁹Derrida, "La Double Séance" 58.

Frequently, especially in book reports and papers on literature, you will refer to only one source in your paper. In this case, fully cite your source the first time; for each subsequent reference, however, you need not use a footnote or endnote. Just put the page number in parentheses *in the text*, followed by a period.

The author goes on to say, "Here eight thousand members of the Oglala subtribe of the Sioux, or Dakota, live on land allotted to them by the government" (115).

Books with Translators.

¹⁰Jean Genet, *Our Lady of the Flowers*, trans. Bernard Frechtman (New York: Grove, 1963) 130.

Books with Editors.   For compilations or collections, put the editor's name first, followed by *ed.*, then proceed.

[11]Feldon Quinn, ed., *Hollywood Writes: The Collected Graffiti of the Stars* (Anaheim: Katella, 1977) 39.

Sometimes an author's work has been edited by someone else. In that case, give the author, the title of the work, then the names of the editor or editors, and proceed.

[12]Harry Stack Sullivan, *The Interpersonal Theory of Psychiatry*, eds. Helen Swick Perry and Mary Ladd Gawel (New York: Norton, 1953) 156.

Anonymous Works. For authorless works — pamphlets, newspaper articles, and so on — start with the title.

[13]"The Bogus Order of Merit," *New Republic* 2 Apr. 1977: 6.

[14]"The Effect of Cotton Candy on the Intestinal Fortitude of the Field Mouse," U.S. News and Information Service, n.d.: 8.

The abbreviation *n.d.* means "no date provided." The abbreviation *n.p.* would mean "no place of publication" or "no publisher provided."

Many instructors prefer slightly different forms for documentation. Make sure you know what your instructor expects.

Bibliography

The form for the bibliography is the same as that for the list of works cited, except that the word *Bibliography* replaces *Works Cited* above the first entry.

The APA Style

The APA style, most common in the social sciences, uses parenthetical text references. Instead of author and page number, however, the basic reference contains the author's last name and the year of publication. Page numbers are not always given because of the frequent necessity of referring to an article or a study as a whole. If you give a page number, precede it with *p.*

Psychoanalysts have generally treated our pleasurable response to works of art as another example of the release of tension (Freud, 1956, p. 133).

Notice that in the APA system a comma goes between the author and the year. If the author's name appears in your text, you need only give the year.

> Freud, like many psychoanalysts before and after him, treated our pleasurable response to works of art as another example of the release of tension (1956, p. 133).

A list of references at the end of the paper contains complete information about each source.

Sample Text References

Here are the most common forms of reference within the text in APA style.

Books by More than One Author. Show all the authors' last names the first time a reference to a multiauthor book occurs; then use the first author's last name and *et al.* for subsequent references. For the first reference:

> Babies start smiling, laughing, and trying to converse at around three months (Miller, Haskell & Golder, 1970).

Later in the text:

> Babies show a preference for bright, striking colors and well-defined patterns (Miller et al., 1970).

Anonymous Works. Use a short title and the year for anonymous works.

> Cardiopulmonary resuscitation training is absolutely essential for the modern lifeguard (*Swimmers,* 1984).

Multiple Works by the Same Author. When you cite two or more works by the same author, use the author's last name and the year.

> Psychoanalysis can be related to language (Edelson, 1972) and to the way in which dreams are generated in the sleeping mind (Edelson, 1975).

If an author has published more than one source in the same year, arrange the sources alphabetically by title and assign each one a lower case letter after the date (1979a, 1979b, 1979c, and so on); use these letters in your references.

Reference List

The reference list is preceded by the word *References* centered at the top of the page. Alphabetize entries by the author's last name, or by the first major word of the title if there is no author. Citations in the APA style differ from the MLA form in four major ways.

1. The APA puts the year immediately after the author's name.
2. The APA does not capitalize after the first word of a title — except proper names and the first word after a colon.
3. Where the MLA uses quotation marks — for titles of articles, chapters, or essays — the APA uses nothing.
4. The APA system uses only initials for authors' first and middle names and uses ampersands instead of the word *and*.

Books by One Author.

Freud, S. (1956). *Delusion and dream.* Boston: Beacon Press.

Books by Two Authors.

Phelps, E., & Drummer, T. (1985). *Whale migration patterns and weather changes.* Miami: Ourania.

Books by Three or More Authors.

Miller, F. L., Haskell, J. K., & Golder, S. (1970). *The growth of perception in the human infant.* Edinburgh: Lanugo.

Books by Corporate Authors.

National Association for Research into Parasitic Diseases. (1981). *Schistosomiasis in the third world.* New York: Harvey.

Anonymous Books.

Swimmers for life. (1984). Huntington Beach: Nereid Press.

Books with Editors.

Mead, M. (1977). *Letters from the field, 1925–1975.* (R. N. Anshen, Ed.). New York: Harper & Row.

Articles.   In journals that paginate continuously throughout the year, use this form.

> Barnet, S. (1955). Some limitations on a Christian approach to Shake-speare. *English Literary History, 22,* 81–92.

In periodicals that paginate each issue separately, follow this style.

> Gordon, G. (1985, May). Micro futures. *Profiles, 2,* 24–30.

In newspapers, follow this style

> Lewis, A. (1985, November 8). White man's lawyer. *New York Times,* p. A27.

REVISING AND WRITING THE FINAL DRAFT

Putting your research paper into final form will call on everything you have learned about writing: style, grammar, and punctuation; paragraphing, persuasion, and documentation; claim, evidence, and warrant. We hope you will refer to this book often in the course of rewriting. Be sure you reread the section "Revising: Getting It Right" in Chapter 1.

Before typing the final draft, read your paper twice, first for content and then again for mechanical correctness. Contrary to popular belief, you cannot read for both content and correctness at once. While hunting down an errant comma, you may miss a faulty warrant. One time-honored method of checking spelling is to start with the last word and read word by word backwards.

Try reading aloud, too.

After you finish revising, your paper will go to your reader. Don't unleash a disheveled paper on the world. Turning in even the most closely reasoned and well-supported paper with incorrect spelling and poor grammar is like going out on a special date with dirty fingernails and greasy hair. If your instructor has given explicit directions regarding title page, binding, footnotes, and the like, follow them. If not, here are twelve guidelines for good form.

1. Use 8½-by-11-inch white paper — not too flimsy and not too easily smeared. Rule out onionskin and certain kinds of erasable pa-

pers. If you use computer paper, remove the perforated sides and separate the pages.

2. Type. Be sure the type is clear, dark, and black. Avoid blue, green, and red ribbons, pretty as they are, and do not use italic types.

3. An inch below the top of the first page and even with the left-hand margin, type your name, your instructor's name, your course title and number, and the date on separate lines, double-spacing between each line. (If you use a cover sheet, center your title about a third of the way down the page. Do not underline it or put it in quotation marks. An inch below the title, type *By* followed by your name. An inch below this line, type the name and number of the course, your instructor's name, and the date, each on a separate, centered line.)

4. Double-space again and type your title in the center of the line. Do not underline the title or put it in quotation marks. Quadruple-space between the title and your first line of text.

5. Number your pages in the upper-right-hand corners, one-half inch below the top of the page and an inch from the right-hand edge. Since papers tend to fly apart, it is also a good idea to give your last name with the page number — for example, "Gerke 6" — from page 2 on.

6. Double-space your text.

7. Leave margins of at least an inch at the top, bottom, and sides.

8. Leave two spaces after any period or other end-of-sentence punctuation.

9. Make sure your references and list of works cited follow the proper form. (See our annotations on Christina Gerke's list of works cited.)

10. If necessary, use correction fluid, but retype a heavily corrected page or passage rather than submit anything sloppy or unreadable.

11. Fasten the pages together with a paper clip or a staple of adequate strength — plastic binders and stiff cardboard can be a nuisance to your reader.

12. Keep all written work away from food and drinks, especially coffee, to which papers seem to have a magnetic attraction. Make a copy of your paper for safekeeping.

A SAMPLE PAPER

Here is a formal outline of Christina Gerke's research paper, followed by the paper itself. Notice that she uses the MLA text reference and list of works cited system of documentation.

The Standardized Testing Controversy   1

By Christina Gerke

English 102

Professor Resnick

May 2, 1985

1. *Title page format.* Gerke includes a formal outline with her paper, so she uses a separate title page. See specifications on page 372. A separate title page is not necessary in a paper that does not have an outline.

The Standardized Testing Controversy   2

Thesis: Since there is still so much controversy about standardized   3

tests, something crucial to many people, employers and insti-

tutions should continue to use them but should de-emphasize

them in favor of other personal factors.

  I. Standardized tests are a fact of life in the United States, but

their design and effects are a matter of continuing controversy.

    A. They determine who graduates from high school, who attends

the best colleges, who gets the best jobs, even who drives a

car.

    B. Educators and experts disagree about their usefulness.

      1. Advocates say they are the best available instrument for

assessing a person's abilities.

      2. Opponents charge that because the tests are biased, they

may do more harm than good.

    C. This paper argues that employers and institutions should

continue to use the tests, but they should de-emphasize them.

 II. The controversy stems from the tests' social origin and social

impact.

    A. The tests have replaced older prejudicial ways of choosing

candidates for college admission and employment.

    B. Advocates praise the tests on two grounds.

      1. The tests have predictive value.

      2. They are reputedly fair.

2. *Outline format.* The outline is placed between the title page and the text. Gerke centers the title of the paper one inch from the top of the page. She skips four lines and types her thesis in a form as close as possible to the way it appears in the paper, while still making sense by itself. This is a formal sentence outline.

3. *Outline content.* Each major point of the outline corresponds to a part of the thesis. Each subdivision relates directly to the main division under which it appears.

C. Opponents, however, point out bias in tests.

1. Minorities score lower.

2. Use of standardized English automatically discriminates against those for whom English is a second language and those who use dialects.

3. Most tests emphasize reading and vocabulary, both of which are culturally linked.

4. Test items can be "differentially attractive."

III. Because of further inherent problems in test design itself, critics doubt the ability of standardized tests to predict future performance, and they question the tests' value in assessing knowledge.

A. Tests ignore personality factors that could influence a person's performance.

B. It is sometimes difficult to ascertain exactly what the tests measure.

1. "Intelligence" is not clearly defined.

2. Tests may measure different abilities in different people.

IV. The Scholastic Aptitude Test (SAT) is a case study in the history and controversy surrounding standardized tests.

A. The SAT is the largest, most widespread standardized test.

B. Students' performance on the SAT may have more to do with which high school they attend than with their intelligence.

C. Minorities and the less affluent perform less well on the SATs.

V. Standardized tests may actually reinforce the subordinate position of minority groups.

4. *Page numbers.* The pages of an outline are numbered with lower-case roman numerals about a half-inch from the top of the page, in the upper-right corner, beginning with *ii* (the first page is counted but not numbered). The pages of the text are numbered with arabic numerals, beginning with the first page.

A. Low scores mean a limited future.

B. Despite efforts to eliminate accidental bias, even minimum competency tests (MCTs) still maintain hierarchies that restrict candidates' future chances.

VI. Still, standardized tests are useful within limits.

A. In general, standardized tests can measure performance, predict future success, and indicate aptitude for various things.

B. SATs can predict students' college success to some extent.

C. It is useful, for better or for worse, to learn how to survive in a white, middle-class world.

VII. We should not, however, rely on tests so much.

A. They are overused, and they have too much power to determine candidates' futures.

B. Some schools are already downplaying the tests in favor of other standards.

VIII. I propose that we adopt an "opportunity quotient" test.   5

A. Such a test would compare a person's opportunity with his or her achievement.

B. An "opportunity quotient" test would present a fairer and more comprehensive picture of a student.

5. *Outline format.* Neither the introduction nor the conclusion is named as a separate part of the outline. Instead, Gerke includes sentences that describe the content of these sections.

1

The Standardized Testing Controversy   **6**

Standardized tests have become an American way of life. They now   **7**
help determine who should be accepted to college; which students must
take remedial classes and which may take advanced classes; who will
make the best soldiers, civil servants, lawyers, state employees--even
who may drive a car. More than 200 million such tests are administered
in the United States each year (Wardrop 16). It may come as a surprise,
then, to learn that something so common is the subject of a national
controversy.

Educators, psychologists, and experts in test design stand on both   **8**
sides of the debate. Advocates argue that standardized tests are still
the best available method of assessing a person's abilities. They
claim that existing tests are "not biased against minority groups"
(Herbert) and are "valid predictors" of a person's future success   **9**
(Eckland 12). In short, they see the tests as services to the community.

Opponents believe that the tests may do more harm than good. In
their eyes, the tests fail to recognize the cultural diversity of our
society. Constructed according to the styles and standards of the
white middle-class male community, the tests, opponents say, are
biased against minorities and less affluent whites. Robert L. Green
and Robert J. Griffore write, "The negative aspects of testing pro-
cedures are especially apparent with respect to racial minorities" (25).   **10**
By failing to recognize cultural diversity, they argue, test makers
permanently handicap large numbers of people whose poor performances

6. *Paper format.* The title is centered between the right and left margins, two inches from the top of the page. The text begins four lines below the title, and is double-spaced throughout (including long quotations, content endnotes, and list of works cited). There is a one-inch margin on all four sides. Paragraphs are indented five spaces, and quotations of more than four lines are indented ten spaces from the left margin.
7. *Introduction.* Gerke devotes four paragraphs to her introduction: one giving general background, two on the controversy (one for either side), and one stating her thesis.
8. *Effective transition.* An idea repeated in slightly different form makes a good transition. The idea of a "national controversy" in paragraph 1 is reflected in "the debate" in paragraph 2.
9. *Integrating sources.* Gerke smoothly combines material from two different sources with her own writing. She puts the authors and page numbers in parenthetical citations, which closely follow the Herbert quotation and the paraphrased information from Eckland. Note also that the reference to the Herbert article does not give a page number since that article is only one page long. This is also true of references to "Jensen's Rebuttal," "Brave New World," and Holden.
10. *Page number in parentheses.* Green and Griffore are already mentioned in the text, so only the page number is given in the parenthetical reference to their work.

land them where they do not belong--in "slow" classes with restricted curricula and even more restricted opportunities.

My discussion will look at both sides of this issue in more detail   12 but will not agree completely with either side. Standardized tests are useful, but they are also very powerful: test scores can affect the course of people's lives, not to mention their self-image and their society's image of them. Until we know more about this crucial yet controversial subject, employers and institutions should continue to use the tests, but they should de-emphasize them.

In the past employers and institutions based their selections on   13 factors such as a candidate's social class and family background. College admissions boards, especially those for private institutions, weighed these values more heavily than proven ability. As late as the 1940s, admissions boards tended to select students from a small number of well-known public and private institutions (Ravitch 55). This practice, obviously unfair to deserving candidates from disadvantaged backgrounds, maintained the homogeneous nature of the colleges.

Standardized tests arose partly to correct such institutionalized prejudices. The French psychologist Alfred Binet originally formulated his Binet scale of intelligence in 1905 to place advanced and handicapped children in special schools (Wardrop 8; Jensen 141-143).   14 Binet's test began the long history of standardized placement examinations.

In the eighty years since, standardized tests have often drawn praise as the most democratic possible means of social selection because they aim only to "predict performance in school and on the job" (Herbert 84). Bruce K. Eckland, professor of sociology at the   15

11. *Running head.* On each page from 2 on, Gerke types her last name along with the page number in case pages are misplaced.
12. *Thesis.* Here, in her thesis paragraph, Gerke distinguishes her position from both sides of the debate. Her thesis promises a workable direction for the paper; it raises some questions to be answered (Why should tests be de-emphasized?) and commits the paper to an argument.
13. *Necessary background.* In the next paragraphs, Gerke gives readers background information explaining why standardized tests became so popular. This section of the paper corresponds to II.A. in the outline.
14. *Multiple sources.* Two different sources are cited for the information about Binet. Both names, separated by a semicolon, are included in a single parenthetical reference.
15. *Introduction to indented quotation.* Gerke establishes the authority of her source by giving his credentials in her excellent introduction to the quotation.

University of North Carolina, gives the standard defense:

> There is no factor that has a stronger, more consistent **16**
> effect in the college attainment process independent of race,
> social class, sex, or any other observed characteristic . . .
> than individual ability as measured by standardized tests.
>
> (12)

Advocates often seem to suggest that this ability to predict exonerates **17**
tests from charges of bias. One defender writes that the tests "can
predict equally well for members of minority groups as for nonwhites"
(Holden), as if this accuracy can somehow sidestep the question of
whether or not the prediction is self-fulfilling.

Yet the charge of test bias against minority groups has become the
central issue in the debate. One consistent trend has proved most
embarrassing to those who favor standardized tests: in general, minorities score lower on standardized tests than do middle-class whites.
On standard IQ tests, for example, the overall difference between
whites and blacks is 15 points, and the gap between rich and poor is
12 points (Jensen 44).

If such figures provide powerful evidence of bias, problems in the **18**
design of the tests are even more telling. One obvious example is the
use of standard English in most tests. Students for whom English is a
second language, or those who speak a dialect like black or Appalachian
English, may have a handicap before they even sit down to take the test
(Farb 162-63). **19**

Further, many tests emphasize reading and vocabulary ability,
which studies have shown to be culturally linked (Ravitch 54)--that is,
a student from a background where reading is either unavailable or not

16. *Indented quotation and use of ellipses.* The passage is indented ten spaces from the left margin. Gerke quotes her source precisely, using ellipses to indicate that she has omitted something from the original. Since Eckland is already mentioned, only the page number appears in the reference, which is placed outside of the indented material, two spaces after the period.
17. *Evaluating sources.* Here and elsewhere, Gerke analyzes and evaluates her sources. This appeal to reason shows that she has thought about what Holden is saying and has something to say in response.
18. *Strong transition.* By suggesting that the next piece of evidence will be more convincing than the first, Gerke pushes the argument forward.
19. *Revision.* In her first draft, Gerke included the Farb information later in the paper. On rereading, however, she realized that it would work more effectively if it were grouped with similar evidence.

encouraged will come to a standardized test at a great disadvantage. And some questions may similarly contain quite accidental bias. Consider this test question:

Collie is to dog as trout is to _____.

The correct answer, of course, is <u>fish</u>, but if a student came from a background where people never used the word trout--or, more likely, used a slang or dialect equivalent instead--he or she would miss the question, not through lack of ability but through being different (Wardrop 53).

20

In the parlance of the experts, certain test items may have characteristics that "are differentially attractive" to different population subgroups. As Janice Dowd Scheuneman, vice president of the Eastern Educational Research Association, states,

21

> Unexpected differences in item performance can occur as the result of . . . urban-rural distinctions, climatic differences, economic advantage or disadvantage . . . cultural characteristics or values . . . Spanish language heritage . . . black English dialects, and the interpersonal style and communication modes of different ethnic cultures. (185)

This means that a person's background shapes his or her perception of the world.

A test constructed by a white, middle-class male will necessarily reflect many of his norms and value assumptions. Obviously, these may differ markedly from those of a lower-class Hispanic woman, who may be penalized for selecting answers that are true for her. Her selection of different answers, however, does not necessarily indicate that she lacks ability or intelligence. Scheuneman gives the example of one

20. *Documenting paraphrased material.* Here Gerke closely paraphrases a passage from Wardrop, keeping the order of the ideas but expressing them in her own language. She still documents her source in a parenthetical reference.

21. *Argument.* Note the argumentative structure of this paragraph. There is a claim and a lengthy quotation for evidence. Gerke condenses the quotation for clarity and maximum concreteness, using ellipses to indicate that she has deleted something from the original. She then concludes with a strong warrant.

test of auditory discrimination in which children were asked to select
a picture of the object which began with the same sound as a word given
by the teacher. In one item,

> the key word was "heart," and the correct choice was [the
> picture of a] "hand." The first option, however, was a
> [picture of a] large, fancy car . . . called a "hog" in
> black dialect . . . this option, in fact, had drawn a
> disproportionately large number of black children. (183-84)

22

Thus, although the answer was technically incorrect, the children
demonstrated that they actually had the skill being tested. Such
built-in inequities may not happen in most test items, but they do
happen often enough to support the conclusion that standardized tests,
while "highly perfected" (Ravitch 13), may not be humanly sensitive.

Bias is not the only point of contention. The great selling
features of standardized tests--their ability to predict future performance and their value in assessing knowledge--are now also under
attack. In a report of the Committee on Ability Testing of the
Assembly of Behavioral and Social Sciences, Alexandra K. Wigdor,
study director of the committee, cites the

23

> limited predictive powers of the tests . . . the
> constraints on assessment introduced by the very process of
> standardization [italics mine], the traditional concentration
> of the tests on a limited range of cognitive skills . . .
> and the inability of the tests to assess adequately other
> important characteristics such as motivation, creativity, or
> perseverance. (6-7)

24

Problems arise, then, whenever we try to measure people by a
single yardstick. Standardization prevents tests from taking into

25

22. *Use of brackets.* Gerke uses brackets to insert material into the quotation for clarity. Bracketed information can also be used to make the quotation fit grammatically with the text of the paper.

23. *Unifying transition.* By referring to *bias* (the umbrella term for the first set of criticisms against the tests), Gerke makes a smooth transition to the next set of criticisms and ties together the various arguments against standardized tests.

24. *Adding emphasis.* Gerke adds italics to emphasize a passage not originally stressed in the source. She puts the phrase *italics mine* in brackets immediately following the material to indicate that this is her addition.

25. *Development of an idea.* Gerke interprets the quotation and then explains further why standardized tests might fail to predict future performance.

account intangible differences among people, differences in personality
factors, such as Wigdor's "motivation, creativity, or perseverance,"
that might be valuable or crucial to a person's success. Most tests
cannot address aspects of character because test takers are often
confined to multiple choice answers ("Jensen's Rebuttal"). Yet any
truly predictive test must measure such qualities, since what people
lack in strictly intellectual or cognitive abilities they can sometimes
offset with other abilities or with hard work and dedication. The
tests may therefore have the serious shortcoming of ignoring significant
predictors of future performance.

Sometimes it is difficult to ascertain exactly what qualities the **26**
tests actually measure. Scientists do not yet agree on a single definition of the word <u>intelligence</u>, for example, and as the meaning of the **27**
word changes so do the tests that try to measure it ("Brave New World").
Furthermore, a test item designed to measure one ability may actually **28**
test different abilities in different people. This accidental shifting
can occur in something as simple as a spelling test.

> Asking for the spelling of a given word may require a
> student who was previously drilled on the word merely to
> recite from rote memory a string of letters but require a
> student who was not taught this word to analyze it into
> syllables and phonemes and then to apply his phonics
> knowledge to the task. (Bormuth 23)

Consequently, a test item aimed at a specific ability (phonics
knowledge) tested something quite different (ability to memorize).
This shifting happened because of the different experiences of the **29**
students being tested, something that no test may ever fully take into

26. *Argumentative paragraph.* Here is the claim.
27. *Evidence.* No warrant is necessary for this, the first piece of evidence.
28. *Evidence.* Here is a second piece of evidence. The quotation that follows makes the evidence more specific.
29. *Warrant.* The warrant explains how the evidence works with the claim. In fact, Gerke makes the warrant very detailed: it takes two sentences.

account. If designers cannot limit what their questions test, their
tests may not really identify specific abilities and test for them
accurately and fairly.

    Inequities occur on the largest scale in one of the grandest
standardized tests of all. The Scholastic Aptitude Tests (SATs)
evaluate high-school applicants to colleges and universities. Taking
SATs has become a senior-year ritual for more than a million students
every year (On Further Examination 1), and, despite the disagreements
over their value, SAT scores are still very important parts of any
college application. SATs aim to measure the student's innate capacity.
However, SAT results may have more to do with one's school than with
intelligence. In an article in New Republic magazine, Ann Hulbert says
that "the SAT is in fact yet another exam that reflects the quality of
the schools students happen to attend, rather than a transcendent test
that measures some ambiguous 'aptitude' they possess" (12). Certain
schools gear the senior and sometimes the junior year to preparing
students for the SATs; others run mock exams or hold classes on how to
use the multiple choice format to help eliminate inaccurate answers.
Thus, the SAT may handicap people who have intelligence and potential
but have not attended schools with these programs.

    Further, the familiar gaps in average score exist between rich and
poor and between racial groups on the SATs as on other tests. Students
from families with incomes under $6,000 per year average about 100
points lower on the verbal and the mathematics parts of the tests than
those from families with incomes over $18,000 per year. Blacks average
100 points below the overall average on the verbal part and 115 points
below on the mathematics (On Further Examination 15).

30

31

32

33

30. *Case study.* The Scholastic Aptitude Tests (SATs) are used as a case study illustrating the strengths and weaknesses of standardized tests.
31. *Abbreviations.* Gerke spells out a term that she will use throughout the rest of the paper and follows the term with its abbreviation in parentheses. In subsequent references she uses just the abbreviation.
32. *Anonymous source.* The title of the book is used in place of an author's name. If the title is very long, a brief form of it, including the word by which it is alphabetized, can be used in the parenthetical reference.
33. *Transitional flag.* Gerke uses the word *further* to make a smooth transition.

The great danger of the SATs and other standardized tests is that they may reinforce social hierarchies by the simple fact that a low test score is a social disadvantage. Because of their low test scores, minority children have often been labeled slow or retarded and placed in special schools or, worse yet, have received no further education. Studies show that such children grow up thinking they are stupid and **34** suffer further hardship, since with no education they can expect fewer prospects in society ("Jensen's Rebuttal").

Even minimum competency tests (MCTs), which were designed to reveal basic skill deficiencies so that they could be rectified (Popham 91), may contribute to the problem.[1] The aim behind these tests was to **35** eliminate the gap between racial and economic groups, but the tests may reinforce class differentiation and hold back deserving students.

Once the system classifies people according to test results, it tends to perpetuate and accentuate the differences among them. Although students are no longer rated "slow" or "fast" learners, a specific number are classified as "pigeons," "hawks," or "eagles" according to their MCT scores (Trusz and Parks-Trusz 17). While "eagles" learn the **36** entire curriculum on which later examinations will test them, "pigeons" are given only a part of it, which causes them to fall further and further behind. The rest of the story is familiar. "Pigeons" could fail to earn a high-school diploma and thus be cut off from further opportunities at school and at work. The handicap of social labeling could ensue: "remediation evokes labelling . . . attaching a negative label to an individual's actions causes the individual to develop a negative self-image. The result is a self-fulfilling prophecy of failure" (Trusz and Parks-Trusz 17). Though they are a result rather

34. *Summary.* This paragraph summarizes much of the article "Jensen's Rebuttal." Only the main sense of the article was needed, not any specific ideas or phrases.
35. *Content note.* The raised number refers readers to a content note at the end of the paper.
36. *Two authors of a single source.* Both names are included in the parenthetical reference.

than a cause of social assumptions, standardized tests begin this
circular pattern.[2]

Despite these problems in design and social sensitivity, standard-   **37**
ized tests have many uses. They can, in general, effectively measure
performance. To some extent they can predict how well you or I will do
in our future lives; within limits, they can also indicate our aptitudes
for various things. For example, SAT scores are good predictors of how
well high-school seniors will do in their first year in college
("Scores" 88). Test design has become a science to itself, and, as it
develops, its products will improve. And even if the critics of SATs
and MCTs are right, the political issue of bias by itself is not enough
to justify doing away with testing. The world of work and school is,   **38**
whether we like it or not, still white and middle class, and, until this
changes, everyone needs to learn how to live and succeed in that world.

We should not, however, rely on standardized tests to the extent   **39**
we do now. We should not use them to pigeonhole people, nor should we
allow them to influence our opinions of them. Even such a proponent as
Arthur Jensen admits that the tests are overused ("Jensen's Rebuttal").
Educator George F. Madaus writes,

> The more one knows about the technology of testing, the more
> one realizes the potential for harm when a test score is
> used as the sole or primary criterion on which to make an
> important decision affecting an individual's future. (93)

Tests may be able to suggest what this or that person's future might be
like, but it would be wrong to let them determine that future.

Some colleges and universities have already begun to downplay   **40**
applicants' test scores in favor of "progressive validity indices"

37. *Qualification and concession.* Gerke lists several ways in which she thinks tests are valuable. This will strengthen her thesis when she reasserts it a final time in the next paragraph.
38. *Critical analysis.* Gerke is not content just to string sources together; she uses her critical faculties and imagination to create a real argument from them.
39. *Return to thesis.* The thesis is reasserted at the end, strengthened by the judicious qualifications in the previous paragraph.
40. *Corroboration.* In a neat argumentative move, Gerke notes that other institutions and people think the way she does. This point again strengthens her thesis.

that balance SAT scores with high-school grades, class rank, and the quality of the high-school program (Ravitch 55). Perhaps this practice will start a trend. Perhaps parents, teachers, and administrators—those who know students as people—will concentrate on getting as comprehensive a picture of each student as they can and passing that picture on.

Ironically, perhaps what we need is another test—one for OQ, or **41** "opportunity quotient." This would compare the amount of opportunity in a person's background with that person's achievements. The motivated but disadvantaged student could score well over 100, while the advantaged but only mildly active student might score below. If this sounds whimsical, it may only be because many of us are not used to thinking in minority ways. An OQ test could reveal people whose drive balances their handicaps in other areas. When they try for that job or that place at Harvard, the Naval Academy, or the foreign service, they should have a dossier that shows them not just as a point along a scale but as a person with potential. **42**

41. *Conclusion.* The conclusion does not restate the major points made previously. Instead, it steps out of the argument, now finished, and makes a proposal — not completely seriously, but well in keeping with the tone and direction of the paper. This ending is a creative way to bring the paper to a well-rounded finish.
42. *Closing sentence.* The paper ends with a strong closing sentence that appeals to the emotions of sympathy and humor.

Gerke 11   **43**

Notes

[1] Popham believes that MCTs will "restore meaning to a highschool   **44**
diploma" (91), but opponents like Anderson and Pipho believe that
"testing minimal competencies primarily affects low achieving students.
. . . It can discourage those who are average or below" (212).

[2] See Jaeger for more information about the relationship between   **45**
standardized tests and student failure.

43. *Format of endnotes.* Endnotes are typed on a separate page, numbered as part of the paper. The heading *Notes* is centered between the left and right margins, one inch from the top of the page. The notes are double-spaced and the first line of each is indented five spaces from the left margin. The number of the note (corresponding to the raised number in the text) is raised a half-space above the note.

44. *Use of endnotes.* This note gives additional information about the MCTs. Gerke originally included arguments about Popham and by Anderson and Pipho in an earlier section of the paper, but she found that she could focus her own argument more clearly by moving the material to a content note.

45. *Bibliographic endnotes.* Endnotes can also refer readers to additional sources of information, as here.

Gerke 12   **46**

Works Cited

Anderson, B., and C. Pipho. "State-Mandated Testing and the Fate of   **47**
Local Control." Phi Delta Kappan Nov. 1984: 209-12.

Austin, Gilbert R., and Herbert Gardner, eds. The Rise and Fall of   **48**
National Test Scores. New York: Academic, 1982.

Berk, Ronald, ed. Handbook of Methods for Detecting Test Bias.
Baltimore: Johns Hopkins UP, 1982.

Bormuth, John R. On the Theory of Achievement Test Items. Chicago: **49**
U of Chicago, 1970.

"Brave New World of Intelligence Testing." Psychology Today   **50**
Sept. 1979: 13.

Eckland, Bruce K. "College Entrance Examination Trends." Austin and   **51**
Gardner 9-34.

Farb, Peter. Word Play. New York: Knopf, 1973.

Green, Robert L., and Robert J. Griffore. "Standardized Testings and
Minority Students." Education Digest Feb. 1981: 25-28.

Herbert, W. "Ability Testing Absolved of Racial Bias." Science News
6 Feb. 1982: 84.

Holden, Constance. "NAS Backs Cautious Use of Ability Tests." Science
19 Feb. 1982: 950.

Hulbert, Ann. "S.A.T.s Aren't So Smart." New Republic 20 Dec. 1982:   **52**
12+.

Jaeger, Richard M. "The Final Hurdle: Minimum Competency Achievement
Testing." Austin and Gardner 223-46.

Jensen, Arthur. Bias in Mental Testing. New York: Free Press, 1980.

"Jensen's Rebuttal." Newsweek 14 Jan. 1980: 59.

46. *Format of the list of works cited.* The works cited list begins on a separate page following endnotes (if there are any). The page is numbered as part of the text. The heading *Works Cited* is centered between the left and right margins, one inch from the top of the page. Entries are double-spaced throughout, with the first line of each entry even with the left margin and subsequent lines indented five spaces. Authors are listed alphabetically, with the first author's name inverted and additional names (if any) in normal order. Anonymous works are alphabetized by the first important word of the title (not *a, an,* or *the*).

47. *Article with two authors.*

48. *A book with two editors.*

49. *A book with a single author.* The name of the press is shortened.

50. *Anonymous article.* The article is alphabetized by the title.

51. *Cross-reference.* Eckland's piece is a chapter in Austin and Gardner. The title of the chapter, in quotation marks, is followed by the name of the book and the page numbers of the chapter. The book itself is cited in full earlier.

52. *Article with noncontinuous pagination.* The number of the first page is followed by + to indicate that the article is not paged continuously.

Madaus, George F. "NIE Clarification Hearing: The Negative Team's
Case." <u>Phi Delta Kappan</u> Oct. 1981: 92-94.

<u>On Further Examination</u>. New York: College Entrance Examination Board,   **53**
1977.

Popham, W. James. "The Case for Minimum Competency Testing." <u>Phi
Delta Kappan</u> Oct. 1981: 89-91.

Ravitch, Diane. "The College Boards." <u>New York Times</u>. 4 May 1975,
Sec. 6: 12+.

Scheuneman, Janice Dowd. "A Posteriori Analysis of Biased Items."
Berk 180-98.

"Scores." <u>Scientific American</u> Sept. 1978: 88+.

Trusz, Andrew R., and Sandra L. Parks-Trusz. "The Social Consequences
of Competency Testing." <u>Education Digest</u> Apr. 1982: 15-18.

Wardrop, James L. <u>Standardized Testing in the Schools: Uses and Roles</u>.
Monterey: Brooks, 1976.

Wigdor, Alexandra K. "Ability Testing: Uses, Consequences, and   **54**
Controversies." <u>Educational Measurement: Issues and Practice</u> 1
(1982): 6-7.

53. *Anonymous book.* The book is alphabetized by the title.
54. *Article in a journal that paginates continuously throughout the year.*

EXERCISES FOR RESEARCH

1. You are doing a research paper on the presidency of John F. Kennedy. What would you take notes on in this passage? Would you quote, paraphrase, or summarize? Why?

Kennedy was called an intellectual very seldom before 1960 and very often thereafter — a phenomenon which deserves explanation.

One cannot be sure what an intellectual is; but let us define it as a person whose primary habitat is the realm of ideas. In this sense, exceedingly few political leaders are authentic intellectuals, because the primary habitat of the political leader is the world of power. Yet the world of power itself has intellectual and anti-intellectual sides. Some political leaders find exhilaration in ideas and in the company of those whose trade it is to deal with them. Others are rendered uneasy by ideas and uncomfortable by intellectuals.

Kennedy belonged supremely to the first class. He was a man of action who could pass easily over to the realm of ideas and confront intellectuals with perfect confidence in his capacity to hold his own. His mind was not prophetic, impassioned, mystical, ontological, utopian or ideological. It was less exuberant than Theodore Roosevelt's, less scholarly than [Woodrow] Wilson's, less adventurous than Franklin Roosevelt's. But it had its own salient qualities — it was objective, practical, ironic, skeptical, unfettered and insatiable.

It was marked first of all, as he had noted to Jacqueline, by inexhaustible curiosity. Kennedy always wanted to know how things worked. Vague answers never contented him. This curiosity was fed by conversation but even more by reading. His childhood consolation had become an adult compulsion. He was now a fanatical reader, 1200 words a minute, not only at the normal times and places but at meals, in the bathtub, sometimes even when walking. Dressing in the morning, he would prop open a book on his bureau and read while he put on his shirt and tied his necktie. He read mostly history and biography. . . . His supposed addiction to James Bond was partly a publicity gag, like Franklin Roosevelt's supposed affection for "Home on the Range." Kennedy seldom read for distraction. He did not want to waste a single second. (Arthur M. Schlesinger, Jr., *A Thousand Days*)

2. The following is a treasure hunt. Find the answers to these questions by consulting the appropriate source in your library. When you have located each answer, report on how you found it and in what source. What sent you to that source in the first place?

What country produced the largest amount of chromium in 1968?

What did movie critics say about *The Jazz Singer* when it first appeared?

How did people do the Big Apple?

How and when was Tanzania formed?

Where did the word *swastika* come from?

Who was the last man Don Larsen faced in his perfect game in the World Series, and how did Larsen get him out?

Who was the second person to walk on the moon?

What was a rumble seat?

What was the latest in women's fashions in 1932?

Why do some Americans say "Gosh!" and "Gee whiz!"? When did these expressions originate?

Which country has the oldest continuously operating form of government?

What was the worst zeppelin crash in Europe's history?

Name all the members of the present Cabinet and report on what they did before becoming Cabinet members.

Who were the members of the Miles Davis Quintet, and why were they important?

Does either Neptune or Uranus have any moons?

Who were the leading man, leading lady, producer, and director of the film *You Gotta Stay Happy*? What was the plot?

Name four cannibal tribes.

3. Look up one of the following names and give a short account of the person's life. Where did you find the information, and why did you go there?

Sigrid Undset	Walter Gropius
Napoleon Lajoie	John Dewey
Alessandro di Mariano Filipepi	Bessie Smith
H. Rap Brown	Harun al-Rashid
Yevgeny Yevtushenko	Bahaullah
Le Corbusier	William Wheeler

4. Find and present an example (through a recording, photocopy, still photograph, plot summary, short excerpt, or other means) of five of the following. Discuss the creators and what makes the works distinctive.

a song by John Dowland	a discovery by Louis Pasteur
a painting by Jan van Eyck	a statue by Constantin Brancusi

a building by Frank Lloyd Wright

a photograph by Edward Steichen

a movie starring Ingrid Bergman

a newspaper article by Damon Runyon

an essay by Jessica Mitford

a mural by José Orozco

an invention by Thomas Edison

a theory by John Maynard Keynes

a discovery by L. S. B. Leakey

an essay by Julian Bond

a poem by Elizabeth Bishop

a study by Mary Douglas

13 / Reading, Interpreting, and Writing about Literature

There are three points of view from which a writer can be considered: he may be considered as a storyteller, as a teacher, and as an enchanter.

– Vladimir Nabokov (1899–1977)
Storyteller, teacher, enchanter

No study is more challenging and rewarding than literature. Many of the most intense and moving moments in our lives have come thanks to literature. It has clarified our thinking and feeling, and changed us in ways we cannot put into words. We have been entertained, taught, and enchanted by it.

The challenges of literature are bracing. Responding to poems, plays, novels, and stories calls for both sensitivity and clarity. It demands an open mind as well as close attention. Yet far from "taking the fun out of literature," accepting its challenges increases both our understanding and our enjoyment.

In the pages that follow, we treat the study of literature as a three-part process of reading, interpreting, and writing.

READING LITERATURE

Reading literature is different from reading a textbook, editorial, or essay. If you tried to use the eight questions in Chapter 2, The Reading Process, on Albert Camus's *The Plague*, T. S. Eliot's *The Waste Land*, or Anton Chekhov's *Three Sisters*, you would not have much success. Literature does not follow the rules of argument. Rather, it presents the world as the writer views it. And it presents this world in a language that is important for itself as well as for what it conveys. To get at the world of the writer and the beauty of its language, the eight questions offer little help.

So — how should you read a poem, a play, a novel, or a short story?

First of all, you should respect the world the work describes. Literature is always a product of a particular time and a particular place. Good readers try to view a work within its own context. Of course, no reader can wholly escape being culture bound; our customs and codes of behavior are too firmly planted. But good readers try to control the bias of their own class and era. They recognize that though values may be eternal, their expression is finite and various. Social relationships may be different. Definitions of acceptable behavior may have changed.

Second, plan to read any work of literature more than once. If you read an expository or argumentative essay carefully, you may well get its whole meaning with one pass — few would read an editorial twice. But literature will not yield its fullness of meaning in one reading. On the first reading, simply read. Don't try to be critical. Give yourself up to the work. Let it possess you.

When reading a poem, read aloud, slowly. Let the rhythms of the poem control the tempo and cadence of your reading. Listen to the music of the poem. Get a friend to read it with you. Never confine a poem to your head. Perform it and listen to the performance. As you read, think about the words themselves, their denotations and their connotations and how the words join with the music to create the total effect.

When reading longer works, set aside at least one, preferably two, hours for uninterrupted periods of reading. Dive in and stay underwater until you get the feel of the work. Whenever you pick it up, give yourself time to settle in. If you only read piecemeal, five pages at a time, you may end up with a piecemeal view of the work.

Keep your mind open during the first reading. Don't try to make the story or poem mean what you expect; let it show you its own meaning. Literature is often startling, outraging, and bewildering. It may ridicule or deny your most cherished beliefs. Do not reject it: learn from it.

On this first reading, don't take notes. They are apt to break your connection with the work by introducing the critical element. If something strikes you, pencil a little check in the margin or circle a phrase. Later you can return to these spots to make full notes.

Warning: no one can skim a piece of literature and expect to get much out of it. You may learn some facts, but you cannot comprehend the quality of the work. Nor can you get much when you rely on the assessments or interpretations of others. There are notes, summaries, and shortcuts on the market today that promise a quick way through novels, plays, and poems. They, too, give facts, but the one thing these shortcuts can never give you is the work itself. There simply is no substitute for a sensitive reading of the text. Don't cheat yourself.

When you have finished this first reading, meditate on what you have read. Think about the ideas, the events, the language. Write a short paraphrase, like these, of the main concern of the work — or your main response to it.

This poem is about the anguish of unrequited love and how its not being returned makes the loved one more attractive.

There are a lot of marriages in this novel but not all are happy because the people are silly or too selfish to adjust.

Thorough readers have been performing such exercises for centuries: they help firm one's hold on the material.

Now re-read the work. This time, annotate the text. Write notes on notecards or in a separate notebook. If you scribble all over your book, your notes will stay unorganized, and you may not be able to find them again.

If the work is long, summarize each chapter. If it is short, paraphrase the whole thing. When you come across one of your checks or circled passages, analyze what struck you the first time. Don't hesitate to go back and forth, to compare different sections. Pause at important junctures. If the characters are confusing, make a list of them. If the language strikes you as unusual, describe its qualities. Take special note of whatever you find arresting. Make exact page references.

General Topics in Literature

What do we look for when we read literature? Literature is so rich that no discussion could possibly cover it. In this section, however, we deal with three important elements common to all literature: theme, symbolism, and language. (Later we will discuss special topics in fiction and poetry.)

Theme. A work always expresses the values of the writer and his or her conceptions of the human condition. But these values and conceptions are rarely simple and obvious. A work of literature cannot be reduced to a simple moral. Nor can it be expressed as a philosophical or sociological treatise. Usually, though, the reader is left with a sense of the point or meaning of a work. This is what we call the theme.

This theme is expressed throughout the work, either as a recurrent idea or a general preoccupation. Examples of a theme might be frustrated desire in Emily Brontë's *Wuthering Heights*, obsession in Herman Melville's *Moby-Dick*, the alienation of modern life in T. S. Eliot's *The Waste Land*. As you read, you can note what changes the theme undergoes and what significance it has either in ᴛne world of the work or in your world.

Symbolism. A symbol is a sign standing for something else. The thirteen stripes in the American flag symbolize the original colonies, and the fifty stars symbolize the fifty states. In literature, a symbol is an image that stands for more than its physical properties indicate. When Hamlet holds up Yorick's skull, that skull stands not just for the remains of a human being but also for death, the certainty that it will come to everyone, including Hamlet.

How can you tell when an image is a symbol? Repetition is one great clue. In *Moby-Dick,* the whale and its whiteness are everywhere and on everyone's mind; they are more than a physical reality. Sometimes the environment of a work will indicate which images you should see as symbolic. When Hamlet holds up Yorick's skull, for instance, he is standing beside a grave and debating death with a grave digger. Hamlet knows his own death is near. You would have to try hard to escape the symbolic function of Yorick's skull in these surroundings. Often shared experiences can lead you to symbols. When you see a human skull, you can hardly avoid thinking of death. When T. S. Eliot, in "The Love Song of J. Alfred Prufrock," writes

Do I dare to eat a peach?

you recognize that it is hardly a brave act to eat a peach, and so you may conclude that eating a peach is symbolic: Eliot is telling you that even such innocent acts can be threatening in our time.

Language. Another common focus of our reading literature is various aspects of language, like tone and imagery. *Tone* is the atmosphere an author creates by the way he or she uses language. It often indicates an attitude toward the subject or toward the audience. When we seek to determine the tone of a work, we are trying to understand the actual voice in which it should be read — serious, sarcastic, playful, or whatever. Edgar Allan Poe begins "The Fall of the House of Usher" with this:

> During the whole of a dull, dark, and soundless day in the autumn of the year, when the clouds hung oppressively low in the heavens, I had been passing alone, on horseback, through a singularly dreary tract of country.

His choice of words, with all those dull *d* sounds, and the slow, ponderous cadence create an atmosphere heavy with threat. Solemn and ominous, the tone shapes our responses.

One very common tone in literature is *irony*. Irony expresses a disparity between opposites: appearance and reality; the ideal and the real; the literal and the implied; what we mean and what we say. Think of the many times you use irony in your daily talk. If someone rams your car, you might say, "That's just great." No one standing by would misunderstand the tone. Or you might resort to understatement, saying "Seems like you left a scratch in the side of my car" when the whole door has caved in.

You will find all kinds of irony in literature. The Eliot line about eating a peach is ironic because there is a disparity between the apparent innocence of the fruit and the fear the speaker expresses. Irony often lends itself to humorous effects. Grace Paley opens her story "The Loudest Voice" this way:

> There is a certain place where dumb-waiters boom, doors slam, dishes crash; every window is a mother's mouth bidding the street shut up, go skate somewhere else, come home. My voice is the loudest.

The irony of the tone is carried through in the plot: Jewish children play leading parts in a school Christmas play.

Sometimes a reader will know something the characters don't know and therefore understands the deeper significance of words and deeds. This situation is called *dramatic irony*. Perhaps the most famous example of this knowing occurs in Sophocles' *Oedipus the King*. The audience knows that Oedipus, by a terrible series of mischances, has slain his father and married his mother. Unaware of these facts, Oedipus wants to discover the truth, and he cries, "I shall not cease until I bring the truth to light." The audience's prior knowledge of what his search will reveal makes his endeavors appear ironic.

Imagery is another important aspect of literary language. Writers seek to stimulate mental images in the minds of readers. Identifying and appreciating such imagery is one of the great pleasures of reading literature. The word *imagery* can refer to pictures, but it is most commonly used to denote the sum of sensual language in a work — the figures of speech and vivid individual images.

Despite its name, an image is not necessarily visual. Several senses are involved in this stanza from Robert Browning's "Meeting at Night":

Then a mile of warm sea-scented beach;
Three fields to cross till a farm appears;
A tap at the pane, the quick sharp scratch
And blue spurt of a lighted match,
And a voice less loud, through its joys and fears,
Than the two hearts beating each to each!

The words that make the passage vivid are images, from simple nouns like *beach* and *farm* to insistently concrete phrases like *the quick sharp scratch/And blue spurt of a lighted match*.

Literature achieves many of its effects through unexpected and startling figures of speech, like *similes* and *metaphors*. A *simile* is an explicit comparison of two things, usually using *like* or *as*. Archibald MacLeish's poem "Ars Poetica," which we discuss in "Special Topics in Poetry," is a series of similes.

A poem should be palpable and mute
As a globed fruit. . . .

A poem should be wordless
As the flight of birds.

Similes occur in fiction also, as you will see when you read Isaac Babel's "My First Goose" in "Special Topics in Fiction." In describing the commander, Babel writes that

His long legs were like girls sheathed to the neck in shining riding boots.

Rather than making an explicit comparison, *metaphor* draws an identity between two things. Toward the end of ''Ars Poetica,'' MacLeish describes the experience of grief in metaphoric terms.

For all the history of grief
An empty doorway and a maple leaf.

We find metaphors in fiction, too, including this one in ''My First Goose'' of a man unable to concentrate on what he reads:

the beloved lines came toward me along a thorny path and could not reach me.

Metaphor's power comes from its unspokenness; it draws us into the possible likenesses between things we had previously assumed were unalike.

We have more to say about similes and metaphors in ''Figurative Language'' in Chapter 7.

Special Topics in Fiction

In addition to theme, language, and symbolism, each kind of literature has its own concerns and terms to be mastered. To prepare for our discussion of the four major elements of fiction — plot, character, setting, and point of view — please read Isaac Babel's ''My First Goose.'' Don't forget to give yourself to it on the first reading and then go back to make notes.

My First Goose

Isaac Babel

Savitsky, Commander of the VI Division, rose when he saw me, and I wondered at the beauty of his giant's body. He rose, the purple of his riding breeches and the crimson of his little tilted cap and the decorations stuck on his chest cleaving the hut as a standard cleaves the sky. A smell of scent and the sickly sweet freshness of soap emanated from him. His long legs were like girls sheathed to the neck in shining riding boots. 1

He smiled at me, struck his riding whip on the table, and drew toward him an order that the Chief of Staff had just finished dictating. 2

It was an order for Ivan Chesnokov to advance on Chugunov-
Dobryvodka with the regiment entrusted to him, to make contact
with the enemy and destroy the same.

"For which destruction," the Commander began to write, smear- 3
ing the whole sheet, "I make this same Chesnokov entirely responsible, up to and including the supreme penalty, and will if necessary
strike him down on the spot; which you, Chesnokov, who have been
working with me at the front for some months now, cannot doubt."

The Commander signed the order with a flourish, tossed it to his 4
orderlies and turned upon me gray eyes that danced with merriment.

I handed him a paper with my appointment to the Staff of the Di- 5
vision.

"Put it down in the Order of the Day," said the Commander. "Put 6
him down for every satisfaction save the front one. Can you read and
write?"

"Yes, I can read and write," I replied, envying the flower and iron 7
of that youthfulness. "I graduated in law from St. Petersburg University."

"Oh, are you one of those grinds?" he laughed. "Specs on your 8
nose, too! What a nasty little object! They've sent you along without
making any enquiries; and this is a hot place for specs. Think you'll
get on with us?"

"I'll get on all right," I answered, and went off to the village with 9
the quartermaster to find a billet for the night.

The quartermaster carried my trunk on his shoulder. Before us 10
stretched the village street. The dying sun, round and yellow as a
pumpkin, was giving up its roseate ghost to the skies.

We went up to a hut painted over with garlands. The quartermas- 11
ter stopped, and said suddenly, with a guilty smile:

"Nuisance with specs. Can't do anything to stop it, either. Not a 12
life for the brainy type here. But you go and mess up a lady, and a
good lady too, and you'll have the boys patting you on the back."

He hesitated, my little trunk on his shoulder; then he came quite 13
close to me, only to dart away again despairingly and run to the nearest yard. Cossacks were sitting there, shaving one another.

"Here, you soldiers," said the quartermaster, setting my little 14
trunk down on the ground. "Comrade Savitsky's orders are that
you're to take this chap in your billets, so no nonsense about it, because the chap's been through a lot in the learning line."

The quartermaster, purple in the face, left us without looking 15
back. I raised my hand to my cap and saluted the Cossacks. A lad with
long straight flaxen hair and the handsome face of the Ryazan Cossacks went over to my little trunk and tossed it out at the gate. Then

he turned his back on me and with remarkable skill emitted a series of shameful noises.

"To your guns — number double-zero!" an older Cossack 16 shouted at him, and burst out laughing. "Running fire!"

His guileless art exhausted, the lad made off. Then, crawling over 17 the ground, I began to gather together the manuscript and tattered garments that had fallen out of the trunk. I gathered them up and carried them to the other end of the yard. Near the hut, on a brick stove, stood a cauldron in which pork was cooking. The steam that rose from it was like the far-off smoke of home in the village, and it mingled hunger with desperate loneliness in my head. Then I covered my little broken trunk with hay, turning it into a pillow, and lay down on the ground to read in *Pravda* Lenin's speech at the Second Congress of the Comintern. The sun fell upon me from behind the toothed hillocks, the Cossacks trod on my feet, the lad made fun of me untiringly, the beloved lines came toward me along a thorny path and could not reach me. Then I put aside the paper and went out to the landlady, who was spinning on the porch.

"Landlady," I said, "I've got to eat." 18

The old woman raised to me the diffused whites of her purblind 19 eyes and lowered them again.

"Comrade," she said, after a pause, "what with all this going on, I 20 want to go and hang myself."

"Christ!" I muttered, and pushed the old woman in the chest with 21 my fist. "You don't suppose I'm going to go into explanations with you, do you?"

And turning around I saw somebody's sword lying within reach. A 22 severe-looking goose was waddling about the yard, inoffensively preening its feathers. I overtook it and pressed it to the ground. Its head cracked beneath my boot, cracked and emptied itself. The white neck lay stretched out in the dung, the wings twitched.

"Christ!" I said, digging into the goose with my sword. "Go and 23 cook it for me, landlady."

Her blind eyes and glasses glistening, the old woman picked up 24 the slaughtered bird, wrapped it in her apron, and started to bear it off toward the kitchen.

"Comrade," she said to me, after a while, "I want to go and hang 25 myself." And she closed the door behind her.

The Cossacks in the yard were already sitting around their caul- 26 dron. They sat motionless, stiff as heathen priests at a sacrifice, and had not looked at the goose.

"The lad's all right," one of them said, winking and scooping up 27 the cabbage soup with his spoon.

The Cossacks commenced their supper with all the elegance and   28
restraint of peasants who respect one another. And I wiped the
sword with sand, went out at the gate, and came in again, depressed.
Already the moon hung above the yard like a cheap earring.

"Hey, you," suddenly said Surovkov, an older Cossack. "Sit   29
down and feed with us till your goose is done."

He produced a spare spoon from his boot and handed it to me. We   30
supped up the cabbage soup they had made and ate the pork.

"What's in the newspaper?" asked the flaxen-haired lad, making   31
room for me.

"Lenin writes in the paper," I said, pulling out *Pravda*. "Lenin   32
writes that there's a shortage of everything."

And loudly, like a triumphant man hard of hearing, I read Lenin's   33
speech out to the Cossacks.

Evening wrapped around me the quickening moisture of its twi-   34
light sheets; evening laid a mother's hand upon my burning forehead.
I read on and rejoiced, spying out exultingly the secret curve of
Lenin's straight line.

"Truth tickles everyone's nostrils," said Surovkov, when I had   35
come to the end. "The question is, how's it to be pulled from the
heap. But he goes and strikes at it straight off like a hen pecking at a
grain!"

This remark about Lenin was made by Surovkov, platoon com-   36
mander of the Staff Squadron; after which we lay down to sleep in
the hayloft. We slept, all six of us, beneath a wooden roof that let in
the stars, warming one another, our legs intermingled. I dreamed:
and in my dreams saw women. But my heart, stained with bloodshed, grated and brimmed over.

Plot.   We call the structure and order of events in a work of fiction
plot. A plot is not just a simple chronology of events, however; it focuses on causation and what forces bring the events about.

We could summarize the plot of "My First Goose" this way:

> A young soldier joins a division of rough Cossacks. As an intellectual,
> he does not fit in. He is ignored or ridiculed. To prove himself and
> earn a place among the soldiers, he bullies an old woman and kills her
> goose for his dinner. He then is accepted. But this incident has taught
> him a bitter lesson about himself.

This is a fairly typical construction, beginning with a situation and
characters, introducing a complication, and then proceeding to a res-

olution. But plots do not always move in such a straight line. They may contain flashbacks to the past, foreshadowings or hints of future events, interruptions, or events seen from several viewpoints.

To get a firm grasp on a story, look at the plot first, especially the beginning. Locate the turning points. Master the chain of causation. Summarize the work. Though it cannot be an essay, a plot summary can be a first step toward understanding the story.

Character. Character is a portrait in words of a person imagined by the writer. This portrait may include physical characteristics, background, and personality. Anything that explains why a person speaks, feels, or behaves as he or she does is part of characterization.

Sometimes the narrator will *tell* us something directly, as in this passage from "My First Goose":

> The steam that rose from it [the cooking pot] was like the far-off smoke of home in the village, and it mingled hunger with desperate loneliness in my head.

At other times the narrator will *show* a character in action, through deeds, dialogue, or interaction with other characters.

> "Oh, are you one of those grinds?" [the commander] laughed. "Specs on your nose, too! What a nasty little object!"

We are in no doubt about the commander's opinion of the narrator or, by extension, about his opinion of learning and intellectuals.

Although much of our understanding comes from what a character says and does, we also learn about character from associated symbols: the specs, the newspaper, the trunk, even the goose. And we also learn about character from the way language is used. The narrator's tone, for instance, changes from the admiring description of the commander to this depressing sentence:

> Already the moon hung above the yard like a cheap earring.

Literature is full of fascinating characters, and it is quite natural to be interested in them. But their personalities are not so much the point as what they cause to happen and what their actions and reactions tell us. Don't think of them as "real people." They are elements with an important role to play in a piece of fiction. In "My First Goose," for instance, the narrator and the Cossacks work through the age-old struggle of the intellectual and the warrior.

Setting. All the events in fiction happen within a time, a place, and specific social circumstances. We call this context the setting. Like all the elements in a story, setting helps determine meaning. The meaning of "My First Goose" is dependent on its setting: a Russian village during the chaotic 1920s, when the Communists were fighting to gain full control of Russia. But you need not know the history to discern the unsettled state of life in the story. The landlady twice says she wants to go and hang herself. The narrator reads a speech by Lenin about shortages. In the foreground are the tensions of a violent, confusing time — a time in which a sensitive person brutally kills a goose.

Because setting is important, be sure that you take it into account during your reading and that you take accurate notes on it.

Point of View. Stories have a storyteller, a narrator, who tells us what happens and sometimes even interprets an event. Since these storytellers are our only source of information, knowing their point of view is important. Point of view refers to the angle from which the story is told, the place from which the reader is allowed to view events. Is the storyteller a participant or only a reporter? Are we allowed to know what one person thinks, or many, or none? Are we close to the action or far from it?

Although there are other possibilities, point of view is generally either first person or third person. In *first person*, we see events through the eyes of a single character. This *I* may be the major character or only a witness or observer. In "My First Goose," he is the main character, that is, the one on whom the events register and to whom they matter most. In other works, like *The Great Gatsby*, an *I* may describe what happens to someone else.

In *third person* point of view, the storyteller is in no way a participant, although sometimes he or she will interrupt a story to make a judgment. Some third-person storytellers, called *omniscient narrators*, know everything and can move from past to present and from the mind of one character to the mind of another. Other third-person storytellers are *limited narrators*, confined to one character's consciousness. This is not necessarily a loss: though we know only one mind, we know it intensely and immediately.

Always note the point of view in a work and pay attention to how it colors your feelings about what happens. Just for fun, try imagining "My First Goose" told by an omniscient narrator who can go into the minds of the Cossacks and the old lady. Do you think that would have made a better story?

Later in this chapter we will use "My First Goose" as an example of how to prepare to write a literary essay.

Special Topics in Poetry

Poems sometimes tell stories that contain characters, plots, and points of view. And poems are as rich in theme as they are in symbolism, imagery, metaphor, and unusual uses of language. Careful readers notice these aspects when reading poems. They also attend to poetry's special domain: the intense world of musicality. In the pages that follow, we discuss this world expressed in rhythm, music, and rhyme.

Before going on, please read aloud, re-read, and take notes on this poem by Archibald MacLeish.

Ars Poetica

A poem should be palpable and mute
As a globed fruit,

Dumb
As old medallions to the thumb,

Silent as the sleeve-worn stone   5
Of casement ledges where the moss has grown —

A poem should be wordless
As the flight of birds.

A poem should be motionless in time
As the moon climbs,   10

Leaving, as the moon releases
Twig by twig the night-entangled trees,

Leaving, as the moon behind the winter leaves,
Memory by memory the mind —

A poem should be motionless in time   15
As the moon climbs.

A poem should be equal to:
Not true.

For all the history of grief
An empty doorway and a maple leaf.   20

For love
The leaning grasses and two lights above the sea —

A poem should not mean
But be.

Rhythm.   Rhythm in a poem is created by alternating strong and weak stresses on syllables in a line. When you read a line of poetry aloud, you can always feel the rhythm.

A poem should be palpable and mute
As a globed fruit,

The stresses force you to attend to certain words and phrases. When you read the lines just quoted, you will hardly be able to ignore the words *mute* and *globed*.

Often a poem will repeat a rhythmic pattern. The word *meter* refers to this measured repetition. MacLeish's line

A poem should be palpable and mute

contains a regular alternation of stressed and unstressed syllables.

Critics often identify unstressed syllables with a ˘ and stressed syllables with a ′. If we used these marks on MacLeish's line, it might look like this:

˘ ′˘   ′   ˘ ′ ˘ ′ ˘   ′
A poem should be palpable and mute

We call this a *metered* line. Each kind of metrical pattern has its own name, depending on the number and arrangement of stresses. (Handbooks on poetry will provide you with detailed information about these patterns.)

Rhythm does more than make reading delightful. It can tell you which words and ideas a poet intends to emphasize. Putting the stress on the word *globed*, for example, emphasizes the fruit's physicality and thus reinforces the point.

"Ars Poetica" plays many games with rhythm and meter. Read these two lines aloud:

Dumb
As old medallions to the thumb,

That solitary, surprising word *Dumb* has a curious sense of finality to it, in part because it hitches the rhythm up short. MacLeish plays off the short one-syllable line against the next longer and more regular line and then comes down hard on *thumb*.

Now read this pair of lines aloud:

Leaving, as the moon behind the winter leaves,
Memory by memory the mind —

You may feel an almost hypnotic rhythm, regular and gradual. And perhaps that will remind you, as it has many readers, of the way the moon climbs in the sky.

Although all poetry has rhythm, not all poetry has meter. Since the mid-1800s, poets have increasingly turned to what is called *free verse*, poetry that does not repeat any rhythmic pattern. Even when reading free verse, however, you should listen for the rhythms that reinforce the meaning. Two lines from a poem by Walt Whitman show the importance of rhythm in free verse; read them aloud.

Out of the cradle endlessly rocking,
Out of the mocking-bird's throat, the musical shuttle,

In these lines you can hear the rhythms of the rocking cradle and of the mockingbird's song. Words alone would not have made them real; words and rhythm together do.

Music. The general term *music* covers the way a poem sounds. In the line

Twig by twig the night-entangled trees,

you can hear the *t* sound repeated. Such repetition of consonant sounds is called *alliteration*. Again, the purpose is more than sound: the poet uses alliteration to point to objects or feelings in the lines. The repeated *t* sound calls up the physical reality of the twigs and trees.

The repetition of vowel sounds is called *assonance*. In these lines, MacLeish repeats the sound of a long *e*.

The leaning grasses and two lights above the sea —

A poem should not mean
But be.

These long *e*'s create a feeling of continuity between the physical world and the poem, which is MacLeish's point. Assonance can also slow the pace of a line. Notice how this line moves:

Leaving, as the moon behind the winter leaves,

Because of all the long vowel sounds, the line is as slow as the moon itself. The brilliant combination of sounds drives the image home. Read the following lines aloud again slowly, shaping your lips around each word, dwelling on the sounds:

A poem should be palpable and mute
As a globed fruit,

The combinations of sound can make you feel as though you were holding the globed fruit in your hand, weight, smoothness, and all.

Rhyme.   When two words terminate in the same sound, they rhyme: *mute/fruit, dumb/thumb, stone/grown.* Most rhymes in poetry happen at the ends of lines and are called *end rhyme*, as here.

For all the history of grief
An empty doorway and a maple leaf.

But frequently poems contain *interior rhyme*, as in these lines written by Gerard Manley Hopkins.

I caught this morning morning's minion, king-
dom of daylight's dauphin, dapple-dawn-drawn Falcon, in his riding

Sometimes sounds are not exactly alike, but are approximate. These are called *slant rhymes.*

A poem should be wordless
As the flight of birds.

A poem should be motionless in time
As the moon climbs,

Like rhythm and music, rhyme directs us to what is important in a poem — the connection, for example, between *grief* and *leaf* and between *wordless* and *flight of birds*.

INTERPRETING LITERATURE

Once you have thoroughly read a work, interpreting it will come naturally. To interpret a work of literature, you say what you think it means, how it achieves that meaning, what values it expresses, what effect it has on the reader, and how it creates that effect. You look at the world the writer presents and at the artistry of the presentation. The aim is both to understand the work and to appreciate the achievement.

Responsible Interpretation

An odd rumor is going around about interpreting literature, namely that all opinions are equally valid: "You can see whatever you want to see in it. You can say just about anything." There is some truth in that — but not much. The range of possible interpretations is indeed large, but it is not infinite. Flights of fancy may be fun, but they usually contribute little to understanding the work.

When MacLeish writes

Dumb
As old medallions to the thumb,

Silent as the sleeve-worn stone
Of casement ledges where the moss has grown —

you could perhaps claim that the medallions are portraits of knights from old castles and that the poem is about the decline of the British Empire. Or when he writes

Leaving, as the moon releases
Twig by twig the night-entangled trees,

you might say he is comparing the poet and the poem to a mother and her child. But such unlikely interpretations are useless. They have strayed too far from the text.

Some readers seem to believe that literature, particularly poetry, contains some hidden meaning, and that interpretation is the deciphering of a riddle. It is true that the significance of a great work is seldom found on the surface. We have to think about it. But literature is not a riddle, and interpretation has little in common with doing crossword puzzles.

One important way in which interpretation is different from doing crossword puzzles is that the puzzles have correct answers, to be published next Sunday. About literature, however, we can never give correct answers. There are no right answers — nor any that are completely wrong. Few writers provide a key to fix a work's meaning forever. Even when a writer does say what a work is about, that is only one interpretation. There will be others, probably just as illuminating. (This may sound like a paradox, but it is true. Virtually all writers acknowledge that there is much more to their work than they have consciously put there.)

Our job as interpreters is not to invent the fanciest answers we can or to discover a secret, but to articulate the meaning of a work.

When interpreting literature, keep two principles in mind.

First, the interpretation must fit the facts. A sound interpretation will not be contradicted by any element or event in the work. In interpreting the lines about the medallion in MacLeish's poem, you can't assert that the poem is about the British Empire when all the evidence points to its being about poems.

Second, the interpretation must be comprehensive. It should account for much of the work and should not neglect any important parts of it. Again, in interpreting MacLeish's poem, you would hardly neglect the facts of rhyme, music, and rhythm. Nor would you ignore the fact that MacLeish illuminates what poetry should do by reference to many physical objects.

Bases for Interpretation

The question is, On what shall we base our readings? There are three possible bases for interpretation: impressionism, factual analysis, and informed speculation.

Impressionism. Some interpretations are all impression. They stray so far from the text that they run off into the land of unbridled feeling. Rather than interpreting, impressionistic readers only treat the emotions they have about a text. Instructors are glad to see students who appreciate what they read. They are not glad, however, to receive personal effusions that sound like *True Confessions.* Here is one:

> Hamlet is as brave as a lonely alpine skier. He thrills to the risks he runs. He's an adventurer, afraid of nothing, willing to take a chance; he's a flyer. He loves speed. He loves to go over the moguls as fast as

he can. But then a blinding snowstorm comes up. He can't make out the trees.

Speed? Moguls? Snowstorm? The problem is obvious: the writer never speaks of Shakespeare's play. He is not articulating meanings within the work: he is conveying pictures that flashed through his mind. There may be some good ideas in here — Hamlet does seem to like risk — but they are submerged in a rush of feeling.

Factual Analysis. Good interpreters start with the facts of the text and stay close to them. Their readings are plausible because their insights are grounded in the text. Good interpreters of MacLeish's poem, for instance, would probably begin with the fact that the poet refers to physical objects to illuminate what poetry should do. And in elucidating that, they would stay close to that idea and use the text to prove it.

The most conservative interpreters stick exclusively to the text. They analyze *only* the facts of the work. In interpreting MacLeish's poem, for instance, a cautious interpreter might discuss the rhyme scheme, the rhythm or assonance, or the repetition of images.

In an essay on *Othello*, a conservative interpreter began this way:

> Iago is the most important character in *Othello*, as we can tell by an examination of the number of lines he speaks and the amount of stage action given to him.

To support her thesis, she went on to present a statistical analysis of the play's lines and action.

The possibilities for this kind of interpretation are large. Facts exist in plots and characters: what actually happens and what causes it; the names, ages, social standings, traits, and number of characters, and how these influence the plot. We can interpret aspects of the setting: whether it is rural or urban, domestic or foreign; whether the time is the present or the past. We can also base interesting interpretations on the physical makeup of the work: number of pages and lines; features of rhythm, meter, sounds, rhyme; use of verbs, nouns, adjectives.

Informed Speculation. The very best interpretation goes beyond the facts. Informed speculation is the most sensitive, delicate interpretation. It is informed because it starts with the facts of the text; it is speculation because it goes beyond the facts to the possibilities they imply. Informed speculation ventures opinions on the meanings behind the words.

Do not worry if you feel insecure about this approach to interpretation. Everyone, no matter how experienced, feels some uncertainty, some risk. It is obviously safer to discuss a rhyme scheme or the use of alliteration than it is to speculate on what the rhyme and alliteration are telling us. When we speculate, we run the risk of being wrong — but we gain the power of offering fresh insights into a work. In any case, informed speculation about a work is the very best way to know literature.

When we speculate we build arguments, not on hard evidence, but on connotations. We might, for instance, discuss the meaning of these two lines:

A poem should be motionless in time
As the moon climbs.

After all, verbs like *climb* imply passage of time. The lines bear scrutiny and interpretation. Or we might analyze the emotional effect of certain words and ideas, like

For all the history of grief

We might interpret the general ideas of a work or build our argument on appeal to shared experiences. We could analyze our impressions or evaluate the author's methods. And always we must identify those places in the text that give rise to our response.

With this kind of interpretation, our intelligence intersects with the text and brings forth fresh meaning.

WRITING ABOUT LITERATURE

When we turn our understanding and enjoyment of literature into writing, we stake out a claim on the work. In accounting for our thoughts and reactions, we take possession of the work. It becomes more deeply and securely ours. Writing about literature, then, is an opportunity to experience more profoundly the art of the storyteller, the teacher, and the enchanter.

Before setting out on your writing, revisit the text and your notes. Return to arresting moments, high points, themes that attracted you.

Meditate a moment. Listen to your inclinations, what likes, dislikes, confusions, or enthusiasms have stayed with you.

You may want to consult outside works. Biographical works can tell you more about the author. Isaac Babel's life, for instance, closely paralleled that of the narrator in "My First Goose." Facts about his life may clarify parts of the story or suggest ideas about it. Historical works will provide information about the setting and social environment of a work. If you want to know more about Lenin, the Cossacks, or the state of Russian society in the early 1920s, you can consult encyclopedias or histories of Russia. Your main source, of course, remains the text.

The best-kept secret about papers on literature is that they are argumentative. When you write about a poem, a play, a novel, a short story, or any other literary work, you argue for your interpretation, using the text as your major evidence.

Now the search is on for a thesis you can argue — an idea that will direct your paper and interest your reader, yet be limited enough to treat within the assigned page limit. Your thesis will present an aspect of your interpretation. To arrive at this thesis, use your favorite form of invention — free writing, clustering, or whatever. (See "Getting Started" and "Subject and Thesis" in Chapter 1.)

Once you have decided on your thesis, return to the text and your notes for evidence. Determine major supporting points and group your evidence from the text under them. During this developing stage, rather than copying out all the quotations, you might want to use page numbers or abbreviations. Just be sure you can go back to the exact quotation you want.

Writing about "My First Goose"

In the pages that follow, we describe the process of preparing to write a six-page essay on "My First Goose."

We can hardly tackle a story like this without being analytical. Without breaking it down into its component parts, we will not be able to say anything significant about it. ("It was great." "It was boring." "It was fun to read.") We can arrive at a worthwhile interpretation only by examining the story under literary topics like the ones we have been discussing.

As we read, we keep in mind plot, character, setting, point of view, theme, symbolism, and language. Some of these topics will attract us more than others. Suppose, for example, that we are particularly drawn to the central figure in the story, the lonely, idealistic young man who kills the goose. We decide to begin with this character.

We do not want to force a thesis, so we return to the story and read it yet again. We want our presentiments to coalesce. When writing about literature, we must go through the same steps again and again, from making notes to reading to thinking to reading to making notes. Nothing appears in exactly the same light twice, for we see the action — the commander's laughter, the slaughter of the goose — differently each time. That is what makes literature so great: it is inexhaustible.

We note the protagonist's characteristics: his admiration for Savitsky, his intellectuality, his "desperate loneliness." We see how he responds to the Cossacks and to the landlady. We observe as the narrator scrambles to gather up his things from his broken trunk, pushes the landlady, and kills the goose. After a few readings, we will have listed many more events and characteristics.

We certainly want to avoid the trap of writing a mere "character study." Having made a list of characteristics, some writers would simply plow through the items, devoting a paragraph to each until the bottom of the list announced the end of the paper. That kind of paper would be mechanical to write and boring to read. Instead, we must account for the character's place in events, and how he illuminates human experience.

Now we confront a second trap: plot summary. From character, we naturally move to thinking about the plot. But the instructor has read the story and need not be told the plot again. Lengthy plot summaries are a waste of everyone's time. What we and the instructor want is critical judgment.

We find ourselves reading the killing scene again, and we ask why the narrator kills the goose. True, he is hungry, but there is more than that. To get at it, perhaps we freewrite about the scene.

> The way the narrator crushes the goose with his boot and digs into it with his sword is too vicious to really have anything to do with that goose. This fellow seemed sensitive, not like the other soldiers, but then this. He becomes just like them, as though he has given in to the brutality he sees around him.

Through reading and analyzing we move closer to a thesis. We now go back to the story to refine what we mean by "the brutality he sees around him." We find all sorts of brutality, though most of it is implied: the commander's insolent power, the jokes about the spectacles, the quartermaster's remarks about soldiers and women, the flaxen-haired lad's insulting behavior, the landlady's despair. We think about the setting of the tale. Brutality seems to be behind almost every action. Why? Perhaps because it is set in a time of upheaval.

With each reading, we learn new things and put them more firmly together. Eventually, we can say something significant about the story based on our analysis.

> In "My First Goose," the killing of the goose signifies the surrender of the young narrator to the brutality of an uncertain time, a brutality that directs the actions of all the characters and permeates the story.

Our early leads changed, and with them changed the direction of our ideas. Our analysis of the character led to the plot and on to a re-examination of the killing scene, which ultimately led to our thesis. This thesis promises that we will show how brutality directs the characters and how the narrator capitulates to this fact of life.

To show this, we must create classifications under which to put evidence. We recognize that examples of brutality occur at every point in the story and on every social level. Commander Savitsky enforces his authority by belittling the narrator. The Cossacks enforce their exclusivity by insults and intimidation. The protagonist bullies the landlady. Examples of the uncertainty of the times are also plentiful: the troubles hinted at in Lenin's speech; Surovkov's remark that truth is to be "pulled from the heap"; the tensions among the characters. We list these examples and prepare to use them in our argument.

Similarly, our reading has prepared us to discuss the ending. The narrator is thrilled to be accepted and exultantly reads Lenin's speech. Later, his exultation falls flat. As in many good stories, the last line here is particularly telling: "But my heart, stained with bloodshed, grated and brimmed over." Now when we make an assertion, we can reach into our notes and pull out an example from the text to support it.

Writing about any work of literature usually follows a pattern much like this: reading, forming a preliminary interest, re-reading, solidifying an idea, perhaps more re-reading, formulating a thesis, collecting and classifying examples, arranging classified material beneath the thesis. Now we can proceed fully equipped to the challenge of making our thinking clear on paper.

Some Do's and Don'ts

Let the structure of your argument take priority over the structure of the text. Too many papers start with line 1 or Chapter 1 and plow through straight to the ending. If you simply follow the text, your argument will have no shape or direction. Organize your argument first, and then arrange your notes and evidence to fit that organization.

Use the language of the text as your evidence. Nothing persuades quite so quickly and thoroughly as the text itself. Sometimes you may need to summarize or paraphrase a section for convenience or clarity, but when you can use the author's own words, do so.

Tie each piece of evidence into your discussion. Warrants are essential in all papers on literature. Some writers pile on quotations without showing how they apply to the argument, as here.

> "Ars Poetica" tries to be the things it portrays. In the first two lines, "A poem should be palpable and mute/As a globed fruit," there are many *p* and *b* sounds.

Not so fast. What is the connection between the claim and the evidence? Until the writer shows *why* those sounds prove the claim, she will not carry her point:

> "Ars Poetica" tries to be the things it portrays. One of the ways it does this is with sound. In the first two lines, "A poem should be palpable and mute/As a globed fruit," there are many *p* and *b* sounds. These sounds force the reader to work the mouth and give the impression of real weight and texture.

This is the form the warrant takes in literary papers — the demonstration that the evidence fits the claim.

Do not praise the text or the author, no matter how great they are. One of the rewards of studying literature is the constant discovery of brilliant insights and technical mastery. But, then, everybody already knows that Honor de Balzac, Thomas Mann, and Virginia

Woolf are "great." Concentrate, rather, on showing how they achieve their great effects.

Write in present tense. By convention, one writes as though the events of the poem, play, novel, or story are taking place in the present.

> When the old lady says, "I want to go and hang myself," the narrator responds by pushing her in the chest.

Give your *interpretation, not that of professional critics.* Most instructors want to know what *you* make of the text. Books of criticism can help to illuminate a difficult text, but use them with great care. Do your own reading and build your own opinions. Do not let experts do the thinking or writing for you. Ask your instructor for suggestions on how to use the experts. And always acknowledge all sources that contributed to your essay.

TIPS FOR READING, INTERPRETING, AND WRITING ABOUT LITERATURE

- Give yourself to the reading the first time through, and make your notes on the second reading.
- Remember that theme, symbolism, and language are concerns in all literary works.
- When reading fiction, think about plot, character, setting, and point of view.
- Read poems aloud, and, as you do, think about rhythm, music, and rhyme.
- Make sure your interpretation fits the facts and does not neglect major aspects.
- Try to go beyond factual analysis to an informed speculation about the meanings in the work.
- Identify what interests you most and use that as a basis for your analysis.
- Develop an essay on literature as you would other argumentative essays, with a thesis, evidence, and warrants.
- Stay close to the text: the best evidence is the author's own words.
- Avoid mere character sketches and plot summaries.
- Remember that your instructor wants your critical judgment of the work.

EXERCISES FOR READING, INTERPRETING, AND WRITING ABOUT LITERATURE

1. Read the following sonnet by William Shakespeare and write an essay in which you first describe the situation presented and then argue for what you believe to be the central anxiety in the speaker's mind. What is the origin of that anxiety? Has the speaker taken any steps at the end of the poem to address his problem? Back up your argument with detailed references to the poem's language, rhythms, and any other technical or thematic material you believe supports your thesis.

Sonnet 138

When my love swears that she is made of truth,
I do believe her, though I know she lies;
That she might think me some untutored youth,
Unlearnèd in the world's false subtleties.
Thus vainly thinking that she thinks me young,
Although she knows my days are past the best,
Simply I credit her false-speaking tongue;
On both sides there is simple truth suppress'd.
But wherefore says she not she is unjust?
And wherefore say not I that I am old?
O, love's best habit is in seeming trust,
And age in love loves not to have years told.
    Therefore I lie with her, and she with me,
    And in our faults by lies we flattered be.

2. Write a page in which you just let yourself go with emotional effusion about the language and symbolism of the sonnet in Exercise 1. Have fun.

3. Analyze the language and symbolism of the sonnet in Exercise 1. Are there metaphors, similes, vivid images? Which words are symbols, and for what ideas?

4. Choose one of the following short stories and identify its central symbol. What makes this symbol significant? What relation does it have to the story's main theme?

    Delmore Schwartz, "In Dreams Begin Responsibilities"
    John Steinbeck, "Flight"
    Nathaniel Hawthorne, "Young Goodman Brown"
    Flannery O'Connor, "A Good Man Is Hard to Find"
    Ernest Hemingway, "The Snows of Kilimanjaro"

5. Analyze the use of point of view in the story you selected in Exercise 4. Write a paragraph describing the advantages or disadvantages of that point of view. Now write another paragraph analyzing the effect a change in point of view would have had.

6. Choose another one of the stories listed in Exercise 4, and write a three- or four-page essay about it. At the end, append a description of where you started your analysis and what route you followed to arrive at your thesis.

14 / The In-Class Essay Examination

Examinations are formidable even to the best prepared, for the greatest fool may ask more than the wisest man can answer.

– *Charles Caleb Colton (1780–1832)*
English writer

When your instructors require an essay examination in a course, they generally have two purposes in mind. First, they want to know how much you have learned about the materials and concepts of the course and how well you can use them. Their second purpose is more educational than evaluative: they want you to synthesize your knowledge and thus to understand it better and possess it more securely. Using knowledge is a superb way of making it yours. An essay exam, then, can be a great learning experience.

Essay exams take many formats. They can last from one to four hours. They can be open or closed book. They can consist of several short essay questions or a single long one. They have in common a premium on time. You must organize information quickly and respond clearly and concisely to the questions posed. Ease in writing in-class essays depends largely on your knowledge of the material and on your physical and mental state at the time of the test. We hope the advice in the pages that follow will help you to get the most out of yourself.

STUDYING FOR THE EXAM

When studying your notes, look for broad themes and patterns. Differentiate major ideas from supporting points. Analyze how the major points are related, and how the evidence supports them. Notice changes and developments.

You may find it helpful to consolidate class notes and reading notes by transcribing them in an orderly way. The act of writing down the information is an excellent reviewing technique. In addition, when you group the information, you improve not only your grasp but also your memory.

A good method for consolidation is to put the basic themes of the course across the top of a sheet of paper as column headings and to list the major divisions of the subject down the left hand margin. In a Western civilization course, for example, you might put major concerns — justice, religion, ethics — across the top and put various philosophers down the side — pre-Socratics, Plato, Aristotle, Cicero, and so on. Under each topic, you would write out the ideas of each philosophical approach. You could then easily compare the major ideas of the course.

As you study and organize your notes, think about what areas of the subject the instructor favored. Try to anticipate test questions. In the Western civilization course, for instance, you might anticipate a question like this one:

Compare Plato's idea of justice with that of Cicero.

or

In what ways is Augustine's idea of freedom a purely Christian concept and in what ways is it a continuation of the Greco-Roman idea of freedom?

Questions, even ones you invent, can help you structure your studying. You may find it both reassuring and informative to share this process with a friend in the class who might have different ideas about the subject.

As you identify probable areas the test will cover, think of major issues and supporting ideas. If, for instance, you think the instructor is particularly keen on the idea of justice, look closely at your reconstructed notes on that subject and know what you think about it. If a major theme remains vague to you, re-read the textbook or the original material. Try to arrive at the exam with ideas that tie the course together.

Avoid anxiety as much as possible. Think about the examination not as just a test but also as a learning opportunity. When you can view the exam as intrinsically worthwhile rather than as an ordeal, you will reduce the concern you feel about it. While studying, try to maintain your usual habits of eating and sleeping. Staying up late, missing meals, or ingesting large amounts of coffee or other stimulants can upset both your memory and your thinking patterns. Cramming may push information you already know out of your mind. Try to take the pressure off. Before the exam, get a good night's sleep. Eat a full breakfast — your brain needs fuel just as your body does.

Immediately before the class, read over your summary notes. Don't try to cram in facts: just remind yourself of patterns and themes. At this point, do not rehearse questions with others. It is too late for that to serve any purpose, and if someone brings up a subject you have not anticipated, it will no doubt increase your anxiety.

Arrive for the exam on time and fully equipped with pen or pencil and scratch paper. Bring a watch with you. Keeping track of time is essential, and you cannot count on a clock or instructor to do it for you. If you have a free choice of seats, sit away from distraction — doors open to the corridor, windows that look out on busy thoroughfares, even other students who might want to socialize.

Relax. If you feel nervous, try one of these methods for relaxing: either breathe in until your lungs are full, add another quick breath, breathe out slowly, and repeat the process several times, or consciously relax each and every muscle of your body, beginning with your little toes. (The first time you try this, you may laugh, which is relaxing in itself.) Clear your mind.

TAKING THE EXAM

Well-prepared, confident, and relaxed, you will be ready, perhaps eager, to show what you know when the instructor says "Go."

When you receive the question sheet, read the instructions and all the questions slowly and thoroughly. Take the time to understand what is expected. Listen to all verbal directions. If you have any problems of interpretation, ask the instructor right away. Know when the test starts and when it will end. Synchronize your watch.

Organizing Your Time

Know exactly how much credit you will receive for each answer and allot your time accordingly.

Start with the question you feel most ready to answer. Not only is this encouraging and even soothing, but also it taps right in on your best ideas. As you write about something you feel fairly confident of, ideas about other questions may occur to you. Be sure to keep your scratch paper handy so that you can jot down these ideas.

Noting Significant Words in the Question

Pay close attention to all command words, key words and phrases, and texts mentioned in each question. These tell you what to do and often how to do it.

Command Words. Command words tell you exactly what the instructor wants you to do: *compare, define, demonstrate, evaluate, isolate, trace,* and so on. These are the action verbs in the question. You might, for instance, receive this instruction in a sociology class:

Define *individualism* in America and trace the development of this concept.

This asks something specific of you: to identify the meaning of the term and to show its origin, its history, and its present application. It does not ask you to compare American individualism with something else or to evaluate it. Be sure you know and follow the exact command.

Some command words — *discuss, explain, explore, describe* — are more general; they put you on your own. In answering a question that uses them, you will have to figure out whether to define, compare, evaluate, and so on. In an American history class, you might be asked to respond to this kind of open-ended question:

> John Adams estimated that one-third of the colonists were loyal to the British Crown during the American Revolution. Discuss the treatment of these loyalists during and after the Revolution.

Don't just start free-associating about the loyalists. Even when the instructor does not tell you exactly what to do, you still must construct a reasoned, organized answer. Figure out your own commands. Here, you might identify who the loyalists were according to economic class, occupation, and geographic location. Then you might trace their history and their fate. Finally, you might analyze their motives and the motives of those who, in punishing them, confiscated their property.

Key Words and Phrases.   With or without clear commands, a question may contain a key word or phrase that can help you organize your answer. This question certainly does:

> What was the origin of the Monroe Doctrine? Examine three occasions before 1900 on which this doctrine was invoked.

The key words and phrases are, of course, *origin, Monroe Doctrine,* and *before 1900.* They strongly suggest a course for a response: define the doctrine, summarize its origin, then turn to the period in question, and select the three occasions. With each occasion, you might say why the doctrine was invoked and what the result was. You might conclude with an evaluation of the doctrine's effectiveness as an instrument of foreign policy in the nineteenth century.

If the key words in a question need definition, define them early and go right to a discussion of why they are significant. Then you can use that definition and evaluation as a basis for your entire answer.

References to Texts.   If the question mentions an author or a text, note them and prepare to treat them specifically in your essay. The instructor is providing you with a focus. Here is a question for a linguistics class that provides a sharp focus:

> Continental linguists criticize Noam Chomsky's theories of language on the grounds that they are based on the behavioristic tradition of J. B. Watson and B. F. Skinner. With reference to Chomsky's *Lan-*

guage and Mind and to Skinner's *Beyond Freedom and Dignity*, evaluate this criticism.

In answering, you would look first at the command word *evaluate*. That word calls for a balanced response, neither enthusiastic agreement with nor dismissal of the criticism. You should express your own opinion, but the command asks you to be alert to both sides. Next, you would turn to the key words *criticism* and *behavioristic tradition*. You would probably define *behaviorism*. Then you would pick up on the authors and texts mentioned. You would describe Chomsky's theories and relate them specifically to those of Watson and Skinner. You would include pertinent analyses of *Language and Mind* and *Beyond Freedom and Dignity*.

Fully understanding the question and identifying the important words in it can carry you a long way toward a persuasive answer.

Shaping Your Answer

The first moments of your exam are important. Once you understand what the question asks, start thinking. It is sheer folly to begin writing your answer the moment the gun goes off. Some good test takers use up to a quarter of the exam time to organize their thoughts before they write their answer. They then have a good idea of what to write and can be cool and collected when they begin.

Remember: an essay examination asks you to write an essay, and an essay has a thesis. Your instructor does not want a mess of unsorted facts or a list of vague feelings. Though the conditions of an exam are somewhat different from those of the usual essay, you can apply much of what you have learned in this book.

Take the first few minutes to formulate your thesis. Use that scratch paper. Employ any of the invention devices. Brainstorm. Free-write. Write down your thesis.

Spend the next few minutes organizing. Make a scratch list of everything pertaining to the question. Don't waste time trying to retrieve something you can't remember. It will either surface or it won't, and it is more likely to if you don't force it.

Turn your scratch list into an outline. Sort out the major ideas. Be ruthless: by combining, condensing, or discarding, reduce your list of major points to three or four. These will be the prominent subheadings under your thesis. Put these points in proper order. If the question lends itself to chronological treatment, as does the one regarding the Monroe Doctrine, use that organizing principle. Otherwise, arrange your answer either according to the order of the relay race, with the second strongest point first and the strongest last, or in ascending order to climax. What you want, of course, is to end on a strong note. (See "Order" in Chapter 3 for a discussion of ordering points.)

You need to flesh out your points. Virtually all graders prefer specific essays to general ones, the concrete to the abstract. The more specific your answers, the better. As you go over your scratch list, identify the support for all your major points. This is a good time to make sure you have identified the major points and have the evidence for them.

Writing the Answer

Write legibly. Illegible handwriting is worse than useless; it is a positive irritant. Use conventional mechanics. Write an economical, plain, direct prose.

If you are using a blue book, skip lines and write on only one side of each page. That way, if you want to add something later you can put it in the empty line or on the blank side of the opposite page with an arrow showing where it fits. The grader will not mind incorporating the new material if its place is clearly designated. In any case, double-spaced writing on one side of the page generally makes reading easier.

Write a brief introduction that contains the general area you will cover in your answer, as well as your thesis. Put your thesis in the last sentence of the introduction and underline it. Don't restate the question. That not only wastes time but also can irritate the grader. A strong thesis will tie your discussion firmly to the question.

Now you are ready to move into your answer. Check the remaining time. Plan so you have ample time to spend on the important points. You don't want to be gasping for breath as you leave this question.

Make paragraphs at important pauses. Write emphatically. Do not be afraid to underline your major point in each paragraph. Construct each paragraph with claim, evidence, and warrant in mind. Your claim will be the major point of the paragraph, perhaps stated as a topic sentence. Support each point with evidence: example, quotation, paraphrase, statistic, or what have you. Be sure you have at least one piece of evidence, and preferably more, for each point. We have never heard an instructor complain of too much evidence in an exam. And clearly tie the evidence to the claim with a short discussion, or warrant.

Write confidently. If a new idea about the subject strikes you, write it. Great revelations can come in the pressure cooker of the essay exam. But don't be diverted from your overall structure. You simply do not have time for digressions or stray points. Discipline is important. Keep the question clearly in mind. If you are to compare and contrast A with B, do not spend 90 percent of your time on A, and do not throw in C.

Leave yourself a few minutes for a conclusion. Ending in style will help any essay. Reiterate what you have said, but try to wrap up the essay with an observation that indicates the importance of what you have written. Your conclusion need not be long, but it ought to have a feeling of finality. Here is the conclusion to an essay analyzing George Washington's warning against getting involved with "foreign entanglements":

> The new United States was still wary from its war with England, and its first president understandably insisted that the country make its own way. But countries cannot exist in a vacuum, and, as the rest of U.S. history has shown, no country can keep out of foreign entanglements for long.

If you can, close each essay answer with a good authoritative last line. (See "Conclusions" in Chapter 4 for more on closing lines.)

If you run into trouble during the writing, don't panic. Just get those juices flowing. Try free writing on scratch paper.

Adding, Reviewing, Polishing

Leave time to review the whole exam. Use the blank sheet opposite your essay for new ideas or for clarifications. Don't forget those arrows to indicate insertions: the grader won't want to reconstruct the order of your ideas. If you run out of space on the blank sheet, go to the end of the blue book.

When reviewing, read your work critically, as though you were the grader. Try to catch inconsistencies, incoherent sentences, unfulfilled promises in your essay. Check your grammar and syntax. But don't make your paper look as if armies of pens and pencils had been in combat over it. Make sure your essay is presentable; then hand it in.

CASE STUDY: A STUDENT EXAMINATION

The following answer was written by Jeri Shikuma in response to the question,

> Drawing on readings and lectures, discuss (1) whether (and in what sense) you think Americans are individualistic and (2) the possible *causes* and *consequences* of that individualism in America's religious origins, stratification patterns, and forms of political power.

Notice how she responds to the command words. In the first paragraph she sets up her thesis and the major topics she will pursue. After the brief introduction she gets right into her argument. Each following paragraph takes up a topic. She carefully develops evidence and always ties it to the claim. She has a strong conclusion. Notice how she bolsters her judgments by reference to sources.

> Individualism has characterized America since its beginnings with the idea of the rugged individualist. This individualism has grown and influenced America's stratification pattern as well as its form of political power.
>
> Americans are individualistic in the sense that they place a great deal of importance on being unique and offering something special. This is manifested in art as well as commerce. Many great American novels portray a hero who must stand alone, outside society, to fight for justice. One such is Herman Melville's *Billy Budd*. Captain Vere accepts the responsibility as well as the loneliness of his command as he sends Billy to his death. Individualism, according to Blumberg, is even manifested in America's architecture. Isolated apartments and one-occupant flats emphasize the individual alone. Even the stress on the nuclear family — mother, father, children — is in opposition to the wider society.
>
> This individualism was probably founded at the very beginning of

the nation with the arrival of the Protestants. According to Weber, the Protestants were deeply ingrained with the sense of the individual alone in the world, and they placed a high importance on individual acts. Calvin's idea of God's being so transcendent that he never interferes with one's life led the Calvinists to believe that they were alone on earth, with no one to turn to for help. Furthermore, because their afterlife was predestined for either salvation or damnation — though they did not know for which — the Doctrine of Proof, in which their proof of salvation showed in their actions, made individual actions very important. Thus, the Protestants, and particularly the Calvinists, perpetuated an ethics of rational, systematic self-evaluation, which grew into a general idea of individualism.

This individualism has permeated every aspect of society. In politics, it manifested itself in pluralistic theories advocating particularistic interests as essential for the health of democracy. To theorists, the pursuit of personal, particular interests in the political arena keeps society from being split down the middle and thus prevents class conflict and, in the long run, tyranny. Mobilization around special interests also prevents deep ideologies from forming and promotes compromise.

Furthermore, individualism has affected stratification patterns. People are inherently different, and, in a society like that in America in which these differences are exploited, stratification is inevitable unless the society directly tries to prevent it through redistributive means. Indeed, as Black said, the idea of individualism in the sense of inherent differences is essential for the justification and legitimation of inequality. Upper-class people can say they have privileges and advantages because they are inherently more capable. The idea simultaneously placates the lower classes by making them feel that they are on the bottom not because of any unfair system but because of human nature. It also lets them feel that they may rise in society if they really try and make the most of their unique talents.

Thus, individualism has been a very prominent force in shaping American society. And though people seem to be caught up in issues of society as a whole, such as unemployment and the arms race, individualism is still important. As Tocqueville recognized in the early nineteenth century, individualism is a deeply ingrained characteristic of American life.

SHORT ANSWERS

Short-answer essay questions require a different strategy from that used in long essays. Scan the identification section of the test.

Note the number of questions and the credit you will receive for each one.

Spend the most time on questions that have the highest number of points. You can afford to botch or omit a five-point question, but not a thirty-five-point one.

Work on questions you know first; save harder ones for later. Generally, people write more easily and quickly on questions about which they feel confident, and much more slowly when they are uncertain.

Write short answers as crisply and specifically as you can. Some instructors want the *shortest* answer possible, and some will stipulate that complete sentences are not necessary. Again, make sure you know what your instructor expects. In any event, vague or general answers lose points. Recall what was said in class about the question at hand. What points did the instructor repeat? What important distinctions or details will he or she probably want to see? Here are two short essay examination answers to a question worth ten points. The first answer, brief and very general, received four points, and the second, more specific one received the full ten.

Question: Identify the term *oxymoron*.
Answer 1: Oxymoron is a figure of speech used in poetry where two words contradict.
Answer 2: Oxymoron is a poetic figure of speech in which two terms seem to contradict. *Seems* is the important word, because although the two words may contradict, together they make a paradox. An example is *loving hate*. The two words seem to contradict, except that there are so many times when love involves feelings close to hatred that the oxymoron makes sense.

TIPS FOR THE IN-CLASS ESSAY EXAMINATION

- Make summary notes of lectures and reading.
- Anticipate the questions or at least the probable areas to be covered.
- Get a good night's sleep and eat a full breakfast before the test.
- Avoid anxiety by breathing deeply and steadily or consciously relaxing each muscle.

- Pay attention to command words, key words and phrases, and texts mentioned in the test question.
- Before beginning, formulate a thesis and organize your answer.
- Write legibly and use conventional grammar, syntax, and mechanics.
- Construct paragraphs with claim, evidence, and warrant in mind.
- Save time for writing a conclusion and adding, reviewing, and polishing.
- Make short answers direct, emphatic, and as specific as possible.

EXERCISES FOR THE IN-CLASS ESSAY EXAMINATION

1. Read these hypothetical essay examination questions. Focus on the command words, key words and phrases, the texts mentioned, the way the questions are put, and any other clues to possible organization. What is each question asking for? How would you organize an answer to it?

   a. Ten days before the San Joaquín revolt of 1886, the duke of Calabria said, "The people will never revolt. They depend too much on us." To what extent did the people of San Joaquín depend on the nobility? Trace the causes of revolt, with reference to Smith's *Urban Armies of Italy.*

   b. Discuss the major differences between a hunter-gatherer society and an early agrarian society.

   c. In recent years the Federal Reserve Board has attempted to control the supply of money in our economy. Compare what a monetarist would say about such efforts with what a supply-sider would say.

   d. Design a program that uses positive reinforcement to help you cure yourself of some undesirable habit. Refer to the steps given in Gibson and Baker.

   e. Would the Athenian citizens have considered the American form of government a democracy? Why or why not?

   f. What was the role of John Foster Dulles in the formation of America's international policy after World War II? Back up your discussion with examples from Raub and Williams.

   g. Read the following passage.

   > But for the moment she was so happy, so lifted up by the belief that her troubles at last were over, that she forgot to be ashamed of her meagre answers. It seemed to her now that she could marry him without the remnant of a scruple, or a single tremor save those that belonged to joy.

Keeping in mind all we have read and learned about American stylists, say whether the passage above was written by Faulkner, Fitzgerald, or James. What aspects of the style led you to make this identification?

2. Your instructor will design an essay examination based on a reading the class will have read in preparation. Before actually taking the exam, the class will discuss how to respond to the question, what clues might help organize the answer, and what the instructor is looking for. The instructor will not confirm or deny anything: the class must reach a consensus before writing.

/appendixes

The Nuts and Bolts:
A Handbook

Glossary of Usage

The Nuts and Bolts: A Handbook

*Grammar, which knows how to
control even kings.*
— Molière (1622–1673)
French dramatist

Thus far, we have concentrated on how to develop a thought with clarity and elegance. Now we turn to the nuts and bolts of persuasive prose: grammar, punctuation, spelling, and mechanics. These conventions are not irrelevancies pedants impose on you to curb your spontaneity and make your life tough. Rather, they guide your ideas. They signal what goes with what, which ideas are important and which are elaborations. They tell the reader how to read your work and they make it easier to do so.

Incorrect use of the conventions delays a reader's understanding. It can permanently obscure the writer's meaning. Errors such as misspelled words, misused semicolons, unclear antecedents are like obstacles in a path, to be walked around or stumbled over. Writers who ignore dangling modifiers, sprinkle commas haphazardly through a paragraph, or indulge in creative punctuation undermine their prose.

In the sections that follow, we do not attempt to exhaust the conventions of English. Rather, we discuss those areas we think many college students find troublesome.

1 / Basic Grammar

Grammar deals with the forms and structures of words and with their conventional arrangement in phrases, clauses, and sentences. In this section you will find definitions of key grammatical terms.

THE PARTS OF SPEECH AND THEIR FUNCTIONS

Nouns

A noun is the name of a person, place, thing, condition, or idea, everything from Mrs. Smith to catfish, from honesty to Albania. *Proper nouns* name a particular person, place, or thing: *Caesar, Utah, Coca-Cola. Common nouns* name general categories: *politician, state, soft drink. Collective nouns* name a number of individuals considered as a single entity: *congregation, covey, jury. Concrete nouns* refer to tangible things: *iron, telephone, fingernails. Abstract nouns* refer to conditions, states, and ideas: *health, consciousness, technology.*

Pronouns

A pronoun is any word that stands for a noun or noun substitute (a word or phrase functioning as a noun). In the passage *Maud shot the sheriff. She shot him with a .44, she* stands for Maud and *him* stands for sheriff. Words like *I, each, him, that,* and *which* are all pronouns.

Every pronoun must have an *antecedent* — that is, a specific noun or noun substitute to which it refers. The pronoun must agree in person, number, and gender with its antecedent. In *Maud bought her gun at a pawnshop when she went to town,* both *her* and *she* agree with the antecedent *Maud.*

Pronouns come in many varieties and perform many tasks. *Personal pronouns* refer to a specific thing or things. The form a personal pronoun takes will depend on *case,* that is, on its function in the sentence. When the pronoun is the *subject* (*She shot the sheriff*), it will take one of these forms: *I, you, he, she, it, we, you, they.*

When a pronoun is the *object* (*Maud shot him*), it will take one of these forms: *me, you, him, her, it, us, you, them.* When a pronoun shows *possession* (*The gun was hers*), it will take one of these forms: *my, mine, your, yours, his, her, hers, its, our, ours, your, yours, their, theirs.*

Intensive and *reflexive pronouns* are *myself, yourself, himself, herself, itself, oneself, ourselves, yourselves, themselves.* An *intensive pronoun* emphasizes a noun or noun substitute (*I myself witnessed the dastardly crime*). It stands beside the noun because it is part of the noun. A reflexive pronoun indicates that a subject is acting upon itself (*Judas hanged himself*). The pronoun follows the verb because it is the direct object.

Relative pronouns are *who, whom, which, that,* and *whose.* A relative pronoun introduces a subordinate clause and relates it to a noun or noun substitute in the main clause. (*Sam, who had never ridden a Brahma bull before, won the rodeo that took place in Amarillo.*)

Demonstrative pronouns are *this, that, these,* and *those.* These pronouns point at the noun and make the reference unmistakable. (*Those plants are poisonous; these are edible.*)

Indefinite pronouns include *all, any, anyone, each, either, everyone, few, most, nobody, none, no one, some, somebody,* and *someone.* These pronouns refer to people or things generally rather than specifically. (*Nobody loves me, everybody hates me, I'm going out in the garden and eat worms.*)

Reciprocal pronouns are *each other, one another, each other's* and *one another's.* They express a mutual relationship. Use *each other* when referring to two people, *one another* for more than two. (*Although we are told we should love one another, those two hated each other.*)

Interrogative pronouns are *what, which, who, whom,* and *whose.* These pronouns introduce questions. (*To whom shall I tell my story?*)

EXERCISE FOR PRONOUNS

1. Choose the correct word in the parentheses.
   a. We looked forward to (them, their) coming home at Christmas.

   b. Men generally misunderstand (we, us) women.
   c. The theme of the essay is clearly expressed in (it's, its) first paragraph.
   d. (We, Us) men are largely misunderstood by women.
   e. We (ourself, ourselves) are happy at the election's outcome.
   f. All the basketball players got in (each other's, one another's) way.
   g. The most valuable player award went to the entire team, including (I, me, myself).
   h. Just between you and (I, me, myself), she has bad breath.

Verbs

Verbs express actions, processes, or states of being. (*He _ran_ outside when the object _appeared_ in the sky, but she _was_ horrified.*) Verbs are the energy at the center of all sentences.

The principal parts of the verb are the *infinitive* (*to sing*), the *past tense* (*sang*), and the *past participle* (*sung*). Changes in verb forms rely on these basic parts. Sometimes the *present participle* is considered a principal part of the verb. It is formed by adding *-ing* to the infinitive (*singing*).

Kinds of Verbs.   We classify verbs according to whether they take a direct object or a complement or help other verbs to perform.

Transitive verbs take a direct object: *The lion _ate_ the wildebeest.*

Intransitive verbs describe activities and states without an object: *Queen Victoria _sneezed_ and the empire _trembled_.*

Linking verbs act as equal signs between nouns and their complements, words that complete the meaning of the sentence: *William _is_ a clown, but he _appears_ miserable.* *To be* is the most frequently used linking verb; other common ones are *appear, become, feel, look,* and *seem.*

Auxiliary verbs, also called *helping verbs,* join with the infinitive or past participle of a verb to form a verb phrase: *The new phone book _has_ arrived.* The verbs *to be* and *to have* are the most common auxiliaries. Others are *can, could, do, may, might, must, need, ought, should, would.*

Tense.   Tense refers to time. All verbs change according to when the action occurs, how it is related to another action, and whether it is continuous.

The *simple tenses* are present, past, and future. *Present tense* indicates current action (*She sings well*). *Past tense* indicates completed action (*She sang that song last night*). *Future tense* indicates action that will be completed later (*She will sing it again tomorrow*). To form the future tense, combine the infinitive with the future tense of the verb *to be*.

The *perfect tenses* indicate an action that was or will be completed after another action. *Present perfect* indicates past action continuing up to the present (*She has sung that song every night*). *Past perfect* indicates action completed before another past activity (*She had sung it nearly fifteen hundred times before her big break came*). *Future perfect* indicates action expected to be completed later (*By July 4, she will have sung that song to a million people*). The perfect tenses are formed by combining the past participle of the verb with the present, past, or future tense of *to have*.

The *progressive tenses* indicate ongoing action (*She was singing, she has been singing, she will be singing, she is singing her life away*). These tenses can indicate ongoing actions past, present, or future. They are formed by combining the present participle of the verb with the appropriate form — present, past, future — of *to be*.

Be consistent with your tenses. Sudden and incorrect shifts can confuse and irritate the reader.

> *Inconsistent*   After Robespierre initiated the Reign of Terror, he controls the revolution and has Danton guillotined.

Because *initiated* is in the past tense, the other verbs should also be in the past tense.

> *Revised*   After Robespierre initiated the Reign of Terror, he controlled the revolution and had Danton guillotined.

Voice.   English has two voices, active and passive. In *active voice,* the subject of the sentence performs the action: *The diva sang an aria from* Aida. In *passive voice,* the subject of the sentence receives the action: *Even the stagehands were moved.* See "Be Active" in Chapter 7 for more on active and passive voice.

Mood. The mood of the verb tells us the speaker's attitude toward the action or state expressed in the sentence. English has four moods. The *indicative mood* makes an assertion: *She will win the race.* The *interrogative mood* asks a question: *Did she win the race?* The *imperative mood* issues a command: *Win that race!* The *subjunctive mood* has several functions: it can express a wish (*I wish I were running*), a statement contrary to fact (*If I were you, I would run faster*), a remote possibility (*I might get in shape someday*), and a command (*I demand that your laughter be stopped*). This form is slowly dying out in English, but careful stylists still use it.

EXERCISES FOR VERBS

1. Write two sentences using a transitive verb, two using an intransitive verb, two using a linking verb, and two using an auxiliary verb.

2. Provide the appropriate form of the verb for each sentence in this paragraph:

   Before the snows have melted, my neighbor (to plant) his garden. He (to work) in his garden every day. He always (to have) tulips and daffodils by April. By the middle of May, the tulips (to begin) to droop. One year, however, they (to bloom) still in June. When he (to work) during the hot summer months, I am often afraid he (to suffer) heat stroke. I think he (to like) flowers.

3. Using a single verb (such as *to race* but not that one), write sentences for all the different moods.

Adjectives

Adjectives are words that modify nouns or noun substitutes: *It was a brilliant idea to build a gravel road.* They answer the question, What kind of person, place, or thing is this? They also tell us how many people, places, and things there are: *Innumerable bum-*

blebees chased the four children. They sometimes follow a linking verb and modify the verb's subject: *The night was brilliant, and the horse looked blue in the moonlight.*

The articles — *a, an,* and *the* — are also adjectives. *The* is the *definite article* and is used to refer to a definite, known thing: *The book was spotted with the orange juice.* *A* and *an* are *indefinite articles* and are used to refer to nonspecific things. *A* precedes nouns that begin with consonants, and *an* precedes nouns that begin with vowels: *To some people a rat is less repulsive than an eel.* One exception is before nouns that begin with a long *u* sound; these take *a* as their article: *Though you may think it an underhanded trick, it is a universal practice.*

To some Americans, the phrase *an historical event* sounds and looks right. If it sounds natural to you, use it. Generally, however, Americans do not use *an* before *h.*

Comparative and *superlative* refer to the degree to which a person, place, or thing possesses an attribute. When a person, place, or thing possesses an attribute more than another does, the adjective is in the *comparative* form: *My daddy is stronger than your daddy.* When he, she, or it possesses the attribute most of any or all, the adjective is in the *superlative* form: *My daddy is the strongest of all people.* Most adjectives simply add *-er* for the comparative and *-est* for the superlative. Some, however, change form with degree (*good, better, best*). And some adjectives of two syllables or more require *more* or *most* to indicate the comparative or superlative form (*Chocolate is more delicious than strawberry; it is the most delicious flavor*). When in doubt, check your dictionary.

Adverbs

Adverbs modify verbs, adjectives, and other adverbs. They indicate how, when, where, why, how often, and in what manner. Most adverbs end in *-ly* (*swiftly, intelligently*), but some do not (*very, beyond*).

Like adjectives, adverbs may be compared, but unlike most adjectives, they require the terms *more* and *most* to signal their comparative and superlative forms: *She ran more swiftly than I did; in fact, she ran most swiftly of anybody.*

EXERCISE FOR ADJECTIVES AND ADVERBS

1. Choose a passage of fifty words and underline all the adjectives and all the adverbs. Provide the comparative and superlative forms for all the underlined words.

Conjunctions

Conjunctions join words, phrases, and clauses. *Coordinating conjunctions* join equal ideas: *Bill and Phil hated the movie, <u>but</u> they liked the popcorn.* You can remember the coordinating conjunctions by remembering *fanboys — for, and, nor, but, or, yet, so.*

Subordinating conjunctions join a dependent clause to an independent clause: *<u>If</u> you hurry, you can still catch the train.* Common subordinating conjunctions are *although, because, if, since, unless, whenever, whereas.*

Correlative conjunctions are pairs of conjunctions that help balance the sentence and relate different parts of it to one another: *<u>Either</u> you leave <u>or</u> I leave.* The correlative conjunctions are *both/and, either/or, neither/nor,* and *not only/but also.* The same grammatical construction must follow both elements of the pair: *Caligula <u>not only</u> destroyed the pride of the Romans <u>but also</u> wasted Rome's resources.*

Conjunctive adverbs provide a logical link between two independent clauses: *You misbehaved, and, <u>therefore</u>, you will have no supper. We guarantee nothing; <u>however</u>, we hope to please.* Common conjunctive adverbs are *however, moreover, nevertheless, therefore, thus,* and phrases like *on the contrary.* Set them off with punctuation. Other punctuation is exactly as if the conjunctive adverb were not there.

EXERCISES FOR CONJUNCTIONS

1. Write seven sentences, using a different coordinating conjunction in each.

2. Write five sentences, using a different subordinating conjunction in each.

3. Write four sentences, using a different pair of correlative conjunctions in each.

4. Write four sentences, using a different conjunctive adverb in each.

Prepositions

A preposition ties a noun or noun substitute to another word in the sentence. In *The baseball rolled into the sewer*, the preposition *into* ties *the sewer* to *the baseball*. Constructing a complete list of prepositions would be nearly impossible — and certainly unnecessary. They range all the way from the common ones like *in, to, with* to the rarer compound prepositions like *inasmuch as, on behalf of*.

A preposition and its object form a prepositional phrase. Such phrases can function in several ways. They can serve as adjectives to modify nouns: *John Maynard Keynes conceived a passion for the ballerina with the long, beautiful legs*. They can serve as adverbs: *On VJ Day, Americans danced in the streets*. They can also serve as nouns: *In the streets was the place to be that day*. Prepositions can combine with verbs to create multiword verbs: *She can't put up with a man who won't give up on a car that always falls apart*.

Unfortunately, prepositional phrases tend to pile up in a sentence, as in E. B. White's famous burlesque: *What did you bring the book I can't stand to be read to out of up for?* When prepositions pile up, rewrite the sentence.

EXERCISES FOR PREPOSITIONS

1. Write three sentences in which the prepositional phrases function as adjectives, three in which they function as adverbs, and three in which they function as nouns.
2. Write five sentences in which you have more than one prepositional phrase.

Interjections

Interjections express feelings, not thoughts. Words like *drat, gosh, hey, oh, ouch, pshaw, say*, and *well* are interjections. They can never constitute sentences on their own and appear only rarely in high informal writing.

PHRASES, CLAUSES, AND SENTENCES

Phrases

A phrase is a group of related words that lacks either a subject or a verb or both. It modifies another word in the sentence or modifies the sentence as a whole: *Standing in the sunlight, the man in the red sweater squinted at the photographer*.

A *prepositional phrase* begins with a preposition and can act as an adjective, adverb, or noun. See the section "Prepositions."

A *verb phrase* is a verb expressed in more than one word: *By this time tomorrow, Los Angeles will have traveled in a 27,000-mile circle*. See the section "Verbs."

A *verbal phrase* is a form of the verb not used as a verb but as another part of speech. An *infinitive phrase* contains the infinitive, its object, and any modifiers. It can function as an adjective, adverb, or noun:

> The Yankees are almost always the team *to beat*. (adjective)
>
> Drew juggled three chain saws *to show his talent*. (adverb)
>
> *To err* is human. (noun)

A *participial phrase* includes a participle, its object, and any modifiers. It functions as an adjective: *Police were on the lookout for a man driving a 1951 Hornet*. A *gerund phrase* is the present participle used as a noun. It functions as either the subject or the object of a verb: *Rising early is healthy, but how I hate getting up*.

An *absolute phrase* modifies a whole clause or sentence, not just a single word: *Weather permitting, we'll boat over the rapids tomorrow*. It contains a participle and a noun or pronoun. Usually, we drop the participle if the verb is *to be*: *Weary and hungry, the field hockey team trudged homeward*.

Clauses

A clause is a group of words that contains a subject and a verb. Clauses can be independent or dependent. When they are *independent*, they can stand alone: *Volcanoes rumble before spewing*. When they are *dependent*, they cannot stand alone: *Whenever volcanoes rumble.* The dependent clause requires an independent clause to complete its meaning: *Whenever volcanoes rumble, the villagers begin to fret.*

A dependent clause (also called *a subordinate clause*) begins with a subordinating conjunction (such as *although, if, whenever*) and can function as an adjective, adverb, or noun:

> The witch doctors, *whose geological training was slight,* said they had nothing to fear. (adjective)
>
> The villagers knew better *when the lava began to flow.* (adverb)
>
> *Whether to flee* was the pressing decision. (noun)

Sentences

A sentence is a complete thought. It contains a subject and a verb. It indicates what happened to the subject or what the subject caused to happen. For a detailed discussion, see Chapter 6, The Sentence from Many Angles.

Sentences come in four constructions. A *simple sentence* contains one independent (or main) clause and no other clauses. It may have a compound subject: *Lewis and Clark explored the Northwest Passage.* It may have more than one verb: *They tried and tried but could not find their way.* As long as it has only one independent clause, it is a simple sentence.

A *compound sentence* contains at least two independent clauses but no dependent clauses. The independent clauses can be joined either by a comma and a conjunction or by a semicolon.

> You take the high road, and I'll take the low road.
>
> Diplomacy without defense is folly; defense without diplomacy is madness.

A *complex sentence* contains only one independent clause and at least one dependent clause.

> When John Adams was president, his wife hung the family wash in the East Room of the White House. (dependent-independent)
>
> On the other hand, George Washington, who preceded Adams in the presidency, never occupied the White House. (independent clause interrupted by a dependent clause)

A *compound-complex sentence* contains two or more independent clauses and at least one dependent clause.

Men over age thirty-five should have a checkup regularly even if they are feeling fine, and they should begin to cut down on the sugar, salt, and cholesterol in their diet. (independent-dependent-independent).

EXERCISES FOR PHRASES, CLAUSES, AND SENTENCES

1. Identify the various kinds of phrases in the following passage.

> Like ill-trained shamans, rock singers manipulated the energies they could scarcely keep in tow. This was closely akin to their self-destructive streak; they loved putting their heads in the lion's mouth, and several were dead before the sixties ended. Janis Joplin was particularly naked in her vulnerability to the audience, in her visible need of them. (Morris Dickstein, *The Gates of Eden*)

2. Write a sentence for each of the different kinds of phrases.

3. Identify the various kinds of sentences in the following passage.

> Anyone who has observed a dog doing his neighborhood rounds and leaving his personal mark on each convenient post will have already guessed how the wolves marked out *their* property. Once a week, more or less, the clan made the rounds of the family lands and freshened up the boundary markers. . . . This careful attention to property rights was perhaps made necessary by the presence of two other wolf families whose lands abutted on ours, although I never discovered any evidence of bickering or disagreements between the owners of the various adjoining estates. I suspect, therefore, that it was more of a ritual activity. (Farley Mowat, *Never Cry Wolf*)

4. Change the following passages as directed:

    a. Into a simple sentence: Thomas Marshall, who was vice-president under Woodrow Wilson, said, "What this country needs is a good five-cent cigar."

    b. Into one complex sentence: Chinese chefs serve food in bite-size pieces. Bite-size pieces cook faster. That saves fuel.

    c. Into a compound sentence: Money is the root of all evil. Few people bury it or burn it.

    d. Into a compound-complex sentence: My uncle said he had a terrific television show to watch, and he insisted on turning to another station, and then he sat in his big green easy chair; he was snoring in five minutes.

2 / Problems in Sentences

SUBJECT-VERB AGREEMENT

The verb of a sentence must agree in number and person with the subject, as in this sentence.

The scarlet macaw lives in the jungles of South America.

The singular noun *macaw* takes the singular verb *lives*.

Macaws have long tails and large hooked beaks.

The plural noun *macaws* takes the plural verb *have*.

Subject-verb agreement can become complicated in constructions like the following.

1. Intervening words. Subject and verb must agree even when other words come between them.

The sight of red and blue macaws thrills the spectator.

Sight is the subject, and *thrills*, the verb, must agree with it, even though *macaws*, a plural noun, is next to the verb. An *intervening clause* with a plural verb can be quite confusing.

The sight of red and blue macaws, which are the largest of all the parrots, thrills the spectator.

Sight is still the subject, and *thrills* agrees with it.

Phrases beginning with prepositions (*along with, as well as, in addition to, like*) are never part of the subject and cannot affect the verb.

President Johnson, as well as Presidents Truman and Kennedy, was once a senator.

What applies to Johnson also applies to the other two, but Johnson alone is the subject and so the verb is singular.

2. Collective nouns. Words like *committee, family, group, jury,* and *team* take a singular verb when you want to emphasize the group as a whole.

The jury has decided.

The family agrees about religion.

These collective nouns take a plural verb when you want to emphasize separate entities.

The jury are in there arguing about the verdict.

The family disagree, however, about sex and politics.

Apply the same rule and reasoning to *majority of, mass of, number of*, and other references to quantity or size. They take the singular to emphasize the totality and the plural to emphasize the separate entities.

The number of mistakes is sometimes disheartening.

But the majority of people make them.

3. Compound subjects. When a compound subject connected by *and* is viewed as separate entities, the verb should be plural.

Harpo and Groucho are my favorites of the Marx Brothers.

When the compound subject is viewed as a unit, the verb should be singular.

Peanut butter and banana is my favorite snack.

When a compound subject is joined by *nor* or *or*, the closer subject determines the verb.

Either the Brownie Scouts or Ms. Peabody was lying about the rampaging bear.

Either Ms. Peabody or the Brownie Scouts were lying about the rampaging bear.

When this rule leads to an awkward construction, rewrite the sentence.

Awkward	Either Clara or I am the worst tennis player on the team.
Revised	Either Clara is the worst tennis player on the team or I am.

4. Numbers. Numbers that act as a unit take a singular verb.

Ninety-five cents is too much to pay for a soft drink.

Numbers viewed as individual items take a plural verb.

Ninety-five dogs in the kennel were barking.

5. Singular words in plural form. Some words ending in -*s* that refer to a single item or idea take a singular verb.

Mumps is usually a childhood disease.

But some take a plural verb.

Scissors are hard to sharpen.

Idiom controls the form. Consult your dictionary.

Some words ending in *-ics* will be singular in one context but plural in another.

Statistics is a branch of mathematics.

Statistics are not always reliable.

In the first example, *statistics* is singular because it refers to a body of knowledge viewed as a unit. In the second, it is plural because it refers to items viewed separately.

6. Noun substitutes. When the subject of a sentence is a phrase or clause used as a noun substitute, the verb is always singular.

Smuggling parrots has become a lucrative business.

Why the smugglers persist is hardly puzzling.

Smuggling parrots is the subject of the first sentence, and *Why the smugglers persist* is the subject of the second. Both require singular verbs. When, however, two or more noun substitutes are the subject, the verb is plural.

Smuggling parrots and selling them are violations of the law.

7. Linking verbs. A linking verb (*to be, appear, feel, look, seem, smell,* and so on) agrees with its subject, not with the noun or pronoun that is the subject's complement.

Pink cockatoos are an Australian native.

Pink cockatoos is the subject; *Australian native* is the complement.

In sentences that begin with *There* or *Here* followed by a linking verb, the verb agrees with the real subject following the verb.

There is a tavern in the town.

There are many customers.

8. Relative pronouns. The singular or plural status of the relative pronouns *that, which, who, whom,* and *whose* is determined by their antecedent, the noun to which they refer.

I love dogs that laugh.

The antecedent of *that* is *dogs*, and so the verb is plural.

I love a dog that laughs.

Now the antecedent is *dog*, and so the verb is singular.

A problem may arise when the word *one* appears in the sentence.

Thomas Mann was one of the German intellectuals who were willing to stand up to Hitler.

Who refers to *German intellectuals* and takes a plural verb.

Mann was not the only one of the German intellectuals who was willing to stand up to Hitler.

Who now refers to *one*, a singular pronoun, and takes a singular verb.

9. Indefinite pronouns. Indefinite pronouns like *any, each, either, everybody, someone*, and so on generally take a singular verb.

Everyone loves fudge.

A few indefinite pronouns (*all, any, few, none, some*) can take either a singular or a plural verb, depending on whether they refer to individual items or the group as a whole.

Some of the fudge has nuts.

Some people make themselves sick gorging on it.

Generally, careful stylists prefer the singular when using *none* and always use the singular when using *no one*.

None was more gluttonous than William, who ate two pounds.

No one was surprised when he got so sick.

EXERCISE FOR SUBJECT-VERB AGREEMENT

1. In the following sentences choose the correct word in the parentheses to make the subject and verb agree:
   a. The list of books (stays, stay) on my table.
   b. The committee (reviews, review) applications at night.
   c. Neither the coach nor the players rewarded (himself, themselves) for the victory.
   d. The collections of antique silver (shows, show) taste.
   e. Either the guards or the warden (was, were) responsible for the trouble.
   f. When measles (is, are) epidemic, I keep my children at home.
   g. The ethics of all who have vaccine (is, are) under scrutiny.
   h. She was one of those brainy people who also (loves, love) sports.

i. The couple living next to the Bishops (drinks, drink) too much.

j. Each one of the dogs that belonged to Jennie Vickers (has, have) fleas.

PRONOUN-ANTECEDENT AGREEMENT

As we said earlier, a pronoun must agree in person, number, and gender with its antecedent, that is, the noun or the noun substitute to which it refers.

Dachshunds require special care because of their long backs.

The pronoun *their* matches in number and person its plural antecedent, *dachshunds*.

Our male dachshund requires special care because of his back.

The pronoun *his* matches in person, number, and gender its antecedent, *our male dachshund*.

Occasionally, a pronoun will precede its antecedent in a sentence.

While performing his tricks, the elephant fell on his nose.

Below we discuss four potentially confusing constructions.

1. Antecedents joined by *and* take a plural pronoun.

As Fido and Rover ate, they snarled at each other.

2. Antecedents joined by *nor* or *or* take singular pronouns when both parts of the antecedent are singular.

Either the flanker or the tight end missed his assignment.

When one of the nouns is plural, the closer noun determines the pronoun.

Neither the coach nor the players admit the mistake.

To avoid an awkward construction, put the plural noun closer to the verb.

Awkward	Neither the Brownies nor Ms. Peabody was able to find her way home.
Revised	Neither Ms. Peabody nor the Brownies were able to find their way home.

3. A pronoun referring to a collective noun (like *audience, committee*) should be singular when the emphasis is on the group as a whole.

The committee has its proposal ready.

The pronoun should be plural when the emphasis is on individual entities within the group.

The audience are slowly taking their seats.

4. Indefinite pronouns (*everyone, some, none*) are usually treated as singular and take singular pronouns.

No one eats her lunch before noon at Miss Blaine's School.

Each of the boys appears in his uniform on Fridays.

Sometimes, however, an indefinite pronoun suggests more than one and should be treated as a plural.

Some of the teachers eat their lunch alone.

When treating the indefinite pronoun as a singular, writers have traditionally used the generic *he, him, his.*

Everyone has his faults.

Many, however, have come to consider this usage sexist. To avoid the problem, recast your sentence.

All have their faults.

(For a general discussion of sexist language, see "Avoiding Sexist Language" in Chapter 7.)

EXERCISE FOR PRONOUN-ANTECEDENT AGREEMENT

1. In the following sentences, choose the appropriate pronoun in the parentheses:

    a. Neither Brecht nor Beckett typed (his, their, theirselves) manuscripts.

    b. The awards committee split (its, their) award between Conklin and (I, me, myself).

    c. The family quarreled with one another because of (its, their) religion.

    d. Some of the members voiced (its, his, their) personal convictions.

 e. Either the manager or his assistants missed (his, their) chance to correct the error.

PRONOUN REFERENCE

A pronoun should refer specifically and unmistakably to one and only one antecedent.

> Lincoln would have had a difficult time in his second term because his cabinet had turned against him.

All the pronouns in this sentence clearly refer to Lincoln. Unclear antecedents can cause the reader to misread the sentence, as in the following six instances.

1. When more than one noun or noun substitute could be the antecedent, the meaning is unclear.

Unclear	After Schmeling fought Louis, he was never the same.

The pronoun *he* could refer to either boxer.

Clear	After he fought Louis, Schmeling was never the same.

Now the pronoun can only refer to Schmeling. The writer revised the sentence so that the second noun is not mentioned until after the pronoun reference is established.

2. When a group of words intervenes between the antecedent and the pronoun, the reference may be unclear.

Unclear	The jury was served doughnuts in the lunchroom that tasted stale.

The lunchroom, we assume, is not what tasted stale. Reframing the sentence so that the pronoun is beside its antecedent clears up the problem.

Clear	In the lunchroom, the jury was served doughnuts that tasted stale.
Unclear	The lawless and intuitive character of modern art is a familiar theme that Professor Longstreth delights in criticizing.

Does Professor Longstreth delight in criticizing the theme, or in criticizing the lawless and intuitive character of modern art?

Clear The lawless and intuitive character of modern art that Professor Longstreth delights in criticizing is a familiar theme.

Now the pronoun stands unambiguously beside the subject that it modifies. It could not be thought to modify *theme*. If, however, the writer had intended the clause to modify *theme*, he or she might have put it this way:

Clear The lawless and intuitive character of modern art is a familiar theme, a theme that Professor Longstreth delights in criticizing.

Repeating the noun *theme* makes the statement unambiguous. Don't be afraid of repeating a word in the interests of clarity.

3. Generally we expect a pronoun to refer to the subject of the previous clause, as this one does:

New models had arrived at the showrooms, and they were all different colors.

We know that the models, not the showrooms, were different colors. When the pronoun refers not to the subject but to some other part of the clause, however, we may be confused.

Unclear If your children refuse to eat their vegetables, slice them up and hide them in a savory beef pie.

What, we may well ask, is to be sliced up? Does the pronoun refer to the subject of the clause, *children*, or to the last noun in it, *vegetables*?

Clear Slice up the vegetables and hide them in a savory beef pie if your children refuse to eat them.

The writer has saved the children from a horrible fate.

4. Demonstrative pronouns like *this, that, these,* and *those* may create confusion, particularly when they begin a sentence.

Unclear Otto nibbled at the frosting and finally took a little slice of the wedding cake and began to eat it. This so angered the bride that she dumped the whole cake on his head.

What angered the bride? The nibbling? Taking a slice? Eating it?

Clear   Otto nibbled at the frosting and finally took a little slice of the wedding cake and began to eat it. Seeing him eating it so angered the bride that she dumped the whole cake on his head.

When using a demonstrative pronoun, be sure its reference is unambiguous.

5. The ubiquitous *it* also can create problems in vagueness when it can refer to more than one antecedent.

Unclear   The sheepdog sniffed the Chihuahua, and then it went to sleep on its side.

Which dog went to sleep? And did it go to sleep on its own side or on the other dog's side?

Clear   The sheepdog went to sleep on its side after sniffing the Chihuahua.

6. Using a pronoun with an unstated antecedent can create confusion.

Unclear   At the New York Stock Exchange, they buy or sell securities listed on that exchange only.

Who is *they*? There is no antecedent.

Clear   At the New York Stock Exchange, traders buy or sell securities listed on that exchange only.

Antecedents implied in adjectives, adverbs, or possessives can also be confusing.

Unclear   She laughed raucously, and that unnerved him.

Raucously is an adverb and cannot function as an antecedent.

Clear   Her raucous laughter unnerved him.

Unclear   Tommy Manville was a much-married millionaire. It was usually to starlets and dancers.

Much-married is an adjective and cannot serve as an antecedent for *it*.

Clear	Tommy Manville was a much-married millionaire. Usually he married starlets and dancers.

In almost all problems of reference, the reader can figure out the meaning, but the writer should make it clear.

COMMA SPLICES AND FUSED SENTENCES

Independent clauses of a compound sentence are joined either by a conjunction and a comma or by a semicolon.

Brutus was careful, but Cassius was cunning.
Jack Sprat could eat no fat; his wife could eat no lean.

When two independent clauses are joined by a comma alone, the error is called a *comma splice*.

Comma splice	I sauntered happily down Connecticut Avenue, it reminded me of my old neighborhood.

Expecting a dependent clause or a phrase to follow a comma alone, the reader may misread. To correct the problem, the writer could add a conjunction or replace the comma with a semicolon.

Revised	I sauntered happily down Connecticut Avenue, for it reminded me of my old neighborhood.

When two independent clauses are joined by no internal punctuation at all, the error is called a *fused* or *run-on sentence*.

Fused	Sudan is the largest country in Africa its land mass is larger than California's.

Absence of punctuation forces the reader to rethink the sentence to figure out the meaning. A comma and a conjunction or a semicolon will do the trick.

Revised	Sudan is the largest country in Africa; its land mass is larger than California's.

The comma splice and the fused sentence can also be corrected by making two sentences.

Revised   I sauntered happily down Connecticut Avenue. It reminded me of my old neighborhood.

EXERCISE FOR COMMA SPLICES AND FUSED SENTENCES

1. Correct the errors in the following sentences:
   a. Walt Whitman's *Leaves of Grass* was poorly received its reception subjected Whitman to embarrassment.
   b. When he was a senator, Nixon's votes on domestic affairs were conservative, his votes on foreign affairs were more liberal.
   c. People call Salinas, California, the lettuce capital of the world also many artichokes are grown in the area.
   d. Jefferson and Adams wrote the Declaration of Independence, they died on the same day.
   e. Comma splices and fused sentences are a problem, they catch us unawares.

SENTENCE FRAGMENTS

From time to time we are all guilty of careless writing. We have a thought, and, before it is completed, another intervenes and knocks the first off the track. The result can be the error called a *sentence fragment*. A sentence is a fragment if it lacks either a subject or a verb, or if it contains a dependent clause but no independent clause.

The building designed by Frank Lloyd Wright
Walked fast in order to get home by dusk
Because I said so

Not complete sentences, these are not complete thoughts. What is being said about the building? Who was walking home and what about it? Because you said so, what? The thought is fragmented, left hanging in midair.

Sometimes you can catch fragments by reading aloud. A sentence lacking either a subject or a verb will sound flat and toneless. A sentence that is only a moorless dependent clause will sound unfinished.

For a discussion of the proper use of a fragment, refer to "Using Fragments" in Chapter 6.

EXERCISE FOR SENTENCE FRAGMENTS

1. Rewrite this passage so that there are no sentence fragments.

> Beyond the maze of alleys was an indoor market. Women guarded the tables. Loaded with fruits, vegetables, and melons. They chatted and nursed babies. Their social life. The mounds of produce came from the big local plantations. A false but incredibly vivid illusion that all was abundance in that poor country.

MODIFIERS: MISPLACED, SQUINTING, AND DANGLING

When we don't make it clear which word a modifier is related to, we run the risk of confusing our readers. The three types of unclear modifiers are misplaced, squinting, and dangling.

1. Misplaced modifiers. Sometimes a modifier is misplaced and seems to apply to the wrong word in the sentence.

Misplaced   Gooey, sticky, and sweet, my friend Celeste put the finishing touches on the Baked Alaska.

At first glance, we have to assume the writer is calling Celeste "gooey, sticky, and sweet." What a friend! But perhaps he meant the Baked Alaska.

Revised   My friend Celeste put the finishing touches on the gooey, sticky, and sweet Baked Alaska.

Sometimes we have to snicker at the effect.

Misplaced   Coming around the corner, the Empire State Building stood before the newly arrived immigrants, then the tallest in the world.

Revised   The Empire State Building, then the tallest in the world, stood before the newly arrived immigrants coming around the corner.

In the revision, the modifiers are placed close to the items they modify, and the meaning is clearer, though not so amusing.

Sometimes even long clauses are misplaced.

Misplaced   People should not toy with knives and forks who are eating their supper.

Revised   People who are eating their supper should not toy with knives and forks.

2. Squinting modifiers. Some modifiers straddle a sentence and seem to "squint" in both directions. The reader cannot know which part of the sentence such a modifier belongs to.

Squinting   That he cleaned up the car thoroughly pleased her.

Did he thoroughly clean up the car, or was she thoroughly pleased?

Revised   That he thoroughly cleaned up the car pleased her.
That he cleaned up the car pleased her thoroughly.

Some adverbs (*just, merely, only, simply,* and so on) often seem to float blithely through a sentence, whimsically dropping between any two words they fancy. *Only* is particularly capricious. Think of all the places it could fall in this sentence.

I have eyes for you.

Be sure to place these adverbs firmly and unambiguously.

I have eyes for only you.

Sometimes a long phrase or clause will squint badly.

Squinting   The coach said while the game was in progress he would make no substitutes.

Did the coach make the statement before or during the game? We couldn't be sure.

Revised   The coach said he would make no substitution while the game was in progress.
While the game was in progress, the coach said he would make no substitutes.

3. Dangling modifiers. Some sentences simply lack the word the modifier is supposed to modify.

Dangling   Before riding the horses, all pets should be tethered.

Reading a sign like that, we do a slight double take: the *pets* will be riding the horses? Then we rewrite the sentence.

Revised   Before riding the horses, riders should tether all pets.

Most of the time, the dangling modifier occurs because the writer has not brought the modified term forward from the previous sentence.

Dangling   We went to the Smiths' last night. The evening passed pleasantly, eating candy and playing music.

Eating candy and playing music dangles because the writer has left *we* in the previous sentence.

Revised   We went to the Smiths' last night. We passed the evening pleasantly, eating candy and playing music.

EXERCISE FOR MODIFIERS

1. Rewrite the following sentences to make clear which words the modifiers modify.
   a. While he told his story to his friends, a boa constrictor coiled menacingly over Conroy's head.
   b. Rationing food and experiencing nightly air raids, the war was extremely difficult for the British.
   c. Some say the German people had themselves only to blame.
   d. Listening to the glorious voice of Leontyne Price, the opera *Aida* was a marvelous occasion.
   e. Second-guessing the coach's strategy, a football game can be a Monday morning social encounter.

PARALLEL CONSTRUCTION

When thoughts are parallel, express them in the same grammatical construction.

To be Italian is to be fortunate.

By so doing, you not only indicate the connection between the thoughts but also create a more vigorous prose. When, on the other hand, you present similar or equally important ideas in grammatically different forms, you make reading more difficult and less interesting. Compare these two sentences:

Nonparallel	France's foreign policy irritates the British because of its arrogance and it is chauvinistic.
Revised	France's foreign policy irritates the British because of its arrogance and its chauvinism.

Ideas in parallel form are more easily grasped. Be particularly careful in constructing a series of equal parts. Whatever form you use for the first part, repeat for each subsequent part.

Nonparallel	Use epoxy to fix broken dishes, for patching cracked glass, if your favorite knickknack is broken, and as a sealant for almost any broken surface.

In this example, each item has a different grammatical construction — and the result is a mess.

Revised	Use epoxy to fix broken dishes, to patch cracked glass, to repair a favorite knickknack, and to seal almost any broken surface.

Sometimes in keeping a list parallel, you may need to repeat a word to maintain clarity.

Unclear	We chased the fox through the woods, the hills, the creek, and a dozen trees.

At first we misread that sentence and thought the chase was through the hills, through the creek, and through a dozen trees.

Revised	We chased the fox through the woods, over the hills, over the creek, and up a dozen trees.

Writers can commit more grievous errors than repetition — confusion for one.

Parallelism is also important in coordinate construction. When you use a coordinating conjunction, be sure you have the same grammatical construction on both sides.

Nonparallel	The woman hated all kinds of music but who loved painting.

In this construction *who loved painting,* a dependent clause, is in a different grammatical form from *The woman hated all kinds of music,* an independent clause.

Revised	The woman hated all kinds of music but loved painting.

When you use a correlative pair (*both/and, either/or, neither/nor,* or *not only/but also*), use the same form following each member of the pair.

Nonparallel	Either he is a genius or a fraud.

In this example, *either* is followed by an independent clause, but *or* is followed only by a noun.

Revised	Either he is a genius or he is a fraud.
	He is either a genius or a fraud.

EXERCISE FOR PARALLEL CONSTRUCTION

1. Rewrite these sentences to make the thoughts parallel.
   a. For years, Ryan had three things on his mind: watching out for his brother's temper tantrums, what his friends thought of him, and how to break away from his overprotective mother.
   b. Many consider Titian the greatest Venetian painter, but some thinking Tintoretto achieved equal greatness.
   c. Either the instructor knows his subject or should be fired.
   d. Not only was Jimmy Carter a farmer, but an engineer.
   e. The mechanic told Mrs. Filoli that the spark plugs ought to be replaced, she needed a new fan belt, and relining the brakes was essential for the car to run well.

3 / Punctuation

When you use periods, commas, semicolons, and other punctuation, you are instructing your reader on how to read your work. Punctuation, therefore, isn't an afterthought or window dressing; it is your practical partner in the effort to be clear. Careful punctuation gets your message across; careless punctuation hinders communication.

ENDINGS

Periods

Periods mark off the endings of sentences. They tell your reader, "This is the end of a complete thought." They also signal abbreviations: *Jan., Feb., Gov., St. Augustine, Ibid., reg. U.S. Pat. Off.* (See the section "Abbreviations.") And they mark off letters and numbers in outlines and figures: *A. Endings*.

Exclamation Points and Question Marks

The exclamation point tells your reader that your sentence is emphatic; the question mark, that it is a question.

I see a ghost! Or is it my kid brother?

In formal prose, use exclamation marks stingily. They are all right in quotations.

When Shelley writes "Oh world! Oh life! Oh time!" he tells us . . .

They are also proper in the rare situation that calls for dialogue.

Newspapers are like a neurotic friend ever at your elbow who cries, at every event whether large or small, "What a decision! What a cataclysm! This is unprecedented!"

But let your own sentences be emphatic without bullhorns. Never double end punctuation. You would not, for example, write

Who wrote *What Price Glory?*?

One question mark is ample.

COMMAS

You will use commas more than any other punctuation mark. They tell your reader how to read your sentences. Commas have many uses. Here are the eleven you will encounter most often.

1. Before coordinating conjunctions. Use a comma before a conjunction that connects two independent clauses; that is, before the *and, but, for*, and so on in a compound sentence.

He liked sports, but he never exercised.

2. In a series. Use a comma between all elements in a series of three or more nouns, verbs, or phrases.

The pen, the pencil, and the typewriter all failed her.

She whistled, tap-danced, and yodeled better than her mother.

Playing jacks, eating candy, and chatting with friends occupied her days.

3. Between coordinate adjectives. Coordinate adjectives are adjectives you can arrange in any order without changing the meaning.

Here we are at the lush, moist, comforting oasis.

Not all adjectives in a series are coordinate, however. The adjective next to the noun sometimes combines with the noun to form a unit and the other adjectives modify the whole unit.

Early fliers hated the long, weary dawn patrols.

Dawn and *patrols* cannot be separated; *long* and *weary* modify *dawn patrols*. To check whether you are dealing with coordinate adjectives, see if an *and* can logically be placed between the last two adjectives, as in the following:

Here we are at the lush and moist and comforting oasis.

Although when you have two coordinate adjectives, you usually separate them with *and*, you can separate them with a comma.

The tall, blond pole-vaulter took off her sunglasses.

4. After introductory material. Use a comma to set off an initial long phrase or dependent clause from the main part of the sentence.

Because of the coldest frost in thirty years, half of Florida's orange crop was lost.

After I had swum across the Amazon River, I dried my hair.

The comma tells the reader to pause and not to run the thoughts together. You can, however, omit the comma after a very short introductory phrase.

After swimming the Amazon I dried my hair.

When in doubt, use your ear and put the comma at the pause.

5. In quotation. Use a comma to separate a direct quotation from its attribution, whether the attribution is at the end, at the beginning, or in the middle.

"We are not amused," said the queen.
The king asked, "Who is not amused?"
"Who," asked the court jester, "wants to know?"

6. For nonessential information. Use commas to tell the reader whether information is or is not essential to the meaning of the sentence.

Use a comma to set off words, phrases, or clauses that provide nonessential information (also called *nonrestrictive elements*).

Harry's wife, Deirdre, was named den mother of the year.

Because Harry has only one wife, the name *Deirdre* is not essential to understanding the sentence and so is set off by commas.

Do not use commas to set off words, phrases, and clauses that provide essential information (also called *restrictive elements*).

As a result, Harry's son Russell became an Eagle Scout.

Because Harry has two sons, the name *Russell* is essential to the meaning of the sentence and therefore should not be set off by commas.

In the following sentence, the commas make a great deal of difference:

All the test pilots, who drink too much, will be grounded without pay.
All the test pilots who drink too much will be grounded without pay.

When *who drink too much* is set off by commas, the sentence means that (1) all tests pilots drink too much, and (2) all will be grounded without pay. When *who drink too much* is not set off by commas, the sentence means that (1) at least some test pilots do not drink too much, and (2) only those who do will be grounded.

7. With parenthetical and interruptive elements. All sorts of expressions and words pop into the middle of a sentence but have no real connection to it. They should be marked off with commas.

Asides	The emu lives, if you want to call it that, in Australia.
	The emu, that flightless bird, runs rapidly.
Interjections and emphatic elements	Well, no, it is not soothing to look at because its neck is, after all, four feet long.
Direct address	What do you think of Steinbrenner, Billy?
Conjunctive adverbs	Moreover, it is almost extinct.
	Its cousin the ostrich, however, is protected for its feathers.

8. Between titles and names. Use commas to separate names from titles that follow, such as *Jr., M.D., Ph.D., Inc.,* and *Ltd.*

Harry Horvath, Jr., and his wife, Deirdre Failin Horvath, M.D., are joint owners of Horvath Chinchilla Farms, Inc.

9. After place names. Use commas after both city and state.

Every year Aunt Hepzibah leaves her boardinghouse in Bent Twig, Wyoming, to visit Harry.

10. For day and year. Use commas to set off the year. Do not use commas to set off only the month and year.

On December 7, 1941, the Royal Japanese Air Force bombed Pearl Harbor.

11. In long, complicated sentences. Use commas to prevent misreading. When a long, twisty sentence threatens to leave your reader behind, you can sometimes break it into readable hunks with a considerate comma.

In my opinion, aerobic exercise helps develop thick, muscular calves, and minds that are well rested and alert.

Because of its structure, this sentence would not automatically get a second comma. As you can see, however, without that comma, we would have thick, muscular minds, as well as calves that are well rested and alert. But be careful to avoid using commas ungrammatically or indiscriminately.

PARENTHESES AND DASHES

Two other ways to mark off parenthetical elements are parentheses and dashes. Each has its own function.

Parentheses

Parentheses are more emphatic than pairs of commas because they decisively block off the material between them.

Years from now (and not too many years at that) the sexual revolution will seem as corrupt as the double standard that preceded it.

Parentheses are a cue to the reader to lower the voice, so to speak. Don't overuse parentheses; no one likes a constant whisperer. Enclose material within them that may be interesting but is really a digression.

Present at Yalta were Joseph Stalin, Franklin D. Roosevelt (who would be dead within two months), and Winston Churchill.

Many people are uncertain about how to punctuate when parentheses are present. Here are two guidelines.

1. When the parentheses are within a sentence, punctuate the sentence exactly as if the parentheses were not there.

Debate used to rage about whether the dog or the cat is smarter (not an unimportant topic for some of us); opinion now leans in favor of Fido.

Be sure not to put the sentence's punctuation inside the closing parentheses.

Incorrect	Sixteen ounces is the equivalent of 454 grams (a ratio of 28.35 to one.)
Correct	Sixteen ounces is the equivalent of 454 grams (a ratio of 28.35 to one).

2. When a complete sentence stands by itself in parentheses — that is, when it is not inside another sentence — the period falls within the parentheses.

Saying the dog is smarter than the cat does not devalue the latter in the eyes of cat fans. (It is doubtful whether anything could.)

In occasional bizarre circumstances a complete and parenthesized sentence can fall within another sentence. In such a case, omit both the initial capital letter and terminal punctuation for the parenthetical sentence.

Beekeeping is hazardous (you always risk being stung) but rewarding.

Dashes

Even more emphatic than parentheses are dashes. They indicate not whispers but shouts.

> Although William Howard Taft was obese — a dinner guest once inquired whether he was expecting — he lived to be seventy-three years old.

Framed by dashes, this joke emerges loud and clear.

Use the dash — sparingly — to indicate interruptions, informal breaks in construction, or special emphasis.

> My best friend — my dog Kent, I mean — has left me forever.

> Muhammad Ali — then known as Cassius Clay — won an Olympic Gold Medal in 1960.

In typing, form the dash with two hyphens. Don't leave a space on either side and do not use any commas, colons, semicolons, or parentheses adjacent to a dash — the dash is the only punctuation needed. When you use a dash before the final element in a sentence, close with the usual period.

> Caesar loved Cleopatra — but not as much as she thought.

Like the other components of writing, these emphatic markers become meaningless if you overuse them. Save them for special occasions.

SEMICOLONS

A semicolon announces a pause in the thought in a sentence. In the strength of pause it is exactly halfway between a period and a comma, and to indicate it a period sits on top of a comma. You can use this pause in two ways.

1. Between independent clauses. Use a semicolon when you want to indicate a close connection between independent clauses.

> The pollsters predicted a close election; the smart money knew otherwise.

Used this way, the semicolon tightly holds together two complete thoughts. It indicates strong likeness or balance.

> He accepted her for her money; she loved him for his soul.

The semicolon is also effective in suggesting a clash of contrast.

He loved biology; he hated math.

You must have independent clauses on both sides of the semicolon in these constructions.

2. In a complicated series. The second use of the semicolon is less common but no less useful. Here, too, you use a semicolon to connect equal elements. When you have a series of items that may have internal punctuation, use the semicolon to separate the items clearly.

At the party we saw Sam, the electrician; Tim, the magician; Bill Jones; Wanda Everts, the land, sea, and air endurance champion of England, China, and Wales; and Everts's dog, Spence.

Without semicolons, this sentence would be hopelessly confusing.

By all means learn to use semicolons; they will add subtlety and grace to your style. Do not overuse them, however, or their power to balance and connect will evaporate.

COLONS

The colon is the vaudeville punctuation mark. Its one task is to introduce: and here it is, folks! A colon comes at the end of an independent clause.

There in the doorway stood something I thought I would never see: my grandfather in a gorilla suit.

A colon can precede another independent clause.

Jealousy serves only one purpose for humanity: it alienates people from those they most dearly love.

It can introduce a series.

Kate visited four Ohio cities: Cleveland, Cincinnati, Columbus, and Toledo.

It can announce a quotation.

Eisenhower said it more than once: "I shall go to Korea."

It can emphasize a single word.

When he asked to borrow money, I knew what to say: No!

Many careful writers do not capitalize after a colon, except for proper names. What follows the colon is not thought of as a new sentence but as an extension of the existing one.

We also use colons to separate hours from minutes in reporting time.

As of this writing, it is 6:34 p.m.

Colons are strong marks: do not overuse them.

APOSTROPHES

Apostrophes serve two important functions: to form possessives and to make contractions.

1. Use the apostrophe to form the possessive of nouns. The *possessive* signifies ownership or association. To make a singular noun possessive, add an apostrophe followed by an *s: Lincoln's beard, the cat's meow, Amos's bee sting, the business's employees*. To make a plural noun ending in *-s* possessive, add only an apostrophe: *the Mohicans' war cry, the girls' crazy hats, the Richards' dinner party*.

Avoid awkward possessives by using *of* or other constructions.

Awkward	After the collision, the Williamses' Cadillac was a wreck.
Revised	After the collision, the Cadillac owned by the Williamses was a wreck.

2. Use the apostrophe to show where you drop letters to contract two words into one. Words frequently *elided*, as this is called, are *can, do, does, have, is, not, will*.

If I can't find my algebra book, I'll flunk.

For the most part, contractions are still limited to informal prose and dialogue. Careful stylists keep them to a minimum. High informal prose should not sound chatty or breezy.

Breezy	Japan couldn't've conquered the whole of Asia because it didn't have the resources.
Revised	Japan could not have conquered the whole of Asia because it did not have the resources.

On the other hand, use contractions when the full form would sound awkward.

Awkward	Is this not the same as claiming that Japan would have been defeated even without the United States?
Revised	Isn't this the same as claiming that Japan would have been defeated even without the United States?

Tiny confusions and mistaken identities plague contractions. The contraction *it's* is often mistaken for the possessive pronoun *its*. There is no apostrophe in the possessive. In the contraction, the apostrophe marks the spot where the second *i* is missing.

Incorrect	Corsica is French, but its often rebellious.
Correct	Corsica is French, but it's often rebellious.
Incorrect	It's main exports are olive oil, wine, and citrus fruits.
Correct	Its main exports are olive oil, wine, and citrus fruits.

Much the same confusion occurs in using *your* and *you're*, and *their* and *they're*. In both cases the first is a possessive form of a pronoun (*you* and *they*), and the second is a contraction of two words (*you are* and *they are*). Perhaps three correct sentences will make the differences clear.

Our beagle always knows when it's time for its dinner.

Your taxi will arrive in five minutes if you're lucky.

They're trying to find their lottery tickets.

You should avoid cutesy apostrophes in your writing. *Steak 'n' eggs* is *steak and eggs, a little bit o' soul* is *a little bit of soul*. Even *rock 'n' roll* suffers little when written *rock and roll*. *Three o'clock*, however, is standard; most of us do not know that it is a contraction for *three of the clock*.

Do not use an apostrophe followed by -*s* to form the plural of abbreviations, capital letters, words used as words, or specific decades unless the *s* alone would be confusing.

His high Cs are sharp, but his low Fs are delicious.

It will take sixteen IBMs to compete with one of our EECs.

In some ways, the 1890s were similar to the 1920s.

But:

> He had difficulty pronouncing S's, A's, and I's.
> Here are the do's and don'ts of windsurfing.

PUNCTUATION OF QUOTATIONS

Punctuation marks seem to congregate whenever a quotation arises. Six standard practices ease the guesswork in such instances.

1. Use double quotation marks to enclose quoted material, titles of essays, articles, short stories, chapters, short poems, and short musical compositions.

> Nixon said, "I am not a crook."
> "Why I Live at the P.O." is a short story by Eudora Welty.
> Chapter 22 is entitled "German Folklore."
> I adore Judy Collins's "Send in the Clowns."

(Titles of other kinds of works require italics. See the section "Italics.")

2. For a quotation within a quotation, use single quotation marks.

> Harry said to Deirdre, "When I said, 'Life would be easier if I were not married,' I was only speaking figuratively."

3. In American writing, periods and commas always come inside quotation marks, whether they are part of the quotation or not.

> When we speak of "the next wave," we mean the same thing our grandparents meant when they said "the latest thing."

4. Colons and semicolons fall outside quotation marks.

> I mean three things when I say "junk food": hamburgers, potato chips, and Twinkies.

5. Place a question mark or an exclamation point inside the quotation marks if it is part of the quotation.

> Betty Rollin wrote "Motherhood: Who Needs It?"

Place it outside if it is not part of the quotation.

> But who wrote "Three Kinds of Thinking"?

6. When quoting a complete sentence, capitalize the first word.

We can sympathize with King Lear when he cries, "How dost, my boy? Art cold?"

Do not capitalize the first word if you are quoting a fragment.

By "different but equal," women's rights advocates still mean "equal."

Do not capitalize if you introduce a short complete sentence with *that* or a similar construction.

When Mark Twain tells us that "training is everything," we should believe him.

Finally, when the attribution comes in the middle of a quoted sentence, do not capitalize after the interruption.

"The only animal ever to be recorded as having been killed by a meteor," Professor Frohling said, "was an Egyptian dog."

ELLIPSES

Ellipses — that is, spaced periods in the body of a quotation — indicate that material has been omitted. They should never be used to change a meaning, but they can help to shorten a long passage that contains material not directly relevant to your purpose.

Here is a passage in which Charles Darwin extols the lowly worm:

Archaeologists ought to be grateful to worms, as they protect and preserve for an indefinitely long period every object not liable to decay, which is dropped on the surface of the land, by burying it beneath their castings. Thus, also, many elegant and curious tessellated pavements and other ancient remains have been preserved; though no doubt the worms have in these cases been largely aided by earth washed and blown from the adjoining land, especially when cultivated. The old tessellated pavements have, however, often suffered by having subsided unequally from being unequally undermined by the worms. Even old massive walls may be undermined and subside; and no building is in this respect safe, unless the foundations lie six or seven feet beneath the surface, at a depth at which worms cannot work. It is probable that many monoliths and some old walls have fallen down from having been undermined by worms. (Charles Darwin, *The Formation of Vegetable Mould, Through the Action of Worms, with Observations on Their Habits*)

By placing ellipses where text has been deleted, you can quote just a part of this passage and still get its point.

> In extolling lowly worms, Darwin says that "they protect and preserve . . . every object not liable to decay . . . by burying it beneath their castings," thus preserving ancient remains. Darwin points out the negative side to this activity, however: "Even old massive walls . . . . have fallen down from having been undermined by worms."

If the deleted material comes in the middle of a sentence, use three spaced periods ("not liable to decay . . . by burying it"); if the deleted material includes the end of a sentence, use four ("Even old massive walls. . . . have fallen down").

Never use ellipses in place of a colon to introduce or set off material.

> *Incorrect*   After miles of wandering, they stood before it . . . the sea.

And finally, never use ellipses to fade in or out of a sentence.

> *Incorrect*   Sunsets are beautiful . . .

OTHER PUNCTUATION

Two relatively rare punctuation marks are brackets and virgules.

Brackets

Whenever you have to change a quotation to fit your context, enclose your words in brackets to indicate the changes.

> *Original*   Darwin says that "a weight of more than ten tons of dry earth annually passes through their bodies. . . ."
>
> *Revised*   Darwin says that "a weight of more than ten tons of dry earth annually pass through their [the worms'] bodies."

Virgules

The virgule, commonly called the *slash*, is used to show that several possibilities are equally appropriate.

King James was a gypsy/god/king.

It is also used to show line breaks in poetry when the lines are not indented but are continuous in the text.

When T.S. Eliot writes, "Set down / This set down / This," the sense of dislocation is breathtaking.

EXERCISES FOR PUNCTUATION

1. Punctuate the following sentences according to proper form.
    a. Heideggers work is difficult I had to read every paragraph several times.
    b. Who was that person shouting help help help outside the police department at six oclock this morning
    c. Her presence her regal walk I mean communicated to us all a sense of confidence poise and financial well-being
    d. Even when I am showered clothed and fed I still have trouble facing up to the mornings most frightening task shaving
    e. Somewhere in a run-down garret in the Spanish-speaking part of Ecuador the most gung ho yodeling choir in the world is practicing for tomorrow nights world championships
    f. All I said to the teacher Bill said was Why are you flunking me you old crow
    g. If you have no money welcome to the club if you do have some lend me five dollars until tomorrow
    h. Monique found three curious items in her grandmothers hope chest a white silk dress still wrapped in the tissue in which it was bought a pair of dancing slippers seemingly made of glass and a jeweled tiara covered with hundreds of fake amethysts
    i. We cant guarantee that you will still be riding your new motorcycle in ten years but we can offer you an insurance policy at very low cost
    j. Oh gosh this is great
    k. Mr. Greaves an old man who has been teaching here for thirty years refers to his rich students as black Porsche philosophers
    l. The black-footed albatross also known as the gooney bird can fly well but has terrible trouble with takeoffs and landings
    m. The career of Upton Sinclair shows that success in one field literature does not necessarily lead to success in another politics
    n. He reached into the aquarium and you wont believe this swallowed both goldfish whole

    o. Sometimes I just go crazy with all the NFLs USFLs NBAs and USHLs dont you

    p. Long before he had told her he would marry someone else

2. Restore the proper punctuation to the following paragraph. Read the passage aloud as a first step.

> To this day we cannot understand how a great civilized nation or at least a considerable part of it could in the twentieth century succumb to its fascination with a ridiculous complex-ridden petit-bourgeois man could fall for his pseudoscientific theories and in their name exterminate nations conquer continents and commit unbelievable cruelties Positivistic science Marxism included offers a variety of scientific explanations for this mysterious phenomenon but instead of eliminating the mystery they tend to deepen it For the cold "objective" reason that speaks to us from these explanations only underlines the disproportion between itself a power power that claims to be the decisive one in this civilization and the mass insanity that has nothing in common with any form of rationality   (Vaclav Havel, "Thriller")

4 / Mechanics

    With punctuation we mark and divide sentences; with mechanics we treat things such as abbreviations, capitalization, italics, numbers, and hyphens. Mechanics are conventions — general and often unspoken agreements about basic procedures — that all writers observe. Your reader will expect you to follow these conventions and may be confused if you deviate from them or are inconsistent. All careful writers learn the proper mechanics to keep their writing clear and correct.

ABBREVIATIONS

    Some abbreviations, which we have grouped in three categories are standard.

1. Many titles and terms — like *Dr., Mr., Mrs., Ms., M.D., J.D.L., Ph.D., AD, BC, a.m., p.m., Hon., Msgr., Rev., St., Jr.,* and *Sr.* — are abbreviated.

2. Institutional names are frequently abbreviated, and most are now written *without* periods: *AFL-CIO, EEC, EPA, GNP, IBM, NAACP, TWA.* If your reader may not know what the abbreviation stands for, write the name out the first time you use it, and follow it with the abbreviation in parentheses.

The journalist's assignment was to cover the Environmental Protection Agency (EPA).

Now you could use EPA throughout the rest of the essay. (On the other hand, IBM is so universally known as *IBM* that many people would not recognize *International Business Machines.*)

Keep abbreviations to a minimum. Clumps of letters and periods make your writing read like a ticker tape. If your audience uses these abbreviations as part of its language, use them. Careful stylists, however, never use *TV* for *television.*

3. Figures and some items in footnotes are often abbreviated: *ed., fig., ft., p., sec.* American practice is tending away from abbreviations in footnotes and figures, although *ed.* for "editor" and *p.* and *pp.* for "page" and "pages" are still common. (See Chapter 12, Writing Research, for explicit information on documentation.)

CAPITALIZATION

Every sentence should, of course, begin with a capital letter. This indicates that you are starting a new thought. The capital has additional uses. We have summarized the uses and misuses in three rules.

1. Capitalize the first letter of each word in the following categories.

Proper names	Michael Jackson
Specific places	Mongolia
Works of art and entertainment:	
Books	*Gone with the Wind*
Movies	*Star Wars*
Plays	*Hedda Gabler*
Paintings and sculptures	*The Last Supper, The Thinker*
Television shows	*Hill Street Blues*

Radio shows	*All Things Considered*
Notable objects and groups:	
Ships	*Queen Elizabeth II*
Planes	*The Spirit of St. Louis*
Famous structures	Golden Gate Bridge
Organizations	United Auto Workers
Institutions	Lehigh University
Religions	Roman Catholic
Ethnic or national groups	Ute Indians
Languages	French, Swahili
Marks on the calendar:	
Days	Wednesday
Months	April
Holidays	Passover
Historical items:	
Eras	Middle Ages
Documents	Magna Carta
Events	Civil War
Sacred beings and terms:	
Deities	God, Allah
Sacred persons	Buddha
Sacred scriptures	the Koran

Capitalize titles of people before their proper names.

Senator Howell Heflin came from Alabama.

Do not capitalize titles standing alone or after the proper name.

The senator from Alabama was Howell Heflin.

Being a senator is hard work.

An exception to this rule is titles of very high and special rank.

Warren Burger is the Chief Justice of the United States.

2. Do not capitalize

Seasons	winter
General groups	the middle class
Abstractions	love, art, nature

3. Some words appear both capitalized and uncapitalized, depending on their use. Capitalize regions.

New Orleans is the gem of the South.

But do not capitalize directions.

Go west, young man.

Capitalize college courses and departments.

Anthropology 119 is the best course offered by the Department of Anthropology.

Do not capitalize the name of general subjects.

I love anthropology, but I don't like mathematics.

ITALICS

To indicate italics on a typewriter, underline the material. Use italics for titles of

Books	*War and Peace*
Periodicals	*Scientific American*
Newspapers	*San Jose Mercury News*
Movies	*Star Wars*
Plays	*Much Ado about Nothing*
Television programs	*Dallas*
Long musical compositions	*Resurrection Symphony*
Foreign words or phrases	*sine qua non*

Avoid underlining as a way of emphasizing. The same writers who are fond of exclamation points also like italics, for with *them* they can *emphasize* every word they think is *crucial.* Let words stand without artificial emphasis. Give your sentences their own punch, and the reader will see the emphasis *without* being *pushed* by shouting, insistent *italics.*

NUMBERS

In nonscientific writing, use figures only for numbers of more than two words.

He was twenty-nine but his great-grandfather was 112.

Spell out any number that begins a sentence.

One hundred and twelve years is a long time to be alive.

HYPHENS

The hyphen is used either to join words or to separate syllables.

1. Use hyphens to join multiword adjectives and nouns.

Harry was a devil-may-care philosopher-poet who claimed he had many out-of-town speaking engagements.

When multiword adjectives follow the noun they modify, however, do not hyphenate them.

Yet he claimed he had many speaking engagements out of town.

There is no hard-and-fast rule governing when to hyphenate compound words. Check the dictionary. If it does not have the entry you seek, write the words without a hyphen.

2. Use hyphens to show where words may be divided at the end of a line.

Houdini was not only an escape artist but a pres-
tidigitator.

If you type carefully, you should not need to divide words often. Never divide one-syllable words and only divide longer words at a syllable break. Check words in your dictionary to determine syllable breaks. When you must divide a word, the last thing on the line should be the hyphen.

Harry retired to Pocatello for a long vaca-
tion because he had just completed a book.

Avoid breaking a word in a way that leaves only one or two letters on either side.

If you do, the letter will look quite a-
lone, and furthermore it will look silly.

3. Use hyphens to attach prefixes to certain root words; for example, a capitalized root word.

She could not decide whether she was a pre-Raphaelite or a postmodernist.

When two prefixes belong to the same word, use a hyphen and a space after the first prefix and attach the second prefix to the word.

She studied both micro- and macroeconomics in college.

More often than not, prefixes are joined to their root words. Again, when in doubt, check your dictionary.

EXERCISES FOR MECHANICS

1. Edit the following sentences for proper form for abbreviation, capitalization, italics, and numbers.
   a. in the winter of 65, people in the midwest were far colder than people in the atlantic states because of a wintry arctic blast
   b. albert appeared on claudia's doorstep last thursday night, smelling of cologne and lisping sotto voce, "Come with me to the casbah — or at least to cinema five. they're showing tracy and hepburn in woman of the year."
   c. in the epic poem gilgamesh, written down around 2000 bc, a sumerian king, gilgamesh of erech, prays to his patron goddess ishtar, and travels to the land of the dead in search of his friend enkidu.
   d. yesterday I read melville's whaling novel moby-dick, hemingway's short story with the lean and revealing dialogue, hills like white elephants, and the new popular mechanics.
   e. when senator gass asked tommy what he wanted to be when he grew up, tommy said he wanted to be a senator just like him and serve in congress.
   f. jack meridge, lld, phd, was first a lawyer for the afl-cio, but then he hooked up with the nfl and the cia, which eventually led to a job with rev harold haines, a leader of the naacp.
   g. is twelve midnight am or pm?
   h. 30,000 buffalo took an average of 5 months to migrate from their winter pastures in new mexico to their summer pastures in montana.
   i. at the salt talks in geneva the ambassador from the united states and the ambassador from the ussr will discuss the abm program and the deployment of medium-range icbms and ss-x-25's.
2. Restore proper mechanics to the passage below.
   on tonight's episode of houston, dr van slyke discovers fifi's plan to sell his ocean liner, the willie mays, to throckmorton gotrocks,

jr, the sixty-seven-year-old former tree surgeon and stunt pilot, in exchange for an autographed copy of his poem, how green the face, six prize st bernard dogs, and 22 us savings bonds. meanwhile, senator rex smith has telephoned his brother roy, governor of the state, to see if he can get free tickets for the exclusive performance of gershwin's porgy and bess, being given by the houston light opera company at the civic center opera house. tonight's episode is based on the short story the big swap by lily upmeier, phd, and is soon to be made into a feature length motion picture, to be entitled grope for gold.

5 / Spelling

English spelling is irregular. Its rules are far from certain and far from complete. Our first and most important tip: use your dictionary. Everything is in there: how to spell a word, how to divide between syllables, and how to join suffixes of all descriptions.

Your dictionary may list two and occasionally three spellings for the same word. Most of the time, the first spelling given is "preferred," and we recommend you use it. When in doubt, however, choose the spelling that is simpler, modern, and American. Write *encyclopedia* instead of *encyclopaedia, theater* instead of *theatre*, and *color* instead of *colour*. Always be consistent. Stick to your choice throughout your writing.

The two most common trouble spots in English spelling are suffixes and homonyms (words that sound alike). Although your dictionary has more information, the following rules will give you some help.

SUFFIXES

Here we set out some guidelines for adding suffixes to words.

Forming Plurals

The plural of most nouns is formed by adding *s*. There are special cases and exceptions.

1. Nouns ending in -*s*. Form the plural by adding -*es*.

 James Jameses   business businesses

2. Nouns ending in -*ch*. Form the plural by adding -*es*.

 match matches   lunch lunches

3. Nouns ending in -*y*. When a word ends in -*y* preceded by a vowel, add -*s*.

 boy boys

When the -*y* is preceded by a consonant, change the -*y* to -*i* and add -*es*.

 trophy trophies

4. Nouns ending in -*o*. When the -*o* is preceded by a vowel, add -*s*.

 studio studios

When the -*o* is preceded by a consonant, add -*es*.

 potato potatoes

5. Nouns ending in -*f* or -*fe*. Some words ending in -*f* or -*fe* take an -*s*.

 fife fifes   chief chiefs

Some change -*f* to -*ves*.

 elf elves   knife knives

There are plenty of exceptions to all this. Check that dictionary.

Doubling the Final Consonant

Is it *traveller* or *traveler*? *Compelled* or *compeled*? Questions like these can sometimes make a writer's head spin. Three factors determine whether you double a word's final consonant before adding an ending.

1. the number of syllables
2. what letters precede the final consonant
3. which syllable is accented

Here are the combinations.

1. Double when a word of one syllable has a single vowel before the final consonant.

 flip flipped   trap trapped

2. Double when a multisyllable word has a final consonant preceded by a single vowel and is accented on the last syllable.

compel   compelling   occur   occurrence
forget   forgetting

3. Don't double when a one-syllable word has two vowels before the final consonant.

peel   peeled   sear   searing

4. Don't double when the word ends in two consonants.

risk   risked   grasp   grasping

5. Don't double when the accent shifts away from the last syllable once the ending is added.

infer   inferential   confer   conference

6. American writers increasingly prefer the single consonant. Therefore, when you encounter words that could go either way, don't double.

focus   focused   travel   traveling

Adding Other Suffixes

1. Adding *-able*, *-ible*, *-alogy*, *-ology*, *-ance*, *-ence*, *-ant*, *-ent*. No hard and fast rules can tell you whether it is *dependant* or *dependent*. If you have not memorized the spellings, use your dictionary.

2. Words ending in *-cede*, *-ceed*, *-sede*. This one is fairly easy. *Supersede* is the only word to end in *-sede*. And only three words end in *-ceed*: *exceed*, *proceed*, and *succeed*. For the rest, use *-cede*: *precede, recede.*

3. Words ending in *-y*. To add a suffix to words ending in *-y* preceded by a consonant, change the *-y* to *-i* except when the suffix begins with *-i*.

happy   happiness   merry   merrily

When the suffix begins with *i*, the *-y* stays put.

carry   carrying

HOMONYMS

Some spelling problems occur because two words are homonyms — that is, they are pronounced similarly or the same way but have different meanings and are spelled differently. Here are some common ones.

accent/ascent/assent	ewe/you
accept/except	incredible/incredulous
affect/effect	loose/lose
brake/break	passed/past
capital/capitol	principal/principle
choose/chose	read/reed
cite/sight/site	right/rite/write
conscience/conscious	stationary/stationery
credible/creditable	straight/strait
desert/dessert	than/then
dew/do	to/too/two
eminent/immanent/imminent	weather/whether

SPELLING GUIDELINES

The following guidelines usually work, but keep your dictionary handy.

1. "*I* before *e* except after *c*, or when sounded like *ay*, as in *neighbor* and *weigh*."

thief   friend   pier

except after c:

ceiling   conceive   conceited

sounds like *ay*

inveigh   skein   sleigh

There are, of course, exceptions, such as *foreigner, height,* and *weird*. Keep your dictionary warmed up.

2. Words ending in final -*e* retain the -*e* before suffixes that begin with consonants.

battle	battlement	shape	shapely
hope	hopeful	cute	cuteness

They drop the -*e* before suffixes that begin with vowels.

believe	believable	scrape	scraping
contrive	contrivance	sanguine	sanguinary

Where confusion could arise with another word, keep the -*e*.

dye   dyeing (instead of dying)

3. Words that end in -*ce* or -*ge* keep the -*e* to retain their soft sound.

change   changeable   notice   noticeable

EXERCISES FOR SPELLING

1. Add the suffixes indicated to the words that follow them. Check your choice of spelling in the dictionary.
   a. Suffix: -able, -ible
      Words: access, commend, defense, excuse, force, response.
   b. Suffix: -ing
      Words: change, commit, pat, prefer, rally, slope.

2. Check the paragraph below for spelling errors. Use your dictionary whenever you are unsure.

> Last night I made the aquaintance of that imminent playright Carol Dermott. This remarkable woman has kept her eye on the changable tastes of her audience for more than twelve years and has never disapointed her fans. She is embarassed by all the adulation and says that it is all exagerrated. Whether she choses to write a tradgedy or an outragous farce, Dermott has shown her independance. Her first play, *Not for Nothing*, portrays a fisherman who sails alone across the Artic Circle. Her prizewinning drama *Lew's Loss* portrays the lonliness of a cemetary gaurd who falls in love with a waitress at a restarant. But it was not until her eigth play, *Unecessarily Yours*, that her rythmic writing, her wierd but mischevious sence of humour, and her briliant satire of modern beaureaucracy recieved the attention they deserved from the American playgoing audiance.

Glossary
of Usage

"When I use a word," Humpty
Dumpty said in a rather scornful
tone, *"it means just what I
choose it to mean — neither
more nor less."*

— Lewis Carroll (1832–1898)
English writer

No one could hope to untangle all the snarls in American usage. In this section, however, we offer advice on how to avoid the common errors. We treat troublesome words that sound alike but have different meanings, words that are frequently used incorrectly, quandaries you may often find yourself in when choosing a word. When we have discussed the problem in the text, we indicate a reference.

a, an Use *a* before words beginning with a consonant sound and *an* before words beginning with a vowel sound. Check the Handbook, p. 459, for a further discussion.

accent marks Accent marks are part of the word and must be used where they are called for, as in *cliché*. Consult your dictionary.

accept, except *Accept* means "to receive" or "to agree to": *Hirohito finally accepted defeat. Except* as a verb means "to leave out" or "to make exception of" and as a preposition means "excluding": *The ravages of war do not except children, the aged, or the feeble. Everyone got out alive except the cat.*

adverse, averse *Adverse* is an adjective meaning "hostile" or "unfavorable": *The adverse effects of alcohol include headache and nausea. Averse* is an adjective meaning "reluctant" or "in opposition": *Repeated hangovers soon made him averse to drinking alcohol.*

advice, advise   *Advice* is a noun meaning "counsel": *Bill went to his broker for advice on the stock market.* *Advise* is a verb meaning "to give counsel": *But Bill's broker was unable to advise him.*

affect, effect   *Affect* as a verb means "to influence" or "to pretend to have": *The oil slick did not seriously affect the beach. Professor Honnicutt affected a Boston accent.* *Effect* as a verb means "to bring about" or "to cause to happen" and as a noun means "result": *Diplomats are trying to effect a peace in Lebanon. The injections had no effect.*

aggravate, irritate   These words are not synonyms. *Aggravate* means "to make worse": *Running in the sprints, Lewis aggravated his hamstring injury.* *Irritate* means "to make impatient or angry": *My little sister irritates me by following me around.*

agree to, agree with   We agree *to* a proposal. We agree *with* a person.

all, all of   When modifying a common noun, use only *all*: *All the world's a stage.* When modifying a proper noun or a pronoun, use *all of*: *When all of his teeth were pulled, all of Hollywood cried.*

all ready, already   *All ready* is an adjective meaning "prepared": *We're all ready to dance.* *Already* is an adverb meaning "prior in time": *Sven had already cooked dinner by the time we arrived.*

all right, alright   Use *all right*; *alright* is a misspelling.

allusion, illusion   *Allusion* means "reference to," as in *The "rail-splitter" was an allusion to Lincoln.* *Illusion* means "deception" or "mistaken idea," as in *He is under the illusion that he is Napoleon.*

almost, most   See *most, almost.*

along with   Phrases introduced by *along with* are parenthetical and do not change the number of the verb: *The mayor, along with the comptroller and the city council, runs a tight ship.* See the Handbook, pp. 465.

although, though   *Although* and *though* are synonyms. Careful stylists, however, prefer *although* in formal writing: *Although he studied for years, Klaus never passed the bar exam.*

altogether, all together   *Altogether* means "entirely": *Einstein was altogether unprepared for the fame his discoveries brought him.* *All together* means "as a group": *Our family stood all together in the dining room for this snapshot.*

ambiguous, ambivalent   *Ambiguous* means "capable of more than one meaning or interpretation," or, more generally, "unclear or confusing": *His statement was ambiguous and I wasn't sure what he meant.* *Ambivalent* means "feeling two ways (usually conflicting) about something": *I was ambivalent about the movie and so stayed home.*

among, between See *between, among.*

amoral, immoral *Amoral* means "without concern for moral standards": *Don Juan was amoral and so felt no guilt about his seductions.* *Immoral* means "in violation of moral standards": *Cruelty to animals is immoral no matter the situation.*

amount, number *Amount* refers to the bulk or quantity of something viewed as a whole: *I have had an adequate amount of back talk from you.* *Number* refers to separate units: *You have made a number of undeserved criticisms.*

and etc. *Et cetera* means "and other things." To place it after *and* means "and and other things," an obvious redundancy.

and/or Avoid this awkward construction. Decide whether you mean "and" or "or." If your sentence contains a third option, add *or both*, as in *We could not decide whether to go to India or China or both.*

ante-, anti- The prefix *ante-* means "before": *Arlington is an antebellum mansion near Washington.* *Anti-* means "against": *If poisoned, find an antidote.*

anxious, eager *Anxious* means "worried, uneasy, brooding": *Most students were anxious about the organic chemistry midterm.* *Eager* means "full of enthusiasm": *Few were eager to take the midterm.* Be careful not to use one when you mean the other.

anybody, any body, anyone, any one *Anybody* and *anyone* are single-word synonyms meaning "any person at all": *Anybody (or anyone) can be a star these days.* The phrase *any body* refers to any item of a particular group of bodies: *You students of surgery may dissect any body you find.* The phrase *any one* means "any single one of a particular group": *Can I choose any one of the cadavers, Professor?*

anymore, any more *Anymore* (less commonly written as *any more*) is an adverb meaning "any longer" and is used in negative situations: *Annie doesn't live here anymore.* Avoid using it in positive constructions to mean "now" or "these days": *Vegetables are certainly expensive now* (not *anymore*). *Any more* usually refers to an addition: *I've had enough sass and don't want any more.*

anyplace, anywhere Careful stylists prefer *anywhere.*

anyways, anywheres Avoid these colloquial variations of *anyway* and *anywhere.*

apt, likely, liable *Apt* means "having a tendency to": *I am apt to be forgetful*. *Likely* means "probable to happen": *I am likely to forget lunch dates*. *Liable* means "legally responsible": *If I don't repair that missing stair, I'll be liable for damages*. Writers sometimes use *liable* when they mean *likely* in situations that have negative consequences: *I'm likely* (not *liable*) *to slip on icy sidewalks*.

as *As* can be a preposition, an adverb, or a conjunction. As a preposition, it means "in the role of": *As a cook, he would make a good tennis player*. As an adverb, it means "equally": *She would be just as miserable in Kathmandu*. As a conjunction, it introduces an adverbial clause: *He smirked as he ate the goldfish*.

Poor *as* is much overused and abused. It is not a synonym for *because*. Prefer *Billy did not attend school yesterday because* (not *as*) *he had a cold*. It is not a substitute for *that*. Prefer *I don't know that* (not *as*) *I care who wins*. It is not a substitute for *to be*. Prefer *The president appointed her to be* (not *as*) *head of the SEC*. (*To be* is usually so strongly implied it may be omitted.)

as, like *As* and *like* are not interchangeable. *Like* is a preposition and can be followed only by a noun or a noun substitute: *Do you think I look like Robert Redford? Like* should not introduce a clause. Use *as*: Do unto others *as* (not *like*) *you would have others do unto you*.

assure, ensure, insure *Assure* usually means "to give confidence": *He assured her that her stuffed goose was delicious*. *Ensure* means "to make certain": *Tying Black Bart with a lasso ensured his detention*. *Insure* means "to get insurance for": *Lloyd's of London refused to insure the trombonist's lip*.

awful, awfully *Awful* is an adjective: *The awful dragon breathed fire*. *Awfully* is an adverb: *The dragon snorted awfully*. Neither should be used in formal writing to mean "very" or "extremely."

awhile, a while *Awhile* (one word) is an adverb and cannot be the object of a preposition: *Let's rest here awhile*. *A while* is a noun phrase and can be the object of a preposition: *I will get moving again in a while*.

bad, badly *Bad* is an adjective that modifies nouns or noun substitutes; *badly* is an adverb. The problem arises with linking verbs, like *feel, appear,* or *look,* that take the complement *bad*: *After eating the pound of chocolate, Hans felt bad* (not *badly*) *enough to call the doctor*.

being as, being that Avoid these colloquialisms. Use *because* or *since*: *Because* (not *Being as*) *I was ill, I could not attend your recital*.

beside, besides *Beside* means "by the side of" or "next to": *The Secret Service agents stood beside the president. Besides* means either "except" or "in addition to": *Besides her, no one volunteered. Three other students besides her received As.*

between, among Use *between* for two things, *among* for three or more, or when the number is unstated: *Between you and me, I think this party stinks. He was first among equals.*

biweekly, bimonthly, semimonthly, semiannually As a prefix indicating time, *bi-* means happening every two periods of time. *Semi-* means happening twice in one period. *We meet biweekly, or every two weeks. We meet bimonthly, or every two months. We meet semimonthly, or twice each month. We meet semiannually, or twice a year.*

bring, take Someone *brings* something toward you and *takes* it away from you: *Bring me some antacid and take away this awful soup.*

bunch Careful writers avoid using this word to mean "many."

burst, bust *Burst* is a verb meaning "to come apart forcefully." Its principal parts are *burst, burst,* and *burst: What will you do if I burst the balloon? I burst the balloon yesterday. I had burst another balloon a week before. Bursted* is incorrect. *Bust* and *busted* are slang.

but hardly, but scarcely, but however, but yet *But* is superfluous. *Hardly, scarcely, however,* and *yet* already carry negative implications.

can, may *Can* indicates capability, as in *I can bench-press 300 pounds on a good day. May* indicates permission, as in *May I please have the salt?* or possibility, as in *I may need salt on my steak.*

can barely, can hardly, can't barely, can't hardly Both *barely* and *hardly* carry negative implications: *I can barely swim and so can hardly save you. Can't barely* and *can't hardly* are double negatives and should be avoided.

cannot, can not *Can not* is not the preferred form; use *cannot.*

can't help but Careful stylists avoid using this colloquial phrase. Prefer *can't help* without *but* or *can't but* without *help: I can't help loving you. I can't but be pleased at that.*

censor, censure *Censor* means "to scrutinize works for unacceptable material": *Some totalitarian countries censor private mail. Censure* means "to scold or criticize": *The Senate censured Joe McCarthy for his conduct.*

center around, center on *Center on* means "to focus or concentrate on": *The FBI hunt centered on the town of Rome, New York. Center* *around* is illogical. Substitute *revolve around: The quest for freedom re-volves around human dignity.*

cite, sight, site *Cite* is a verb meaning "refer to": *To prove that the world is round, I need only cite that famous explorer Columbus. Sight* is a noun meaning "a view": *I'm sure Columbus found America to be a beautiful sight. Site* is a noun meaning "place" or "location": *Was Rhode Island the site of his landing?*

climactic, climatic *Climactic* refers to a peak or high point: *Bogart's farewell to Bergman is the climactic love scene in* Casablanca. *Climatic* refers to weather: *His voice changed according to climatic conditions.*

compared to, compared with *Compared to* suggests a similarity between two things not usually thought of together: *My boyfriend compared me to Jessica Lange. Compare with* suggests an analysis of differences and similarities: *His essay compared Roosevelt's presidency with Lincoln's under the headings of wartime leadership, intellectual ability, and personal integrity.* As an intransitive verb, *compare* always takes *with*, as in *Today's presidents just don't compare with yesterday's greats.*

complement, compliment As a verb, *complement* means "to complete" or "to match," as in *The green sweater complements his green eyes.* As a noun, *complement* means "a word or phrase that completes an idea": *"Sweet" is often the complement of "sugar."* As a verb, *compliment* means "to praise": *The mayor complimented the fire department's quick work.* As a noun, it means "a bit of praise": *"You've lost a ton of weight" doesn't sound like much of a compliment to me.*

compose, comprise To *compose* means "to form the parts into a whole": *I composed a poem in praise of toothpaste.* The whole *comprises* or *consists of* the parts, as in *The Congress comprises (consists of) the Senate and the House of Representatives.* Careful stylists, therefore, would write *Twelve teams compose the National League*; and *The National League comprises twelve teams.*

conscience, conscientious, conscious, consciousness *Conscience* is a noun referring to our sense of right and wrong: *My conscience hurt because I ate the whole cake by myself. Conscientious* is an adjective meaning "scrupulous, careful": *He was conscientious about homework and did it every night. Conscious* is an adjective meaning "aware of self and surroundings": *He was conscious of the lipstick smear on his cheek. Consciousness* is a noun referring to the state of being aware: *After the blow on her head, she lost consciousness.*

continual, continuous   *Continual* means "happening repeatedly": *His job as jackhammer operator gave him a continual headache. Continuous* means "uninterrupted or unbroken": *The Apennines form a continuous ridge of mountains.*

could of, should of, would of   Avoid all of these. They are incorrect ear-spellings for *could have, should have*, and *would have.*

council, counsel   *Council* refers to an administrative or legislative body, and *councilor* to a member of that body. *Counsel* refers to advice or to a legal adviser, and *counselor* refers to anyone who advises. *Counsel* can also be a verb, as in *Ghandi counseled his followers to resist without violence.*

couple of   In formal English, don't use this phrase to mean "several" but only to mean "two that are connected, a pair": *A couple of horses pulled the cart.*

credible, creditable, credulous   *Credible* means "giving sufficient reason to be believed": *After a vigorous cross-examination, the jury found her a credible witness. Creditable* means "worthy of praise or esteem": *Mattingly did a creditable job at first base. Credulous* means "ready to believe on slight evidence": *He was so credulous I convinced him I'd been to the moon.*

criterion, criteria   *Criterion* is the singular. *Criteria* is the plural. *Stamina is the main criterion for good running. Stamina and will are the main criteria for good running.*

datum, data   *Datum* is the singular form and *data* is the plural. *The data shows a 15 percent decrease* should be *The data show a 15 percent decrease.*

different from, different than   Many people say, and some write, *different than*, but careful stylists prefer *different from: Being a teenager is different from being an adult.*

differ from, differ with   *Differ from* means "to show unlikeness": *California bagels differ from Boston bagels in color and price. Differ with* means "to disagree with": *Oppenheimer differed with Teller over the hydrogen bomb.*

discreet, discrete   *Discreet* means "prudent" or "able to be silent": *He was so discreet about his poker losses that his wife never found out. Discrete* means "separate" or "distinct": *Each country has its own discrete culture.*

disinterested, uninterested *Disinterested* does not mean "to have no interest," but "to have nothing personal at stake and thus to be impartial": *The dispute between Japanese and Soviet fishermen has been handed over to a disinterested Swiss arbitrator.* *Uninterested* means "apathetic," or "uncaring": *Harry took Deidre for a fishing trip, but she was obviously uninterested.*

doesn't, don't *Doesn't* is the contraction of *does not*, and *don't* is the contraction of *do not*. Be sure you don't use *don't* when you mean *doesn't*: *He doesn't* (not *don't*) *feel well today.*

due to, because Avoid using *due to* as a synonym for "because": *Because of* (not *due to*) *rain, the game was called.* Save *due to* for bill paying.

due to the fact that This long running jump means *because.* Use *because.*

each, every *Each* means "one of a group": *Each carton of milk undergoes careful inspection.* *Every* refers to all members of a group: *Every writer wishes for fame.* Both take a singular verb.

effect See *affect, effect.*

e.g., i.e., etc. These are abbreviations from Latin: *e.g.* stands for *exempli gratia*, which means "for the sake of example": *i.e.* stands for *id est*, which means "that is"; and *etc.* stands for *et cetera*, which means "and other things." These Latin abbreviations are fading from use in formal writing. Stick to the English equivalents.

either, neither Both of these words can function as an adjective, a pronoun, or part of a correlative conjunction. As an adjective, *either* means "one or the other": *Guard dogs stand on either side of the gate.* As an adjective *neither* means "not one or the other": *Neither dog has on a muzzle.* As pronouns, *either* and *neither* take singular verbs: *Either is enough to scare off burglars. Neither makes the postman cheerful.* As a correlative conjunction, *either* is followed by *or* and *neither* by *nor.* For a further discussion, see the Handbook, pp. 460 and 480.

elicit, illicit *Elicit* is a verb that means "to pull forth" or "to evoke": *Ted Williams's homer in his last time at bat elicited a huge roar from the crowd.* *Illicit* is an adjective that means "not allowed": *Ormsby was arrested for possession of illicit drugs.*

eminent, imminent, immanent *Eminent* means "respected, high-ranking, outstanding": *Ben Franklin was the most eminent statesman of his day.* *Imminent* means "impending": *An imminent storm darkened the horizon.* *Immanent*, a rare term of philosophy, usually means "inherent" or "resting within": *Romantic philosophers thought divinity was immanent in nature.*

enthuse   Careful stylists avoid using this colloquial term in formal prose. Prefer *enthusiastic: New York City was very enthusiastic about baseball in 1955.*

etc.   See *e.g., i.e., etc.*

everybody, every body, everyone, every one   *Everybody* and *everyone* are indefinite pronouns referring to all members of a group. Both take singular verbs: *When everybody plays well, everyone cheers loudly. Every body* is a phrase in which the noun *body* is modified by the adjective *every: You will find a heart in every body of a mammal.* In *every one,* the pronoun *one* is modified by the adjective *every: Every one has lungs as well.*

everyday, every day   *Everyday* is an adjective: *At five each morning, she rose to do her everyday chores.* The phrase *every day* acts as an adverb: *I see him every day.*

everywheres   Avoid this colloquial version of *everywhere.*

except   See *accept, except.*

explicit, implicit   *Explicit* means "stated outright": *I made an explicit offer to buy his car. Implicit* means "unstated but suggested": *Implicit in my offer was that he throw in the whitewall tires and a gallon of gasoline.*

farther, further   Use *farther* to express physical distance: *Is it farther to his house or to yours?* Use *further* to express abstract distance: *Newton probed further into the nature of the universe than any thinker before him.*

few, fewer, less, lesser   *Few* and *fewer* refer to countable items: *We have few friends, and with that attitude, we'll have fewer. Less* and *lesser* refer to a whole not divisible into individual countable units: *I have less money than you, but you are the lesser talent.*

first, firstly   *Firstly, secondly,* and *thirdly* have pretty much faded from use. Prefer *first, second,* and *third: First, the state of our economy is weak. Second, our foreign policy is in disarray . . .*

flaunt, flout   *Flaunt* means "to make an ostentatious display": *The Smiths flaunted their new car in front of the neighbors. Flout* means "to treat disrespectfully" or "to scorn": *The banker flouted convention by coming to the bank in jeans and sneakers.*

former, latter   These words can help avoid repetition. Use them only when you are referring to two things: *Mr. Hobson and his dog are so alike that I sometimes mistake the former for the latter.*

get, got, gotten   *Got* is the past tense of *get: Millions of Americans got their income tax forms in the mail yesterday.* The past participle of *get* is either *got* or *gotten*, hence the confusion. Either is acceptable English: *Have you got a tennis racket? I have gotten to bed late every night this week.*

Americans use *gotten* more often, especially to signal a progression: *The moral standards of the United States have gotten steadily worse.* We also use *got* in informal English as an intense form of *must: You have got to help us.* Our advice: don't overuse *get* in formal writing. Although a necessary verb, it can be an easy way out of the search for good verbs.

good, well   *Good* is a noun: *I stand for the true, the good, and the beautiful. Good* is also an adjective: *Wouldn't we all love to be good writers? Well* is an adverb: *She plays the bassoon well.* The problem arises, as with *bad* and *badly*, with linking verbs like *feel* or *sound*, which take *good* as a complement. *Whenever she ran ten miles, she felt good* (not *well*). In this sentence *good* modifies the subject *she*, not the verb.

good and   Avoid this colloquial equivalent of *entirely* or *very: You should be very* (not *good and*) *mad.*

had ought   Avoid this colloquial equivalent of *ought.* Prefer *You ought* (not *had ought*) *to study.*

hanged, hung   As past participles, the word *hanged* is used with people, and the word *hung* with objects: *In the old West, outlaws were hanged. Pictures are hung all over my house.*

hardly   See *can barely, can hardly, can't barely, can't hardly.*

have, of   Do not use the preposition *of* when you mean the verb *have: She shouldn't have* (not *of*) *done what she did.*

hopefully   *Hopefully* is an adverb meaning "in a hopeful manner" and modifies the verb, as in *The sick man waited hopefully for the doctor.* This means "As he waited, he was hopeful." The term is frequently misused: *Hopefully, we should arrive at the summit by two.* This means that when the climbers get to the top, they will be full of hope. The speaker meant: *I hope we arrive at the summit by two.* Be careful: this misuse is a pet peeve of many people.

house, home   A *house* is an edifice; a *home* is an emotional entity where you live: *A house is where the kitchen is. A home is where the heart is.*

however   This word means "in spite of" or "no matter": *We do not have the exact style you ordered; we do, however, have a similar one.* When used as a conjunctive adverb this way, *however* should be set off by punctuation. Never use this word in a clause beginning with *but*: that would be redundant. Careful stylists do not begin sentences with *however*.

human, human being   *Human* is an adjective: *Her dog had a human smile.* Although *human* is acceptable as a noun, careful stylists prefer *human being*: *Her dog was almost like a human being.*

i.e.   See *e.g., i.e., etc.*

if, whether   In speech, we often say *I'll find out if he's home or not.* A better word here is *whether: I'll find out whether he is home or not. Whether* indicates a choice or alternative. *If* indicates a contingency: *If he doesn't shut up, I'll scream.*

imminent, immanent   See *eminent, imminent, immanent.*

impact   Avoid using this word as a verb. Prefer a more specific word: *Years of war depleted (not impacted on) the treasury of Venice.*

imply, infer   *Imply* means "to suggest" or "to indicate," as in *By shaking her head, she implied disapproval. Infer* means "to conclude" or "to understand," as in *I inferred from her nodding that she agreed.*

individual, person, party, people   *Individual* emphasizes singularity or separateness: *Our government must protect the individual. Person* emphasizes the actual self or personality: *A person could develop a cough. Party* means a group of people assembled for a purpose. *Our party arrived fifteen minutes late. People* refers to a nation, congregation, class, or company: *Of the people, by the people, and for the people. People* is also used to refer to human beings in general: *People do the darnedest things.*

infer, imply   See *imply, infer.*

ingenious, ingenuous   *Ingenious* means "especially inventive" or "clever": *With an ingenious contrivance, King Frederick had the kitchen raised into his bedroom. Ingenuous* means "childlike" or "innocent": *When my daughter said I looked a hundred, I forgave her because of her ingenuous smile.*

irrespective, regardless, irregardless   *Irrespective* and *regardless* are synonymous and mean "whether taken into account or not," as in *We are all equal irrespective of sex, color, or creed. I am leaving regardless of her opinion. Irregardless* is incorrect.

is when, is where   Avoid these awkward constructions. Revise *A double elimination tournament is when teams losing twice are eliminated.* Prefer *In a double elimination tournament, teams losing twice are eliminated.*

it's, its   Because the spelling is so close, these two words are often confused with each other. *It's* is always a contraction of *it is: It's lovely weather if you're a duck. Its* is a possessive pronoun: *My duck is looking for its bowl.* See the Handbook, p. 488.

-ize verbs   Many verbs that end in *-ize* are essential, like *organize* and *civilize.* Try, however, to avoid made-up *-ize* verbs that take the place of better verbs. Prefer *moisten* to *moisturize, finish* or *complete* to *finalize,* and *use* to *utilize.*

kind, kinds   *Kind* is singular and takes a singular modifier and verb, as in *This kind of novel bores me. Kinds* is plural and takes a plural modifier and verb, as in *These kinds of novels bore me. These kind of cars is* incorrect.

kind of, sort of   In formal writing, avoid using *kind of* and *sort of* to mean "to a degree" or "less than completely." If you cannot indicate the exact degree, prefer *somewhat* and *rather: Murray's poems are rather* (not *sort of*) *elusive. Kind* is never followed by *a. He is kind a tough* is incorrect.

lay, lie   *Lay* is a transitive verb and thus takes a direct object. Its principal parts are *lay, laid,* and *lain: That comedian will lay an egg tonight, just as he laid one last week, and just as he has lain one every night for the past five years. Lie* is an intransitive verb and thus does not take an object. Its principal parts are *lie, lay,* and *lain: I will lie on the beach today; I lay there yesterday, and I feel as though I have lain there all my life.*

lead, led   The verb *lead* becomes *led* in the past tense: *You lead me down the mountain today. I led you up yesterday.*

leave, let   *Leave* means "to depart"; *let* means "to allow." They are interchangeable only when both meanings apply, as in *Let* (or *leave*) *me alone.*

lend, loan   Careful stylists use *loan* only as a noun, as in *The interest on the loan is 12 percent.* The verb is *to lend,* as in *Will you lend me a dime?*

less   See *few, fewer, less, lesser.*

liable   See *apt, likely, liable.*

like, as   See *as, like.*

loose, lose   *Loose* means "unbound" or "free from restraint": *Electricians traced the blackout to a loose wire. Lose* means "to become unable to find": *Don't lose your train ticket.*

lots, lots of, a lot of, alot   These are all colloquial equivalents of *much, many,* or *a great deal.* Avoid them in your college writing: *Many* (not *a lot of) steamships sailed from Le Havre.*

majority   Use this word to refer to more than half a group of countable items: *The majority of voters stayed home.* Use words like *most* when the subject cannot be divided into countable items: *Most of the sky is clear.*

may, can   See *can, may.*

may be, maybe   The phrase *may be* is the subjunctive of *is: The aliens may be laughing at us right now. Maybe* is an adverb meaning "perhaps": *Maybe they think our taste in clothes is strange.*

medium, media   *Medium* is the singular form: *Television is the fastest growing news medium in the world. Media* is plural: *Newspapers and network news are the two most important news media.*

moral, morale   *Moral* is an adjective meaning "conforming to a standard of rightness or goodness": *Helping poor nations is a moral thing to do. Morale* is a noun meaning "mental or emotional condition": *After the Battle of the Bulge, Allied morale was high.*

most, almost   *Most* is an adjective meaning "the greater part": *Most people like finding hidden money. Almost* is an adverb meaning "close but not quite": *We are almost home.* They are not interchangeable. *I see him most every day* is incorrect.

myself   This is a reflexive or intensive pronoun. As a reflexive, the actor also receives the action: *I hurt myself jogging.* As an intensive, it emphasizes a point: *I guess I myself will have to do it.* See the Handbook, p. 455.

nauseous, nauseating, nauseated   *Nauseous* and *nauseating* mean the same thing; that is, "causing nausea": *That wig is nauseating. I can't stand any more of his nauseous quips. Nauseated* means "feeling nausea": *She is a little nauseated after riding the Ferris wheel.* A sentence like *That hotdog made me nauseous* would mean you were causing others to feel nausea.

none   *None* is almost always singular, as in *Of four candidates, none was female.* Treat *none* as a plural, however, when you wish to consider the members of the group as separate entities: *Of all the varieties of life on earth, none are hardier or more resourceful than the insects.*

nowheres   Avoid this colloquial equivalent of *nowhere*.

number, amount   See *amount, number*.

off, off of   *Off* is sufficient, as in *Get off my bunion*. Adding *of* is unnecessary.

OK, O.K., okay   Avoid these in your college writing.

on, upon   These words are synonyms. To many people, *upon* sounds pretentious.

on account of, because   *On account of* should be reserved for partial payment of a debt. Use the shorter and more direct *because*.

one, you   *One* is the third person impersonal pronoun: *One never knows where one stands these days. You*, the second person pronoun, is often used in its place. *You never know where you stand these days.* Neither is perfect. *One* has the drawback of being associated with pretentious speakers; *you* has the drawback of being a little too chatty for formal prose. Careful stylists still prefer *one*, though they use it sparingly. Sometimes it is simply better to say *I* when referring to your own experience. Don't use *you* unless you are directly addressing the reader.

only   To avoid confusion, place *only* in front of the word you intend it to modify: *Why did you buy only two bananas?* See the Handbook, p. 477.

pair   Use a singular verb when you are considering the pair as a unit: *A pair of wild horses is hard to control.* Use a plural verb when you wish to indicate that the two elements of the pair are separate. *Our new pair of puppies are getting along well with each other.*

per   This Latin word means "for each." Prefer the English equivalent: *My Oldsmobile gets fifteen miles to a* (not *per*) *gallon. I sent the letter by* (not *per*) *Express Mail.*

percent, per cent, percentage   *Percent*, now used more commonly than *per cent*, must follow a numeral: *The bond paid 9 percent.* *Percentage* means "part" or "portion." Do not use it by itself to mean "a small part or portion." It requires an adjective to give it meaning: *A high percentage of injuries in football are to the knee.*

person   See *individual, person, party, people*.

phenomenon, phenomena, phenomenal   *Phenomenon* is a noun meaning "an observable fact or event": *A hurricane is a frightening phenomenon. Phenomena* is the plural: *Hurricanes are frightening phenomena. Phenomenal* is an adjective meaning "extraordinary": *Her skill in doing calculus was phenomenal.*

plenty of   Careful stylists avoid using *plenty of* to mean a large number or amount: *Philip Johnson has designed a great many* (not *plenty of*) *fine buildings.*

plus   Use *plus* only when adding numbers. Careful stylists never use it in place of *in addition to* or *and.*

precede, proceed   *Precede* means "to go before": *Women and children precede the men into the lifeboats. Proceed* means "to continue on": *Proceed directly to the boarding gate.*

presently   Use this word to mean "in a little while": *I'll return presently.* Do not use it to mean "now."

pretty   Avoid this colloquialism in formal writing. *Mr. Elton is rather* (not *pretty*) *drunk.*

principal, principle   *Principal* as a noun means "chief officer," as in *The principal sent Ralph home from school for keeping a frog in his book bag.* As an adjective, it means "foremost" or "most important": *Our principal objective is to defend the ridge until dawn. Principle* (note the spelling difference) is a noun that means "rule" or "truth": *The first principle of long-distance running is relaxation in the midst of arduous physical exercise.*

quote, quotation   *Quote* is a verb, not a noun: *Newspapers often quote rock stars out of context. Quotation* is the noun: *Reporters scramble to get good quotations* (not *quotes*).

real, really   *Real* is an adjective: *A real crocodile lay on the bank. Really* is the adverb: *It was sleeting really* (not *real*) *hard.*

reason is because, reason is that   *Reason is because* is a redundancy, though it is often seen: *The reason Hamlet waits so long to kill Claudius is because there is so much uncertainty in the court of Denmark.* Use *reason is that: The reason Hamlet waits so long to kill Claudius is that there is so much uncertainty in the court of Denmark.*

regarding, in regard to, with regard to, as regards   All these words are synonyms for *concerning.* Avoid using *in regards to*, a cross between *in regard to* and *as regards.*

sensual, sensuous   *Sensual* means "preoccupied with bodily pleasures": *The voluptuous Polynesian women in Gauguin's paintings look sensual. Sensuous* means "appealing to the senses": *I love the sensuous colors in Gauguin's paintings.*

shall, should, will, would   *Shall* was once the correct future tense auxiliary for the first person (*I shall be home shortly*), but in American usage it is now reserved for emphasis (*I shall return*) or a request for an opinion or consent (*Shall we see each other again tomorrow night?*) For most purposes, *will* functions as the future tense auxiliary for all persons. *Should* was once the past tense of *shall* but now indicates obligation: *He should occasionally volunteer to do the dishes. Would* was once the past tense of *will* but now indicates the conditional: *If she played softer music, I would attend her parties.*

should See *shall, should, will, would.*

should of, should have See *could of, should of, would of.*

sit, set *Sit* is intransitive — that is, it takes no object: *Ever since I bruised my coccyx, I have found it difficult to sit. Set* is transitive — that is, it takes an object: *We set the piano in your kitchen.*

situation This word is much overused and often unnecessary. Whenever possible, use a concrete word to indicate what the *situation* is: *Congress has done nothing to combat the worsening deficit* (not *worsening situation*). When the word is unnecessary, avoid it: *They found themselves in danger* (not *in a dangerous situation*) *high on the rock face.*

so This word can be an adverb, an adjective, or a conjunction. As an adverb, it usually means "in order to" or "to the degree": *She kept the door open so that she could hear the baby.* As an adjective, it is a vague intensifier. Careful stylists prefer *very* or *intensely: Michael Jackson is very* (not *so*) *good looking.* As a conjunction, it indicates result: *The river is still cold, so the fish are still jumping.* Careful stylists avoid starting sentences with *so.*

somebody, some body, someone, some one Both *somebody* and *someone* are indefinite pronouns meaning "an unspecified person": *Won't somebody* (or *someone*) *answer the phone? Some body* is a phrase meaning an unspecified body: *Some body of government ought to examine this problem. Some one* is a phrase that means "an unspecified one": *Some one of the guests committed the murder.*

someplace, somewhere These two words mean "an unspecified place." Careful stylists prefer *somewhere.*

sometime, some time, sometimes *Sometime* is an adverb that means "at an unspecified time": *Come up and see me sometime. Some time* is a phrase that means "an unspecified length of time": *I haven't seen jai alai for some time. Sometimes* is an adverb that means "occasionally": *Cockroaches appeared sometimes one place, sometimes another.*

somewheres Avoid using this colloquialism in your writing.

sort of See *kind of, sort of*.

split infinitives An *infinitive* consists of *to* and the main form of the verb, like *to deny*. To *split* an infinitive means to place an adverb or a phrase between the *to* and the verb *(to categorically deny)*. When a writer places a long phrase between the *to* and the verb, the split infinitive can make comprehension difficult: *I want to categorically and without fear of contradiction from anyone deny all charges*. Careful stylists are known to strenuously object to any split infinitive.

stationary, stationery *Stationary* is an adjective meaning "not moving or moved": *Scientists in antiquity once thought the earth stationary and the universe revolving*. *Stationery* is what we write letters on.

suppose to, supposed to Use *supposed to* in your writing to indicate what is expected to happen: *The total eclipse is supposed to* (not *suppose to*) *begin tomorrow*.

sure, surely, certainly Avoid using *sure* to mean "surely" or "certainly." *Sure* is an adjective that means "confident": *The scoutmaster was sure we were near the camp*. *Surely* is an adverb that means "without doubt": *Though cantankerous, Grandpa surely loved his family*. *Certainly* is even more assured: *He was certainly good at getting people to agree with him*.

take, bring See *bring, take*.

than, then Note the difference in spelling between these two words. *Than* introduces a comparison: *My father is stronger than your father*. When using *than* with a pronoun, be sure the pronoun is in the right case. One method of making sure is to fill in all the words: *He liked her better than [he liked] me. He liked her better than I [liked her]*.

that, which Use *that* to introduce clauses containing essential information: *The red hat that I lost yesterday was found*. I have other red hats; this sentence refers to the one I lost yesterday. Use *which* to introduce clauses containing nonessential information: *The red hat, which I lost yesterday, has been found*. I have only one red hat and therefore it is not essential to identify the hat further. The words *restricted* and *nonrestricted* are frequently used to make this distinction. See the Handbook, p. 483, for more on the distinction between essential information and nonessential information.

their, there, they're *Their* is the third person plural possessive: *The models put on their eyelashes*. *There* is an adverb of place: *I saw the baboon over there in the parking lot*. *There* can also introduce an expletive: *There wasn't a police officer to be found. They're* is a contraction of *they are: They're not eager to accost big animals.*

theirselves Avoid this colloquialism.

this, these These demonstrative adjectives must agree in number with the noun they modify: *This kind of day is my favorite. These sorts of dresses are always expensive. Those silk scarves cost a fortune.*

this here, these here, that there, them there Avoid these colloquial expressions.

through, thru Use *through* in your writing. *Thru* is informal.

till, until, 'til *Till* is acceptable, but *until* is preferable. *'Til* is incorrect.

to, too, two *To* is a preposition: *I propose a toast to all the night watchmen of the world. Too* is an adverb meaning "also" or "more than enough": *He was too conceited to notice that everyone was smirking. Two* is a number: *One plus one equals two.*

toward, towards Careful stylists prefer *toward.*

try and, try to *Try to* is preferable: *Scuba divers should never try to* (not *try and*) *swim alone.*

unique *Unique* does not admit of degree or comparison: a thing cannot be more or less or very unique, only unique. At all events, *unique* is much overused these days. It means "only one of a kind," "singular." Reserve it for things you have never seen the like of before.

upon, on See *on, upon.*

use, utilize, utilization *Utilize* is an overused -*ize* verb. Prefer *use: We must use* (not *utilize*) *every means at our disposal.* Similarly, prefer the noun *use* to *utilization: China condemned any use* (not *utilization*) *of biochemical warfare.*

use to, used to Past tense is the preferable form when you mean "did habitually": *I used to* (not *use to*) *scream at horror movies.*

viable The adjective *viable* means "capable of living or growing": *Anaerobic microbes are not viable in oxygenated environments.* Avoid using it to indicate that something will work: *Hydroelectric energy is a practicable* (not *viable*) *alternative to nuclear power.*

way, ways Avoid using *a ways* to mean "a great distance." Prefer *a way: Africa has a way* (not *a ways*) *to go before it can compete with industrialized nations.*

well, good   See *good, well.*

where, where at, where to   In some regions of America it is quite common to hear *Where are you going to?* and *Where is the shoe at?* In writing, however, never use *to* or *at* after *where.* <u>*Where are you going?*</u> is sufficient.

whether   See *if, whether.*

which, that   See *that, which.*

would   See *shall, should, will, would.*

you're, your   *Your* is a possessive pronoun: <u>*Your heart is in the right place.*</u> Do not confuse it with *you're,* a contraction of *you are:* <u>*You're coming to the show tonight, aren't you?*</u> See the Handbook, p. 489.

Index